"This collection of studies by Kimlyn Bender showcases both very fine dogmatic talent and impressive theological maturity and responsibility. Engaged across a wide ecumenical front even as it delves deeply into the particular riches of Barth's theological legacy, Bender's work brings much needed light to some of the most acute debates of the present moment in English speaking Protestant theology. It invites readers to secure important gifts for the life, preaching and mission of the church precisely in and through the joyful labor of substantive theological reflection and careful dogmatic argument. The lucidity with which these essays are written is surely a mark of Bender's great gifts as a theological teacher."
Philip G. Ziegler, University of Aberdeen

"In this absorbing work, Kimlyn Bender offers a series of doctrinal studies that exemplify the art of thinking *with* esteemed figures from the theological tradition—in order then to think *after* them for the purpose of the church today. The collection attends primarily to themes in ecclesiology, Scripture, and Christology in dialogue with Karl Barth and Friedrich Schleiermacher; but in truth its dogmatic remit is far broader, and its discourse embraces a wide array of challenging conversation partners. Bender writes with his characteristic precision and verve throughout, and his measured contributions are as insightful as they are thoughtful. This volume comes highly recommended."
Paul T. Nimmo, University of Aberdeen

"In these well-crafted, incisive and penetrating essays, Kimlyn Bender provides ample demonstration of the ongoing significance of both Karl Barth and Friedrich Schleiermacher for theology and confession in the present time. An outstanding contribution to the literature of contemporary theology in service to the witness of the church."
John R. Franke, Yellowstone Theological Institute

"*Confessing Christ for Church and World* brilliantly declares 'Jesus is Lord' in the contemporary North American context in dialectical fashion. In this fine collection of essays, Kimlyn J. Bender masterfully explores the significance of Karl Barth's theology in conversation with Friedrich Schleiermacher and other notable interlocutors on a wide range of important subjects. The reader will come away challenged and enlightened by the depth and breadth of this ecumenical endeavor that grounds contextual theology in the scandal of gospel particularity."
Paul Louis Metzger, Multnomah Biblical Seminary

"More than just a description of Karl Barth's theology, Kimlyn Bender's erudite collection of essays explores a variety of topics and interlocutors engaging Barth as a persuasive conversation partner. These essays are theologically sophisticated and written in a lively and intellectually engaging style, discussing topics in ecclesiology (Reinhard Hütter), Christology (Schleiermacher), Scripture and theology (von Harnack and Bart Erhman), natural theology (William James and Alasdair McIntyre), and atheism (Feuerbach and the 'new atheism'). Ecumenical in tone, Bender's arguments are shaped by a strong Reformation sensitivity and written in an 'ad hoc' apologetic style (or what Barth calls 'good apologetics'), demonstrating the truth of confessing Christ in the church and the world. This book is highly recommended for scholars in Barth's thought yet accessible to non-experts, especially Catholic and evangelical observers, who seek to think more critically about their own commitments and traditions."

David Haddorff, St. John's University

Confessing Christ
for Church and World

Studies in Modern Theology

Kimlyn J. Bender

IVP Academic

An imprint of InterVarsity Press
Downers Grove, Illinois

InterVarsity Press
P.O. Box 1400, Downers Grove, IL 60515-1426
World Wide Web: www.ivpress.com
Email: email@ivpress.com

InterVarsity Press® is the book-publishing division of InterVarsity Christian Fellowship/USA®, a movement of students and faculty active on campus at hundreds of universities, colleges and schools of nursing in the United States of America, and a member movement of the International Fellowship of Evangelical Students. For information about local and regional activities, write Public Relations Dept., InterVarsity Christian Fellowship/USA, 6400 Schroeder Rd., P.O. Box 7895, Madison, WI 53707-7895, or visit the IVCF website at www.intervarsity.org.

Scripture quotations, unless otherwise noted, are from the New Revised Standard Version of the Bible, *copyright 1989 by the Division of Christian Education of the National Council of the Churches of Christ in the USA. Used by permission. All rights reserved.*

Cover design: Cindy Kiple
Interior design: Beth McGill
Images: The crucifixion: The way of the cross, Jesus dies upon the cross by Eric Gill at The Museum of New Zealand Te Papa Tongarew, Bequest of P. Martin Hill, 2007. The Bridgeman Art Library.
    Burlap: © Roel Smart/iStockphoto

ISBN 978-0-8308-4059-5 (print)
ISBN 978-0-8308-9674-5 (digital)

Printed in the United States of America ∞

Library of Congress Cataloging-in-Publication Data

Bender, Kimlyn J., 1969-
  [Works. Selections]
  Confessing Christ for church and world : studies in modern theology
/ Kimlyn J. Bender.
    pages cm
  Includes index.
  ISBN 978-0-8308-4059-5 (pbk. : alk. paper)
  1. Barth, Karl, 1886-1968. 2. Theology—History—20th century. I.
Title.
  BX4827.B3B38 2014
  230'.044--dc23

                                                                  2014033342

P	23	22	21	20	19	18	17	16	15	14	13	12	11	10	9	8	7	6	5	4	3	2	1
Y	33	32	31	30	29	28	27	26	25	24	23	22	21	20	19	18	17	16	15	14			

For my teachers and my students

*We thank God for giving us brethren who live by his call,
by his forgiveness, and his promise.*

Dietrich Bonhoeffer,
Life Together

Contents

Abbreviations

BTBF   *Bound to Be Free*
Reinhard Hütter. *Bound to Be Free: Evangelical Catholic Engagements in Ecclesiology, Ethics, and Ecumenism.* Grand Rapids: Eerdmans, 2004.

CD   *Church Dogmatics*
Karl Barth. *Church Dogmatics.* Edited by G. W. Bromiley and T. F. Torrance. Translated by G. W. Bromiley, G. T. Thomson, et al. Four volumes in 13 parts. Edinburgh: T & T Clark, 1936–1977.

CF   *The Christian Faith*
Friedrich Schleiermacher. *Der Christliche Glaube.* Edited by H. Martin Redeker. 2 vols. Berlin: de Gruyter, 1960. ET: *The Christian Faith.* Translated and edited by H. R. Mackintosh and J. S. Stewart. Edinburgh: T & T Clark, 1989.

ET   English translation

GD   *Göttingen Dogmatics*
Karl Barth. *The Göttingen Dogmatics: Instruction in the Christian Religion.* Volume 1. Edited by Hannelotte Reiffen. Translated by Geoffrey Bromiley. Grand Rapids: Eerdmans, 1991.

KGSG   *The Knowledge of God and the Service of God*
Karl Barth. *The Knowledge of God and the Service of God According to the Teaching of the Reformation: Recalling the Scottish Confession of 1560.* Translated by J. L. M. Haire and Ian Henderson. Eugene, OR: Wipf & Stock, 2005. Originally published by Hodder & Stoughton, 1938.

NT   New Testament

OT   Old Testament

SDT   *Suffering Divine Things*
Reinhard Hütter. *Suffering Divine Things: Theology as Church Practice.* Grand Rapids: Eerdmans, 2000. Originally published as *Theologie als kirchliche Praktik.* Gütersloh: Chr. Kaiser/Gütersloher Verlaghaus, 1997.

TRC   *The Theology of the Reformed Confessions*
Karl Barth. *The Theology of the Reformed Confessions, 1923.* Translated by Darrell L. Guder and Judith J. Guder. Louisville, KY: Westminster John Knox, 2002.

Introduction

The following chapters, some previously published, attempt to reflect on what it means to confess that Jesus Christ is Lord in our day. They explore issues of ecclesiological conversation in ecumenical encounter, scriptural authority in relation to tradition and confession, and christological determination of creation and covenant. This exploration is undertaken by examining two of the most significant theologians of the modern period, Karl Barth and Friedrich Schleiermacher, and by placing them in dialogue with Catholic, mainline Protestant, evangelical and Free Church traditions—key traditions of the current American religious landscape. The focus of most of the following essays is directed toward the theology of Barth, though Schleiermacher is a significant if secondary figure. It is my belief that these theologians stand as two towering pinnacles of the modern period, and that their theological achievements still affect the world in which we live, whether we prefer to deem that world modern or postmodern. Most of the following studies are historical in nature, though they flow into commentary on how the theology of Barth in particular can speak into our own time and how it continues to provide resources that might assist the church in its confession of the gospel within our world. In brief, these studies argue for the ongoing relevance of Barth's Protestant ecclesial vision in engagement with these traditions.

As stated, these essays fall into three primary divisions. The first, "Church and Conversation," focuses on matters of ecclesiology and ecumenicity. Here Barth's ecclesiology is examined in light of its inner content, formal structure and ongoing relevance, and with an eye towards its future promise.

These essays truly span the ecumenical spectrum, at least in representation, ranging from Roman Catholic to American evangelical concerns. Barth speaks across the spectrum, but his mature, distinctive and developed Protestant sensibilities stand as an alternative and in contradistinction to both a Catholic substance that sees the church as an extension of Christ's own person and agency, as well as to alternative forms of low church and evangelical voluntarism and populism that lose the theological identity of the church as the body of Christ in generic models of community and sociality.

The second division of essays, "Canon and Confession," focuses on questions of Scripture, biblical authority and tradition. The distinctive Christian commitments regarding Scripture as canon are grounded in and given intelligibility by convictions of Christology, yet these convictions are often implicit rather than explicit in expositions of the doctrine of Scripture. At times these scriptural commitments are unmoored from Christology altogether and are given a new home in discussions of theological epistemology or, alternatively, general hermeneutics—both of which, at their worst, are presented as a kind of apologetic foundationalism on one side or symbolic expressivism or literary theory on the other. These essays attempt to give voice to the distinctive christological convictions that lay behind Barth's understanding of Scripture as canon, and how such convictions arose in Barth's thought and shaped his debates with historical criticism in the past. They move on to consider how his thought might illumine such debates in the present and provide resources for a postcritical reading of Scripture. That the Bible stands in a unique place between Christ and the church's confession is one of Barth's central convictions, a conviction here placed into conversation not only with Catholic understandings of the relation of Scripture and tradition but with Free Church ones as well. Also in this section are essays that address contemporary questions which impinge on Christian confession today, such as the rise of popular biblical skepticism and certain resurgent forms of atheism.

The final division of essays, "Christ and Creation," focuses on matters of Christology, creation and covenant. These essays have Christology at their center (in reality all the essays in this book do), but with a specific focus on how the doctrines of creation and Christology are related, as well as how such questions influence understandings of natural theology and the sciences. To consider the natural world from a center in Christology may seem strange and to some quite mistaken, but if Christ's identity and his mission are intertwined, then in him the Actor and the Play become one, such that there is an identity of Actor and Role in the divine drama—a drama itself played out on the stage of creation and history.[1] The final chapter on Schleiermacher's Christology is, careful readers will note, something of a farewell.

I will not in this introduction provide further synopses of the chapters. The arguments they make do not lend themselves well to abridgement and are best experienced in their exposition and aggregate effect. Read this way, there are themes that emerge from these essays providing them with a coherence and cumulative form of argumentation. This unity amid their diversity, and despite their different occasions and times of composition, is both real and perceptible though not based on a systematic form of organization. Not all of these themes were entirely evident to me when I wrote these essays, but as I look back on the time, spanning more than a decade, in which they came to be, such themes are unmistakable.

The most important of all of the themes is a deep commitment to the scandal of the gospel and to its radical particularity, expressed in its earliest and most succinct form in the confession that "Jesus Christ is Lord." At the heart of this commitment is a radical centering on God's singular revelation in Jesus Christ reflected in an attendant understanding of the Spirit's ongoing work and of the enduring place of Holy Scripture in the life of the church. This central conviction is accompanied by a quiet commitment to a humble ecclesiology that for all its humility is no less urgent in its call for the church to be faithful and obedient in its confession and life in and for our time. That the Protestant vision remains a viable, distinctive and important witness in our day is another secondary conviction that also arises out of these essays. There are other important themes and convictions, most of which unmistakably if discursively unfold from the central one of the gospel's scandal, but these are perhaps best left to their discernment in reading the essays themselves (and ferreting them out of

---

[1]As recognized not only by Barth but also articulated by von Balthasar, himself drawing on Theodor Haecker. See Hans Urs von Balthasar, *Theo-Drama: Theological Dramatic Theory, Volume 1 Prolegomena*, trans. Graham Harrison (San Francisco: Ignatius Press, 1988), pp. 645-46.

footnotes). None of them, however, overshadows their center, which is nothing less than a full embrace of what Ralph Waldo Emerson deemed the great error of historic Christianity, namely, its "noxious exaggeration about the *person* of Jesus."[2] I am hoping this book can provide some small help, encouragement and exhortation to Christians to prolong this noxious exaggeration in our time.

If there are other guiding commitments governing the composition of these chapters that should be noted at the outset, the following are conscious to me and significant in shaping their form and content. The first is that while distinctives of the modern and postmodern periods can be roughly distinguished, they are not neatly demarcated, as no periods ever are, nor are their characteristics tidily listed. I therefore am less interested in defining precisely what it means to say that Schleiermacher or Barth are modern theologians than I am in looking at the specific ways that they define and conduct the theological task as they understand it in engagement with the spirit of their own age. When this is done the richness and complexity of their thought becomes all the more evident, while the labels of modern or postmodern become less helpful, particularly with reference to Barth.

The second guiding commitment is to acknowledge and address the social location that provides the context for these studies, which is the church as found in all of its diversity in North America (with nods to the Old World of Europe). To acknowledge as much is not to say that these essays should not or cannot be read with interest and benefit elsewhere, nor should it in any way be taken to discount the importance of the riches of the global church. To locate their origin and primary audience is only to confess that all theology is contextual, and the context for these studies is North America. This is also not to ignore the original (Continental, German) context from which the work of Schleiermacher and Barth arose. But there is a unique perspective that comes with reading Barth and Schleiermacher in an American context, as there would be with reading them in any particular

---

[2]Emerson states: "Historical Christianity has fallen into the error that corrupts all attempts to communicate religion. It has dwelt, it dwells, with noxious exaggeration about the person of Jesus." Ralph Waldo Emerson, "Divinity School Address," in *The Portable Emerson*, ed. Carl Bode, new ed. (New York: Penguin, 1981), pp. 78-85, quoted in Stanley Hauerwas, *With the Grain of the Universe: The Church's Witness and Natural Theology* (Grand Rapids: Brazos, 2001), p. 81. Emerson contrasted this christological focus with one that exalted in the divinity of humanity.

context. These essays try to place Barth particularly in conversation with the current religious diversity of America.

The third commitment follows from the second, which is that theology must speak not only within a particular confessional tradition but across the horizontal spectrum of the churches (which includes, for any who are interested, not only Roman Catholic, Anglican, Lutheran and Reformed communities, but also the plethora of Free Church and Pentecostal ones—the latter, sadly, getting left out of this collection, though perhaps not in spirit—see chapters two and eight). It also entails, however, that theology must speak not only within the quiet studies of professional theologians but to the concerns of the persons who sit week in and week out in the pews, persons whose questions may be quite different from those of the academy, and questions often taking their rise from the magazines and books that seem so prominently displayed in the stores, airports and websites that these persons frequent, as well as the other media they encounter—questions about Scripture and its reliability; questions about who Jesus really was, that is, questions of the "Jesus of history" and the "Christ of faith"; questions about the New Atheism that seems to be everywhere; questions about science and its relationship to faith; and so forth.

For this reason, there are essays here that might raise the eyebrows of some in the academy—a chapter on Jesus, the Bible and historical criticism as addressed in Bart Ehrman's slew of popular books; a chapter on the New Atheism, a theme revisited in a discussion of current forms of scientific reductionism and materialism in a later chapter; and a chapter on the question of whether the entire Reformation is at an end and what its legacy might be. The chapters range widely and yet are again centered on but a few themes.

C. S. Lewis provides an image I would like to invoke for how these chapters are to be approached and understood. In his short essay "Meditation in a Toolshed," Lewis distinguishes between "looking at" a beam of light and "looking along" the beam to the objects such a beam illuminates.[3] While not using this image in the exact way Lewis did, I find it a fitting one for how I hope these chapters will be read. On the first level, they are "looking at" Schleiermacher and Barth, historical and expositional studies of

---

[3]In C. S. Lewis, *God in the Dock*, ed. Walter Hooper (Grand Rapids: Eerdmans, 1970/1999), pp. 212-15.

the content, coherence and meaning of their theological work. In this sense, Schleiermacher and Barth are the objects of such essays, such that the essays are exercises in historical theology.

But what should be clear to the reader is that these studies are really "looking along" with Schleiermacher and Barth to the reality they were trying to describe, which for both of them meant (though in radically different ways) the reality of God's revelation in Jesus Christ. In other words, these essays are attempts to look along with Schleiermacher, and especially Barth, at what they were attempting to attest. So while they may take the form of historical studies that "look at" Barth's thought (or Schleiermacher's) —and as works of historical theology have their own scholarly integrity— they nevertheless move beyond such historical investigation and exposition to "look along" with Barth to the true object, which was really a Subject (*die Sache*) that Barth himself attempted to witness: nothing less than God's glorious breaking into our world in the person of Jesus Christ, the true object of our faith, our hope and even our love.

One of the greatest perpetual temptations for theology is to turn the witnesses to truth from the past into primary objects of study, and thus to confuse theology with history.[4] The reason for such a temptation is not difficult to discern, for theologians, like all persons, value safety and security above all things. For Barth, however, such an exchange was a betrayal of theology's true task. This is not to say that historical study is of no value, but it is not the only theological task, and certainly not an end in itself for the church, regardless of its place of study in the academy. What interested Barth as he himself studied the past was not to make the mothers and fathers of the church (including the apostles) *themselves* the primary objects of our study, but to think and reflect and consider *along with* them what they themselves tried to point to and give witness to—God's revelation in Christ through the Spirit, God's own active presence within our world. Such thinking might also mean that one must think not only *along with* but

---

[4]So many of the temptations alluded to in the essays below, including those of historicism and scientism (including its reductive materialism), can be summarized as "looking at" something without "looking along" it. This was, and remains, one of the quintessential and captivating temptations, and delusions, of the modern and postmodern world. Lewis's short essay was an attempt to get at the heart of this temptation and its attendant misconception that one could trade all "looking along" for "looking at."

beyond our fathers and mothers, and to do so is to honor them rightly in spirit and truth, rather than in simple imitation of the letter. Yet to so honor them, one must first understand them rightly and respectfully, and thus historical study is unavoidable, the first step on a path that extends beyond historical study itself. To walk this path is the goal of these essays: to pay respect to Barth best by moving from attending to his thought to consider what it tried to attest. This is what it means to "look along" with him, rather than simply to "look at" him.

In this sense, a student is not greater than his teacher, though he must go his own way. All of these chapters were written in great debt to my own teachers. I have been truly blessed in life having had wonderful teachers, not least of all those who first led me to the wonder of the gospel, including above all my parents, as well as those pastors and teachers of my youth, many now long departed. To try to list my teachers all by name would only leave some out, but a few do deserve special mention: James Edwards, Dennis Ockholm and Gary Watts (these three, for introducing me to a faith that could seek understanding as a form of obedience and vocation); Timothy Bratton (for showing me the riches of history); Don Taylor (for doing the same for me with literature); and Jim McClendon, Nancey Murphy, John Thompson, Colin Brown, Dan Migliore, Bruce McCormack, George Hunsinger and Diogenes Allen (the formative teachers of my graduate studies). The list certainly contains my colleagues at the University of Sioux Falls and now those at George W. Truett Theological Seminary and Baylor University, from whom I have learned so much and whose friendship I cherish. Such a list could grow quite long if it included persons from whose books I have learned deeply, evident in the footnotes throughout. I have gained from all of my teachers, though I have traveled my own path, as these chapters show as well. My teachers are not at fault for this book's deficiencies.

I am a teacher as well. I dedicate this book not only to my teachers but also to my students, with the hope that they, too, will become teachers of others, as they have already taught me so much. It is my students who provided me with the quotation on the dedication page. It is a fitting one that expresses my thanksgiving to God for a life marked by wonderful teachers and wonderful students.

A few final words. All quotations and citations from Barth's *Church Dog-*

matics are from the English edition edited by G. W. Bromiley and T. F. Torrance. Where German text is provided or other translations offered, they are from the *Kirchliche Dogmatik*, 4 volumes, 13 parts (Zollikon-Zürich: Evangelischer Verlag AG, 1932–1967). I am thankful for the patience and wisdom that David Congdon has shown as my editor, and I am grateful to him and to InterVarsity Press for bringing this work to publication. Dean David Garland and Associate Dean Dennis Tucker of Truett Seminary have done much to make my scholarship possible and rewarding. I appreciate and value their encouragement, as well as that of all of my other Truett colleagues. Jamie McGregor, my graduate assistant, was a great help in researching and formatting the chapters. I am very grateful for all of his work to bring this volume to press; his patience and cheerfulness through it all was a gift to me. A special word of thanksgiving must be reserved for my family. I am ever thankful for my wife, Trudy, and my children, Andrew, Stephen and Karalyn. They have taught me most of all, and they bring me joy throughout the lessons.

PART ONE

Church and Conversation

1

Karl Barth's Doctrine of the Church in Conversation with American Theology Today

✠

The English-speaking world is presently witnessing a notable resurgence of interest in the theology of Karl Barth, evidenced in a fresh outpouring of new studies addressing Barth's wide-ranging corpus of dogmatic work.[1] While early examinations of Barth's theology centered especially on questions of method and Barth's doctrines of revelation, the Trinity and Christology (still topics of enduring and wide attention), recent years have seen a notable rise in the specific areas of Barth's ecclesiology and ethics, focusing on Barth's understanding of the church and of human moral agency and activity.[2] My purpose here is to introduce and survey recent studies of the former topic, though the second impinges on the first, for as any investi-

---

This chapter appeared in an earlier form as "Karl Barth's Doctrine of the Church in Contemporary Anglo-American Ecclesiological Conversation," *Zeitschrift für dialektische Theologie* 20 (2005): 84-116. Reprinted by permission.

[1]The reasons for this resurgence of interest are complex, many and varied. For one attempt to address this question, see Bruce L. McCormack, "The Barth Renaissance in America: An Opinion," *Princeton Seminary Bulletin* 23 (2002): 337-40.

[2]With regard to the latter, notable studies of the recent past include John Webster, *Barth's Ethics of Reconciliation* (Cambridge: Cambridge University Press, 1995); Webster, *Barth's Moral Theology: Human Action in Barth's Thought* (Grand Rapids: Eerdmans, 1998); Nigel Biggar, *The Hastening That Waits: Karl Barth's Ethics* (Oxford: Oxford University Press/Clarendon Press, 1993); David Clough, *Ethics in Crisis: Interpreting Barth's Ethics* (Aldershot: Ashgate, 2005); Paul T. Nimmo, *Being in Action: The Theological Shape of Barth's Ethical Vision* (Edinburgh: T & T Clark, 2007); Gerald McKenny, *The Analogy of Grace: Karl Barth's Moral Theology* (Oxford: Oxford University Press, 2010); and David Haddorff, *Christian Ethics as Witness: Barth's Ethics for a World at Risk* (Portland, OR: Wipf & Stock, 2011).

gation into Barth's doctrine of the church reveals, ecclesiological and ethical matters are intertwined.

This chapter will first outline in broad detail the material content and formal structure of Barth's mature ecclesiology. Such a description must be general and brief.[3] In light of this description, I will turn to recent examinations of Barth's ecclesiology in American theological circles (primarily mainline Protestant and Roman Catholic) with an eye toward presenting and assessing their criticisms of Barth's ecclesiology. In light of this appraisal, I conclude with a prospect for future reflection on Barth's understanding of the church.

BARTH'S CHRISTOLOGICAL ECCLESIOLOGY

Barth's doctrine of the church may be described as christological in both its material content and formal structure as well as shaped by inalienable trinitarian patterns. In regard to content, Barth's ecclesiology is centered on the image of the church as the body of Christ, his "earthly-historical form of existence" (*irdish-geschichtliche Existenzform*).[4] Barth does not see this image as simply symbolic or metaphorical but as an ontic description of the church's true nature and reality.[5] Barth's mature ecclesiology can be seen as an attempt to systematically examine and describe the meaning and significance of the central dogmatic conviction that the church is the body of Christ, and while Barth does attend to other biblical and traditional images for the church, these take a secondary position to this christological one.[6]

The material content of Barth's doctrine of the church. Barth's mature ecclesiology is found in its most developed form in the doctrine of election

---

[3]For a detailed description of the formal logic and material content of Barth's ecclesiology in light of its historical development, see Kimlyn J. Bender, *Karl Barth's Christological Ecclesiology* (Aldershot: Ashgate, 2005; reprint, Eugene, OR: Cascade Press, 2013). The current chapter draws openly and extensively on this work.

[4]*CD* IV/1, p. 661.

[5]*CD* IV/1, p. 666.

[6]Barth's predominant reliance on the image of the "body of Christ" (overshadowing all other images) leads Nicholas Healy to categorize Barth's doctrine of the church as a type of "blueprint ecclesiology" that attempts to derive a systematic presentation of ecclesiology from a single controlling image. See Healy, *Church, World and the Christian Life: Practical–Prophetic Ecclesiology* (Cambridge: Cambridge University Press, 2000), pp. 26-29. While Barth's unrelenting focus on this christological image provides coherence and richness to his exposition, such a narrow range can present its own questions.

in the *Church Dogmatics*[7] as well as in the doctrine of reconciliation,[8] though the church is a recurrent theme throughout Barth's magisterial work. In the second volume of the *Dogmatics*, Barth grounds the church not in a historical event but in the eternal will of God, so that the church stands under the election of Christ while preceding the election of the individual. The church thus stands, by eternal decree, between Christ and the Christian, and correspondingly, between Christ and the world. As Barth writes:

> The community is the human fellowship which in a particular way provisionally forms the natural and historical environment of the man Jesus Christ. Its particularity consists in the fact that by its existence it has to witness faith in Him. Its provisional character consists in the fact that in virtue of this office and commission it points beyond itself to the fellowship of all men in face of which it is a witness and herald. The community which has to be described in this way forms so to speak the inner circle of the "other" election which has taken place (and takes place) in and with the election of Jesus Christ. In so far as on the one hand it forms this special environment of the man Jesus, this inner circle, but on the other hand it is itself of the world or chosen from the world and composed of individual men, its election is to be described as mediate and mediating in respect of its mission and function. It is mediate, that is, in so far as it is the middle point between the election of Jesus Christ and (included in this) the election of those who have believed, and do and will believe, in Him. It is mediating in so far as the relation between the election of Jesus Christ and that of all believers (and vice versa) is mediated and conditioned by it.[9]

By grounding the church in the doctrine of election (and thus within the doctrine of God, for Barth places election itself there), Barth preserves the divine initiative in relation to the church. He thus ensures that the church is viewed as part of God's eternal covenantal intention and decision, and not simply as a corporate body composed of individuals who willingly join themselves together on the basis of a shared religious experience. For this reason, Barth insists that the proper descriptive mode for understanding the church must be theological, rather than sociological or historical.

If the doctrine of election provides the basis and ground for the doctrine

---

[7]*CD* II/2.

[8]*CD* IV/1, IV/2, IV/3.

[9]It should be noted that, for Barth, the elect community enfolds both Israel and the church (*CD* II/2, p. 196; cf. pp. 205-6).

of the church, it is the doctrine of reconciliation where Barth's ecclesiology is given its primary material content. There, Barth presents his most detailed description of the church under three headings: "The Holy Spirit and the Gathering of the Christian Community";[10] "The Holy Spirit and the Upbuilding of the Christian Community";[11] and "The Holy Spirit and the Sending of the Christian Community."[12] In the first part-volume,[13] Barth's primary though not sole focus is on the being and nature of the church. Central to this discussion is Barth's conception of the church as both invisible and visible. Barth does not think of these terms along traditional Augustinian and Calvinist lines, in which the organized visible church on earth is contrasted with the body of true believers known only to God. Rather, the invisible church is the miraculous working of the Spirit which gives rise to a visible congregation in history.[14] Barth rejects both an exclusively invisible church that takes flight from history (which he equates with a docetic ecclesiology), as well as a solely visible church in which the unique spiritual reality of the church is sacrificed and exchanged for a purely historical and sociological explanation of the church's existence (which Barth equates with an ebionitic ecclesiology). The church consists as the unity of both an inner spiritual activity and reality and a visible manifestation and embodiment. The church is thus the union of a divine work of the Spirit and a historical concrete visible life in analogy to the singular and irreplaceable miracle of the incarnation. To confess faith in the church is thus to confess "faith in the invisible aspect which is the secret of the visible."[15] Barth writes:

> Faith in His community has this in common with faith in Him, that it, too, relates to a reality in time and space, and therefore to something which is at bottom generally visible. If, then, we believe in Him, we cannot refuse—however hesitantly or anxiously or contentiously—to believe in His community in its spatio-temporal existence, and therefore to be a member of it and personally a Christian.[16]

---

[10]*CD* IV/1.
[11]*CD* IV/2.
[12]*CD* IV/3.
[13]*CD* IV/1.
[14]*CD* IV/1, pp. 652-56.
[15]*CD* IV/1, p. 654.
[16]Ibid.

The relationship between the invisible and visible church is thus tied to the highly dialectical notion of the church as both event and institution, as both an ever-recurrent calling of the church into existence by the Spirit and an ongoing historical corporate life that exists through time. The relationship between these is one of the most complex and controversial aspects of Barth's ecclesiology, and a common criticism of Barth is that he has sacrificed the latter to the former, as will be seen below.

In the second part-volume,[17] Barth turns to questions pertaining to the church's form and order (though, again, not exclusively to such questions). There he takes up the theme of the nature of the church's life in the world. A central aspect of the church's concrete historical existence is the question of church law.[18] With regard to such law, Barth rejects both a formless ecclesiastical antinomianism and a rigid ecclesiastical jurisprudence. He refuses either to absolutize such law (such that it becomes a binding universal norm that cannot be revised) or to relativize it (so that the church becomes formless and void of visible organization and structure). Barth's markedly dialectical conception of church law is therefore akin to his dialectical understanding of church dogma. Both church doctrine and ecclesiastical law are relative rather than absolute authorities, the latter type of authority belonging to Christ alone and secondarily to his living voice in Scripture, which stands above both the church's dogma and law and serves as their criterion. Church dogma and law are seen as necessary yet provisional, authoritative yet reformable, understood as a response of human obedience to divine revelation, rather than equated with revelation itself.[19] Barth maintains that the church's law should be derived from the "christologico-ecclesiological concept of the community."[20] It is thus christologically grounded and construed:

> As such, all valid and projected Church law, if it is true Church law, will be clearly and sharply differentiated from every other kind of "law." In great things and small, in all things, true Church law arises from adhering to the voice of Jesus Christ. Neither formally nor materially does it arise elsewhere.

---

[17]*CD* IV/2.

[18]*CD* IV/2, pp. 676ff.

[19]Barth's understanding of the relative and circumscribed authority of church dogmas, doctrines and confessions is outlined in *CD* I/2, pp. 585-660.

[20]*CD* IV/2, p. 681.

> To seek and find and establish and administer this law is an integral part of
> the action with which the community is charged in and in relation to the
> world. For this reason, too, we cannot eliminate the question of true Church
> law, or treat it as a question of minor importance.[21]

Such law serves not only to give shape to the church's own life in worship
and service but also should exist as a pattern on which all other human law
may be predicated. Church law is, in Barth's memorable term, "exemplary
law," and as such is paradigmatic "for the formation and administration of
human law generally, and therefore of the law of other political, economic,
cultural, and other human societies."[22]

In the last major section on the church, "The Holy Spirit and the Sending
of the Christian Community,"[23] Barth turns to the church's mission and
vocation. The church does not exist for itself, but in service to God and for
the world. While the community lives within the world, it is also set apart
from the world by God in order to carry out its divinely-appointed task,
which is to witness to the world regarding its own alienation and point it
to God's reconciliation and salvation in Christ.[24] Barth can go so far as to
say that the church has no independent existence apart from its Christ-
appointed ministry to the world.[25] He states:

> As God exists for it [the world] in His divine way, and Jesus Christ in His
> divine-human, so the Christian community exists for it in its own purely
> human. All ecclesiology is grounded, critically limited, but also positively
> determined by Christology; and this applies in respect of the particular
> statement which here concerns us, namely, that the Church exists for the
> world. The community neither can nor should believe in itself. Even in this
> particular respect, there can be no *credo in ecclesiam*. Yet as it believes in God
> the Father, the Son and the Holy Ghost, it can and should believe and confess
> its own reality: *credo ecclesiam*, and therefore the reality rather than the mere
> ideal that it exists for the world.[26]

Barth's ecclesiology is thus considerably determined by a teleological, rather

---

[21]*CD* IV/2, p. 682.
[22]*CD* IV/2, p. 719.
[23]*CD* IV/3.
[24]*CD* IV/3.2, pp. 762-63.
[25]*CD* IV/3.2, pp. 795-96, 830-31.
[26]*CD* IV/3.2, p. 786.

than purely ontological, concern, and Barth defines the church's nature by its activity. Indeed, for Barth these are inseparable, for the church's being is determined in and by its action.[27] Moreover, the church is defined not solely by its self-constituting practices (as it is by the Augsburg Confession, for example),[28] but by its missionary and evangelistic task. It must be stated that this task is predominantly described by Barth in terms of witness rather than mediation. Barth does not see the church's ministry and mission as either an extension or supplement of Christ's own salvific work but as a witness and proclamation of a prior event, Christ's finished and perfect atonement. The church is not an extension of the incarnation, nor does the church re-place Christ in the economy of salvation following the ascension. Barth insists that even with regard to its "invisible essence," the church "is not Christ, nor a second Christ, nor a kind of extension of the one Christ."[29] Because Christ is the sole redeemer and Lord of the world, the church's ministry is always the humble ministry of service and proclamation, never one of lordship or co-redemption. It is therefore not surprising, given Barth's proclivity for speaking of the church as witnessing to, rather than bearing, God's grace, that the church is portrayed as most closely aligned with the prophetic, rather than priestly or kingly, form of Christ's threefold office.[30]

The ministry that the church undertakes not only for itself but also on behalf of the world is comprised of a number of concrete "forms of ministry" categorized under the twofold witness of the community in speech and action. Barth lists twelve such forms, six of speech and six of action. The practices of the church's speech are (1) the praise of God, (2) the procla-mation of the gospel (preaching), (3) instruction in Scripture and the faith, (4) evangelization to the surrounding culture, (5) mission to the nations and

---

[27]Such a conception of the church may rightly be described as a form of actualism. For a discus-sion of actualism in Barth's theology, see George Hunsinger, *How to Read Karl Barth: The Shape of His Theology* (Oxford: Oxford University Press, 1991). For a discussion of actualism in relation to the doctrine of God, on which all other instances of actualism are dependent and for which they serve as analogies, see Eberhard Jüngel, *God's Being Is in Becoming: The Trinitarian Being of God in the Theology of Karl Barth*, trans. John Webster (Edinburgh: T & T Clark; Grand Rapids: Eerdmans, 2001).

[28]"The church exists where the Gospel is purely proclaimed and the sacraments rightly adminis-tered" (Augsburg Confession, Article 7).

[29]*CD* IV/3.2, p. 729.

[30]*CD* IV/3.2, p. 790.

(6) the discipline of theology.[31] It is in fact theology that examines the appropriateness not only of the other practices of the community's speech (such as praise, preaching, instruction, evangelization and missions) but also of its action. The six practices that comprise the church's action are (1) prayer, (2) the cure of souls (pastoral care), (3) the production of exemplars of Christian life, (4) the rendering of service (diaconal ministries that address physical needs and that include within them a place for Christian social criticism), (5) the prophetic action of the community based on the discernment of current events and (6) the establishment of fellowship.[32] Barth outlines each practice in brief detail. What is of primary significance for us here is that each practice serves two functions. First, the practice provides concrete determination of the identity of the church by serving as a defining characteristic of the community. But second, each practice serves not only the church itself but also gives witness to the world. All therefore serve the church's missionary task. Barth's emphasis and recovery of mission as central to the church's very identity remains one of his distinctive and lasting contributions to ecclesiological thought.

The formal structure of Barth's doctrine of the church. Having provided a broad and admittedly cursory overview of the content of Barth's ecclesiology, we now turn to examine its underlying grammar. Barth's mature ecclesiology is ruled by a christological logic which governs its internal structure and gives shape to its content. While other patterns are discernible as well (the most notable being the trinitarian ones), it is the christological ones that are in general inclusive of the others, not surprising when one considers the centrality of Christology for Barth's theology. Indeed, Barth states: "All ecclesiology is grounded, critically limited, but also positively determined by Christology."[33] So while Barth places the doctrine of the church under the subjective side of the work of the atonement, and therefore under the third article of the creed as a doctrine of the Holy Spirit,[34] this discussion itself takes place under the more inclusive doctrine of reconciliation, and thus within the framework of the second article.[35]

---

[31]*CD* IV/3.2, pp. 865-82.
[32]*CD* IV/3.2, pp. 882-901.
[33]*CD* IV/3.2, p. 786.
[34]*CD* IV/1, p. 643.
[35]*CD* IV.

Three primary elements comprise the christological logic that provides the formal governance of the material substance of Barth's doctrine of the church. These elements are related in an inclusive fashion, in that the second element serves as a further detailed explication of an aspect of the first, and the third as a further detailed explication of an aspect of the second. They are therefore unfolding elements, each intricately related to the other.

The first and most comprehensive element is what George Hunsinger has identified as the Chalcedonian pattern.[36] This pattern serves first and definitively to describe the unique union of God and humanity in Christ as grounded in the hypostatic union of the incarnation, but it is also applied by Barth as the regulative pattern and paradigm governing all divine and human relationships that exist in an analogical relation to the incarnation itself.[37] This pattern is comprised of a unity, a differentiation and an asymmetrical relation between the divine and human natures in Christ, and by analogy between the members, or terms, of the other designated relations. In regard to ecclesiology, such strict ordering entails that Christ, who is Lord of the church, and the Spirit, who gives it life and calls it into existence, freely take up the church's life and proclamation for their own service and self-communication, yet neither can Christ (or the Spirit) and the church be confused. They exist in an ordered, asymmetrical and irreversible relation, in which the distinction between Christ and church (and the Spirit and church) is never sacrificed, and in which the first remains Lord, while the church remains servant, utterly dependent on its Lord for its existence. The church cannot take the place of Christ, nor can its life and activity be directly identified with that of his Spirit. Christ and the church thus exist in the union of head and body such that the communion of both is preserved ("without division"), but they are not identified in such a way that the integrity of either is sacrificed ("without confusion"). The church for Barth is neither to be granted an autonomy such that its reliance on Christ and the Spirit is lost, nor is it to be denied its own rightful place in the economy of

---

[36]See Hunsinger, *How to Read Karl Barth*, pp. 85, 173-80, 185-87, 204-5, 286-87, et al. See also James Y. Holloway, ed., *Barth, Barmen and the Confessing Church Today: Katallegete* (Lewiston, NY: Edwin Mellen Press, 1992/1995), pp. 289-92.

[37]Hunsinger states that "there is virtually no discussion of divine and human agency in the *Church Dogmatics* which does not conform to this scheme" (*How to Read Karl Barth*, p. 187).

grace by negating it through a type of divine determinism or monism.[38]

The second element of the christological logic follows from this final aspect of the Chalcedonian pattern. In essence, it may be described as a further exposition clarifying the nature of the asymmetrical relation itself with primary reference to the personal union of Word and flesh in Christ and then to the communion of the natures, and with secondary application to defining the relationship between divine and human subjects. This element is articulated in terms of the patristic *anhypostasia/enhypostasia* formula in Christology understood along Reformed lines.[39] This doctrine, as Barth understood and articulated it, made two statements, one negative and one positive. The negative assertion, expressed by the *anhypostasis*, is that the human nature of Christ has no independent existence apart from the Word in the incarnation. This safeguards both the divine freedom and initiative as well as the utter dependence of the creature on the Creator. It therefore protects against any form of adoptionism. The positive assertion, expressed by the *enhypostasis*, is that the human nature does have a real, true and complete existence in the Word. This ensures the integrity and wholeness of the creature, that Jesus was a complete human being. The christological couplet preserves both the sovereign freedom and benevolent goodness of the divine self-giving in the incarnation, as well as the wholeness and bestowed dignity of the creature, thus expressing "the essential logic in the irreversible movement of God's grace."[40]

When applied by analogy to the church, then, this christological formula

---

[38]"The Chalcedonian pattern is used to specify counter positions that would be doctrinally incoherent (and also incoherent with Scripture). 'Without separation or division' means that no independent human autonomy can be posited in relation to God. 'Without confusion or change' means that no divine determinism or monism can be posited in relation to humanity. Finally, 'complete in deity and complete in humanity' means that no symmetrical relationship can be posited between divine and human actions (or better, none that is not asymmetrical). It also means that the two cannot be posited as ultimately identical" (Hunsinger, *How to Read Karl Barth*, p. 204).

[39]For Barth's understanding of this formula, see *CD* I/2, p. 163; cf. *CD* IV/2, pp. 49-50, 90-91. A discussion of the place of this couplet in Barth's Christology is provided by Thomas F. Torrance, *Karl Barth, Biblical and Evangelical Theologian* (Edinburgh: T & T Clark, 1990), pp. 198-201, 125. In reference to this couplet, Torrance writes: "As Barth used it . . . this was a technically precise way of speaking of the reality, wholeness and integrity of the human nature of Jesus Christ in the incarnation, without lapsing into adoptionism, and of speaking of its perfect oneness with the divine nature of Christ without lapsing into monophysitism" (Torrance, *Karl Barth*, p. 200).

[40]Torrance, *Karl Barth*, p. 199; cf. p. 125.

entails that the church and its work have no independent existence apart from the divine initiative but at the same time ensures that the church does have a real and true existence and activity in the covenant of grace, which Barth sees preeminently in terms of witness to God's gracious act in Christ. As noted above, the church and its action cannot in any way be seen as a substitute for Christ; Barth eschews all notions of a vicarious role for the church and indeed eschews church offices themselves.[41] Nor can the church's work be seen as a supplement to Christ's own; Barth rejects all such synergistic accounts of salvation. Nevertheless, the church does have its own true identity and role, a unique dignity established by Christ. The church exists on a different plane from its Lord, and its work is better described as a witness to a completed work rather than a participation in salvation itself. Barth's *anhypostatic-enhypostatic* christological formula when applied to ecclesiology preserves both the integrity of the church and its activity on the one hand and the superiority and uniqueness of Christ on the other.[42] It also entails that the church exists, and only exists, in dependence on the Spirit.

This understanding of the *anhypostasia/enhypostasia* formula applied to ecclesiology is complemented by a distinctly Reformed christo-ecclesiological interpretation. The asymmetry of the relation between Christ and the church entails that neither the doctrine nor the activities of the church can be directly identified with the Spirit's work. For Barth, the church's doctrine and teaching, as well as its activities and practices, can never be directly identified as God's own work, that is, as revelation itself, though they can be indirectly so identified, for it is the Spirit which calls the church (and its historical life) into existence. Yet, this existence is that of men and women, and therefore a creaturely existence. Just as the Spirit gave rise to Christ's human nature, yet this nature was a human nature (rather than a divinized one), so also the church, as the body of Christ called into existence by the Spirit, exists as a divinely established human reality. For Barth, there could be no confusion on this score. Consequently, Barth carried out a radical desacramentalizing of the church and its activities, seen in his highly con-

---

[41]Barth's aversion to any vicariate role for the church and such offices is witnessed at least as early as his dogmatic lectures in Göttingen; see *Unterricht in der christlichen Religion, Dritter Band* (Zürich: Theologischer Verlag Zürich, 2003), pp. 372-77.

[42]See *CD* IV/2, pp. 59-60; see also *CD* I/2, p. 348.

troversial, though arguably consistent, doctrine of baptism in CD IV/4.1. Barth never sacrificed his deeply-held conviction that while history can become a predicate of revelation, revelation can never become a predicate of history.[43] This is evidenced when he writes:

> No concrete form of the community can in itself and as such be the object of faith. Even the man Jesus as such, the *caro Christi*, cannot be this, just as the individual Christian cannot believe in his faith as a work. The community can believe in itself only when it believes in its Lord and therefore in what it is, in what it really is in its concrete form. The work magnifies the master. The visible attests the invisible. The glory of the community consists in the fact that it can give God the glory, and does not cease to do so. Its glory can appear only where there appears the glory of Jesus Christ and the sinner justified by Him. But as long as time endures, until the final manifestation of God and man in the future of Jesus Christ, the place where this takes place is hidden in its concrete form, with which it is only indirectly and not directly identical. For that reason this occurrence must be believed in the concrete form of the history which is visible to all.[44]

The asymmetry of the relationship between the Lord and the church is therefore demonstrated in that while the church can exist only because of Christ's action through the Spirit, Christ cannot be directly identified with the church or be made dependent on it so that his freedom is sacrificed. Barth writes:

> There can be no thought of the being of Jesus Christ enclosed in that of His community, or exhausted by it, as though it were a kind of predicate of this being. The truth is the very opposite. The being of the community is exhausted and enclosed in His. It is a being which is taken up and hidden in His, and absolutely determined and governed by it. The being of the community is a predicate of His being. As it exists on earth and in time in virtue of the mighty work of the Holy Ghost, it is His body; and He, its heavenly Head, the incarnate Word, the incomparable Holy One, has in it His own earthly-historical form of existence; He Himself, who is not yet directly and universally and definitively revealed to the world and it, is already present and at work in

---

[43]Karl Barth, "Church and Theology," in *Theology and Church: Shorter Writings 1920–1928*, trans. Louise Pettibone Smith (New York: Harper & Row, 1962), p. 292.
[44]CD IV/1, p. 658.

it. The community is not Jesus Christ. But He—and in reality only He, but He in supreme reality—is the community. He does not live because and as it lives. But it lives, and may and can live, only because and as He lives. . . . The sequence and order are all-important. But in this sequence and order it may and must be affirmed that Jesus Christ is the community.[45]

Barth thus demonstrates a firm commitment to an ecclesiological *extra Calvinisticum*. While it can truly be said that "Where Christ is, there is the church," it is improper, Barth contends, to say "Where the church is, there is Christ," at least without careful and extensive qualification.[46] Such an unqualified reversal would fail to respect the asymmetrical relation between the partners, a strict ordering in analogy to the strict and irreversible ordering of "The Word became flesh." It could only lead to confused understandings of Christ and the church, as well as to synergistic and supplemental accounts of salvation.

The final element of the christological logic follows from the two preceding. It further describes the nature of the human life of Christ in relation to his divine life, and thus describes the character of the real, true and whole human existence that is established by the divine Word in material rather than purely formal terms. Barth answers the question as to the positive relation of the second term to the first, of Christ's human life to his divine life, by positing the notion of correspondence (*Entsprechung*).[47] Correspondence itself includes both ontological and ethical aspects and is related to the epistemological concept of the analogy of faith (*analogia fidei*).[48] It is a specifi-

---

[45]*CD* IV/2, p. 655.

[46]Barth's understanding of the irreversibility of the relation between Christ and the church can be seen by comparing it with such a reversal, stated by Anders Nygren: "Christ and his Church are inseparable entities. Just as the Church is nothing without Christ, so also Christ is nothing without his Church" (Nygren, *Christ and His Church*, trans. Alan Carlsten [Philadelphia: Westminster Press, 1956], p. 90). This citation is quoted approvingly by Carl E. Braaten in "The Special Ministry of the Ordained," in *Marks of the Body of Christ*, ed. Carl E. Braaten and Robert W. Jenson (Grand Rapids: Eerdmans, 1999), p. 135. Whatever one's estimation of Barth's ecclesiology, one thing is certain: he could never utter such a sentence.

[47]For a discussion of Barth's concept of correspondence and the accompanying concepts of "parable" (*Gleichnis*) and "analogy" (*Analogie*), see Helmut Gollwitzer, "Kingdom of God and Socialism in the Theology of Karl Barth," in *Karl Barth and Radical Politics*, ed. George Hunsinger (Philadelphia: Westminster Press, 1976), pp. 97-99. See also Webster, *Barth's Ethics of Reconciliation* and *Barth's Moral Theology*.

[48]Correspondence may be thought of as the ontological and ethical parallel to the epistemological "analogy of faith" (*analogia fidei*) in Barth's theology. Referring to the concept of correspondence and to the related one of parable in Barth's theology, Gollwitzer concludes: "It is indicative of

cally christological notion, however, for it is defined by and refers first and preeminently to the manner in which Christ's human life mirrors and indeed re-presents the divine life of God and reflects the divine will in history, and thus how his human nature reflects his divine nature in its own proper sphere of being and activity.[49] It is then applied by analogy to obedient human activity that reflects the divine will as established by grace.

When applied by Barth to the church, the concept of correspondence speaks neither of an identity, continuity and cooperation between divine and human action nor of a purely radical separation, opposition and contradiction between them. It is neither univocal nor equivocal but analogical in nature. It guards against any type of identification or conflation of divine and human activity, excluding any synergistic or cooperative understandings of salvation. Divine activity and human activity remain distinct and do not exist on the same plane. Positively, it entails that human actions not contradict but reflect the divine will and activity in a manner appropriate to the creature, neither replacing nor supplementing the divine activity.[50] And it is for this positive affirmation that the negative judgment is made: human activity is relativized and limited not so that it is to be set aside as irrelevant or purely sinful, but so that it might be given its own proper place as a truly human work, rather than the work of God. For this reason, Barth does not see his "de-sacramentalizing" of the church's action as a denigration of the church's activity but as a clarification of the church's real, true and rightful dignity as a human response of obedience to the grace of God.[51] Barth can even refer to such action as a cooperation with God, though in a highly qualified and circumscribed manner:

> Within the limits of its creaturely capacity and ability it [the church] is or-
> dained and summoned to co-operate with Him in His work [. . . *zur Mitar-*

---

academic theology's idealist way of thinking that it is not these concepts, but their correlate from the theory of knowledge—the concept of analogy—which has held the center of attention in the discussion and interpretation of Barth. . . . *Analogia fidei* corresponds at the theoretical level to 'parable' at the level of social praxis; the former is necessary in that it grounds and secures the correct occurrence of the practice of the Christian life" ("Kingdom of God and Socialism," p. 97).

[49]*CD* IV/2, p. 166.

[50]Gollwitzer, "Kingdom of God and Socialism," pp. 97-99.

[51]For the radical implications of Barth's understanding of the church's ministry, see Eberhard Busch, "Karl Barth's Understanding of the Church as Witness," *St. Luke's Journal of Theology* 33 (1990): 87-101; also Webster, *Barth's Moral Theology*, pp. 125-50.

beitershaft an seinem Werk bestimmt und berufen]. And since His work is on and in the world, in its own place and manner it, too, is pledged to the world and made responsible for what is to become of it. Different though its action may be from His, in its own definite function and within the appointed limits it, too, is summoned and freed and commissioned for action in and towards the world.[52]

This human life and activity corresponds, or lives in analogy to, the divine life, but does so only in light of the previous logic whereby the radical asymmetry between the partners and their work is affirmed, and the complete and utter dependence of the human on the divine is safeguarded. Barth's notion of correspondence describes the character of the human life and activity that exists enhypostatically in the divine Word in the incarnation, and by analogy the character of the life of the church and the Christian established by God within the covenant of grace. It thus ties the theological and the ethical, the vertical and the horizontal, together. An analogous relationship of being-in-act and a correspondence of activity are made possible by divine grace rather than a natural human capacity. The action of the church does not replace or supplement the divine activity, but it does have a real, true, and important place that reflects and bears witness to God's salvific work. There is nothing insufficient in the divine activity that requires completion in the church's life, but the church does by grace accompany and serve the divine activity as a witness.

Once again, correspondence is first and foremost a christological principle before it is an ethical one in that the correspondence of the creature to the Creator finds its ultimate and normative archetype in the humble obedience of Jesus Christ to God, the life of the New Adam lived in conformity to the Father's will. This is seen preeminently in the fact that Jesus Christ is not only the electing God but also the elect human being, not only the humble and obedient Son of God but also the exalted and glorified Son of Man. Yet this christological correspondence is complemented by an ecclesiological one, in that the church is to attempt and bear within its life and in the life of each member "an imitation and representation [*Nachahmung und Darstellung*] of the love with which God loved the world."[53]

---

[52]*CD* IV/3.2, p. 777.
[53]*CD* III/4, p. 502.

These christological elements of the Chalcedonian pattern, the *anhypostasia/enhypostasia* formula and the motif of correspondence, serve not only the constructive purpose of giving shape to Barth's ecclesiology, but a critical one as well. They do so in providing criteria that assist in criticizing and avoiding mistaken positions whether conceived on the theological left or right. The close affiliation between Christology and ecclesiology in Barth's thought is made evident in that these mistaken ecclesiological positions are construed by Barth in terms of christological heresies. For Barth, to consider the true church to be an invisible reality behind the visible institution, and indeed opposed to and in contradiction with it, was to succumb to a docetic ecclesiology. On the opposite side, to conceive of the church solely and purely as a historical phenomenon and as one human society among others, without regard to its grounding in the activity of the Holy Spirit as an eschatological event, was to fall into an ebionitic heresy. While Barth explicitly identified these errors as docetic and ebionitic, he also speaks implicitly of a third error: that of confusing the historical institution, life and practices of the church with revelation itself, what might be termed a Eutychian heresy. Here the dialectical relation itself is sacrificed so that history is divinized and revelation is historicized in a confused and amalgamated relation. The first error sacrifices the historical form to the divine event, thus failing to account for the enhypostatic character of the church. The second sacrifices the divine event to the historical form, thus failing to account for the anhypostatic character of the church. The third sacrifices the dialectical character and confuses the realities, so that the asymmetrical and irreversible character of the relation is lost, the correspondence of the church giving way to a synergism of cooperation.[54]

As should by now be evident, Barth's own position is to speak of the church as both divinely constituted and historically situated, a reality com-

---

[54]For an insightful description of ecclesiology in terms of the relationship between divine event and historical form and duration, see Martin Honecker, "Kirche als Gestalt und Ereignis: Die sichtbare Gestalt der Kirche als dogmatisches Problem," in *Forschungen zur Geschichte und Lehre des Protestantismus*, ed. Ernst Wolf, no. 10, v. 25 (München: Chr. Kaiser Verlag, 1963), pp. 1-238; esp. pp. 11-15. Honecker identifies this relationship between eschatological event (*Ereignis*) and historical form (*Gestalt*) as central to the Reformation understanding of the church and states that the defining theological problem pertaining to this relationship can be stated succinctly: "the church stands in history but does not originate from history" (*die Kirche in der Geschichte besteht, aber nicht aus der Geschichte stammt*) (p. 12).

prised of both an inner mystery of the Spirit and a society of human persons in fellowship and joint activity. The church is for Barth both invisible and visible, so that the inner mystery is not sacrificed to the external form, or vice versa, thus maintaining the integrity of each. Barth seeks neither to confuse nor separate the divine event and the historical and sociological form, presented in a highly dialectical construal of the relation between divine action and historical duration. He regularly defines the church dialectically with reference to rejected and opposing dyads—the church is neither docetic nor ebionitic, neither idealized nor historicized, neither antinomian nor legalistic, neither sacralized nor secularized.

In sum, Barth's doctrine of the church, in all of its varied and multifaceted complexity, is best understood when its christological logic is delineated and understood, and its strengths and deficiencies can be assessed more fairly and accurately when the deep substructure of Barth's doctrine of the church is kept in view. When they are not, mistakes and missteps can only ensue.

BARTH'S ECCLESIOLOGY IN THE LIGHT OF RECENT CRITICISMS

Having provided a necessary if somewhat terse account of Barth's doctrine of the church, we can turn to recent engagements with his ecclesiology. Contemporary discussions of Barth's ecclesiology among mainline Protestant theologians (and some Roman Catholic ones) are for the most part both appreciative of Barth's achievement and critical of apparent shortcomings. While limitations of space render it impossible to survey such studies of Barth's ecclesiology exhaustively and in fine detail, it is possible to present the central and recurrent criticisms of Barth's understanding of the church and the general arguments proffered for them under a few major headings.

Barth has subsumed pneumatology into Christology. Specifically, he has so identified the Spirit with Christ that the distinctive personhood and agency of the Spirit is sacrificed. One of the criticisms of Barth's theology in general, with special application to ecclesiology in particular, is that he has subsumed pneumatology into Christology and thus sacrificed a real and significant place for the Holy Spirit in the economy of salvation. While such a charge may at times be overdrawn, it arises out of a significant concern.

The manner in which Barth construes the relationship between the Holy Spirit and Christ with particular reference to the church is related to his answer to the problem of speaking of both the presence and absence of Christ during the time between Christ's ascension and return, between his first and second advents. Barth is reticent to speak of Christ as absent during this intervening time, for this might imply that the community needs to make him present through some form of sacramental mediation, a position Barth rejects. Christ is present, not absent, Barth insists, and therefore he has no need of vicars or representatives in the world. Nor can he be subsumed into the church's proclamation, faith or community, or be replaced by them.[55] Yet, as Barth concedes, Christ is of course not physically present in the world today, having ascended and now delaying his second advent, and therefore the question of his absence cannot be ignored.

Barth's solution to this conundrum is to speak of Christ as present through the Holy Spirit in a manner that closely joins and nearly identifies the Spirit and Christ, and in a way that sees Christ to be present in his community as the "earthly-historical form of his existence." The time between Christ's first advent and his second one is therefore not a period marked by Christ's absence, requiring the church to act as a mediator or vicar on the earth, but as the time of Christ's presence precisely through the power of the Spirit in the community, the time of Christ's second form of existence. It is thus another form of the *parousia* of Jesus Christ. The Holy Spirit on this account is nearly identified with Christ himself. Barth can even go so far as to assert that the Holy Spirit is "Jesus Christ Himself in the power of His resurrection."[56]

With this solution Barth can on one hand deal realistically with the absence of Christ as the eschatological problem in this time between the first and second advents, while on the other hand he can speak of a real presence of Christ during this epoch, though it is a presence mediated by the Spirit.[57]

---

[55]*CD* IV/3.1, pp. 349-50.

[56]*CD* IV/3.1, pp. 352, 353. Elsewhere Barth writes: "It is crucial that the Holy Spirit should not in any sense be understood as a relatively or absolutely independent and independently operative force intervening between Jesus Christ and the man who is called by Him, but as His Spirit, as the power of His presence, work and Word, as the shining of the life of which He is the fullness." Further: "The presence and action of the Holy Spirit are the *parousia* of Jesus Christ in the time between Easter and His final revelation" (*CD* IV/3.2, p. 503).

[57]See *CD* IV/2, p. 652. Barth speaks of the time between the first and second advents as the time of the community, the time in which the church lives as a provisional representation, and thus as a real and true, though imperfect and incomplete, reflection of the sanctification of humanity in Christ (*CD* IV/2, p. 649; also *CD* IV/1, pp. 725-39).

Barth writes: "Where the man Jesus attests Himself in the power of the Spirit of God, He makes Himself present; and those whom He approaches in His self-attestation are able also to approach Him and to be near Him."[58]

This close identification of Christ and the Spirit solves a dilemma for Barth, namely, the problem of Christ's seeming absence and the need for ecclesiastical mediation in the present in light of this absence. His solution, however, raises some oft-noted questions. While Barth is not far from Calvin on this question of Christ's presence through the mediation of the Spirit, at points Barth seems to come very close to identifying Christ with the Spirit and subsuming the Spirit into Christ. In the passages within the *Church Dogmatics* where Barth specifically addresses the question of the Trinity, there can be no doubt as to the integrity and distinctiveness of all three persons, or, as Barth prefers, "modes of being" (*Seinsweisen*). Yet in Barth's ecclesiological thought, some take Barth to be close at times to subsuming the person and work of the Spirit into Christ's person and work in a modalist fashion, making the Spirit simply the manifestation of Christ's presence in the community today. This would leave Barth not with a Trinity but a Binity, and although without doubt this is not Barth's intention, it is a question that hangs over his seeming identification of the Spirit as "Jesus Christ Himself in the power of His resurrection" and equation of the person and work of the Spirit with Christ's own "spiritual being and work."[59] Here some ask whether Barth's pneumatology has been unduly influenced by his fear of ecclesiastical and sacramental mediation, and whether the Holy Spirit has received short shrift in Barth's ecclesiology so that his theology is one-sided.[60]

It is indeed this charge of one-sidedness that often is raised when Barth's description of the church is deemed pneumatologically deficient. Reinhard Hütter can thus write that Barth "is able to articulate the Holy Spirit *only* as

---

[58]*CD* IV/2, p. 654.

[59]*CD* IV/3.1, pp. 352-53; *CD* IV/1, p. 147.

[60]Robert Jenson, "You Wonder Where the Spirit Went," *Pro Ecclesia* 2 (1993): 296-304; see esp. pp. 302-4. For a defense of Barth on this score, see George Hunsinger, "The Mediator of Communion: Karl Barth's Doctrine of the Holy Spirit," in *Disruptive Grace: Studies in the Theology of Karl Barth* (Grand Rapids: Eerdmans, 2000), pp. 148-85. For a critical introduction to Barth's pneumatology as it bears on other doctrines within his theology, see Daniel Migliore, "Vinculum Pacis: Barth's Theology of the Holy Spirit" (unpublished English manuscript, 2000), published in German translation as "Vinculum Pacis—Karl Barths Theologie des Heiligen Geistes," *Evangelische Theologie* 6 (2000): 131-52.

a *mode* [of God] rather than as *Spiritus Creator* having its own salvific-economic mission and its own work."[61] He later continues: "This [Barth's] pneumatology makes it impossible for any genuine salvific-historic work of the *Spiritus Creator* to be related to or even distinguished from the salvific-economic mission of the Son. Because of this Barth's theology cannot really establish any firm *ecclesiological* position."[62]

In a similar vein, Joseph Mangina states that while Barth's manner of closely uniting Christology and ecclesiology, Christ and the church, has many strengths, it nevertheless "is flawed in its failure to acknowledge the Holy Spirit as a distinctive divine economy." He continues: "Since Barth treats the cross as bringing history to a close, the Spirit's work is 'short-circuited.' The Spirit can only appear as a predicate of Christ's reconciling work, a *manifestation* of the latter rather than an *agency* of its own."[63] Barth's ultimate deficiency, therefore, rests for such interlocutors in an under-developed pneumatology that fails to provide the Spirit with a distinctive and independent identity and agency in the history of redemption. This broad accusation underlies the other more definite criticisms that follow.

In construing the finality of Christ's saving work on the cross in such a way that salvation history is thus brought to a close, Barth fails to attribute distinctive agency and unique work to the Spirit in the history between the resurrection and the second advent. Specifically, Barth fails to identify the dogmas and practices of the church as the direct and distinctive workings of the Spirit in the life of the church. We might ask, "What is it that the Spirit is to accomplish in the economy of salvation that Barth ignores?" One answer that is sometimes given is that Barth fails to recognize that the Spirit provides the church with normative and binding dogma as well as its concrete practices and forms of life.

---

[61]Reinhard Hütter, *Suffering Divine Things: Theology as Church Practice* (Grand Rapids: Eerdmans, 1999), p. 111, originally published as *Theologie als kirchliche Praktik* (Gütersloh: Chr. Kaiser/Gütersloher Verlaghaus, 1997), hereafter cited as *SDT*. Hütter is a native of Germany but now teaches in the United States and thus is appropriately included in this study of North American mainline reactions to Barth's ecclesiology. This appropriateness is in no way undermined by the other qualification that must be noted, namely, Hütter's conversion to Roman Catholicism.
[62]*SDT*, p. 112.
[63]Joseph L. Mangina, "Bearing the Marks of Jesus: The Church in the Economy of Salvation in Barth and Hauerwas," *Scottish Journal of Theology* 52 (1999): 270. He later states that Barth "has left precious little for the Holy Spirit to accomplish" (p. 300).

This is a central tenet of Hütter's criticism of Barth's dialectical construal of the relation of the Spirit and the church. Barth's refusal to identify church dogma with the work of the Spirit in a direct (that is, nondialectical) manner, and his deep conviction that such confessional doctrine is not directly the Spirit's work but a human response to revelation, leads Hütter to judge Barth's position to be an inherently unstable and volatile one. He writes: "The construction does not provide for the Holy Spirit to tie itself to such a confession or for such a confession to express human action 'in' the Spirit such that the confession itself might be understood as a work of the Holy Spirit."[64] What Barth ultimately fails to do, according to Hütter, is identify the doctrines of the church as the work of the Spirit in a direct manner so that they might be rightly recognized as binding and irreformable. Instead, his dialectical understanding of the relation between Spirit and church in effect undermines church dogma, rendering it relative and replaceable. Barth's strict *diastasis* between God and humanity, between Spirit and church, is therefore responsible for undercutting any normative doctrine with the result that its guiding authority is sacrificed. Barth's position is unable to provide the church with the constancy that only guiding and fixed confessional statements and practices supply, a constancy necessary for the church's historical identity and life to be sustained in the midst of surrounding change. Hütter writes:

> Barth is unable to interpret or render ecclesiologically fruitful in any pneumatologically relevant fashion what he calls the "mediate forms," and his development of the relational nexus of church, church doctrine, and theology ultimately remains ecclesiologically unstable because the pneumatology itself remains deficient. The relation between Holy Spirit and church turns out to be the core problem.[65]

Hütter contends that Barth's dialectical and eschatological understanding of dogma must ultimately be rejected, for it leads not only to an unstable center

---

[64]*SDT*, p. 107. Hütter examines Barth's position in light of the debate between Barth and Erik Peterson in the 1920s over the question of church doctrine. See *SDT*, pp. 95-115; also Reinhard Hütter, "The Church as Public: Dogma, Practice and the Holy Spirit," *Pro Ecclesia* 3 (1994): 334-61.

[65]*SDT*, pp. 112-13. Elsewhere Hütter writes: "Barth's understanding of theology is pneumatologically sophisticated yet ecclesiologically deficient precisely because the relationship between Spirit and church is far from clear" ("Church as Public," p. 345).

for theology but ultimately into the dangers of "spiritualistic individualism."[66]
He writes: "If indeed all human action per se can at best refer either antici-
patorily or in response to this event, and yet if God's action in principle has
never nor will it ever tie itself to any human action, then God's actions can
be conceived only as becoming evident as God's self-manifestation in the
interiority of the believer."[67] The public nature of the church thereby dissi-
pates into subjectivism. In the end, Barth's position can only recognize an
absence, rather than a real presence, of the Spirit in the church.[68]

In contrast to Barth, Hütter states that one should not understand church
doctrine to be dialectical but to be the real work of the Holy Spirit and thus
to be a concrete and binding authority for the church.[69] He states that "the
church, as the work of the Holy Spirit . . . is also characterized by duration,
concreteness, and visibility, and as such is identical with distinct practices
or activities, institutions, offices, and doctrines."[70] The Holy Spirit has bound
himself to the church, and the doctrines and practices of the church are
constitutive for the church and are in fact binding and immutable because
they themselves are first and foremost the work of the Spirit, and only secondarily of the church itself.[71]

Hütter's criticism of Barth's dialectical relationship between the Spirit and
the church is echoed by others and is not idiosyncratic to him. Mangina
raises similar points of contention with Barth's concept of the church and

---

[66]*SDT*, pp. 112-15. Barth's position, which Hütter here calls Barth's "christological-pneumatological
actualism" (p. 113) and which he elsewhere calls Barth's "dialectical catholicity," in which the
work of the Spirit and the confession of the church are never directly identified, must give way,
according to Hütter, to a stable position where such dialectical understandings of doctrine are
replaced by a non-dialectical "concrete catholicity." It is such a "concrete catholicity" that Hütter
believes marks both the Roman Catholic and Reformation understandings of the church in
contrast to Barth. See Reinhard Hütter, "Karl Barth's 'Dialectical Catholicity': *Sic et Non*," *Modern Theology* 16 (2000): 137-57, esp. pp. 149-52.

[67]*SDT*, p. 109.

[68]Ibid., pp. 106-7. It is not insignificant that Hütter contends that Barth's application of Chalcedonian
christological patterns to all areas of theology (and thus beyond the bounds of Christology proper)
is mistaken. If this is so, Hütter's disagreements with Barth perhaps run deeper than he himself
may realize. He writes concerning the Chalcedonian logic: "What doubtless constituted a meaningful regulative in a substance-ontological context does not in an action-determined context
automatically apply" (p. 106). What is indeed problematic with this statement itself is that Barth's
own Christology was not predicated on a "substance" ontology but on an actualistic one.

[69]"Precisely from the perspective of the *Spiritus Creator*, theology must be conceived undialecti-
cally 'in' the presence of the Spirit" (ibid., p. 114).

[70]Ibid., p. 119.

[71]Ibid., pp. 27, 125-26, 132, 176, et al.

posits that an ecclesiology that corrects Barth and provides the "concrete pneumatology" that he lacks requires "the possibility of acknowledging developments in the life of the post-apostolic church as binding and, perhaps, irreversible. From a Reformation point of view, the important thing is to maintain a lively sense of God's judgment *over against* the church, yet without denying the reality of God's gifts *to* the church."[72] Mangina, like Hütter, thus sees Barth's fundamental problem as rooted in his dialectical understanding of the relation between the Spirit (and Christ) and the church, for such a dialectic moves "between the poles of complete identity and complete non-identity" and thus cannot provide a stable center and norm for ecclesiastical life.[73] In the end, what Barth's doctrine of the church seems to lack, according to his critics, is concreteness, and this leads to a further criticism of Barth's ecclesiology.

By refusing to identify the concrete activity of the church with the Spirit's work, Barth in turn fails to take the church's historicity seriously. Specifically, Barth fails to give adequate attention to the church's socially embodied existence and its particular and constitutive practices and in turn provides an abstract and dehistoricized ecclesiology. This charge may indeed be characterized as the other side of the coin to that which faults Barth for neglecting to identify the Spirit's work with the constitutive doctrine and practices of the church, an ecclesiological "tails" to the pneumatological "heads" of the coin. In short, it is the charge that Barth does not take the concrete existence of the church seriously enough—he is so concerned to preserve the Spirit's freedom against that of the church and maintain the distinction between the Spirit's agency and that of the church that he ulti-

---

[72]Mangina, "Bearing the Marks of Jesus," pp. 301, 269-305. It is difficult to know how to reconcile this reference to "binding and irreversible developments" with Mangina's later statement: "The vulnerability of *any aspect* of church life to critique is a function of the lordship of Christ; the doctrine functions 'hermeneutically' because and in so far as it articulates this material conviction" (p. 303, emphasis added). One here wonders if such "binding and irreversible developments" fall within the category of "any aspect" of the church's life. If they do not, Mangina's statement appears to be false; if they do, in what sense are they then "irreversible" (even if in another sense "binding")?

[73]Mangina, "Bearing the Marks of Jesus," pp. 301-2. Elsewhere he writes that this "aversion to identifying the Spirit's work with persistent, enduring social forms or practices marks a problematic area in his [Barth's] thinking"; see Joseph Mangina, "The Stranger as Sacrament: Karl Barth and the Ethics of Ecclesial Practice," *International Journal of Systematic Theology* 1 (1999): 333.

mately relativizes the church's historical existence and its activity.[74] Nicholas Healy has made the claim (though he now seems to have backed away from it) that Barth "bifurcates" the church between the invisible real church and the visible and sinful church in history so that the latter with its concomitant earthly activity is rendered extraneous to the church's true reality: "*What people do, as such, is not a constituent element of the church's identity*."[75] Echoing Healy, Mangina maintains that "while Barth emphasizes the church's task as a witness to Christ it is not clear that the church *as a configuration of human practices* makes much difference to this task."[76]

For many, this shortcoming is in concert with Barth's penchant to see the true church as "event" and not as a historically continuous community or as a subject in its own right. Therefore, Hütter states, Barth fails to realize that for the church to be a church at all, it must be a "public," that is, a concrete and historical community within the world that manifests a particular life enduring through time. For the church to be such a public, it requires both binding doctrine and concrete practices which give it a specific form of life and enduring shape of existence.[77] This concreteness is precisely what Barth lacks, for Barth emphasizes the invisible work of the Spirit in the church rather than its manifestation in the church's particular and visible practices, an emphasis in evidence with an almost exclusive commitment to theological rather than social descriptions of the church's identity. In light of such charges, Barth's view of the church has been criticized as possessing a

---

[74]See Nicholas Healy, "The Logic of Karl Barth's Ecclesiology: Analysis, Assessment and Proposed Modifications," *Modern Theology* 10 (1994): 253-70. In fairness to Healy, it should be noted that he seems to have retracted his strong criticisms of Barth's ecclesiology after further investigation. See Nicholas Healy, "Karl Barth's Ecclesiology Reconsidered," *Scottish Journal of Theology* 57 (2004): 287-99. Nevertheless, while this point should be constantly kept in mind, the influence of Healy's earlier article on later examinations of Barth's ecclesiology requires that it, too, be included here.

[75]Healy, "Logic of Karl Barth's Ecclesiology," p. 260. Healy writes: "In sum, we have found that Barth selects either of two options in those passages of the *CD* devoted more specifically to the human aspects of the church. On the one hand . . . Barth bifurcates the church into two separate entities, the human church and its spiritual counterpart. On the other hand, when describing the human aspects of the church in their relation of dependency upon the Holy Spirit, he discusses these actions in an abstract and formal manner, bare of concrete descriptions of the 'human phenomena' involved" (p. 263).

[76]Mangina, "Bearing the Marks of Jesus," p. 278. See also Healy, "Logic of Karl Barth's Ecclesiology," p. 260.

[77]*SDT*, pp. 115, 119; see also Hütter, "Church as Public."

"strong tendency towards an abstract and reductionistic ecclesiology."[78]

In sum, some contend that what is missing in Barth's ecclesiology is precisely the thick historical and sociological description of the church's concrete life established by the Spirit that is required to adequately describe its reality and guide its action. Barth's failure to provide a "concrete pneumatology" is thus paralleled by his failure to provide a concrete ecclesiology.[79] This entails a number of ramifications. One is that Barth "dehistoricizes" the church by emphasizing its theological reality and union with Christ in such a way that its own historical agency and life is neglected.[80] Another is that Barth does not sufficiently appreciate the fact that the doctrines and practices of the church themselves "constitute the church," that is, truly make the church what it is and provide its uniqueness and defining identity.[81] Such an identity embodied through such convictions and practices in turn shapes the identity and character of the church's constituent members. As Hütter states, the church is "first of all *a way of life*, i.e., a distinct set of practices interwoven with normative beliefs, concretely and distinctly embodied."[82] Barth's failure is that in providing a safeguard against a "one-sided sociological description" of the church, he has now fallen into the opposite error, that of providing a "one-sided doctrinal description."[83] By making such a strong distinction between the inner reality of the church and its historical reality, Healy states, Barth has transgressed Scripture, in which these are united.

Hütter's criticisms are stronger still. Ultimately, he contends, Barth's dialectical starting point not only undercuts the public nature of the church but in essence precludes it, for Barth's "dialectical catholicity," as an intrinsically critical position, can be used to criticize and test positive ecclesiastical in-

---

[78]Healy, "Logic of Karl Barth's Ecclesiology," p. 263.

[79]Mangina, "Bearing the Marks of Jesus," p. 301. Hütter can also speak of Barth's theology in terms of a "disembodied pneumatology" and "bifurcated ecclesiology" ("Karl Barth's 'Dialectical Catholicity,'" p. 151).

[80]Mangina, "Bearing the Marks of Jesus," pp. 277-78.

[81]See *SDT*, p. 133.

[82]Hütter, "Karl Barth's 'Dialectical Catholicity,'" p. 149. This description of the church closely describes the ecclesiology of Stanley Hauerwas, and it is not insignificant that Hauerwas is posited by Mangina as providing the "temporal and historical thickness" that Barth lacks ("Bearing the Marks of Jesus," pp. 270, 282-92).

[83]Healy, "Logic of Karl Barth's Ecclesiology," p. 263. Again, whether Healy would maintain such criticisms is questionable in light of his later article.

stantiations but cannot be seen to comprise such a tradition itself. In other words, such a "genuine Protestantism" may be "employed over against all real existing churches" as a critical principle but itself cannot "exist in an ecclesially embodied form." Why is this the case? "Because critical principles by definition cannot be embodied, but are to be applied in relationship to concrete embodiments."[84] The result is that Barth's ecclesiology must remain a "disembodied" one. When all is said and done, Hütter seems to say, Barth's dialectical ecclesiology could never find a true instantiation in a real church, for its critical element would relativize and destabilize the very doctrine and practices which are needed to give it temporal constancy and duration. Indeed, Hütter contends, what needs to be taken up, in contrast to Barth's "disembodied pneumatology and critical ecclesiology," is a type of "concrete catholicity." He discovers this catholicity in Luther, and specifically in Luther's practices defined in *On the Councils and the Church*.[85]

Barth fails to make the church a necessary part of God's salvation, thus denigrating its true place in the salvific economy. Specifically, Barth's sole reliance on the notion of "witness" not only overshadows and ignores the church's "mediation" but also in effect renders any real and substantive place for the church irrelevant beyond announcing a finished event. This charge is not unrelated to the prior ones. If Barth has not provided a distinct role for the Spirit in the economy of salvation, and has likewise not sufficiently attended to the concrete social practices that constitute the church, he has in a similar and related fashion not retained a significant place for the church and its action in the economy of salvation. This is presupposed in his construal of the atonement as bringing salvation history to a close. Barth therefore refuses to see the church's work as anything but witness to a past event, rather than a participation in salvation history itself. This is a criticism of Barth's emphasis on witness and dismissal of the notion of sacramental mediation. Barth's strong emphasis on the distinction between divine and human action, coupled with his emphasis on the finished work of salvation in Christ, entails that Barth leaves little not only for the Spirit but also for the church to do.[86] Furthermore, for some, this implies that the

---

[84]Hütter, "Karl Barth's 'Dialectical Catholicity,'" p. 147.
[85]Ibid., pp. 148, 149-52; also *SDT*, pp. 128-45.
[86]That Barth's "pneumatological deficiency" and "ecclesiological deficiency" are seen as two sides

difference between the church and the world in Barth's theology is primarily one of knowledge of salvation, not of a real ontic change.[87]

This argument can be transposed into another key and made more forcefully. Stanley Hauerwas asserts that while Barth sees the importance of the church for the proclamation of the gospel, he does not see the church itself as a part of the gospel proclamation, indeed as constitutive of it.[88] For Hauerwas, the church is not simply a herald of grace but the manifestation of God's grace in the world in the form of a new community, and this latter viewpoint is precisely what Barth ignores. Hauerwas writes: "Barth, of course, does not deny that the church is constituted by the proclamation of the gospel. What he cannot acknowledge is that the community called the church is constitutive of the gospel proclamation."[89] Mangina insightfully summarizes the issue in two juxtaposed questions: "Does the Christian community itself constitute a part of the gospel it confesses? Or is the church simply the human response to a gospel that can be formulated quite apart from the community?"[90] What Hauerwas and Mangina both contend is that Barth's position is best described by the second question, so that the church is extrinsic, rather than intrinsic, to the message of the gospel itself.[91] This should not be construed to mean that they think that Barth denies the

---

of one problematic coin for many of Barth's critics is witnessed in the following: "It is in Barth's theology of the Church, in fact, that all the difficulties in his pneumatology are accentuated. Most prominent among these is the lack of mediation which is attributed to the members of the Church, let alone to all mankind, in the accomplishment of the Spirit's mission of bringing about the consummation of the world" (Philip Rosato, *The Spirit As Lord: The Pneumatology of Karl Barth* [Edinburgh: T & T Clark, 1981], p. 185).

[87]See Healy, "Logic of Karl Barth's Ecclesiology," p. 265; also Hütter, "Karl Barth's 'Dialectical Catholicity,'" p. 150.

[88]Stanley Hauerwas, *With the Grain of the Universe: The Church's Witness and Natural Theology* (Grand Rapids: Brazos, 2001), p. 145. See also Mangina, "Bearing the Marks of Christ," p. 292.

[89]Hauerwas, *With the Grain of the Universe*, p. 145.

[90]Mangina, "Bearing the Marks of Jesus," p. 292. Mangina continues on to quote Robert Jenson as posing a variation of these very questions: "Granted that there would be no gospel to believe, did not the church preach and administer sacraments; granted even that faith in the gospel would be impossible except in the community of the church, can the church be unthematic for faith once present? Are faith in Christ and identification with the church-community distinguishable spiritual acts? Or is the Christ who is both the ground and object of faith the *totus Christus*, the embodied person whose body is the church?" (Robert Jenson, *Unbaptized God* [Philadelphia: Fortress, 1992], p. 97, quoted in Mangina, "Bearing the Marks of Jesus," pp. 202-93).

[91]"Barth sets the community in a completely 'eccentric' relation to the story to which it bears witness" (Mangina, "Bearing the Marks of Christ," p. 295).

church's visible existence. This is not a charge of docetism. What is at issue is not that Barth possesses a docetic ecclesiology but that the concrete visible and social existence of the church is not intrinsically related to the message of the gospel or identifiable with the Spirit's activity. For Hauerwas, the net result is that Barth's ecclesiology is "not sufficiently catholic," which results from Barth's inability (or refusal) to acknowledge that "through the Holy Spirit, we are made part of God's care of the world through the church."[92] This is a central criticism of Hauerwas against Barth's ecclesiology, and he states it in an even more powerful manner, in effect questioning the necessity of the church for Barth:

> Barth says that we may venture three statements: "1. the world would be lost without Jesus Christ and His Word and work; 2. the world would not necessarily be lost if there were no Church; and 3. the Church would be lost if it had no counterpart in the world." If the world is not necessarily lost without the church, then it is by no means clear what difference the church makes for how we understand the way the world is and, given the way the world is, how we must live.[93]

In its basic form, the final criticism of Barth's ecclesiology here considered is that he has denied a role of sacramental mediation to the church. In its strongest form, it seems to question whether Barth's theology has any significant role for the church in God's salvation at all.

EVALUATION OF THE CRITICISMS

It would be a mistake to conclude from the previous discussion that Barth's interlocutors are solely critical of Barth's ecclesiological work. In truth, most are deeply appreciative of his achievement. Yet, a survey such as this one is best served not by focusing on agreement but in attempting to get to the heart of disagreement, and while criticisms of Barth's ecclesiology range

---

[92]Hauerwas, *With the Grain of the Universe*, p. 145. Mangina makes a similar though more qualified point: "The church is constituted by the Spirit as the social activity of witness to the life, death, and resurrection of Jesus Christ; as witness to *him* it acquires a definite internal structure, law, and way of life; but the latter are purely human responses to the work of the Spirit, rather than divinely-willed coordinates that help to define the Spirit's action" ("Bearing the Marks of Jesus," p. 295).

[93]Hauerwas, *With the Grain of the Universe*, p. 193. See also Mangina, "Bearing the Marks of Christ," pp. 280-81. The quotation from Barth is from *CD* IV/3.2, p. 826.

over a number of concerns, most center on the issues addressed above. It is now time to turn our sights on the criticisms themselves.

The question of subsuming pneumatology into Christology. As this is the most general charge, and one that goes far beyond the limited scope of the topic at hand, comments must be limited and somewhat provisional. As noted above, Barth does at times come close to identifying Christ and the Spirit and this does raise questions for his ecclesiology. Whether he subsumes the latter into the former is a valid question. Nevertheless, it must be stated that the heart of the issue for Barth is not to deny that the Spirit is distinct from Christ (a conviction he certainly could affirm elsewhere—Barth was no proponent of a binitarian faith), but that the Spirit's work is not distinctive from that of Christ if this means that the Spirit (or the church) must supplement the work of Christ in such a way that the latter is shown to be somehow deficient. Most important for understanding Barth's close association of Christ and the Spirit is to recognize his central conviction that the Spirit cannot be construed as an independent agent in salvific history.[94] Such a view would both deny the trinitarian nature of salvation itself (*Opera trinitatis ad extra sunt indivisa*), as well as overlook the fact that the Spirit does not testify to himself but to Christ.[95]

Another historical concern resides below the surface. Quite simply, Barth was wary of any attempt to separate Christ and the Spirit because of a general fear of anthropology overtaking theology (a fact noted by his critics as well as admirers). Separating the Spirit from Christ could only lead to a confusion and eventual identification of the human spirit with the divine Spirit, the spirit of the church with the Spirit of God. Barth's close union, if not identification, of Christ and the Spirit was therefore driven by a legitimate concern, namely, that the Spirit could be divorced from Christ in a form of mysticism or existentialism so that the objectivity of Christ is sacrificed and replaced by an anthropologically construed present experience of salvation. Barth himself glimpsed the former in Schleiermacher and the latter in Bultmann, and for Barth this subjective turn was the hallmark of Protestant

---

[94]*CD* IV/3.2, p. 503.

[95]As George Hunsinger writes: "The significance of the Holy Spirit is not found directly or independently in himself," and later, "In short, the saving activity of the Holy Spirit, as understood by Barth, is always Christ-centered in focus" ("Mediator of Communion," pp. 157, 162, respectively).

liberalism past and present. Some may consider Barth's solution to be a
pendulum swing too far in the other direction, the direction of a hard soteriological objectivism—he himself noted that a legitimate theology of the
third article could be written but that this remained for others to achieve.[96]
Barth's own christological concentration was thus an attempt to change the
course of a long tradition, and it should not be surprising that such course
corrections can lead to overcompensation and one-sidedness. Barth himself
was not unaware of such one-sidedness in his thought.[97] Nor did he think
such one-sidedness mistaken.

Here we must take great care. As John Webster has noted, it may be that
in regard to pneumatology Barth is "not so much deficient as different—
less committed to a pluralist trinitarian theology, less anxious to identify
the demarcations between the actions of Christ and the Spirit in the world."[98]
In sum, we may well be faced here with an "either-or" between Barth and
his critics. Certainly Barth's doctrine of election as well as his Christology
(in which reconciliation and redemption are both accomplished in Christ)
impinge on his pneumatology and leave no room for traditional conceptions of ecclesial mediation that some of his critics seem to espouse and for
which they accuse Barth of one-sidedness. Here the issue may not be a
question of deficiency in pneumatology but of disagreement based on other
dogmatic convictions.

---

[96]See Karl Barth, *Theology of Schleiermacher*, ed. Dietrich Ritschl, trans. Geoffrey W. Bromiley
(Grand Rapids: Eerdmans, 1982), pp. 277-79. It should also be noted that Barth's doctrine of
redemption, the proposed volume 5 of the *Church Dogmatics*, was never completed. This would
no doubt have contained a more developed and detailed account of pneumatology, following
Barth's trinitarian structure of the doctrines of creation (*CD* III), reconciliation (*CD* IV) and
redemption (the unfinished *CD* V). There Barth may well have spoken of the Holy Spirit more
as an agent in his own right (see Hunsinger, "Mediator of Communion," p. 161). This would
address Jenson's concern that in the doctrine of reconciliation the Spirit disappears whenever
"he would appear as someone rather than as something" (Jenson, "You Wonder Where the Spirit
Went," p. 304).

[97]In response to a student's inquiry in the 1950s as to why the Holy Spirit was largely absent in
Barth's section on the "revealed Word," Barth responded: "You must remember the theological
situation in 1932. At that time I wanted to place a strong emphasis on the objective side of
revelation: Jesus Christ. If I had made much of the Holy Spirit, I am afraid it would have led
back to subjectivism, which is what I wanted to overcome. Today I would speak more of the
Holy Spirit. Perhaps I was too cautious. You students should not make that mistake in your
polemical writings!" (John D. Godsey, *Karl Barth's Table Talk* [Edinburgh: Oliver and Boyd,
1963], p. 27).

[98]John Webster, *Karl Barth* (New York: Continuum, 2000), pp. 138-39.

The question of the dogma and practices of the church as the works of the Spirit. There can be no denying that Barth remained committed to a dialectical notion of revelation from beginning to end. It is also true that Barth places the church's dogma and confessions, as well as its "forms of ministry," on the side of human response rather than divine revelation. But such commitments do not entail that Barth thinks that the Spirit has no role in their origination. Barth certainly agrees that the Spirit gives rise to the church's confession, for it is the Spirit who reveals the Word to the church, thus resulting in the church's confession and the task of doctrinal formulation. For Barth, it was a fresh hearing of the Word (in the midst of crisis) that led to the drafting and adoption of the Barmen Declaration. Nevertheless, he does not concede that such creeds or confessions, or the doctrine that they communicate, are identical with the Spirit's work or that they are absolutely binding. For Barth, their authority always remains relative and they themselves remain provisional, open to correction in light of a fresh hearing of the Word of God.

Therefore, Barth refused to identify the work of God and that of the church, whether in dogma or practices. Perhaps more accurately, these could not be directly, but only indirectly, identified, for to do otherwise would ultimately undermine the distinction between Christ and his church.[99] To directly equate them, rather than indirectly relate them, Barth maintained, would be to confuse them, to divinize human things, and then, consequently, to insulate them from criticism, seen in irreformable dogma and irrevisable practices. "A Church which maintains that its official decisions are infallible can commit errors which are irreformable. It has more than once done so."[100] Such a statement leaves little to the imagination. Here it seems Hütter (and others who make similar claims) do not misunderstand Barth so much as simply disagree with him.[101] This is the rub—there is no reconciliation of Barth's position and that of Hütter. For in effect, Hütter calls for a nondialectical construal of the relationship between the Spirit and the church, or, to sharpen the point, between the working of the Spirit and

---

[99]Barth certainly would not agree that "dogma is the prolongation of the body of Christ," as Hütter seems to espouse ("Church as Public," pp. 351-52).

[100]*CD* IV/1, p. 626.

[101]Healy, "Karl Barth's Ecclesiology Reconsidered," p. 289.

the working of the church expressed in dogma. The heart of Hütter's call is that such dogma be "binding" and irreformable. If forced to choose, Hütter would side with Peterson over against Barth, and follows the same path. In the end, Hütter (and those who argue along similar lines) reject one of Barth's deepest convictions: that the relation between the Spirit and the church must be understood dialectically according to a christological pattern of unity, differentiation and asymmetry. And so Barth's strict adherence to the dictum *finitum non capax infiniti*, itself christologically redefined, is also a point of contention.

Perhaps a way to examine the issue is not to pit a dialectical understanding of dogma over against a nondialectical one but to ask the question, "What is lost when such a dialectical relationship is set aside?" We might address this question by in turn posing a number of questions to Hütter's ecclesiological proposal.

First, it might be asked whether the church really is "identical with distinct practices or activities, institutions, offices, and doctrines," as Hütter contends.[102] Is there not something more to the church than this visibility? What difference does the Holy Spirit really make in Hütter's ecclesiology when the church is equated with its visible and historical life and practices?[103] Could this not lead to a confusion of the work of the Spirit and that of the church, and, in the end, to a loss of the Spirit's freedom in relation to the church? Furthermore, if the doctrines and practices of the church are primarily the work of the Spirit (and only secondarily those of humanity), it is unclear on what grounds they might be criticized. Here Barth's statement regarding "infallible decisions and irreformable errors" seems to come back with a vengeance. Of course, because Hütter sees dogmas as the work of the Spirit is precisely why he states that they are binding and irreformable. This binding character in turn is seen to serve as the guarantee against an unstable position in danger of a disembodied ecclesiology and subjectivism. Yet it might rightly be asked whether such instability is not inescapable for any embodied church that is committed to *ecclesia semper reformanda*. Such instability also may be seen as a blessing, not as a curse.

---

[102]*SDT*, p. 119. Healy himself has backed away from such an identification and has become more sympathetic to Barth's position; see "Karl Barth's Ecclesiology Reconsidered," esp. p. 295 n. 13.
[103]I am indebted to Healy for this way of phrasing this question.

This leads to a second set of related questions. If "binding" dogma means dogma that is immutable and unquestionably authoritative, we might ask whether this position places the church's doctrine and core practices on the same par as Scripture.[104] For if they are not primarily to be thought of as human responses to revelation, but the work of the Holy Spirit, isn't this the same as calling them inspired? Another way to put this question is to ask whether the difference between Scripture and doctrine is a quantitative or a qualitative one. If it is qualitative, how are we to understand this in light of the statement that dogma itself is the work of the Holy Spirit?[105] And if Scripture is the voice of Christ in the church today, as Barth maintains, in what way does Christ stand over and at times over against dogma?[106] It is questionable whether such a nondialectical conception of dogma can retain any real substance for *sola Scriptura*. While Hütter does seem to want to preserve a place for a critical voice for Scripture over against the church, it is unclear whether his description of the doctrine and practices of the church as works of the Spirit allow him to do so convincingly.[107]

Barth and Hütter are certainly in agreement that the church must be visible and give rise to doctrinal confessions and concrete forms of ministry. Indeed, in light of our initial examination, Barth can even speak of the necessity not only of dogma but also of church law. The question therefore is not whether the church must be concrete, but whether the concrete dogma and practices of the church can be directly equated with the reality of the

---

[104]This point is substantiated when we consider that Hütter can list Scripture among other "works of the Spirit" in a sequential manner without drawing attention to a distinction between them. He can thus place under the category of dogma the following: "scriptural canon, the creeds, the dogmatic decisions of the ecumenical councils, and the confessions" ("Church as Public," p. 346). Now a number of questions might be raised of such lists: (1) Is each member of the list on the same authoritative plane, and if not, how are they to be distinguished? (2) How are they to be chosen for acceptance, when some indeed appear to make mutually exclusive claims (for example, the differing confessions of the differing churches)? (3) If Scripture alone is insufficient to provide the stability and constancy required for the church's "public" nature, how will the supplementation of Scripture with binding confessional documents eliminate the hermeneutical problems that give rise to various interpretations of Scripture in the first place? Are not the confessional documents themselves open to various interpretations? Is this not a shift, rather than a solution, of the hermeneutical problem? Such questions could be multiplied. It is not clear that Hütter has provided the resources to answer such questions, though he rightly recognizes the brokenness of the church and how only the Spirit can overcome this (p. 360).
[105]*SDT*, pp. 131-33.
[106]See *CD* I/2, pp. 475, 544, 585.
[107]*SDT*, p. 139.

church and directly identified with the activity of the Spirit. Here Barth and Hütter truly do seem to be in disagreement.

Perhaps some limited rapprochement, though, is possible. While Barth does not see church dogma and confessional decisions as binding and irreformable in the absolute sense that Hütter seems to see them, this does not mean that he understands them as entirely and unqualifiedly relative and easily overturned. Barth was fully aware of the dangers of subjectivism and individualism and certainly did not consider revelation and confession as ultimately reducible to the "interiority of the believer," Hütter's terms and charge notwithstanding.[108] He simply rejects Hütter's solution, that is, that the only defense against such subjectivism is irreformable dogma. For Barth, such an antithesis was a false alternative because both positions fail to listen to the living voice of Christ in Scripture. Barth could, however, speak of a real and enduring, though relative and provisional, authority for church confessional decisions. Two immediate examples come to mind, though more are possible.

First, Barth's deep appreciation for Chalcedonian Christology witnessed to his conviction that it served as a unique norm for the church; it could be abandoned only at great peril (though here, too, what Barth found of lasting significance was not its ancient ontology but its grammar). Nicene and Chalcedonian conciliar decisions were in Barth's thought and estimation enduring and invaluable "guiding lines" for christological thinking.[109] The second example is that of the canon, a topic to be revisited in a later chapter. Barth holds that the canon is open in principle because its boundaries cannot be "fixed" by the immutable decrees of a council but only by the Spirit who attests these books and no others to be the primary witness of God's revelation in Christ. Nevertheless, the history of the church in hearing God's Word in precisely these books, a hearing acknowledged in the past

---

[108]Barth indeed places the faith of the individual under that of the church's own faith: "Put pointedly and to be taken *cum grano salis*, there exist over against Jesus Christ, not in the first instance believers, and then, composed of them, the Church; but first of all the Church and then, through it and in it, believers. . . . And when we say 'Church,' we do not mean merely the inward and invisible coherence of those whom God in Christ calls His own, but also the outward and visible coherence of those who have heard in time, and have confessed to their hearing, that in Christ they are God's. The reception of revelation occurs within, not without, this twofold coherence" (*CD* I/2, p. 211).

[109]*CD* IV/1, p. 127.

decisions of the church regarding the determination of the canon, has so much weight behind it that Barth finds it difficult to conceive that circumstances could arise which would require a change in the canon's composition and an overturning of the church's decisions of the past. Such is not impossible, but it would require a true consensus of the church, and Barth does not seem to expect such an occurrence. On this question, Barth comments that the "so far unaltered judgment of the Church radically precedes as such the judgment of the individual, even if it is the judgment of quite a number of individuals who have to be reckoned with seriously in the Church."[110] If this is the case, Hütter's absolute authority and Barth's relative authority for confessional dogma may at points differ little in practice, though greatly in principle. It would seem, moreover, that the list of such "binding" decisions would be much shorter on Barth's side.

The question of the church's concreteness. Barth and his interlocutors agree that the church is embodied in a concrete and visible form of life. Where Barth seems to differ from them (at the very least in emphasis, if not in outright disagreement) is with regard to the claim that this concrete embodiment constitutes the church, that it is identical with the church's full reality. Barth refuses to reduce the church to its visible existence, for the church is a true church only as it is so constituted by the Holy Spirit and is *not* guaranteed simply by the existence of the church's institutions, traditions and reformations.[111]

In contrast to an undialectical equation of the true church with the visible church, Barth's carefully constructed dialectical ecclesiology preserves a place for both the invisibility *and* the visibility of the church, for both its transcendent and historical qualities, and construes their relation according to christological norms. Barth certainly does not want to dehistoricize the church anymore than he wants to historicize it. He firmly insists that the visibility and temporality of the church are central to its identity and rejects any ecclesiological docetism, while equally rejecting a flight into visibility that simply equates the church's essence with its historical and social existence.

Yet, it must be admitted that while Barth preserves the integrity and unity of both the invisible and visible church, the priority of the first strand does

---

[110]See *CD* I/2, p. 479.
[111]*CD* IV/1, p. 654.

at times overshadow the second in a way that reveals the underdeveloped nature of the latter term. It is not that Barth chooses the invisible over the visible church, or the church as event over the church as institution. It is, rather, that with regard to the latter some important themes are sometimes absent.[112] For example, notably missing in the *Dogmatics* is a sustained discussion of ordained ministry. Barth disdains strong clergy-lay distinctions and rightly focuses on the ministry that each member must undertake in the community. Nevertheless, if hierarchical offices are rejected, the questions of ordination and ministerial roles are all the more inescapable in ecclesiology. The absence of an extensive discussion of these matters in the *Dogmatics* therefore is significant. Furthermore, as Webster has noted, in regard to the church Barth "has a rather slender account of the moral processes of common life."[113] Here, a rightful fear of casuistry can tend "to leave the processes of moral reasoning rather opaque" and the practices of moral formation unspecified.[114] In response to such charges, it might reasonably be said that Barth may well have taken up such matters in more detail in the ethics of reconciliation (which remained incomplete) and in the ethics of redemption (which was never written). Nevertheless, this incompleteness and lack of specificity lies at the root of the criticism that Barth's ecclesiology lacks concreteness (and is in fact a more accurate way of putting what is truly at issue).

If such a criticism is made, it must be very carefully articulated, however. It would be false to maintain that Barth precludes historical continuity in his definition of the church's substance. Barth does not simply set an invisible, true church of event over against a visible, false institutional church. It is precisely such a dichotomy that Barth's ecclesiology attempts to overcome, and most of Barth's modern-day critics do not repeat this earlier criticism. It was not the visible church that Barth opposed, for the true church was both invisible and visible. What Barth opposed is a sociological understanding of the church that fails to discern its true theological character. So to state that Barth has a low ecclesiology, one that relativizes the visible, and to assert that for Barth the church "is not a qualitatively distinct

---

[112]As Healy rightly notes in "Logic of Karl Barth's Ecclesiology," pp. 257-58; cf. pp. 266-68.
[113]Webster, *Karl Barth*, p. 161.
[114]Ibid.

entity, for it has neither unique powers nor a distinctive ethos that would give its members the opportunity to engage in the most adequate way of life or response and witness to Jesus Christ," is to put matters in a way that is quite difficult to defend.[115] For Barth, the church is a distinct entity, for it is in fact called into existence by the power of the Holy Spirit, and it is this power that not only gives rise to the church but also sets it apart from every other historical society. In short, the church is a mystery (in analogy to the supreme mystery and miracle of Christmas itself) which can be recognized only by faith. Furthermore, the church is distinct because it does have a unique way of life, a way that is the normative pattern for all other familial, social and political forms of life, and normative precisely because it exists in correspondence to Christ's own life. Church law is exemplary law. It is thus not the case that for Barth the church's empirical distinctiveness is in effect relativized and its historical reality and embodiment of no importance.

Barth is rightly concerned that the church not simply be described in sociological terms, or that such description be substituted for theological exposition itself. For Barth, this is a concomitant error to the mistake of subsuming revelation into history and thus confusing them, precisely the problem that Barth perceived in his early opponents. Certainly Barth could at times set theological and sociological descriptions of the church against one another in competition and as mutually exclusive, rather than integrating the latter into the former.[116] Such exclusivity is the real basis of truth in the charge that Barth's description of the church at times appears formal and abstract.[117] Yet such a charge itself should be made only after taking note of a number of factors that greatly qualify it.

First, while Barth's ecclesiology may be open to criticism for its emphasis on formal relations and sparse description of specific practices, such a criticism should only be made after a thorough examination of Barth's descriptions of precisely such practices in *CD* IV/3.2 has been conducted. Barth's

---

[115]Healy, "Logic of Karl Barth's Ecclesiology," p. 265. Once again, Healy now seems ready to withdraw such claims in "Karl Barth's Ecclesiology Reconsidered."

[116]A classic example of this competition may be seen in Barth's early essay of 1926, "Church and Culture," in *Theology and Church*, pp. 334-54; see esp. pp. 334-37, though whether this competitive viewpoint entirely disappears from the *Church Dogmatics* is debatable.

[117]Healy, "Logic of Karl Barth's Ecclesiology," pp. 263-64; also Hütter, "Karl Barth's 'Dialectical Catholicity,'" p. 148.

ultimate criterion for the church's identity is theologically described in terms of God's action in Christ through the Spirit to call the Christian community into existence. Nevertheless, this divine action calls into existence a particular fellowship with particular forms of ministry, some of which Barth can even say are universal, demanded "always, everywhere and in all circumstances."[118] Indeed, they are in this sense even constitutive, for they are required by the church's very nature and "cannot indeed be lacking in so far as they are generally posited by God."[119]

Second, that Barth's descriptions at times appear markedly formal and abstract may be due to his insistence that all forms of ministry must arise from particular circumstances, and therefore the theologian cannot in fact prescribe a timeless system of such practices. Barth maintains that investigation of specific forms of ministry belongs to practical, rather than dogmatic, theology, the multiplicity of forms making a systematic presentation impossible.[120] In light of charges of a lack of concreteness in his description of the church's historical life, we can imagine that Barth might respond that such critics themselves are not thinking concretely enough. It is precisely the variation of specific circumstances across time and space that make a complete description of church order and forms of ministry impossible. All that dogmatic theology can do is to outline the enduring and general principles of order and forms of ministry, for their concrete embodiment belongs to the individual Christian communities to determine in light of their own concrete circumstances, and these cannot be dictated by the theologian.

Third, there is room for reading Barth as not ruling out detailed sociological description but simply ruling it out of the realm of dogmatics. Barth holds that sociological description, as well as a complete investigation of the church's order and forms of ministry, belongs not to dogmatics but to practical theology and to canon law.[121] While this observation may not allay all criticisms, it does provide a rationale for Barth's rather general and formal

---

[118]CD IV/3.2, p. 864.

[119]CD IV/3.2, p. 859.

[120]CD IV/3.2, pp. 859-60.

[121]See, for example, CD IV/3.2, pp. 859-60; also CD IV/2, p. 678. Barth elsewhere makes a similar distinction between "theological ethics" and "Christian ethics," the former concerning itself with the general ethical principles to be examined by dogmatics and the latter addressing the concrete ethical application of these principles to actual human situations (CD II/2, p. 542). I thank Daniel Migliore for drawing my attention to this latter insight.

description of the church's concrete practices. This complements Barth's recognition that these practices cannot be given in detail in dogmatics because they will vary greatly over time and from one location to the next. A dogmatics that is too specific may therefore also be too provincial.

Finally, one must recognize that Barth's fears of sociological description were not unfounded. Reductive sociological understandings of the church were prevalent in the nineteenth and early twentieth centuries, and Barth justifiably reacted against them. Against sociological reductionism, Barth strongly maintained the irreducibly theological character of the church. He would no doubt be uncomfortable with modern descriptions of the identity of the church as coextensive with the particularity of its historical and sociological existence and forms of life.

These observations mitigate and lessen the force of the criticism that Barth's ecclesiology lacks concrete historical description and fails adequately to outline detailed and explicit forms of order and ministry. They do not eliminate all concerns, however, for by excluding specific questions of definite church order and forms of ministry from the realm of dogmatics, the danger always looms that such order and practices will in fact be determined and shaped not by the inner logic of the gospel but rather by alien and foreign principles.

The question of ecclesial mediation. There is indeed some truth in the claim that for Barth redemptive history is portrayed as coming to a close with the cross, so that the resurrection adds nothing more to redemption than to reveal its true character, which in turn seems to undermine a significant role for the church and its activity in history.[122] Yet, it is mistaken to conclude that Barth leaves no place for ecclesial and human agency, and few would go so far as to make such a claim. Such an accusation can be made only by overlooking Barth's rich notions of witness and correspondence.

It is indeed much more accurate to say that Barth excludes a certain type of human and ecclesial agency than that he excludes human agency altogether. The issue is not that Barth has provided a purely monistic account of agency, excluding the human for the sovereignty of the divine and relegating the church's activity to inconsequence in the face of the finality of

---

[122]See Mangina, "Bearing the Marks of Jesus," pp. 275-78; see also Webster, *Karl Barth*, p. 139.

Christ's all-sufficient sacrifice. As Barth himself constantly reiterated, the dictum that "God is everything and humanity is nothing" is not only false but nonsense. The issue is, rather, that he describes human agency in general, and ecclesial agency in particular, in terms of correspondent witness rather than direct cooperation or mediation. This is the basis of the church's vocation.

Barth's understanding of ecclesial agency can be understood only by a serious examination of his notion of correspondence, an idea crucial to his thought. Barth strongly maintains that the work of Christ requires no supplementation, which is first and foremost the case because Christ's work encompasses both reconciliation and redemption, and because Christ is not absent, but present, and thus requires no mediation by the church to make him present. This assertion of Christ's presence does raise the problem of the Spirit's distinctive role in the economy of salvation and may also be read as a denial of ecclesial agency. Yet such a reading would be inaccurate, for Barth relativizes the work of the church in order to establish it, insofar as by ridding it of the untenable task of divine mediation, Barth believes it may be free for its true human vocation of witness.[123] Barth's concept of correspondence allows him to provide a place for concrete and material obedience by the church in its very visible and historical existence, giving his ecclesiology, as his theology as a whole, an essential ethical character.

Furthermore, correspondence guards against seeing the church as irrelevant in light of a divine monergism and christological monism, and as triumphant and independent in light of a human and ecclesial autonomy.[124] For this reason, Barth's articulation of the relationship between Christ and the church is not solely exhausted by moving "between the poles of complete identity and complete non-identity,"[125] but in fact speaks of an analogical

---

[123] As Webster states: "The move Barth is making here at one and the same time relativizes and establishes the activity of Christian witness. 'Relativizes,' because it asserts the entire adequacy of Jesus' own self-declaration; 'establishes,' because the willed form of that self-declaration includes its echo in human declaration" (*Barth's Moral Theology*, p. 144). This relativization is thus a liberation for the church to fulfill its proper task without burdening it with the work of what God alone can accomplish, a fact Webster believes Hütter has underestimated (see p. 146; also p. 170).

[124] Cf. Webster, *Barth's Ethics of Reconciliation*, p. 57. While Webster applies this description specifically to Barth's ethics, it is equally applicable, with only slight qualification, to Barth's ecclesiology.

[125] Mangina, "Bearing the Marks of Christ," pp. 301-2.

relation between them that is defined neither by identity nor contradiction but by correspondence. In correspondence to Christ, the church receives its true task of witness and attestation to the reconciliation of the world accomplished solely by Christ.

Yet here again, such comments do not eliminate all questions. Barth's strength is preserving the distinction and irreversibility between divine and human agency, as well as that between the work of Christ and the church. He is perhaps less successful in describing their relation and inseparability and articulating how the Holy Spirit works in, and not simply parallel to, the working of the church. Barth often speaks of a parallelism of action, rather than an embodied action, so that divine and human activity are portrayed in conjunction, rather than in terms of the divine acting in and through the human, Christ acting in and through the church.[126] The point might be illustrated by asking whether Christ comes to us through the proclamation of the church or alongside it.

Barth had good reason to fear the loss of Christ's distinct place as Subject in relation to the church, as well as an ecclesial sacramental manipulation of grace. The activity of God and the activity of the church are distinct and are therefore to be carefully distinguished. In good Reformed manner Barth attempted to protect and clarify the distinction. Less successful, perhaps, is his attempt to articulate how they are united and conjoined. As often noted, what is largely missing is an account of how the activity of the church is not only a response to the gospel but also a means taken up by God for its transmission. For some, this deficiency points to the inadequacy of the concept of witness and correspondence to describe the church's task exhaustively.[127]

Once again, however, such a judgment may point not so much to a deficiency in Barth but to a real and irreducible difference between him and his critics. Were he here today, he might well retort: "What does it mean to say that witness is not enough?" For Barth, the church's attestation to Christ is in fact the church's true glory, so that in trying to do more than this the church does not become greater, but less. Certainly Barth might fear that an emphasis on the church's necessary and intrinsic role within the gospel itself may lead to the church proclaiming itself rather than Christ.

---

[126]I owe this insight to George Hunsinger.

[127]See Mangina, "Karl Barth and the Ethics of Ecclesial Practice," pp. 332-33.

Such an observation should not lead one to conclude that Barth excluded the church from the gospel altogether. It is included in the covenant of grace insofar as the church is a part of God's eternal election. Indeed, Christ's own history includes the church's own: "Salvation history is the history of the *totus Christus*, of the head with the body and all the members."[128] The chief question is therefore not whether the church is intrinsic or extrinsic to the gospel for Barth. The primary question hinges, rather, on how the history of Christ and the history of the church are related, and for Barth, the answer is always that these two histories are inseparably conjoined through divine decree, yet they are irreducibly differentiated, with the second existing only in complete dependence on the first and united to it in an asymmetrical and irreversible relation.

It is this deep inalienable asymmetry between Christ and the church which seems to be missing in some of Barth's commentators, such as Hauerwas. Hauerwas takes issue with Barth's statement that the world may not be lost without the church. This statement requires clarification, for Barth certainly did not see the church as expendable or of no consequence for belief. This fact should be clear when Barth's privileging of the church's faith over that of the believer is recalled. Rather, Barth's own position in distinction from Hauerwas is best seen in Barth's pronouncement: "While God is as little bound to the Church as to the Synagogue, the recipients of His revelation are."[129] What Barth has, and Hauerwas seems not to have, is an ecclesiological *extra Calvinisticum*. In other words, while the church is necessary for us because God has freely chosen it and freely joined himself to it, it is not necessary for God, nor is God's salvific activity limited to the church by some type of necessity.[130] Such would betray God's freedom and perhaps the sufficiency of Christ's salvific work itself. To put this in the language of Hauerwas, the story of the church must always be made subservient to the story of Christ. They do not stand on the same plane, nor is the former simply an extension of the latter. Christ does not leave the world and leave behind the church to take his place.

---

[128] *CD* IV/3.1, p. 216.

[129] *CD* I/2, p. 11.

[130] *CD* IV/3, p. 790. This element of Barth's ecclesiology may well be what leads Hauerwas to say that Barth has an "overly cautious account of the role of the church in the economy of God's salvation" (*With the Grain of the Universe*, p. 202).

Despite such real disagreement, here too some rapprochement may nevertheless be possible, for on some issues, the difference between Barth and Hauerwas may not be as great as it appears. Hauerwas's ecclesiology may be an attempt to provide the rich historical description that Barth lacks. One would not want to overestimate the differences between them. Yet on this matter of ecclesial mediation, there does seem to be genuine disagreement.

Looking Ahead . . .

Barth's ecclesiology is often looked at through the lens of a central conviction of Barth's theology, namely, God's freedom. Because of the freedom of God, the church's life, along with its doctrines and practices, cannot be directly identified with Christ's own action, or the Spirit tied in any way to the church so that this divine freedom is sacrificed. God's freedom is a central tenet in his theology, and it is one worth exploring with regard to an American theology, as Barth himself noted on his one and only trip to the United States. Certainly God's freedom over against the lordless powers and against the sins both of triumphalism and desperation is a theme in Barth's theology that has much to teach us. But it is not the only one.

If there is a theme in Barth's thought that seems in need of reexamination, it is his deep and abiding conviction that God is faithful. Barth's justified and outspoken emphasis on the freedom and lordship of God is so evident in his work that his quiet yet unshakable confidence in God's faithfulness is at times missed. It is a consideration of divine freedom without faithfulness that may be the reason some regard Barth's theology in general, and his ecclesiology in particular, as inherently unstable, occasionalistic, or ahistorical, and ultimately incapable of providing truly viable guidance and direction for an embodied ecclesial life. It is this need for stability and constancy which seems to follow from a deep if at times unspoken anxiety expressed in many quarters of the American (and European?) church today regarding its self-preservation in the midst of cultural uncertainty.[131] The search to alleviate this anxiety is nowhere as evident as in the search for a stable objectivity in both Protestant and Roman Catholic circles, an objectivity attempted in the flight to irreformable dogma, an infallible church

---

[131]See also Healy, "Karl Barth's Ecclesiology Reconsidered," pp. 297-99.

office or inerrant biblical text, an irrevocable ministry of historic apostolic succession or a hierarchically arranged ecumenical alliance. All of these flights to authority will appear in later chapters.

Barth quite simply followed none of these flights (indeed he opposed them all), yet he feared neither subjectivism nor the loss of the church's relevance. We would do well to ask why. The answer seems to lie in his deep and firm conviction that not only is the Spirit free, but the Spirit is also faithful. On the faithfulness of God the church could stand. Such faithfulness could not be played against God's freedom. The faithfulness of God was not a buttress with which to prop up a false objectivity itself, nor was it an excuse to cast off objectivity altogether into some form of gnostic spiritualism. Such faithfulness did not exempt the church from the need to display and struggle for its own faithfulness in its own life—indeed, its concrete life. Nonetheless, for Barth anxiety was not an option, for the Spirit is both free and faithful. Barth provides the following postscript, words perhaps particularly prescient for our time of calls for renewed ecclesial norms:

> The Creed offers little externally to the Church, and is certainly not a protection against creeping degeneration. The power which originated it is the power of the Holy Spirit, and that power is also the power of its continuing endurance and effectiveness. It has no other power, but that power it has.[132]

If we understand this last line (and *really* understand it), we understand the secret of Barth's own firm and quiet confidence in the freedom and faithfulness of God for the church.

---

[132]Barth, "The Desirability and Possibility of a Universal Reformed Creed," in *Theology and Church*, p. 118.

2

Karl Barth's Doctrine of the Church in Conversation with American Evangelicalism

✛

To ask whether Karl Barth and American evangelicals are friends is an in-teresting question to pose regarding two contentious partners. Certainly the actual relationship between them did not begin well, and the first challenge to answering such a question in any affirmative way entails that this history be overcome.

Barth's own interaction with American evangelicalism during his lifetime cannot be described as auspicious by any stretch of the imagination, with one particular episode especially significant and telling. At the request of the editor of the evangelical magazine *Christianity Today*, Geoffrey Bromiley wrote Barth in the summer of 1961 asking whether he would be willing to answer questions from three prominent American evangelical theologians, questions that Bromiley forwarded with his letter.[1] Having surveyed the questions sent, some of them from Cornelius Van Til—who had already chastised Barth severely in print—Barth's reply to Bromiley was genial but also terse.[2] He must be forgiven, he said, if he could not and would not

---

This chapter appeared earlier as "The Church in Karl Barth and Evangelicalism: Conversations Across the Aisle," in *Karl Barth and American Evangelicalism*, ed. Bruce L. McCormack and Clif-ford B. Anderson (Grand Rapids: Eerdmans, 2011), pp. 177-200. Reprinted by permission.

[1]Barth's response to Bromiley's letter, as well as the questions posed, are included in Karl Barth, *Letters 1961–1968*, ed. Jürgen Fangmeier and Hinrich Stoevesandt, trans. and ed. Geoffrey W. Bromiley (Grand Rapids: Eerdmans, 1981), pp. 7-8, 342-43.

[2]Cornelius Van Til's criticisms of Barth appear in *The New Modernism* (Philadelphia: P & R, 1947). He would continue these criticisms in *Christianity and Barthianism* (Philadelphia: P & R, 1962).

answer the questions, for he was busy with his teaching and writing responsibilities during his last semester as a professor before retirement. Yet even if he had the strength and time, Barth related, he would not enter a discussion based on such questions. A discussion would presuppose a serious attempt to understand what he himself had written in the *Church Dogmatics* about related matters. But in his estimation, this prerequisite was conspicuously missing, readily apparent from the questions themselves, which Barth found superficial and trivial.[3]

But there was an even more important reason from abstaining from dialogue, as he writes:

> The decisive point, however, is this. The second presupposition of a fruitful discussion between them and me would have to be that we are able to talk on a common plane. But these people have already had their so-called orthodoxy for a long time. They are closed to anything else, they will cling to it at all costs, and they can adopt toward me only the role of prosecuting attorneys, trying to establish whether what I represent agrees or disagrees with their orthodoxy, in which I for my part have no interest! None of their questions leaves me with the impression that they want to seek with me the truth that is greater than us all. They take the stance of those who happily possess it already and who hope to enhance their happiness by succeeding in proving to themselves and the world that I do not share this happiness. Indeed they have long since decided and publicly proclaimed that I am a heretic, possibly (van Til) the worst heretic of all time. So be it! But they should not expect me to take the trouble to give them the satisfaction of offering explanations which they will simply use to confirm the judgement they have already passed on me. . . . These fundamentalists want to eat me up. They have not yet come to a "better mind and attitude" as I once hoped. I can thus give them neither an angry nor a gentle answer but instead no answer at all.[4]

While such a letter provides little hope for a fruitful dialogue between

---

[3]Barth, *Letters 1961–1968*, p. 7. Barth writes: "I sincerely respect the seriousness with which a man like Berkouwer studies me and then makes his criticisms. I can then answer him in detail. But I cannot respect the questions of these people from *Christianity Today*, for they do not focus on the reasons for my statements but on certain foolishly drawn deductions from them. Their questions are thus superficial."

[4]Ibid., pp. 7-8.

Barth and evangelicals, things are quite different today. Since the time of this letter, much has changed on the evangelical side of the aisle (Barth himself is no longer with us to answer from his own side, of course). Just as Barth could mellow in his old age, so evangelicalism seems to have mellowed (at least in some circles) with regard to Barth.[5] Within the past few decades especially, evangelicals have come to appreciate Barth as a fruitful dialogue partner, even if there remains an implicit and some- times explicitly expressed wariness regarding his theology.[6] Yet the challenge pertaining to the question of the relation of evangelicals and Barth is no longer one of a problematic history but one of identity. To be specific: What is evangelicalism? To place Barth in a dialogue with American evangelicalism requires that we know what evangelicalism itself is.

This question itself may seem trite, but it is important to recognize that evangelicalism is a contested concept. The multifarious and complex nature of evangelicalism as a subculture has been much discussed and readily doc- umented.[7] Indeed, evangelicalism is such a slippery term and so conten- tious a concept that some from both the Wesleyan and Reformed wings of the movement have in effect called it meaningless and requested a mora- torium on the use of the term.[8] Nevertheless, despite such minority voices, the majority of American historians and theologians continue to preserve it

---

[5]It is also important to remember that Bromiley, the great translator and devotee of Barth and one of the most important persons for Barth's early reception in North America, may be described as an evangelical and taught at an evangelical institution, Fuller Theological Seminary.

[6]See especially Bernard Ramm, *After Fundamentalism: The Future of Evangelical Theology* (San Francisco: Harper & Row, 1983); Gregory G. Bolich, *Karl Barth and Evangelicalism* (Downers Grove, IL: InterVarsity Press, 1980); Phillip R. Thorne, *Evangelicalism and Karl Barth: His Recep- tion and Influence in North American Evangelical Theology* (Allison Park, PA: Pickwick Publications, 1995); Sung Wook Chung, ed., *Karl Barth and Evangelical Theology* (Grand Rapids: Baker Aca- demic, 2006); and David Gibson and Daniel Strange, eds., *Engaging with Barth: Contemporary Evangelical Critiques* (Nottingham, UK: Apollos, 2008).

[7]Randall Balmer, *Mine Eyes Have Seen the Glory: A Journey into the Evangelical Subculture in Amer- ica*, 4th ed. (New York: Oxford University Press, 2006); Joel A. Carpenter, "The Fellowship of Kindred Minds: Evangelical Identity and the Quest for Christian Unity," in *Pilgrims on the Saw- dust Trail: Evangelical Ecumenism and the Quest for Christian Identity*, ed. Timothy George (Grand Rapids: Baker Academic, 2004), pp. 27-42; and Mark Noll, *American Evangelical Christianity* (Malden, MA: Blackwell, 2001), p. 14.

[8]Donald W. Dayton, "Some Doubts About the Usefulness of the Category 'Evangelical,'" in *The Variety of American Evangelicalism*, ed. Donald W. Dayton and Robert K. Johnston (Downers Grove, IL: InterVarsity Press, 1991), pp. 245-51; D. G. Hart, *Deconstructing Evangelicalism: Con- servative Protestantism in the Age of Billy Graham* (Grand Rapids: Baker Academic, 2004).

as a useful if imperfect designation for a broad consensus among a variegated grouping of American Christians.[9]

Evangelicalism is then usually defined in one of two ways: according to a narrative history that traces its genetic development, or by means of a list of key convictions that seeks to capture its essential nature. The first is a historical and sociological approach, while the latter strives for a theological definition. With regard to the first, it must be noted that while the narrative history is itself disputed, there is a broad consensus among historians that American evangelicalism arose as a movement with roots in the Protestant Reformation, the confluence of Puritanism and Pietism in the Great Awakenings and revivalism of eighteenth- and nineteenth-century America, and the Fundamentalist and Modernist controversy of the early twentieth century. These are, in fact, the periods in which the term "evangelical" came to prominence. This history is told a bit differently depending on denominational perspective (for example, Wesleyan or Reformed, dispensational or Pentecostal, confessional or pietist).[10] Indeed, few concepts in American religious history are as disputed and amorphous as that of evangelicalism.[11] The history of evangelicalism is even traced by some all the way back to the first century and to those who embraced the *euangelion* of Christ, entailing that the first great divisive event in the church was not that between Protestant and Catholic, nor even Catholic and Orthodox, but between Chris-

---

[9]While the usefulness and meaningfulness of the term has been called into question, many historians and theologians defend the term while recognizing that it is nevertheless an "essentially contested concept." For example, see Robert K. Johnston, "American Evangelicalism: An Extended Family," in Dayton and Johnston, *Variety of American Evangelicalism*, pp. 253, 252-72. Johnston argues that while no uncontested definition for evangelicalism can be given, there are "family resemblances" between different denominational groups that allow them to be categorized under a common term: "evangelical." So also Richard Lints: "Evangelicals are like a collection of many siblings connected by some loose family resemblances. The differences between them are often as important as the similarities. The unifying strands will almost always admit of exceptions, and when the analysis becomes too fine-grained, it will lose some of its explanatory power" (*The Fabric of Theology: A Prolegomena to Evangelical Theology* [Grand Rapids: Eerdmans, 1993], p. 32). For a history of evangelicalism with special reference to its particular theology, see Roger Olson, *The Westminster Handbook of Evangelical Theology* (Louisville, KY: Westminster John Knox, 2004), pp. 1-66.

[10]Kenneth J. Collins, *The Evangelical Moment: The Promise of an American Religion* (Grand Rapids: Baker Academic, 2005), pp. 19-40.

[11]As Collins notes, there is no definitive "evangelical metanarrative" but only smaller narratives that are combined through family resemblances and shared common themes (*Evangelical Moment*, p. 22).

tians and Jews.[12] Such a definition of evangelicalism is so broad as to render the term devoid of any meaning or usefulness. More common, however, is a historiography that begins in the Reformation and marks evangelicalism as distinctly Protestant in nature. In its most strict form, evangelicalism refers to the neo-evangelicals, such as Harold John Ockenga and Carl F. H. Henry, of American post–World War II society who attempted to reform fundamentalism and overcome the deficiencies of its separatism and anti-intellectualism. Evangelical divisiveness and plurality are an inheritance of Protestant divisiveness and plurality and not unrelated to them. Evangelicalism is thus a reform movement within Christianity itself.

The other way of defining evangelicalism is by means of an essentialist, rather than historical, approach. The defining doctrines or convictions are most often stated as (1) an authoritative and normative place for Scripture in determining all of faith and practice; (2) the necessity of conversion; (3) the centrality and definitive nature of Christ's atonement; and (4) the imperative of evangelism.[13] This evangelical quadrilateral has gained much acceptance as an accurate description of evangelical theological identity, and though other lists do exist, they usually amplify, rather than differ from, these four basic convictions.[14]

In brief, it is this prevalent definition of evangelicalism as a post–World War II phenomenon with roots in American Puritanism, Pietism and revivalism—and as defined by these four convictions—that I will assume, rather than argue for, in this chapter. Nevertheless, it should be noted that it serves better as a descriptive rather than as a strictly definitional term as well.

If we are then to answer the question of whether Barth and American evangelicals are friends or foes, we have to keep these challenges of history and identity in our purview. But this chapter asks this question with regard to a specific theme, namely, that of ecclesiology as the topic of comparison between these dialogue partners, and here we reach a challenge that surpasses those of a troubled history and an elusive identity. This challenge can

---

[12]Ibid., pp. 22ff.

[13]Ibid., pp. 21, 41-61; this quadrilateral was definitively articulated by David W. Bebbington, *Evangelicalism in Modern Britain: A History from the 1730s to the 1980s* (London: Unwin Hyman, 1989), pp. 1-19.

[14]For example, see Lints, *Fabric of Theology*, p. 49; also Olson, *Westminster Handbook to Evangelical Theology*, pp. 6-7; and Johnston, "American Evangelicalism," p. 261.

be illustrated by a bit of humor shared among some evangelicals involved in formal dialogue with Roman Catholics. As they put it: "The main difference between us and the Catholics is ecclesiology. They have one and we don't."[15] As Mark Noll comments, the joke is funny because it is at least partially true. Indeed, one evangelical theologian has even floated the idea that "evangelical ecclesiology" may be an oxymoron.[16]

To see why this strange statement makes a bit of sense, we again must return to the question of identity. For unlike Lutheran, Reformed, Baptist, Congregationalist and other communions, evangelicalism is not a confessional tradition, nor is it an institutional church or denomination, though George Marsden famously argued that it was.[17] It is a movement, and movements do not have ecclesiologies—churches do.[18] Remember that the list of four defining convictions for evangelicalism provided above did not include any specifically addressing ecclesiology. That absence is telling, for evangelicalism by its very nature is not a church (whether we understand a church in the sense of a local community of believers, a confessional or denominational body or as an institutional structure) but rather is a movement that coalesced around a set of convictions and issues shared across various communions and denominations.[19] This is not to overlook the fact that evangelicals do belong to particular churches with particular ecclesiologies, so that we ought perhaps more accurately to speak of evan-

---

[15]Recounted in Mark Noll and Carolyn Nystrom, *Is The Reformation Over? An Evangelical Assessment of Contemporary Roman Catholicism* (Grand Rapids: Baker Academic, 2005), p. 145.

[16]Bruce Hindmarsh, "Is Evangelical Ecclesiology an Oxymoron?" in *Evangelical Ecclesiology: Reality or Illusion?* ed. John G. Stackhouse Jr. (Grand Rapids: Baker Academic, 2003), pp. 15-37. Hindmarsh believes that evangelicalism has its own "ecclesial consciousness," if not a developed specific ecclesiology per se.

[17]George M. Marsden, "The Evangelical Denomination," in *Evangelicalism and Modern America, 1930–1980*, ed. George M. Marsden (Grand Rapids: Eerdmans, 1984).

[18]This is not to deny that ecclesiologies differ even within traditions, and that not only evangelicalism but also confessional traditions themselves, are contested. For example, what does it mean to be Reformed? (And what is Reformed ecclesiology?) Van Til and Barth (both Reformed) would no doubt give quite different answers. Alasdair MacIntyre reminds us that all traditions are contested traditions, for a tradition is but "an historically extended, socially embodied argument." See MacIntyre, *After Virtue*, 2nd ed. (Notre Dame, IN: University of Notre Dame, 1984), p. 222. For the diversity of Reformed thought since its inception, see Philip Benedict, *Christ's Churches Purely Reformed: A Social History of Calvinism* (New Haven, CT: Yale University Press, 2002).

[19]The word *church* itself is of course a multivalent term. See Erwin Fahlbusch, "Church," in *The Encyclopedia of Christianity: Volume 1 A-D*, ed. Erwin Fahlbusch, Jan M. Lochman, et al., trans. Geoffrey W. Bromiley (Grand Rapids: Eerdmans, 1999), pp. 477-78.

gelical ecclesiologies in the plural rather than in the singular. Yet evangelicalism itself is both smaller than, and larger than, churches, while having its own unique ecclesial consciousness.[20]

First, evangelicalism is marked not so much by an ecclesiology as by *ecclesiolae in ecclesia*, a fellowship of persons within churches. At its most extreme, it trades the church for Philipp Jakob Spener's *collegia pietatis*, a college of piety, though it may also focus on doctrinal nonnegotiables. Evangelicalism thus is smaller than churches insofar as it exists within them. It unites persons with shared convictions within traditional churches. Indeed, the ecclesiology of evangelicalism has often been an ecclesiology of division and separation as new denominations emerged from older ones in formal schism due to doctrinal differences or disagreements about the necessity of conversion. Separatism has been a recurrent feature of evangelical ecclesiologies.[21]

Evangelicalism is also larger than churches. It is marked by a penchant for producing large nondenominational and pan-denominational alliances and parachurch organizations that unite persons from various Protestant and even Catholic confessions for common ministry, evangelism and social action and service. Evangelicalism thus spans ecclesial borders. Indeed, its transdenominationalism is sometimes added as a fifth element to the four doctrinal marks above in order to identify what makes it most distinctive from other forms of Protestantism.[22]

If we do not understand evangelicalism as a movement both smaller than and larger than particular churches and confessional fellowships, we cannot make sense of both its sectarian proclivities and ecumenical achievements. These seem to be mutually exclusive, but they are not. Evangelicalism achieves the coalescing of a shared doctrinal and/or experiential identity within established churches. At times, the confessional and denominational identity of a particular church and its evangelical identity are functionally coextensive. At other times, however, an evangelical subconstituency forms

---

[20]I borrow this term from Hindmarsh; see note 16 above.

[21]Carpenter, "The Fellowship of Kindred Minds," p. 33; for an insightful discussion of evangelicalism's peculiar ecclesial existence, see also Stanley Grenz, *Renewing the Center: Evangelical Theology in a Post-Theological Era* (Grand Rapids: Baker Academic, 2000), pp. 287-324.

[22]For example, John G. Stackhouse Jr., *Evangelical Landscapes: Facing Critical Issues of the Day* (Grand Rapids: Baker Academic, 2002), pp. 48-50; cf. pp. 163-65.

its own identity that is more central and determinative than its confessional heritage (when one identifies oneself first as an evangelical, rather than as Reformed or Baptist). This new forged identity, when joined to disillusionment with and opposition to denominational directions and stances, may even lead to a separation from these confessional churches and the formation of new congregations and even denominations. Hence the sectarian element of evangelicalism.[23]

But along with such sectarian proclivities, evangelicalism has also contributed to some of the most significant ecumenical achievements of the modern period, as Christians from numerous confessional and denominational traditions, from various churches, have joined with one another in both formal organizations and informal alliances to achieve shared evangelistic and activist goals in mission and relief. Such proclivities were already evident in the early British evangelicals, such as George Whitefield and John Wesley, who worked with those from various Christian traditions even while separated from them by confessions and other theological convictions. Such ecumenical endeavors led then, as now, to consternation among those less ecumenically inclined.[24] Evangelicalism is marked by sectarianism as well as ecumenism, by a demand for doctrinal purity that can lead to separation from mainline denominations, while at the same time downplaying confessional doctrines in favor of a shared conversional piety that transcends denominations themselves. Both of these must be recognized for us to consider evangelicalism honestly and accurately.[25]

The four-sided nature of evangelical ecclesial consciousness as sectarian and ecumenical, as well as pietistic and parachurch, lies at the root of evan-

---

[23]Leaving a confessional heritage or denomination can be done for less serious reasons as well. Stackhouse can write: "Many evangelicals . . . feel free to leave one congregation, or even an entire denominational tradition, to find what to them is most important in a church: usually some combination of the right basic doctrines, good preaching, good programs for the kids, and so on. Indeed, only among evangelicals does one encounter the revealing cliché, 'church shopping'" (*Evangelical Landscapes*, p. 28).

[24]For an account of Whitefield's and Wesley's openness is this regard, see Mark Noll, *The Rise of Evangelicalism: The Age of Edwards, Whitefield and the Wesleys* (Downers Grove, IL: InterVarsity Press, 2003), pp. 13-21; also Hindmarsh, "Is Evangelical an Oxymoron?" pp. 22-23; and Grenz, *Renewing the Center*, pp. 292-93.

[25]That Gary Dorrien sees only the sectarian, rather than the ecumenical, side of evangelicalism is thus a deficiency in his analysis of it. See *The Remaking of Evangelical Theology* (Louisville, KY: Westminster John Knox, 1998), p. 3. I owe this insight to Stackhouse, *Evangelical Landscapes*, p. 183 n. 35.

gelicalism's historical indifference to the institutional church and its general neglect of ecclesiology as a theological topic.[26] There can be no denying that evangelicalism has had significant effects on American ecclesial life, not the least of which is a weakening of denominational and confessional identity. Whether one sees this as a positive or negative development depends on one's particular perspective and consideration of specific cases and aspects of this outcome.[27] Such a weakening can lead to a spiritualistic individualism that neglects the visible church and its sacraments, ordinances and practices, as well as to a theological minimalism that dilutes rich and hearty confessional stews into a kind of thin theological gruel owing more to the market and to cultural trends than to the developed theological heritage of the churches. Such a weakening can also be due, however, to a recognition by Christians within one communion of a common confession of Christ and fellowship with others beyond the narrow confines of one's own denomination, accompanied by a newfound freedom from captivity to the confessional polemics of the past. Evangelical biblicism can foster both the bane of vacuous individualism, doctrinal indifference and theological shallowness, as well as the benefit of freeing Christians to hear the voice of God anew and the freedom to circumvent, if not overcome, hard and fast confessional divisions of the past in common Christian witness for today.[28] Evangelicalism is unique, and it is uniquely puzzling.[29]

---

[26]As Marsden notes: "One of the striking features of much of evangelicalism is its general disregard for the institutional church." See George Marsden, *Understanding Fundamentalism and Evangelicalism* (Grand Rapids: Eerdmans, 1991), p. 81, quoted in Grenz, *Renewing the Center*, p. 288, who then writes: "The lack of a full-orbed ecclesiological base is related to the 'parachurch' character of evangelicalism, which in turn has shaped the movement's particular ecumenicity. . . . The parachurch nature of evangelicalism has resulted in an unmistakable minimizing of ecclesiology" (pp. 288-89).

[27]Stackhouse analyzes both the positive and negative effects of the increasing importance of parachurch organizations within evangelicalism in *Evangelical Landscapes*, pp. 25-36. As he argues, "parachurch organizations cannot provide the full-fledged alternative cultures that Christian families, Christian small groups, and Christian churches can provide. . . . When Mr. and Mrs. Evangelical try to cope with a problem or succeed with an opportunity, InterVarsity and Focus on the Family and World Vision cannot talk with them in their living room, but local Christians bound to them in covenant *will* be there" (p. 20).

[28]See ibid., p. 174.

[29]I would argue that evangelicalism at its best is a movement that may include doctrinal and conversionist themes but that most positively serves as an ecumenical vision—it allows persons to transcend the feverish and narrow confines of their traditions, which must be nevertheless where all must live. Evangelicalism serves most significantly as a public space not for minimalist doctrinal commitments but for ecumenical encounter and shared service and mission. In this, it serves

There can therefore be no simple answers when evaluating evangelical achievements and deficiencies with regard to ecclesiology. Even some of the significant elements of both Continental and British evangelicalism, as well as that of America, that weakened traditional confessional identities cannot be simplistically judged and condemned. For example, the renewed missionary impulse of the eighteenth and nineteenth centuries led to the formation of ecumenical foreign missionary societies that up to that point had no parallel, and that then-current ecclesiological structures could not themselves provide. Such societies were the forerunners of modern parachurch organizations.[30] These societies provided for leadership opportunities outside hierarchical denominational structures and thus for greater lay involvement and leadership, thus lending them democratic and populist appeal. For no one was this more the case than for women. One of the often overlooked facts of the history of women in ministry is the place of these evangelical missionary societies, which were often organized, ad ministered and led by women, long before the ordination of women in mainline denominations.[31]

All of this to say that evangelicalism has historically been loosely tied to traditional ecclesiological structures, most often existing within such structures (*ecclesiolae in ecclesia*) or in organizations spanning alongside and across them (parachurch organizations). This fact does not mean that evangelical organizations, both within and spanning across the churches, need

---

as a hallway, to borrow an image from C. S. Lewis, or perhaps better as a parlor, where Christians dedicated to their individual churches, denominations and traditions can meet for cordial (and sometimes heated) conversations as well as common mission. It is evangelicalism's institutions, such as its seminaries, and its publications, such as *Christianity Today*, and its publishing houses, such as Eerdmans, Baker and InterVarsity, that serve as vehicles for theological discussions across denominational barriers and, I would argue, across evangelical and mainline divides (for example, Eerdmans crosses such barriers by publishing authors who unabashedly claim the evangelical label and those who would reject that label entirely).

[30]Carpenter, "The Fellowship of Kindred Minds," p. 34. "These new voluntary societies were to have profound implications for the churches. Like parishes or congregations, they were designed to bring people within hearing range of the gospel and to bring them into the church, but they did not fit into ecclesiastical systems of governance. So a new type of church organization grew up alongside old ones, and was parasitically related to them, but not under their authority. In the nineteenth century, there was an explosion of voluntary societies, as zealous evangelicals immediately saw opportunities to put these new organizational tools to work, for the reformation as well as the evangelization of their homelands" (pp. 34-35).

[31]Ibid., p. 35. See also Justo L. González, *The Story of Christianity: The Early Church to the Present Day*, vol. 2 (Peabody, MA: Prince Press, 2001), p. 308.

be competitive with the churches; such organizations may work synergisti-
cally alongside of them.[32] Nevertheless, evangelicalism's unique character
has historically led many evangelicals to downplay the church and certainly
to neglect its centrality as a theological category (evangelicals have focused
much more on the themes of Christ, atonement and Scripture, and in doing
so are heirs of the Reformers in this regard). Stanley Grenz can thus state
that ecclesiology is "the neglected stepchild of evangelical theology."[33] Only
now, among second- and third-generation neo-evangelicals, and in light of
the increasing importance of ecclesiology in non-evangelical Protestant
circles, have the ecclesiological deficiencies of evangelicalism been faced
head on and ecclesiology taken up as a significant area of study.[34] More and
more studies by evangelicals on ecclesiology are appearing, and this new
wave of scholarship will have to address whether an evangelical ecclesiology
is or is not an oxymoron.[35]

As I mentioned above, movements lend themselves to sociological description and perhaps even theological analysis. But movements themselves
are not churches, and thus it takes some straining to argue that they possess
ecclesiologies in their own right beyond those of the churches of their constitutive members. Nevertheless, setting aside this very large qualification,
for the rest of this chapter I want to focus on what Barth might criticize in,
sympathize with and contribute to contemporary evangelicalism and its

---

[32]Stackhouse, *Evangelical Landscapes*, p. 32.

[33]Stanley Grenz, *Revisioning Evangelical Theology* (Downers Grove, IL: InterVarsity Press, 1993),
p. 165.

[34]Vanhoozer comments, "The doctrine of the church has, in the last decade or so, moved to the
forefront of theological research and writing, primarily among non-evangelicals—so much so
that ecclesiology has effectively displaced the doctrine of revelation as 'first theology.'" Kevin
Vanhoozer, "Evangelicalism and the Church: The Company of the Gospel," in *The Futures of
Evangelicalism: Issues and Prospects*, ed. Craig Bartholomew, Robin Perry and Andrew West
(Grand Rapids: Kregel, 2004), p. 63.

[35]Some of the most important recent studies of evangelical ecclesiology are the papers collected
in Stackhouse's *Evangelical Ecclesiology*, as well as those in *The Community of the Word: Toward
an Evangelical Ecclesiology*, ed. Mark Husbands and Daniel J. Treier (Downers Grove, IL: Inter-
Varsity Press, 2005). See also Vanhoozer, "Evangelicalism and the Church," pp. 40-99, as well as
Grenz, *Renewing the Center*, pp. 287-324. Howard A. Snyder has argued that evangelical ecclesiologies are patchwork amalgams of the Anglo-Catholic and Reformed/Lutheran-Catholic
heritage, the Radical Reformation and Free Church tradition, the revivalist tradition, American
democracy and American entrepreneurship; see Snyder, "Marks of Evangelical Ecclesiology," in
Stackhouse, *Evangelical Ecclesiology*, pp. 92-96. With such a mongrel pedigree, it is no wonder
that it is so difficult to speak of a coherent evangelical ecclesiology.

understanding (or understandings) of the church. I will divide my comments into three broad headings: (1) areas where Barth would be quite critical of evangelicalism's understanding of the church and parachurch organizations, and how evangelicals might possibly respond to Barth; (2) areas where Barth can make a contribution to evangelicalism's understanding of the church today; and (3) areas where Barth might be quite sympathetic to evangelicalism and its understanding of the church and where they might share common ground. Let me also tip my hand at this point: I think that Barth provides evangelicalism with significant resources for a revitalized, rich, evangelical understanding of the church, and I want to encourage evangelicals to take Barth's ecclesiology with utmost seriousness. So for the rest of this chapter, I address three elements that Barth presents to evangelicalism: criticisms, contributions and areas of consensus.

Let us begin with the problems. Insofar as evangelicals (not all, of course, but a significant number) neglect the visible institutional church, and insofar as they align themselves more with parachurch movements and neglect or even denigrate the concrete assembly of believers in a church of word and sacrament or ordinance, Barth would spare no criticism. Such a judgment is not difficult to defend, and one piece from Barth's corpus is sufficient to ground it, namely, a short article addressing the Oxford Group Movement of the 1930s.[36] Barth's opposition to the Oxford Group Movement was not unrelated to the connections of some of its leaders to members of the Nazi Party, and I am not in any way implying that in this sense the Group Movement and evangelicalism can be compared or are at all similar. But as a renewal movement within the church, the Group Movement does provide an interesting test case for how Barth might respond to certain aspects of contemporary evangelicalism when Barth's specific charges against the Oxford Group Movement are examined.[37] In fact, a number of Barth's crit-

---

[36]For an introduction to Barth's background with the Oxford Group Movement, see Christoph Dahling-Sander, "Karl Barth—Emil Brunner: An Uneasy Correspondence from the Very Beginning," http://karlbarth.unibas.ch/fileadmin/downloads/letter2.pdf. Barth's opposition to the movement was tied up with his fight against National Socialism. Though this is the case, there is here absolutely no implication that Barth's criticisms of evangelicalism would have any correspondence to this aspect of the Group Movement.

[37]For the following discussion, see Karl Barth, "Church or Group Movement?" *The London Quarterly and Hoborn Review* January (1937): 1-10. This article was originally published in *Evangelische Theologie* 6 (1936): 205ff.

icisms of this movement appear prescient for those who know American evangelicalism's weaknesses well.

First, Barth criticizes the Oxford Group for substituting a movement for the church. For those who were abandoning the church for the charisma and promise of the Oxford Group Movement, Barth indeed had stern rebuke. He writes: "Preaching, doctrine, teaching, pastoral work and the building up of the Christian congregation have nothing whatever to do with a 'movement.'"[38] Moreover, regardless of its shortcomings, the problems of the church could never entail its abandonment. When Barth himself in his early pastorate was enthralled with a movement, namely, the socialist movement, and was also quite critical of the church, he nonetheless did not abandon the church for socialism's call to action, to the chagrin of some of his socialist friends. Despite his harsh criticisms of the church in his commentary on Romans, leaving the church was never a serious question for him.[39] As he wrote to his friend Eduard Thurneysen in 1925, the protest against the church in those early years was a protest from within the church itself.[40] Barth's commitment to the church would never waver in this regard.

Second, Barth is very troubled by the anthropological starting point of the Oxford Group, in which the needs and contemporary situation of the modern person are determinative for the shape that the gospel message is to take and which in fact, in his estimation, stand in judgment over it. He writes: "The Groups have put the 'world' in the position of a 'bank cashier' who tests

---

[38]Ibid., p. 4.

[39]Barth writes: "The description of the Church which we have just given is often blamed as being typical of those who oppose the Church or who, at least, hold themselves aloof from it. But blame such as this does not affect us. When, however, our critics go on to propose that we ought to leave the Church if we think of it thus, we are bound to state that we could not contemplate such a proposal, and would do our best to dissuade others from even considering it. It would never enter our heads to think of leaving the Church. For in describing the Church we are describing ourselves." See Karl Barth, *Der Römerbrief*, 2nd ed. (München: Chr. Kaiser Verlag, 1923), p. 355; ET: *The Epistle to the Romans*, trans. Edwyn C. Hoskyns (Oxford: Oxford University Press, 1968), p. 371. For the development and content of Barth's ecclesiology, see Kimlyn J. Bender, *Karl Barth's Christological Ecclesiology* (Aldershot: Ashgate, 2005). Barth could later look back on his early reflections regarding the church during the *Romans* period as unduly harsh and one-sided: "It was a part of the exaggerations of which we were guilty in 1920 that we were able to see the theological relevance of the Church only as a negative counterpart to the Kingdom of God which we had then so happily rediscovered" (Karl Barth, "The Humanity of God," in *The Humanity of God*, trans. John Newton Thomas [Richmond: John Knox Press, 1960], p. 62).

[40]James D. Smart, ed., *Revolutionary Theology in the Making: Barth-Thurneysen Correspondence, 1914-1925*, trans. James D. Smart (Richmond: John Knox Press, 1964), p. 216.

the gold coin, i.e. the genuineness of the Christian proclamation."[41] For Barth, the gospel must be prior to such needs of the moment and cannot be captive to current blowing winds. To fail in this regard is to trade the Word of God for "a beautiful and moralistic programme" that can only be self-serving.[42] Barth wholly rejects such an apologetic of experience, whether moralistic or mystical, for Scripture's truth.[43]

In a related vein, Barth is also deeply distressed with both the triumphalism and the secular methods of the Groups in their attempt to Christianize the world. Barth, who opposed ecclesiastical and cultural triumphalism in any form, writes: "I do not know how long the world will submit to being conquered for Christ in such a secular way. But this I do know, that the creation of this magic land composed of secular values and standards has nothing to do with prayer, with hope and with the message of the Christian Church, and that the Church can only be compromised by the Groups." For Barth such triumphalism joined to worldly methods is a denial of the freedom and mystery of grace and the secularization of the church itself.[44]

Fourth, Barth also has a wariness of the cult of personality that the Groups seem to foster: "If a man with a title such as 'Secretary of State for the U.S.A.' utters only the very vaguest word in their favour, this becomes—I do not know why—a really magical testimonial."[45] Here again, the worldly position and standing of the testifier is seen to add credibility to the testimony, and this standing is being exploited by the Oxford Movement. For Barth, such could appear as little more than fawning for endorsements.

Finally, Barth is very disturbed by a movement that seems to lay more emphasis and weight on the testimonial of a changed individual than the gospel of Christ. Here Barth's fear of an anthropological starting point, more commonly encountered in his interaction with Friedrich Schleiermacher, Emil Brunner and Rudolf Bultmann (though also tellingly prefigured in his ambivalence to Pietism), is readily evidenced in relation to a contemporary evangelical movement. As Barth accuses the Oxford Group:

---

[41]Barth, "Church or Group Movement," p. 4.
[42]Ibid., p. 8.
[43]Ibid., p. 9.
[44]Ibid., pp. 5, 9-10.
[45]Ibid., p. 4.

Should one take the miraculous reports of the Group as an adequate and acceptable supplement to the Christian message? According to that very message Jesus Christ is the end and the way to the end. The way of the Group is not Jesus Christ, but the ostensibly changed man and what this man is pleased to report about himself. In this case can Christ be indeed the end of all things? I do not see a supplement here, I only see a contradiction.[46]

Against such a movement, Barth poses the church, which "points away from the man who receives grace to the grace of God Himself."[47] For Barth, one had to choose between the church and the Group movement in an either/or decision. His own answer was to side with the church and exhort it to be and become the church which God would have it to be.[48]

Reading this short and little-known piece from many years ago is illuminating for the present. Barth's opposition to any denigration and abandonment of the church for participation in a movement, to evangelistic triumphalism and the conflation of the church's mission with a cultural program, to secular methods driven by the needs of the time rather than from reflection on the gospel itself, to the reduction of the gospel to a pragmatic moralism, to a cult of personality and to aggrandized testimonials often heavily salted with emotionalism as well as to a not-so-latent individualism—all are directly pertinent to a discussion of modern evangelicalism, at least in terms of its excesses often documented by many of its own adherents. In short, Barth's list from the past can only make many of us wince in the present. Certainly this is not to say that all of evangelicalism would fall under such criticisms, and as noted above, many evangelicals themselves have made similar ones of the modern movement. But such criticisms are worth noting nonetheless.

Though Barth's criticisms were meant for a movement long ago, they do

---

[46]Ibid., p. 6. He also states: "The Groups' praise of God is too self-centered to be genuine praise; in the Bible it is *God's* help alone which is praised" (p. 8). Dahling-Sander summarizes Barth's criticisms of the movement this way: "Barth placed the Oxford-Group-Movement together with its Swiss branch, the 'Middle-Party' in the church struggle in Germany as well as the Young Reformation Movement in the category of 'natural theology,' which he fought against. Practically, it became for him the embodiment of the ambiguous nature of man, which seeks to justify and sanctify itself and, in so doing, take control of God. It deceives itself subjectively and 'acts' instead of allowing God to act" ("Karl Barth—Emil Brunner," p. 13).

[47]Barth, "Church or Group Movement," p. 8; also p. 10.

[48]See ibid., pp. 1, 2, 4.

illustrate what Barth would no doubt oppose in much of current evangelical ecclesial life. Evangelicals themselves, however, might want to retort that Barth has overstated his case and offer their own questions to Barth. For instance, need the relation between Christian renewal movements or parachurch organizations and the church always be portrayed as one of conflict? Could there not be genuine harmony and cooperation? Moreover, there is good biblical precedent, they might justifiably argue, for "becoming all things to all people" so that they might be saved (1 Cor 9:22), as well as for recounting one's own encounter with God not in order to glorify the self but turn others toward this God "who raises the dead" (2 Cor 1:8-11). Did not the chief of sinners (as portrayed in Acts) often recount his inglorious past in order to point toward God's glorious future by speaking of a blinding light, a changed life and a new destiny (Acts 22; 26)?[49] Evangelicals would not have to start from scratch in forming their own questions and countercriticisms. Variations of the very ones I have just mentioned were raised by the distinguished Oxford New Testament professor B. H. Streeter, who defended the Oxford Movement in an April response in the same journal to Barth's January article.[50] I do not believe that Streeter provides anything that would make Barth retract his criticisms, although against Barth, Streeter made the astute point—and one that is to me irrefutable and too often forgotten—that the professor's lecture and the pastor's sermon can lend themselves to egoism as readily as an individual's testimonial.[51] Nevertheless, it is not hard to imagine that were Barth here today to converse with evangelicals, the discussion might sound something like the jousting between Barth and Streeter. I am not, however, going to try to stage such a debate or adjudicate it—a debate quite tied to how the objective and subjective poles of salvation are related. Instead, I want to move on to what Barth might uniquely contribute to evangelicalism's understanding of the church.

Most significantly, Barth provides a rich theology of the church that evangelicals may want to study and consider.[52] Barth's ecclesiology presents

---

[49]One might also consider the final four chapters of 2 Corinthians in this regard.

[50]B. H. Streeter, "Professor Barth v. The Oxford Group," *The London Quarterly and Hoborn Review* (April 1937): 145-49. Barth's and Streeter's short articles read together make for interesting reading.

[51]Ibid., pp. 148-49.

[52]For a comprehensive discussion of Barth's theology of the church, see Kimlyn Bender, *Karl Barth's Christological Ecclesiology* (Aldershot, UK: Ashgate, 2005; reprint, Eugene, OR: Cascade,

evangelicalism with an alternative to two mistaken approaches to which it has at times been prone, namely, a flight into visibility in which the theological nature of the church is sacrificed to sociological approaches, and a flight from the visible altogether by recourse to a doctrine of the invisible church. In other words, these are the problematic approaches of an ebionitic and a docetic ecclesiology, respectively. Let me address these in turn.

To say that evangelicals have neglected ecclesiology is not to say that they have neglected the church altogether. What they have neglected, rather, is a rich theological account of the church. An honest evaluation of evangelicalism must conclude that evangelicals have oftentimes conceded ecclesiology to sociology, history and, in the worst instances, to entrepreneurship. Evangelicalism to a great degree does not have a richly trinitarian, christological and pneumatological understanding of the church, though there are ever-increasing attempts to address this deficiency. There are at the very least two reasons for this lack of rich theological description. First, evangelicalism is most often understood as a sociological and historical movement, perhaps partly due to the prominent place that its historians play rather than its theologians. This view of evangelicalism in turn translates into a sociological view of the church, rather than a theological one. Second, practitioners more interested in pragmatic and numerical success than theological reflection are often the ones who shape evangelical ecclesiology. In the words of Barth, they are often more impressed with extensive rather than intensive growth, numerical rather than spiritual increase (though, as Barth himself noted, these need not be mutually exclusive).[53] Nevertheless, to treat the church as a society among societies, as an organization among organizations, as a sociological entity marked by visible success accounted for by secular methods, is to take flight into the visible church and sacrifice its theological identity. What is required is a much more robust theological doctrine of the church.

Now it must be said that evangelical theologians are very aware of this. In his excellent essay, "Evangelicalism and the Church," Kevin Vanhoozer contends: "The church cannot be adequately understood unless one gives

---

2013); also the essays by John Webster in Husbands and Treier, *Community of the Word*, pp. 75-95, 96-113.

[53]*CD* IV/2, p. 648.

an appropriately 'thick description,' one that goes beyond the human categories of sociology, even beyond the notion of 'community practices.' To describe all that the church is, one must have recourse to properly theological categories. For the church is, in the final analysis, a *theological community*."[54] In contrast, he states, "evangelicals by and large do not know what they believe about the church—neither about what it is, nor what it should be doing."[55]

Such an appeal to fundamental unawareness may overstate the case, confusing ignorance with an alternative view of the church, one that is sociological rather than theological in nature, an ecclesiology "from below" wherein the church is an aggregate of individuals self-chosen in a voluntary society.[56] But evangelicalism is marked not only by a flight into the visible church but also oftentimes by a flight from it.

In contrast to the former sociological understanding of the church, evangelicalism is often marked by a disregard for the visible church altogether and an embrace of a spiritual, invisible church.[57] Such a view sees the visible church with its obvious difficulties as at best indifferent to and at worst deleterious for the spiritual life. It is the invisible church, the church as a "spiritual fellowship of the truly converted," that matters, such that involvement within the visible church becomes optional because it is in the

---

[54]Vanhoozer, "Evangelicalism and the Church," p. 71; cf. pp. 70-71.

[55]Ibid., p. 42.

[56]As George Hunsberger writes, evangelical ecclesiology tends to see the church as "the modern social form of a *voluntary organization* grounded in the collective exercise of *rational choice* by its members rather than the form of a communion of saints that is made such by the will of the Spirit of God. There need be no dichotomy between the choices of God and the responses of those whom God calls, of course. But that dichotomy is precisely what emerges from a sense of Christian identity that is first and foremost individual rather than one that knows that human identity is both personal and relational, both individual and communal" ("Evangelical Conversion Toward a Missional Ecclesiology," in Stackhouse, *Evangelical Ecclesiology*, pp. 118-19). For critiques of evangelicalism's individualism in relation to the church, see also C. Norman Kraus, "Evangelicalism: A Mennonite Critique," in Dayton and Johnston, *Variety of American Evangelicalism*, p. 198, and Vanhoozer, "Evangelicalism and the Church," p. 58. Reformed thinkers in America at times criticize evangelicalism for its low ecclesiology and penchant to use a parachurch definition of voluntary association united for practical purposes as an adequate ecclesiological description of the church. See Mark Noll and Cassandra Niemczyk, "Evangelicals and the Self-Consciously Reformed," in Dayton and Johnston, *Variety of American Evangelicalism*, p. 216.

[57]For evangelicalism's proclivity to abandon the visible church for the invisible one, see Vanhoozer, "Evangelicalism and the Church," pp. 46-48; also Grenz, *Renewing the Center*, pp. 297-99.

end soteriologically irrelevant.[58] This viewpoint is evident when some evangelicals witness to others by contrasting the new life in Christ with the failures of the church. Such a viewpoint is of course not the case for many evangelicals. But it does seem to be the case for many American self-designated evangelicals answering George Barna's surveys.[59] One does not have to dig very hard in evangelicalism to find indifference toward the visible church, if not a flight from the visible church altogether.

Against both a flight into and from the visible church, against both reductive sociological and pragmatic understandings of the church on one hand and platonic and spiritualistic ones on the other, Barth presents a fully theological understanding of the church, a church that is divinely constituted, in which, as he says already in the *Göttingen Dogmatics*, the "invisible-becomes-visible" (*sichtbarwerden*).[60] The church is thus more than the visible, for it is divinely called and not simply humanly constituted. But it is never less than visible, for its visibility is indeed part of its divinely ordained existence. The doctrine of the church as both invisible and visible, with the first functioning as the basis of the second in an irreversible relation, thus exists in analogy to the doctrine of the person of Christ in Christology.[61] The church is the body of Christ, an image which Barth understands not as a weak metaphor but as an ontological reality in which the church truly exists as Christ's "earthly-historical form of existence" (*irdisch-geschichtliche Existenzform*).[62] Christ and the church are joined together in the *totus Christus*, Christ with his body, and Barth provides a place for the church in God's economy of salvation that is an important corrective to much of evangelicalism's reductive sociological description of the church in which the church is a collection of individuals, a solely voluntary society, and little else.[63]

Barth's ecclesiology is also a corrective, however, for ecclesiologies that

---

[58]Vanhoozer, "Evangelicalism and the Church," p. 47.

[59]See *The Barna Update*, "Americans Have Commitment Issues, New Survey Shows" (April 18, 2006), www.barna.org/culture/155-americans-have-commitment-issues-new-surveyshows# .U2Fx9setteI4.

[60]Barth, *Unterricht in der christlichen Religion*, 3: *Die Lehre von der Versöhnung/Die Lehre von der Erlösung*, ed. Hinrich Stoevesandt (Zürich: Theologisher Verlag Zürich, 2003), p. 364. This was Barth's first dogmatics and originated from his first professorship in the early to mid-1920s.

[61]Ibid., p. 366.

[62]*CD* IV/1, p. 661.

[63]*CD* IV/2, pp. 59-60; see also *CD* IV/3.1, p. 216.

trade concrete visibility for spiritual fellowship and personal piety and make the church peripheral or even irrelevant to God's saving activity. Against such a view, Barth presents a very different one, making the faith of the believer dependent on the prior witness of the church, as when he states regarding the subjective reality of revelation in the first volume of the *Church Dogmatics*: "God himself and God alone turns man into a recipient of His revelation—but He does so in a definite area, and this area . . . is the area of the Church."[64] As he then continues:

> Put pointedly . . . , there exist over against Jesus Christ, not in the first instance believers, and then composed of them, the Church; but first of all the Church and then, through it and in it, believers. While God is as little bound to the Church as to the Synagogue, the recipients of His revelation are. They are what they are because the church is what it is, and because they are in the Church, not apart from the Church and not outside the Church. And when we say "Church," we do not mean merely the inward and invisible coherence of those whom God in Christ calls His own, but also the outward and visible coherence of those who have heard in time, and have confessed to their hearing, that in Christ they are God's. The reception of revelation occurs within, not without, this twofold coherence.[65]

Against the excesses of evangelical individualism, Barth posits the corporate reality of the church, a reality that is not peripheral to the economy of salvation but grounded in God's sovereign election.[66] And against the evangelical penchant to downplay or even disregard the visible church and take flight to an invisible one, Barth posits that the church is necessarily visible and concrete as the "outward and visible coherence of those who have heard in time," ideas included in extensive sections of the *Church Dogmatics* where Barth speaks of such concrete issues as church law and church practices.[67] In short, Barth's ecclesiology is thoroughly grounded in God's free election of grace and integrated into the work of God's act of reconciliation rather than simply functional and peripheral to them. Barth provides a rich theological account of the church as a corporate and concrete people that

---

[64]*CD* I/2, p. 210.
[65]*CD* I/2, p. 211.
[66]*CD* II/2, pp. 195ff.
[67]*CD* IV/3.2, pp. 865ff.; see also CD IV/2, pp. 676ff.

can serve as a resource to protect against current deformities of ecclesiology resulting from an overemphasis on pragmatism and the rising tides of a recently resurgent gnosticism.[68] Yet Barth's ecclesiology is more than a remedy for recent concerns.

What Barth provides is a richly developed ecclesiology that attempts to overcome a deficiency already latent to some degree in the Reformation bifurcation of soteriology and ecclesiology.[69] The bifurcation was perhaps unavoidable in its day, and the debate between Luther and the likes of Cajetan and Prierias was a necessary one, but it came with a price, namely, a division between soteriology and ecclesiology in which the former was used against the latter, evidenced in a minimalist Protestant ecclesiology that evangelicalism has attenuated still further. Luther and Calvin certainly labored to retain the centrality of the church in God's plan of redemption and cannot be pinned with today's individualistic excesses. But the times often dictated that the doctrine of salvation and that of the church were locked in a tragic zero-sum game, so that ecclesiology was even for the Reformers often defined in a negative and reactive rather than constructive manner. Their successors were much less successful than they. What Barth provides is a reuniting of soteriology and ecclesiology by getting at the heart of the matter, namely, the relation of Christ, and thus the gospel, to the church. His is an attempt to undo what was at the time a needed division but one that cannot last. Yet, and this cannot be stressed enough, this reunification is undertaken in a thoroughly Protestant manner, for Barth is after nothing less than articulating an ecclesiology equal in development and scope to that of Tridentine Catholicism, but one faithful to the Protestant vision, to join again together what in the Reformation was rent asunder, but to join them in a rightly ordered relationship—to take Ephesians as seriously within the canon as Romans and Galatians.

Barth was keenly aware of the failure of the Reformation and post-Reformation to put forth an ecclesiology that was rich and developed, a

---

[68]Evangelicalism is always in danger of gnosticism, which seems, along with individualism, to be America's quintessential heresy. See Harold Bloom, *The American Religion: The Emergence of the Post-Christian Nation* (New York: Simon and Schuster, 1991). There is something perennially tempting about a gospel of simple knowledge, simply held, for an escape from a doomed world.

[69]One way to state this is that the Reformers traded Augustine's ecclesiology for his soteriology. See Diarmaid MacCulloch, *The Reformation* (London: Penguin, 2003), p. 111.

failure in no small part due to its protest against the robust ecclesiology of Roman Catholicism. The answer to such a robust view of the church, Barth realized, could never be an ecclesiological minimalism but a fully formed and compelling Protestant alternative to it. Just as the *Church Dogmatics* is in some respects on a par with Thomas's *Summa Theologica* in seriousness, weight and scope (for Barth never repudiated the scholastic impulse of comprehensiveness in theology), so Barth's doctrine of the church provides an ecclesiology for Protestantism as high as that of Roman Catholicism. It is thus a serious resource to be considered for an ecumenical ecclesiology for Protestantism today that stands between the organic ecclesiology of Roman Catholicism and the self-selected sociological ecclesiology of so much of evangelical Protestantism. What Barth gives us is a rich ecclesiology that aspires to be catholic even as it is thoroughly evangelical (in the widest sense of the term), Protestant in nature and congregational in form. To borrow from Richard Dawkins in a way that he would no doubt despise, Barth may provide a significant resource for remaining an "intellectually fulfilled Protestant" by providing an ecclesiology that is sufficiently serious and compelling to be a viable alternative to those of the Catholic and Orthodox traditions.

Barth can provide this due to a theology of the church that fully incorporates the church into the economy of grace without making it the steward of grace. In other words, while Barth takes seriously the unity of the *totus Christus*, the unity of Christ and the church in a way that evangelicalism often has not, this unity always remains for him a unity in distinction, never a simple unity. Christ is united with his church, but he is never subsumed into it. In other words, Barth never ceases to be a Protestant in his ecclesiology even while correcting Protestant deficiencies. He provides a truly catholic evangelical (over against, for example, a Roman Catholic or evangelical catholic) doctrine of the church.

Certainly it must be said that the distinction between Christ and the church is carefully preserved in evangelicalism, but it is often preserved by making the church peripheral to God's act of reconciliation. What Barth provides is an ecclesiology in which there is a true union of Christ and the church, but where this union remains ever differentiated and irreversible in nature, where Christ is never subsumed into the being and agency of the church, where the church is a witness to, but not an extension of, the incarnation, and thus a proclaimer, rather than a dispenser, of grace. This ecclesiology is one in which the church is both divine event and human institution, but with these also in an irreversible order, the first giving rise to the second. The second is never the church without the first. In short, what Barth offers evangelicals to consider is a doctrine of the church that once again sees the church as a mystery and an article of faith. This in the end may be Barth's greatest contribution to evangelicalism regarding the question of the church, if evangelicals are willing to take him seriously on this score. Such a consideration need not mean that evangelicalism's unique and best contributions to ecclesiology cannot be preserved. Perhaps even evangelicalism's voluntarism and its emphasis on the individual (though not its individualism) could thus be theologically transformed and reconstituted by being grounded in the freedom of God and the priesthood of all believers, respectively, though this is a topic for another time.[70]

In closing, I want to add that I think this conversation can get off the ground and that Barth and evangelicals can even be friends, in spite of the significant differences that continue to exist between them. I believe this can take place because Barth and evangelicals are very close on a number of central and important issues, of which I will mention three. The first is that both embrace the scandal of the gospel, namely, the centrality of Christ and his unique and supreme and irreplaceable identity standing at the heart of all the ways and works of God. This sets them apart from so many others today, sadly. If the great divide in modern American Christianity is between those who embrace and those who reject the scandal of the gospel, then Barth and evangelicals stand together on one side of the aisle.

Second, in correspondence to this christological particularity, Barth and evangelicals both give evidence of a shared commitment to a radical particularity in ecclesiology, in that the primary agent of God's work in the world is not the institutional structure of a church per se but is the concrete congregation of believers in a particular place and time. If all politics are

---

[70]For a provisional attempt at such a reconfiguration, see Roger Olson, "Free Church Ecclesiology and Evangelical Spirituality: A Unique Compatibility," in Stackhouse, *Evangelical Ecclesiology*, pp. 161-78. I believe that precisely such a reconfiguration could establish the great contributions of the Baptist tradition specifically on a firmer theological (rather than philosophical, sociological, political or anthropological) footing.

local, and the church as the concrete sign of the kingdom is a divinely actualized event that gives rise to a new form of politics in the world, then the
church, too, is local. The universality of the church is therefore found in its
radical particularity and the fundamental nature of the church is related not
first and foremost to an institutional or denominational structure but to the
local body of believers, for the church is before all else an event that gives
rise to a historical existence in a particular location, and thus the church is
first and foremost a congregation rather than an institution (hence Barth's
preference for the German *Gemeinde* rather than *Kirche*).[71] In a manner that
could no doubt be embraced by most evangelicals, Barth articulates this
conviction when he states: "When I say congregation, I am thinking primarily of the concrete form of the congregation in a particular place. . . .
Credo ecclesiam means that I believe that here, at this place, in this visible
assembly, the work of the Holy Spirit takes place."[72] Moreover, like Barth,
many evangelicals are not likely to be swayed by an argument that the answer
to today's secularism can effectively be held off with an appeal to a new
creedalism or recovery of an episcopal ministry and return to strong clergy
and laity distinctions.[73] Creeds and bishops may have helped in the past and
may have value in the present, but they are not enough and may even be
more harm than good (may one assume that Bishop John Shelby Spong says

---

[71]See Barth's address at the Amsterdam Assembly of the World Council of Churches in 1948 in
Man's Disorder and God's Design (New York: Harper & Brothers, 1948), pp. 67-76; see also Barth's
discussion of the difference between these terms in *Evangelical Theology: An Introduction*, trans.
Grover Foley (New York: Holt, Rinehart and Winston, 1963), p. 37. For a robust and compelling
defense of an evangelical congregationalism, including a theological defense of a chastened
emphasis on the individual and of voluntarism, see Olson, "Free Church Ecclesiology and Evangelical Spirituality," pp. 161-78.

[72]Karl Barth, *Dogmatics in Outline*, trans. G. T. Thomson (New York: Harper & Row, 1959), pp.
142-43. Elsewhere he can say: "We assume that by the Christian community or Church is not
meant an establishment or institution organized along specific lines, but the living people
awakened and assembled by Jesus Christ as the Lord for the fulfillment of a specific task" (*CD*
III/4, p. 488). Such a view of the church as local and concrete does not deny the reality of the
universal church, but it does prioritize and respect the integrity of the local congregation and
refuse to universalize forms and structures of community life that are best left to local and
indigenous decision.

[73]Barth's opposition to hierarchical vicariate offices can be seen at least as early as his dogmatic
lectures in Göttingen; see Barth, *Unterricht in der christlichen Religion* 3, pp. 372-77; see also *CD*
III/4, pp. 488-90 and *CD* IV/2, pp. 690-95. For an early commentary on the limitations of creedalism, see Barth's "The Desirability and Possibility of a Universal Reformed Creed," in *Theology
and Church: Shorter Writings 1920–1928*, trans. Louise Pettibone Smith (New York: Harper &
Row, 1962), p. 118.

the creed in the liturgy?). So Barth and evangelicals may find a common cause in a commitment to a very different catholicity and a very different ecclesial concreteness than the high church and highly centralized and hierarchical ecclesiology espoused by the so-called evangelical catholics of today, one that focuses on concrete congregational existence rather than institutional offices and structures, as well as one that is eschatological, rather than romantic, regarding questions of ecumenism.[74]

The final similarity between Barth and evangelicals is that both define the church not only by its self-constitutive practices (as does the Augsburg Confession, for example) but make mission as evangelism and service central to the church's existence, though for evangelicals mission is often thought of as what the church does, whereas in Barth's actualistic ecclesiology mission is what the church is.[75] Nevertheless, evangelicals, who often are much stronger in their practice than their theory, would no doubt completely concur with Barth's statement that "The Church is either a missionary Church or it is no church at all."[76] Evangelicals indeed now seem to live this out significantly more than their mainline counterparts.

Barth himself regretted that this missionary impulse was not to be found in the magisterial churches of his day, while readily evident in the sects, as he referred to them.[77] But the end of Christendom, which Barth saw as occurring around him, has now come to pass in the West, so it is perhaps best to retire Ernst Troeltsch's categories once and for all and recognize similarities among all like-minded missional Christians. And when we retire such categories, perhaps this too can remove one more barrier to making conversations between Barth and modern evangelicals possible and productive.

---

[74]For such an example of an evangelical-catholic approach, see Carl E. Braaten, "The Special Ministry of the Ordained," in *Marks of the Body of Christ*, ed. Carl E. Braaten and Robert W. Jenson (Grand Rapids: Eerdmans, 1999), pp. 123-36. Braaten has little regard for evangelicalism, it seems (see p. 134). For a very different assessment of episcopal ministry than Braaten's by one within both the high church and evangelical traditions, see Paul F. M. Zahl, "Up the Creek: Paddling in the Maelstrom of the Mainline," in George, *Pilgrims on the Sawdust Trail*, pp. 177-81, as well as his response to the articles in Stackhouse, *Evangelical Ecclesiology*, pp. 213-16.

[75]See *CD* IV/3.2, esp. pp. 795-96.

[76]*CD* III/3, p. 64. Barth claimed to have recovered this missionary impulse not from magisterial Protestantism but from Anabaptism and Pietism (*CD* IV/3.1, pp. 11-38, esp. pp. 25, 28).

[77]*CD* III/4, p. 505.

3

An Old Debate Revisited

Karl Barth and
Catholic Substance

✠

Of all the critical investigations of Barth's ecclesiology appearing in recent years, one of the most significant is that of Reinhard Hütter. In his work *Suffering Divine Things: Theology as Church Practice*, as well as in a number of essays now collected and revised in *Bound to Be Free: Evangelical Catholic Engagements in Ecclesiology, Ethics and Ecumenism*, Hütter interacts with Barth constructively and appreciatively but in the end finds Barth's understanding of church and dogma deficient and untenable for providing a theology with the richness, vitality and concreteness necessary to sustain a church through time and in the face of the waves of modernity.[1] Though he expresses sympathy for Barth's dialectical theology, he ultimately concludes that Barth's ecclesiological project, with its dialectical understanding of church doctrine, is in the end a nonviable proposal for an embodied church and an ecumenical future, concluding that it is "a quite seductive but ultimately abstract catholicity."[2] Against what he calls Barth's "dialectical catholicity," Hütter proposes a "concrete catholicity." In what follows, I will

---

This chapter draws upon and expands material in "Karl Barth's Ecclesiology in the Light of Recent Reconsiderations," a paper presented at the Karl Barth Society of North America Section of the American Academy of Religion National Meeting, Atlanta, Georgia, 2003.

[1]Reinhard Hütter, *Suffering Divine Things: Theology as Church Practice* (Grand Rapids: Eerdmans, 1999), hereafter cited as *SDT*; and *Bound to Be Free: Evangelical Catholic Engagements in Ecclesiology, Ethics and Ecumenism* (Grand Rapids: Eerdmans, 2004), hereafter cited as *BTBF*.

[2]*BTBF*, p. 4.

extend the examination of the first chapter and consider what Hütter's own proposal for a concrete catholic ecclesiology might entail.

Rethinking the Timeline

Before assessing Hütter's criticisms of Barth and his own constructive proposal, however, we have to note that his assessment of Barth's theology suffers from a problem of (chronological) emphasis. Hütter contends that Barth's early dogmatic theology, first given systematic expression in the *Göttingen Dogmatics*, was shaped in a significant way by his interaction with Roman Catholic theology, for as soon as Barth took up the dogmatic task, and "to seriously study and engage Reformation theology (especially that of Calvin), he began to engage Roman Catholic theology as a decisive counterpart."[3] This claim is not without some warrant, but it does require significant qualification in light of Barth's actual encounter with Roman Catholic theology during this time.

While Barth was aware, of course, of the basic outlines of Roman Catholicism and possessed many of the typical Protestant stereotypes of his time as a young pastor, he became more acquainted with Catholicism in the early 1920s as witnessed in three primary developments.[4] The first development was Barth's new awareness of the vibrant renewal of Roman Catholicism in Germany in the early years of the twentieth century, an awareness followed by a curious appreciation (as a Protestant outsider) for this growing Catholic revitalization.[5] The second development was a new friendship with Erik Peterson while in Göttingen and Barth's attendance of Peterson's seminar on Thomas Aquinas in 1923, coupled with his own sus-

---

[3]Ibid., p. 81.

[4]For Barth's early encounters with Roman Catholicism, see Amy Marga, *Karl Barth's Dialogue with Catholicism in Göttingen and Münster: Its Significance for His Doctrine of God* (Tübingen: Mohr Siebeck, 2010); Eberhard Busch, *Karl Barth: His Life from Letters and Autobiographical Texts*, trans. John Bowden (Grand Rapids: Eerdmans, 1994), pp. 126-98; Keith Johnson, *Karl Barth and the Analogia Entis* (London: T & T Clark, 2010); Johnson, "A Reappraisal of Karl Barth's Theological Development and His Dialogue with Catholicism," *International Journal of Systemic Theology* 14, no. 1 (2012): 3-25; Benjamin Dahlke, *Karl Barth, Catholic Renewal and Vatican II* (New York: T & T Clark, 2012), originally published as *Die Katholische Rezeption Karl Barths, Theologische Erneuerung im Vorfeld des Zweiten Vatikanischen Konzils* (Tübingen: Mohr Siebeck, 2010); and Kimlyn J. Bender, *Karl Barth's Christological Ecclesiology* (Aldershot, UK: Ashgate, 2005), pp. 45-68, 82-92.

[5]Marga, *Karl Barth's Dialogue with Catholicism*, p. 3.

tained reading of Thomas during that and the following year.[6] Finally, Barth's serious engagement with the Reformation heritage in the early 1920s did indeed cause him to reflect on Roman Catholicism insofar as Barth's engagement with the theology of the Reformers and the Reformed Confessions led him to work out a distinctively Reformation position that served as an alternative to Roman Catholic conceptions of Scripture, church and dogma.[7]

---

[6]While Peterson's conversion to Roman Catholicism did not occur until 1930, his stance was such that already in 1925 Barth took him to represent a "catholicizing phenomenology," i.e., a Roman Catholic position. See Barth, "Church and Theology" in *Theology and Church: Shorter Writings 1920–1928*, trans. Louise Pettibone Smith (New York: Harper & Row, 1962), p. 288. Thus in 1925 Barth clearly perceived that he stood between two positions he had to reject. He wrote: "If one accepts Schleiermacher without blushing, then Thomas Aquinas is equally acceptable. Both are equally far from Luther and Calvin" (ibid., p. 288).

[7]For Barth's work on these topics during this period, see note 12 below. Barth only began to engage Catholicism in earnest during his time in Münster (1925–1930), evidenced not only in his serious reading of Catholic theology during this time but also in his interactions with a Catholic lay discussion group which he joined there (see Marga, *Karl Barth's Dialogue with Catholicism*, pp. 33-35). The most famous engagement, perhaps, is Barth's interaction with the Catholic theologian Erich Przywara in 1929 and the infamous debate over the *analogia entis* that ensued. Barth had, however, already given serious thought to Roman Catholic theology before that encounter, evidenced not only in his provisional thoughts in the 1925 essay "Church and Theology," addressing Peterson's work, but also in the later essays of the following years: "The Concept of the Church" (1927) and "Roman Catholicism: A Question to the Protestant Church" (1928). These essays can be found in *Theology and Church*, pp. 272-85 and 307-33; for an examination of these essays, see Marga, *Karl Barth's Dialogue with Catholicism*, pp. 37-44; also Bender, *Karl Barth's Christological Ecclesiology*, pp. 45-58. That Barth's essays of 1927 and 1928 are often given little weight in understanding Barth's relation to Catholicism during this period is perhaps best attributed to the fact that Barth's development is so often seen only through the lens of theological method and its focus on epistemology and the doctrine of revelation (and the *analogia entis* debate), rather than in relation to a wider range of questions, including ecclesiological and ethical ones that also greatly consumed Barth during his early years. Therefore, no matter how important Barth's interaction with Przywara was for the question of the development of Barth's theological method (as incisively examined in the works of Johnson cited above), it was not decisive for Barth's Reformation commitments, more akin to their fruition than their impetus. Marga puts this well: "Barth emerges from the Thomas Seminar even more committed to the Reformation theology than he had in the past, and its categories spread through his own work" (*Karl Barth's Dialogue with Catholicism*, p. 136). In short, even though Barth stated in 1932 that only the *analogia entis*, as the "invention of Antichrist," separated Protestantism and Roman Catholicism, such that all other reasons for not becoming Catholic were "short-sighted and trivial" (*CD* I/1, p. xiii), this statement needs to be read in a wider context and taken as hyperbolic overstatement in the heat of a particular battle. Barth certainly had quite a number of ecclesiological and soteriological reasons for the ongoing relevance of protest that he had articulated earlier not only in the two essays previously mentioned but in others as well, and none of these reasons were seen by him as trivial (see, for instance, those essays referenced in notes 22 and 23 below, as well as the 1927 and 1928 essays here referenced; see also *GD*, p. 212, where Barth states that it is the Scripture principle that keeps one from becoming Roman Catholic). In fact, even with respect to Przywara, one could make the argument that it was not solely

Nevertheless, when one looks at where Barth was spending his focused mental and productive energy during the years of his conscious break from liberalism and his years in Göttingen, it was not with Roman Catholic theology. Barth's early lectures and seminars focused on the exposition of books of the Bible, on the theology of the formative figures of liberal Protestantism (especially Schleiermacher) and on the theology of his newly discovered and appreciated Reformed heritage (evidenced in lectures on the theology of Calvin, Zwingli, the Heidelberg Catechism and the Reformed confessions).[8] While Roman Catholic thought was never outside of his purview, it nearly always came secondhand, and a close examination of his Göttingen lecture cycle gives witness to an engagement primarily with past Reformed and Lutheran sources, as well as a running commentary and debate with his liberal inheritance. Barth himself would later comment on the important place that Heinrich Heppe's *Dogmatics* (along with the Lutheran equivalent of Heinrich Schmid) had on his own development of this early dogmatic cycle.[9] Moreover, even though Thomas makes numerous appearances in the Göttingen lectures, he is referenced more as one from whom Barth could learn, a source for reflection on a prior point or in support of such a point, than as a spokesperson for Catholic orthodoxy or a church father who shaped Barth's discussion of the theological *loci* under examination. Thomas is one who

---

the *analogia entis*, but equally his conception of the *incarnatus prolongatus*, i.e., the church understood as the prolongation of the incarnation and the mediator and pattern of all God's relations with the world, that was the crux of Barth's reaction to and rejection of his theology; see Johnson, *Karl Barth and the* Analogia Entis, pp. 89-91; see also Przywara's lecture given at Barth's seminar, published as Erich Przywara, "Das katholische Kirchenprinzip," *Zwischen den Zeiten* 7 (1929): 277-302. At the very least, an appreciation of this history demonstrates that epistemological and ecclesiological questions cannot be separated in understanding Barth's development, and particularly understanding his interaction with and relation to Roman Catholicism. Certainly the history of Barth interpretation has often made him out to be singularly concerned with theological epistemology and method to the neglect of these other themes.

[8]For the topics of Barth's lectures and seminars during his time in Göttingen and later Münster and Bonn, see Bruce McCormack, *Karl Barth's Critically Realistic Dialectical Theology: Its Genesis and Development* (Oxford: Clarendon Press, 1995), pp. 293-94, 378, 415-16; see also Busch, *Karl Barth*, pp. 126-98. For Barth's appropriation of the Reformed tradition while in Göttingen, see Matthias Freudenberg, *Karl Barth und die reformierte Theologie: Die Auseinandersetzung mit Calvin, Zwingli und den reformierten Bekenntnisschriften während seiner Göttinger Lehrtätigkeit* (Neukircher-Vluyn: Neukirchener Verlag, 1997); and John Webster, *Barth's Earlier Theology: Four Studies* (London: T & T Clark, 2005).

[9]See Barth's foreword to Heinrich Heppe, *Reformed Dogmatics—Set Out and Illustrated from the Sources*, rev. and ed. Ernst Bizer, trans. G. T. Thomson (London: George Allen & Unwin, 1950), p. v.

Barth always treated with respect, but one who is engaged and consulted not only with appreciation but also at times with criticism, and sometimes brought in simply for illustration, a source among sources, and often of interest only as a source for later Protestant orthodoxy.[10] Barth certainly could recognize Thomas's normativity for Catholic theology, but Barth himself does not treat him in this way for his own, even as he learns from him.[11]

Furthermore, Barth's productivity during this time in Göttingen was marked by published essays that focused on developing his own theology of proclamation and Scripture through an appropriation of the Reformed tradition. This was itself carried out with a concomitant conversation with Luther and the Lutheran tradition on one side, as well as with past or present figures of the liberal theology from which Barth was distancing himself apace on the other (such as essays on Luther as well as Schleiermacher and Herrmann, or his famous debates with Harnack and Tillich, both in 1923).[12] Therefore, while recognizing Barth's serious interaction with Aquinas in the early part of the 1920s, one is nevertheless warranted to conclude that Barth's first truly substantive interactions with Roman Catholic theology on its own terms did not occur until the mid- to late 1920s, and that, contrary to Hütter's contention, his first dogmatic lectures were primarily shaped by interactions with other dialogue partners.[13]

This is not to overlook that Barth was indeed engaged with questions of Roman Catholicism during this time. He could note with curious appreciation that Roman Catholic reviewers had often understood his *Römerbrief* better than contemporary Protestant reviewers.[14] He could also note with amazement, in letters to his friend Thurneysen, the true weight of Catholic thought in

---

[10]See *GD*, pp. 3, 10, 12, et al.

[11]*GD*, p. 238; cf. Marga, *Karl Barth's Dialogue with Catholicism*, pp. 28-33; also p. 135.

[12]For Barth's published work on these figures during this period, see *Vorträge und kleinere Arbeiten 1922–1925*, ed. Holger Finze (Zürich: Theologischer Verlag Zürich, 1990); for the period immediately following, see *Vorträge und kleinere Arbeiten 1925–1930*, ed. Hermann Schmidt (Zürich: Theologischer Verlag Zürich, 1994); a number of these essays appear in *The Word of God and Theology*, trans. Amy Marga (London: T & T Clark, 2011), and *Theology and Church: Shorter Writings 1920–1928*.

[13]Marga notes: "The Münster dogmatic lectures, begun in October 1926, are the first place in Barth's dogmatic theology where he can be seen taking Catholic concerns seriously in a systematic and sympathetic way" (*Karl Barth's Dialogue with Catholicism*, p. 36).

[14]See the foreword to the fourth edition of the commentary on Romans: Karl Barth, *The Epistle to the Romans*, trans. Edwyn Hosyns (Oxford: Oxford University Press, 1968), p. 21.

comparison with so much of contemporary Protestantism.[15] Yet at this point of his career, Roman Catholic theology was not the center of Barth's attention. Barth's earliest theology leading up to his first dogmatics was the product of critical interaction with a number of significant influences on his thought. Roman Catholic theology was present, but not high, on this list, the top places taken by other influences, of which the following were decisive.

First, though often mentioned but seldom truly appreciated, Barth's rediscovery of the Bible must head the list of influences and elements that shaped the theology he developed immediately following his break from liberalism. This period was one marked by sustained and extensive exegesis of biblical texts, most notably in the *Römerbrief* of 1919 and in the revised edition of 1922, but also in lectures while in Göttingen on Ephesians, James, 1 Corinthians, 1 John, Philippians, Colossians and the Sermon on the Mount.[16] Barth's interaction with the Bible, and the central place he gave to it for both dogmatics and preaching, remained a constant throughout his theological development.

Second, Barth was engaged in polemical interaction with his liberal inheritance and what he believed to be the failure of neo-Protestantism.[17] This critical engagement was mirrored in the putting forth of a constructive and alternative proposal for a Protestant theology, one shaped by both theological and philosophical (Kantian and Kierkegaardian) convictions. Here, Barth displayed an ever-increasing appreciation for the role that preaching was to play in such a constructive proposal (alongside Scripture).[18] Barth's

---

[15]Karl Barth, *Revolutionary Theology in the Making: Barth-Thurneysen Correspondence, 1914–1925*, trans. James D. Smart (Richmond: John Knox Press, 1964), pp. 161-62, 168, 175.

[16]McCormack, *Karl Barth's Critically Realistic Dialectical Theology*, pp. 293-94. For Barth's interaction with the Bible as a defining element of his theology, see Donald Wood, *Barth's Theology of Interpretation* (Aldershot, UK: Ashgate, 2007); Webster, *Barth's Earlier Theology*; and Barth's essays "The New World in the Bible" and "Biblical Questions, Insights and Vistas," in *Word of God and Theology*, pp. 15-29, 71-100, respectively.

[17]In addition to Barth's commentary on Romans, see his essays in *Word of God and Theology*, and those on Schleiermacher, Herrmann and Ritschl in *Theology and Church* (pp. 136-58, 159-99, 200-216, 238-71), as well as his lectures on Schleiermacher in *The Theology of Schleiermacher*, ed. Dietrich Ritschl, trans. Geoffrey Bromiley (Grand Rapids: Eerdmans, 1982).

[18]For the significance of preaching in Barth's early theological thinking and its place in the dogmatic task, see "The Need and Promise of Christian Proclamation" and "The Word of God as the Task of Theology" in *Word of God and Theology* (pp. 101-29, 171-98, respectively), and "Menschenwort und Gotteswort in der christlichen Predigt," in *Vorträge und kleinere Arbeiten 1922–1925*, pp. 426-57; also *GD*, pp. 3-22, 23-41.

first dogmatic cycle took preaching as the raw material for dogmatics, and he could state that it is in preaching that a "direct point of contact for dogmatic reflection" is found.[19]

Third, Barth found his own theological and ecclesial identity in a rediscovery of the Reformed tradition, and it was a rediscovery that itself was enjoined to an investigation of Lutheran theology set over against this tradition. Barth steeped himself in discovering his Reformed ancestry during his first professorate at Göttingen, having been appointed to a chair in Reformed theology. There he gave courses on the Heidelberg Catechism and the Reformed confessions, as well as Calvin, Zwingli and Schleiermacher, as noted above.[20] In finding this identity, the primary dialogue partner became the sister Protestant tradition of the Reformed, namely, the Lutheran tradition. All of this exegetical, polemical and historical work culminated in the first dogmatics lecture cycle in Göttingen. Only after these three strands of Barth's work were in place did Barth engage Roman Catholicism in a significant way (in the mid- to late 1920s in Münster), and by then his constructive program and its primary commitments were well formed, though they would continue to undergo significant development.[21] Indeed, Barth read Roman Catholicism through eyes trained by and then turned against

---

[19]GD, p. 26.

[20]For Barth's recovery of the Reformed tradition while in Göttingen, see Freudenberg, *Karl Barth und die reformierte Theologie*; Webster, *Barth's Earlier Theology*; as well as Barth's now published lectures on the Reformed confessions: *The Theology of the Reformed Confessions, 1923*, trans. Darrell L. Guder and Judith J. Guder (Louisville, KY: Westminster John Knox, 2002), hereafter cited as *TRC*; on Zwingli: *Die Theologie Zwinglis: Vorlesungen Göttingen Wintersemester 1922/23*, ed. Matthias von Freudenberg (Zürich: Theologischer Verlag Zürich, 2004); on Calvin: *The Theology of John Calvin*, trans. Geoffrey Bromiley (Grand Rapids: Eerdmans, 1995); and those aforementioned on Schleiermacher (note 17 above). See also his essays "The Substance and Task of Reformed Doctrine," *Word of God and Theology*, pp. 199-237; "The Desirability and Possibility of a Universal Reformed Creed," *Theology and Church*, pp. 112-35; and "Schriftprinzip der reformierte Kirche," *Vorträge und kleinere Arbeiten 1922-1925*, pp. 500-544.

[21]McCormack also does not want to overemphasize the place that Roman Catholic theology played in Barth's early theology, but when he states that "during his time in Göttingen, Barth did indeed work 'exclusively in the triangle' created by his Kantian epistemological commitments, his retrieval of the older Protestantism, and his ongoing debate with neo-Protestantism," he has left out something too important to overlook, namely, Barth's ongoing conversation with the Bible, an element at least as important to his thought (and to my mind, much more) than his Kantianism (see Bruce McCormack, *Orthodox and Modern: Studies in the Theology of Karl Barth* [Grand Rapids: Baker Academic, 2008], p. 300). If Hütter had argued that McCormack had neglected the role of the Bible in Barth's Göttingen period, rather than Roman Catholicism, he would have been able to make a stronger case. See *BTBF*, p. 244. For a similar assessment of McCormack along these lines, see Wood, *Barth's Theology of Interpretation*, pp. 2-4.

neo-Protestantism, and it is not entirely surprising that the criticisms Barth used against the latter were along the same lines as those against the former. Indeed, Barth could see the mistakes of Schleiermacher as analogies to those of Roman Catholicism.[22]

Now, the distinctions of these three strands should not be misconstrued as hard and fast divisions between them. Certainly Barth's understanding of the Scripture principle, for example, was influential not only for his view of Scripture but grew out of his appreciation of the Reformed tradition and provided a mark of demarcation for his theology from the liberal theology of his youth, thus serving a critical and polemical as well as constructive purpose in his theology. Moreover, to acknowledge that it was the biblical and Reformed strands (as engaged with and set over against the Lutheran and neo-Protestant traditions) that were primary in Barth's theological development is, of course, not to overlook that Barth had certain instincts about what he objected to in Roman Catholicism already evident in the early 1920s.[23] Nor is it to deny the fact that Catholicism grew to have an increasing role as an interlocutor as time went on (indeed, it increased as neo-Protestantism decreased, such that there seemed an inverse proportion between the two).[24] But this does not entail that Barth's formative period was singularly marked by an interaction with Catholicism as the most important influence for Barth's constructive proposals. When Hütter states: "As soon as Barth had to teach theology and, in the course of his preparation, to seriously study and engage Reformation theology (especially that of Calvin), he began to engage Roman Catholic theology as a decisive counterpart," this overplays the influence of Catholicism

---

[22]See Barth's 1927 essay "Rechtfertigung und Heiligung," in *Vorträge und kleinere Arbeiten 1925–1930*, p. 75; and Barth, "Church and Theology," p. 288; cf. *CD* I/1, p. 34.

[23]Quite evident in Barth's "Need and Promise of Christian Proclamation," pp. 112-16, and in "Schriftprinzip," pp. 500-544, as well as throughout the *GD*.

[24]Evident in Barth's statement in 1928 that if forced to choose between Protestant liberalism and Roman Catholicism, he would choose the latter; see "Roman Catholicism," in *Theology and Church*, p. 314 n. 1. Marga writes of this essay: "Barth's lecture on 'Roman Catholicism as a Question to the Protestant Church' displays his very conscious and public decision to stop encountering Roman Catholic theology as a modern *Protestant* theologian, and start encountering it as a theologian of the Reformation" (*Karl Barth's Dialogue with Catholicism*, p. 41). If true, it is at this point for the first time that Barth can be seen as taking Roman Catholicism seriously on its own terms, and with decisive significance for his own theology. It was also from this point forward that Barth's criticisms of Roman Catholic theology grew more pointed, and these criticisms remained consistent throughout his career (see ibid., p. 42).

on his earliest development.[25] Barth's decisive counterparts for his earliest period were the neo-Protestant tradition and the Lutheran tradition, over against each of which (though not equally) Barth developed his constructive program. Barth's earliest formative period included but was not dependent on a dialectical engagement with Roman Catholicism, and attention to the sources Barth actually cites in the *Göttingen Dogmatics* displays that Barth was primarily drawing on Reformation, Protestant orthodox and modern Protestant sources.[26] Certainly, once Barth began to engage the question of ecclesiology in force, Roman Catholicism did become a very significant dialogue partner.[27] Yet his engagement with Roman Catholicism was quite peripheral when one looks at the works Barth was actually citing and his own publishing output and teaching preoccupations in these years in Göttingen. It was not until his time in Münster and the late 1920s, with his seminar on Aquinas and his interaction with Erich Przywara, that Barth engaged Catholicism with singular attention, and by this time, his central convictions were firmly in place.[28] That this is so can be seen already in his response to Erik Peterson in 1925.[29]

This narrative of Barth's development is told for more than historical curiosity and interest, for its central claim has important constructive ramifications. Barth's program was not simply parasitic on Roman Catholicism (just

---

[25]*BTBF*, p. 81.

[26]It is thus hard to agree with Hütter when he states that a close study of the *GD* displays an "inner, theological urgency to engage Roman Catholicism" (*BTBF*, p. 242). Certainly it is true that by going back to the ancient dogmas Barth was visiting a common heritage of Catholic and Protestant traditions, but to claim that Roman Catholic theology was the major dialogue partner in the mid-1920s is to overstate the case. For a similar assessment, see McCormack, *Orthodox and Modern*, pp. 230-31, 298-302.

[27]Kimlyn J. Bender, *Karl Barth's Christological Ecclesiology*, pp. 45-89. Catholicism thus became an important dialogue partner only after Barth was well established in his basic theological convictions. As Marga writes: "After four years of teaching in Münster, Barth came to see Catholicism and the theology of Thomas less as teachers and conversations [sic] partners and more as the most important opponent that modern Protestantism would have to face if it were going to be true to its Reformation roots" (*Karl Barth's Dialogue with Catholicism*, p. 10). Yet if so, then Marga herself overreaches when she states in reference to Barth's reading of Thomas in 1923/1924: "From this time on, Thomas became as important a theologian in Barth's dogmatic theology as Luther or Calvin" (p. 30). Certainly Barth did not see things this way and always reserved a particular place of honor for Luther and Calvin that Thomas could never reach; see *CD* I/2, pp. 603-20, esp. pp. 609, 612-14.

[28]For Barth's interaction with Przywara, see Marga, *Karl Barth's Dialogue with Catholicism*, pp. 123-52, and Johnson, *Karl Barth and the* Analogia Entis.

[29]Barth, "Church and Theology," pp. 286-306. For Barth's response and Peterson's own claims, see *BTBF*, pp. 19-42; Marga, *Karl Barth's Dialogue with Catholicism*, pp. 84-90; Bender, *Karl Barth's Christological Ecclesiology*, pp. 87-89.

as it was not on neo-Protestantism), nor was it a reactionary one set over against Catholicism as if Catholicism from the first provided for Barth some kind of privileged baseline of comparison. Certainly Barth's appropriation of the ancient church pushed out the boundaries of Reformation resources in his first dogmatic lecture cycle. Yet Barth read these resources through a particular Reformed hermeneutical lens. Moreover, while Barth indeed came to find in Roman Catholicism a serious partner, and in time, the most serious partner, to his retrieval and renewal of a Reformation theology, his own theological development and program was not simply a critical and reactionary one.[30] If it was, then Hütter might be correct that it itself could not provide a true ecclesial existence but serve only a prophetic, dialectical and judgmental function, set over against and within an enduring, viable and normative concrete ecclesial one in Catholicism. But Barth's project was in fact a constructive reappropriation of the Reformed tradition (including within it a particular appropriation of the patristic one), and this tradition itself was an ecclesially embodied one, and perhaps one not best captured by the term "dialectical catholicity."[31] It was not an "endless dialectical play, a ceaseless critical oscillation between neo-Protestantism and Roman Catholicism,"[32] though the question of whether it was ecclesially concrete is a significant one we will have to revisit below. At this point, it is simply important to note that Barth did believe that the Reformed tradition, like the Lutheran one, was ecclesially concrete in the churches of the Reformation and their faithful descendants, though its witness had been greatly attenuated and compromised in the Protestant churches that had embraced the liberal tradition.

Peterson's Arguments Reborn

With this historical work in view, we can move on to a more direct engagement. Hütter's own proposal for a constructive ecclesiological program

---

[30]Barth would state how seriously he had come to take Roman Catholic theology as the primary rival to Protestant theology, the "only conversation partner of Protestant theology worthy of serious consideration" (*den einzigen wirklich ernst zu nehmenden Gesprächsgegner der evangelischen Theologie*), in his pointed exchange with Georg Wobbermin in 1932 in relation to the conversions to Catholicism of Erik Peterson and Oskar Bauhofer. See Karl Barth, *Offene Briefe 1909–1935*, ed. Diether Koch (Zürich: Theologischer Verlag Zürich, 2001), p. 227.

[31]*BTBF*, p. 83. Hütter himself seems to realize this, noting that Barth's goal is nothing less than to restore a genuine form of Protestantism having lost its way in modern neo-Protestantism.

[32]Ibid., p. 85.

is to put forward a more substantive pneumatology than Barth's own, one that "takes the Holy Spirit's distinct economy into account," and that, following Eastern Orthodox theology, sees the "church's existence and mission in the closest connection with the Holy Spirit's person and mission."[33] Hütter's own proposal is to argue that the church must be a "public"—a concretely embodied social reality marked by distinctive and binding teachings and practices. This concreteness is of key importance for Hütter, for it is only such binding dogmas and practices that define and constitute the church as a public such that the church is the embodiment of such teachings and practices which are themselves creations of the Spirit.[34] This alone can provide a viable existence for the church, one that can stave off the threats of secular modernity.[35]

Hütter's goal is a "pneumatological ecclesiology in which the binding nature of the church's doctrine and core practices is understood to be not 'against' the Spirit" but as the product of the Spirit.[36] Through a historical investigation by which he sides neither with what he describes as Adolf von Harnack's subjectivism nor Erik Peterson's objectivism, but with Barth, he concludes that Barth's own proposal is inadequate for providing the concrete ecclesiology needed for the church to be a viable public.[37] He finds the beginning of such a viable ecclesiology in Luther's list of constitutive practices in *On the Councils and the Church*.[38]

Yet, when one reads Hütter's actual examination of the Barth and Peterson dialogue, it is very difficult not to conclude that Hütter does in fact decisively side with Peterson against Barth.[39] His own judgment of Barth's inadequacies read like Peterson *redivivus*. As Hütter writes:

> Yet despite Barth's constructive pneumatological response to Peterson's challenge, I think all the questions Peterson places on the doorstep of Protes-

---

[33]Ibid., p. 49.

[34]Ibid., pp. 20-21, 31, 37-38, et al. Hütter draws on social and political theory to explain what he means to say that the church is a "public," as he writes: "Any public is defined by a particular set of normative convictions, embodied in constitutive practices, and directed toward a distinctive telos" (p. 30). The practices of the church thus are "constitutive of the church" (p. 35).

[35]*SDT*, p. 171.

[36]*BTBF*, p. 37.

[37]Ibid., pp. 24-28.

[38]Ibid., pp. 35-36, 49-50.

[39]Ibid., p. 235 n. 27.

tantism are still to be answered. The reason for this is that Barth failed—despite his pneumatological advance—to make his theology ecclesiology, in other words, to interpret the concrete mediating forms in a way that shows their ecclesiological relevance.[40]

Barth's theology is thus "pneumatologically sophisticated yet ecclesiologically deficient precisely because the relationship between Spirit and church is far from clear."[41] He has provided an insufficient doctrine of the Holy Spirit, one marked by "the eclipse of the distinct economy and mission of the Holy Spirit."[42] Furthermore, this pneumatological deficiency leads to an instability of both doctrine and ecclesial life, in that its dialectical character cannot provide the concreteness necessary for either a binding teaching authority in dogma or for intractable and constitutive practices, both of which provide a viable public character to the church. What Hütter deems Barth's "dialectical catholicity" cannot provide such stability but is torn by a constant back-and-forth between identity and non-identity and thus renders only an abstract, rather than concrete, ecclesiology. We are left, then, simply with Barth the ecclesially disembodied individual theologian.[43] In sum, Barth failed to revive a church in which his theology could find a permanent embodied home.[44] Hütter sees in Barth the danger of Harnack's subjectivism reborn, and, though not without qualification, sides with Peterson's objectivism, even though he wants to get beyond both.[45] The only viable

---

[40]Ibid., p. 28.

[41]Ibid.

[42]Ibid., p. 47.

[43]Ibid., p. 48; see also pp. 88-90.

[44]"The deep problem now is that Barth's 'genuine Protestantism' cannot really exist in an ecclesially embodied form. 'Genuine Protestantism,' for Barth, rather serves as a critical theological principle to be employed over against all real, existing churches. Dialectical catholicity is the concrete strategy through which this critical principle takes shape in light of the opposing principles of neo-Protestantism and Roman Catholicism. Yet it is precisely in its very dialecticity that this principle has to remain abstract from each concrete ecclesial body. Why? Because critical principles by definition cannot be embodied but are to be applied in relation to concrete embodiments" (*BTBF*, pp. 88-89). Now there is at least one problem, if not two, with this assessment. The first is that Barth did not see Protestantism simply as a critical principle but also as a concrete form of life that took this principle seriously. The second implicit problem is that Protestant churches are seemingly defined out of existence simply because they are not hierarchically arranged societies of authoritative offices and irreformable dogmas.

[45]*BTBF*, p. 30. Hütter consistently seems to fear subjectivism and individualism more than authoritarianism and a reified objectivism.

ecclesiology, Hütter concludes, is one of binding authority, what he terms "concrete catholicity" (over against Barth's "dialectical catholicity"). Furthermore, not only Barth, but also Protestantism itself, cannot provide such an unquestioned and dogmatic authority. It is thus no surprise that Hütter follows Peterson not only in argument but also in his real-life conversion to Roman Catholicism.

Hütter's estimation of Barth's deficiencies amounts to a serious charge, yet not without warrant. Barth himself was quite uncertain as to the future of Protestantism in the late 1920s, a concern nowhere as close to the surface as in his lecture on Roman Catholicism in 1928, where he stated that if forced to choose between neo-Protestantism and Roman Catholicism, he would choose the latter.[46] But what must be remembered as well is that Barth did not think that neo-Protestantism was the legitimate outworking of the Reformation, nor did he ever become tempted by the Catholic answer, even in his later years.[47] One reason is that Barth's own concrete ecclesiology was not initially worked out in dialogue with Catholicism in the late 1920s but was actually birthed a few years earlier in his lectures on the Reformed confessions in 1923.

Barth's ecclesiology and understanding of dogma was not in fact simply a vacillation between identity and non-identity, as Hütter claims.[48] Certainly such a dialectic was present in Barth's early theology and was never entirely abandoned in his thought. Nevertheless, Hütter's charge fails to take into account the positive role of dogma in Barth's thinking as Barth came to see the distinction between the Creator and the creature, and thus of revelation and church, as one of correspondence, not simple contradiction, and came to understand church dogma as having its own relative (if not irreformable and absolute) authority, and correspondingly church law as a required aspect of ecclesiological existence (yet again, with relative rather than

---

[46]See Barth, "Roman Catholicism: A Question to the Protestant Church," in *Theology and Church*, p. 314.

[47]To think otherwise is to fail to examine with care Barth's later writings on Catholicism, where, even in moments of appreciation, his strong opposition to Catholic answers continued to shine through. For examples of this, see Karl Barth, *Letters 1961–68*, ed. Jürgen Fangmeier and Hinrich Stoevesandt, ed. and trans. Geoffrey W. Bromiley (Grand Rapids: Eerdmans, 1981), pp. 312-14, 333-35; also Karl Barth, *Ad Limina Apostolorum*, trans. Keith R. Crim (Richmond: John Knox Press, 1968).

[48]*BTBF*, p. 87.

absolute authority).[49] For how could dogma (as the church's teaching) or church law (as the church's ordering of its life) have any enduring value or real (if relative) authority if they were only contradiction? Hütter has not taken the role of correspondence in Barth's thought seriously enough, nor, it seems, Barth's mature thought on dogma and church law.[50] Correspondence (like the analogy of faith) preserves the Creator-creature distinction without falling into a constant vacillation between identity and difference. In other words, Barth's mature dialectical understanding is not one of judgment and grace, law and gospel, with a constant movement between them.[51] There is a real correspondence in time, a real history, to the church, so that even while Barth refuses to trade the church as event for the church

---

[49]Hütter writes: "What Peterson conceives in strict continuation of the incarnate logos in unbroken continuity, Barth conceives in a fundamental diastasis (God—human being; heaven—earth) in which the various elements, although certainly related to one another, nonetheless remain strictly separated within this relationship" (SDT, p. 104). The question might be posed why such human responses have any authority at all for Barth if this is true. What Hütter overlooks is that not only is there a diastasis, but there is also a correspondence, such as when Barth stated that the concrete authority of the church's teaching in creeds and confessions must be obeyed but only "as far as they conform to the authority of Christ" (Barth, "Church and Theology," p. 296). Barth therefore does recognize an authority in the church's teachings, though it is a relative, rather than absolute, one. Barth's mature expression of his understanding of authority in the church in relation to doctrine is found in CD I/2, pp. 538-740. For his later reflections on church law along similar lines, see CD IV/2, pp. 676-726.

[50]Hütter seems quite indifferent to this point nonetheless when he states: "It is ultimately of no consequence for the heuristics of this inquiry into the relation between church, church doctrine, and theology whether the Church Dogmatics overcomes the pneumatological deficit in Barth's response to Peterson or not" (SDT, p. 108). Hütter's indifference lies in his conviction that the answer cannot be found in the CD because Barth was consistent there with his earlier theology. There is truth here—there is real consistency and continuity of thought. But there is also a real development and progression (see Bender, Karl Barth's Christological Ecclesiology, pp. 79-80). And if true, Barth's own solution may not be as problematic and flatfooted as Hütter makes it to be, and may in fact be worthy of more serious attention than is given.

[51]BTBF, p. 90. Hütter is constantly caught in such false dichotomies, reading the Peterson and Barth debate as a straightforward debate between institution and charisma: "The controversy between Erik Peterson and Karl Barth concerning the nature and task of theology as a church activity in its relation to church and dogma exemplifies the debate between the two alternatives of institution and charisma, alternatives still providing the two basic options for Western theology since the Reformation. This particular controversy demonstrates that theology as a church practice can only remain an unstable undertaking as long as its relationship with church doctrine is not clarified, and also demonstrates that the two alternatives similarly are unpersuasive because both remain pneumatologically deficient in their 'either/or'" (SDT, p. 95). Perhaps there is no sign that Hütter has profoundly misread Barth as self-evident as this flat juxtaposition of charisma and institution with the conclusion that Barth's ecclesiology can simply be seen as the making of a choice for charisma versus institution. Such a view can make no sense of Barth's extensive discussions of the invisible and visible church, or of church dogma and law, in the CD (and already witnessed in the GD).

as institution, these are not opposed to one another as a divine invisible church set against a sinful visible one.[52]

What Hütter has raised is the question of whether Barth's understanding of the church as event can provide a place for the church as historical duration and institution. The answer is that it can and does, though not in a way in which Hütter might be satisfied.[53] Barth did, nonetheless, have a concrete ecclesiology, though of a particular Reformed and low church variety. Hütter's contention that Barth consistently bifurcated the church between the true church that was invisible and the false church that was visible is wrong on two counts.[54] First, it fails to see that Barth never saw the visible and the invisible church as separated or opposed, even if these aspects remain irreducibly distinguished, and this commitment to unity-in-distinction was in place as early as his first dogmatic cycle of lectures in Göttingen. The true church is, as Barth put this point in the lectures, the "invisible-that-becomes-visible."[55]

Second, to see Barth's relation of the invisibility and visibility of the church as one simply of opposition and contradiction is a false reading of Barth's understanding of the *Scheinkirche*, which never meant for Barth (*contra* Hütter's reading) the visible church per se as set over against an invisible, divine one, but rather described a church that had turned away from its Lord.[56] The true church is nothing other than the real and human visible church in time that has been called into existence by God's act as predicated on an eternal decision. To call Barth's ecclesiology "bifurcated" is to overlook the deep christological logic that undergirds it, a logic born out of Barth's conviction that the church is both invisible and visible, and one at the heart of Barth's constructive (rather than simply reactionary)

---

[52]Bender, *Karl Barth's Christological Ecclesiology*, chaps. 5-6.

[53]Hütter sees Barth as rarely providing a concrete ecclesiology and as bifurcating the church between God's act as the true church and the false church in history. To see how problematic such conclusions are, see Bender, *Karl Barth's Christological Ecclesiology*, esp. chaps. 5-6, 9.

[54]See *BTBF*, pp. 91-92.

[55]Karl Barth, *Unterricht in der christlichen Religion*, 3: *Die Lehre von der Versöhnung/Die Lehre von der Erlösung, 1925/1926*, ed. Hinrich Stoevesandt (Zürich: Theologischer Verlag Zürich, 2003), pp. 356-64. For Barth's ecclesiology in these first dogmatic lectures, see Bender, *Karl Barth's Christological Ecclesiology*, pp. 66-82. Barth reiterates these early thoughts, now greatly developed, in *CD* IV/1, pp. 650-725.

[56]*BTBF*, p. 91. For the problems with this reading, see Bender, *Karl Barth's Christological Ecclesiology*, pp. 271-72; for Barth's understanding of *Scheinkirche*, see pp. 154-61, 172-74.

theological project. Hütter states that Barth's ecclesiology is predicated on
a dialectical strategy of employing a critical principle against neo-Protestantism and, more substantively, against Roman Catholicism.[57] Yet such a
charge is not ultimately effective; this description itself is inadequate because it overlooks Barth's constructive account of ecclesiology in his
mature thought.

To characterize Barth's understanding of the church as "transcendental
ecclesiology" thus grossly mischaracterizes it.[58] It may be an under-
standable judgment of Barth's ecclesiology in the *Romans* commentary of
1922 (though it would not be entirely accurate even there). It is, however,
a judgment that can make no sense of Barth's rejection of what he termed
the docetic ecclesiologies of Emil Brunner and Rudolph Sohm, or of
Barth's emphasis in his mature ecclesiology that the church requires
visible order and even law.[59] Nor can it make sense of the fact that Barth
can speak not only, in his central image, of the church as the body of
Christ, but also of it as Christ's "earthly-historical form of existence"
(*irdisch-geschichtliche Existenzform*).[60] Moreover, it cannot render Barth's
appropriation and description of Christ's relation to the church as that of
the *totus Christus* intelligible.[61] Perhaps the judgment is made because so
much of Barth's corpus is overlooked. For instance, in criticizing Barth's
lack of ecclesiological concreteness, Hütter does not attend to the concrete practices of the church that Barth in fact outlines in his mature
ecclesiology, which, on investigation, are quite akin to those Hütter finds
so helpful in Luther.[62] Nevertheless, regardless of the reason for the
judgment, this assessment does not accurately depict Barth's actual ecclesiological thought. Yet while Hütter's description of Barth's ecclesiology
can be questioned, perhaps more attention should be paid to Hütter's own
alternative proposal, what he terms "embodied pneumatology," over

---

[57]*BTBF*, p. 93. Hütter writes: "Yet Barth's dialectical catholicity as a distinct and pervasive methodological strategy turns out to be a deeply problematic and ambiguous phenomenon, one that
is inherently linked with his disembodied pneumatology and therefore bifurcated ecclesiology."
[58]Ibid., p. 90.
[59]*CD* IV/2, pp. 676-80. Barth writes: "The Church never has been and never is absolutely invisible" (*CD* IV/1, p. 653).
[60]*CD* IV/2, p. 643; passim.
[61]*CD* IV/2, pp. 59-60; cf. *CD* I/2, p. 348.
[62]*CD* IV/3.2, pp. 864-901.

against what he takes to be Barth's deficient pneumatology, disembodied ecclesiology and abstract catholicity.[63]

The Church as the Body of the Spirit

Hütter's proposal calls for an "embodied pneumatology" in which the church exists as a public within the world, a public comprised of concrete traditions, dogmas and practices. If there are two adjectives that form the heart of his proposal, it is that ecclesiology must be *concrete* and that its concreteness must be expressed in dogmas and practices that are *binding*. In speaking of ecclesiology, Hütter is proposing a movement from the area of Christology to pneumatology, and to a particular construal of their relation. More specifically, Hütter is interested in the relation between Christ and the Spirit as this is itself translated and interpreted as one between Christ and the church. This shift is not unimportant, because Hütter moves effortlessly between describing the first relation of Christ and the Spirit and that of the second between Christ and the church. If so, Spirit and church maintain the same placeholder in the formal christological relation, and indeed, their own relation to each other becomes, as we shall see, one of near identity. The importance of this fact cannot be overestimated—yet to grasp its full significance may require an explication of the other christological relations themselves. Therefore, we must begin by considering the relation between Christ and the Spirit, and, correspondingly, between Christ and the church, as Hütter outlines them.

For Hütter, the church itself appears to be that which forms the bond between Christ and the Spirit, the church being not only the extension of Christ in the world but also the distinct sphere of the Spirit's activity and indeed identified with the Spirit's own action. Thus, on the one hand, the church, and specifically its doctrine, is "the prolongation of the body of

---

[63]*BTBF*, pp. 1-5, 19-42, 78-94; *SDT*, pp. 1-37, et al. Hütter finds the intrinsic problem of Barth's deficiency in Barth's Chalcedonianism as it is transferred to every area of theology so that Barth's position fails to take a particular pneumatological unity of Spirit and church seriously enough: "The construction does not provide for the Holy Spirit to tie itself to such a confession or for such a confession to express human action 'in' the Spirit such that the confession itself might be understood as a work of the Holy Spirit" (*SDT*, p. 107). Yet while Hütter himself thinks that Barth's failures lie in the fact that his Chalcedonianism applies only to a "substance-ontological" context and not an "action-determined context," this itself misconstrues Barth's mature Christology, which is predicated on an actualistic ontology (*SDT*, pp. 106-7).

Christ" understood pneumatologically and eschatologically.[64] On the other hand, the church can be understood in light of "the Spirit's embodiment in the concrete traditions, doctrines, and practices of the church."[65] Once again, not only are these doctrines and practices concrete, they are binding, for they are nothing less than the work of the Spirit itself, the Spirit's own creation and indeed embodiment.[66] All of the problems in Hütter's own proposal arise from these simple axiomatic statements.

First, we are faced with the question of how Christology and pneumatology (and Christ and Spirit) are not only related (which Hütter finds missing in Barth), but distinguished. What does it mean to talk about an "embodied pneumatology"? Certainly Hütter does not want to speak of a second incarnation? If not, then the unity of Christology and pneumatology as he conceives them seems to fall apart—the church on the one hand cannot be a prolongation of what is, over against it, a unique and unsubstitutable reality—namely, the hypostatic union in Jesus Christ. On the other side, the unique unity of this relation of Word and flesh in Jesus Christ entails that it cannot be replicated in the area of pneumatology. In other words, the work of the Spirit and the work of the church are not hypostatically joined and therefore the latter can never be directly identified with the former, so that in turn some form of dialectical relation between them seems inevitable.[67]

If Hütter intends "embodied ecclesiology" simply to mean that the Spirit calls the church into concrete and visible existence, then his proposal is in fact not really very different from Barth's own understanding. However, if he wants to say that the dogmas and practices of the church are directly the work of the Spirit and thus identical to the Spirit's own work (for this is what ensures their binding character), then his position is indeed quite different from Barth's, and a careful reading of Hütter's work seems to entail the latter. This claim itself raises a number of christological and pneumatological concerns. As traditionally understood, in the incarnation, we are speaking

---

[64]BTBF, p. 34.

[65]Ibid., p. 15.

[66]Ibid., pp. 21, 37.

[67]Not even in the hypostatic union is direct identity the case. The divinity and humanity of Christ uniquely and inseparably joined but not identified—a conviction central to the Chalcedonian definition.

about one agent, the Logos in flesh. But if we are talking about the church, we are speaking about two, the Spirit and the church (and its members), and these cannot be directly identified, even though they are united through the Spirit's work. For how can we speak of the sinfulness of the church if we equate the church with the direct work of the Spirit? Again, Hütter is aware of this problem, for he wants to speak not only of the Spirit's embodiment in the church but also of the church's brokenness.[68] Nevertheless, in order to achieve the concreteness and stability he deems necessary for ecclesial life, Hütter rejects an indirect, or dialectical, identity of the work of the Spirit and the work of the church. And so, while he wants in some sense to preserve their distinction, his rejection of an indirect and dialectical relation makes it difficult not to equate them.[69] If then the relation of Christology and pneumatology may be deemed the formal problem of Hütter's proposal, the relation of Christ to the church (and of the Spirit to the church) may be understood as the unifying basis for a host of other material problems that arise, of which the following are most significant.

First, it may sound good in principle to speak of binding and irreformable doctrines, but which are such? If Hütter constricts the circle to include only the Apostles' and Nicene Creeds, his proposal is for the most part uninteresting. No great moves are needed to reach ecumenical consensus on such a minimalist view of dogma in the West, though even here, the Eastern church does not use or accept the Apostles' Creed, nor do all Free Churches explicitly embrace either.[70] If, however, Hütter is arguing for a richer conception of catholic substance, namely, the development of a great tradition

---

[68]*BTBF*, p. 93.

[69]Hütter does in fact prevaricate on this point, at times equating the Spirit's activity with that of the church but at other times attempting to preserve a distinction between them; see *SDT*, pp. 127-28. In one sense, this proclivity to identify them can be regarded as Hütter's embrace of a Lutheran understanding of the Lutheran *finitum capax infiniti* doctrine which equates the divine Word and the church's human word. But in his ready acceptance of the church as an extension of the incarnation itself and immersion of Scripture into the broader stream of church tradition, Hütter has in fact adopted an ecclesiology much more akin to a Roman Catholic one.

[70]Hütter seems to be arguing in places for such a limited sense of dogma but also for an expansive sense of doctrine: "The pre-schismatic ecumenically acknowledged form of church doctrine is 'dogma.' Hence, only the teachings declared binding by the early ecumenical councils will in the following be called 'dogma' in the strict sense. Moreover, I understand 'doctrine' to be an unfolding and specification of its constitutive source, the *doctrina evangelii*, that is, the preaching and teaching of the gospel as the church confesses it in the Apostles' and Nicene Creeds" (*BTBF*, p. 21).

as a whole in some kind of Newmanesque sense, then he runs into a very different type of problem—not only to explain the reality of doctrinal development and change (a difficult question unto itself), but more pointedly, to explain how the mutual confessions of various ecclesial traditions, many of which run counter to each other and express mutual anathemas, are to be reconciled with one another and understood as direct workings of the Spirit. The irony is that while Hütter states that only by turning to and embracing the church's "concrete ecclesial traditions, doctrines, and liturgical, communal, and moral practices" can the church face up to its brokenness, the reality seems that sometimes these traditions themselves are the problem.[71] Perhaps no one has put this more succinctly than John Howard Yoder when he writes: "Roman Catholics cannot ask Protestants to share the decisions of Trent. Lutherans cannot expect the 'anabaptists,' whom their *Confessio Augustana* condemns five times, to share that text as an identity marker. The canonical Scriptures are, at least on pragmatic grounds, the primary court of appeal."[72]

---

[71]*BTBF*, p. 93. Hütter is not unaware of these difficulties, noting that discernment is necessary to acknowledge those doctrinal formulations and practices that "point to, promote, and even embody the church's unity—and thereby become again, in the mode of an ongoing ecumenical *metanoia*, vessels of the Holy Spirit's teaching and remembering" (p. 40). He observes that Barth rightly opposed Peterson's appeal to the corporal punishment of heretics, yet one wonders if Hütter fully appreciates the historical precedent and trajectory that his appeal to the keys to uphold irreformable dogmas actually took (pp. 33-34). For if one wants to speak of an attempt to maintain ecclesial discipline without political coercion, then one must look in history to a very different kind of concrete ecclesiology than that of papal keys and binding irreformable dogmas altogether. Not even the magisterial Reformers could escape from the Constantinian picture in this regard, with the Reformation tied by Luther to the princes in Germany and Calvin's participation in the trial leading to the burning of Servetus in Geneva. What Hütter will need to answer is in what sense such dogmas are "binding" when there is no arm of civil enforcement to uphold and enforce subscription to them. In like regard, Hütter sees only two possibilities for a Protestant church—either a political state church or cultural "people's church" (*Volkskirche*) on one side, or a devolution into a "private religious association" on the other. The two options are thus either an established church or pietistic inwardness and individualism (*SDT*, pp. 8-12). But is this not a challenge for any church in a free society, Protestant or Catholic, that rejects coercion? Interestingly, Barth himself rejected both of these choices for Protestantism. His own call was for a confessing church that rejected both establishment and individualism. Such a church did produce confessions that had a real if relative (not infallible or irreformable) authority, and it was precisely their reformability that made ecumenical progress possible. Hütter is certainly correct that it remains to be seen, however, whether Protestantism will steer between these two alternatives of establishment and subjectivism.

[72]John Howard Yoder, "Walk and Word: The Alternatives to Methodologism," in *Theology Without Foundations: Religious Practice and the Future of Theological Truth*, ed. Stanley Hauerwas, Nancey Murphy and Mark Nation (Nashville: Abingdon, 1994), p. 89. For a particular discus-

Yoder's appeal to the canon raises then a second problem with Hütter's proposal. If one takes a viewpoint that sees dogmas and creedal or confessional statements as the direct work of the Spirit, how can one then distinguish them from Scripture? Hütter does want to claim a superior authority for Scripture, but his listing of Scripture together with creeds, dogmas and ecclesial practices as members of a class, one bound by the fact that all are (without distinction?) works of the Spirit, entails that he has not spelled out how they really can be distinguished.[73] Perhaps most problematic of all, this sacrifice of the Scripture principle (and Hütter never really displays signs of appreciating its significance in the development of Barth's theology) entails that Scripture truly cannot stand in judgment over such developments.[74] For how can the Spirit judge itself? Hütter's conception of Scripture and dogma entails that the church is unable to criticize itself or allow itself to be corrected precisely because its own work is directly equated with that of the Spirit. In other words, Scripture is simply the first member of a class of tradition, rather than set apart and over against it in some way, a point Barth made in his 1925 treatise on the Scripture principle. Hütter himself wants to guard against seeing the church as "managing" the Spirit, possessing the Spirit by means of its doctrine and practices. Yet if the work of the Spirit and the doctrines and practices of the church are directly identified, it is difficult to understand how the former can or need test the latter, or how Scripture can stand over against dogma and not simply adjacent to it.[75]

This position may then lead down paths Hütter does not intend. For him, the Spirit is free for new action only if there are ecclesial realities that are binding: "The Spirit can do a 'new thing,' guide the church into all the truth (John 16:13), only if there is a binding set of doctrines and practices in the

---

sion of the difficulties of the Augsburg Confession from the Roman Catholic, rather than Yoder's Anabaptist, perspective, see Yves Congar, *Diversity and Communion*, trans. John Bowden (Mystic, CT: Twenty-Third Publications, 1985), pp. 145-48.

[73]Hütter can often place Scripture among other authorities such as creeds, confessions and the decisions of ecumenical councils without distinguishing it as unique from the others; see *BTBF*, pp. 29, 31, passim.

[74]For Barth's understanding of the Scripture principle, see his essay of 1925, "Schriftprinzip," pp. 500-544; this essay was the culmination of work in his 1923 lectures found in *TRC*, pp. 38-64.

[75]Thus the church as the work of the Holy Spirit is "characterized by duration, concreteness, and visibility, and as such is identical with distinct practices or activities, institutions, offices, and doctrines. In this way the work of the Spirit acquires its own, eschatological extension 'in time'" (*SDT*, p. 119).

church."[76] Yet we might ask as to whether this freedom is only truly re-
spected when we pay attention to an even greater particularity, namely, that
Scripture and Scripture alone is binding in this way, such that its particular
witness allows the voice of Christ to be heard through his Spirit not only
within but also over and above the church and its dogmas and practices.
Here Barth would no doubt provide his own alternative questions to Hütter.
For Barth, a church that cannot hear the voice of judgment against itself is
a church that cannot truly be renewed. It is a church that is only having a
conversation with itself.[77] Such a difficulty arises from an ambiguity and
confusion as to whether the gospel finds its definitive expression in Scripture,
in dogma or in both.[78] Moreover, if there is not a distinction between
Scripture and the church (and thus between the voice of Christ and that of
the church's own voice, and, correspondingly, between the Spirit's work and
the church's own dogma, activity and response), it is difficult to see how
doctrinal developments can truly be tested, judged and reformed. As Barth
pointedly noted, "A Church which maintains that its official decisions are
infallible can commit errors which are irreformable. It has more than once
done so."[79]

Third, and now coming full circle, Hütter's penchant for speaking of "the
Spirit's embodiment in the concrete traditions, doctrines, and practices of
the church" is deeply problematic and an extension of a prior problem.[80]
The failure to distinguish Christ from the church, in which the latter is understood to be an extension of the former, is thus mirrored in a rejection of
the Scripture principle and of a distinction between Scripture and dogma.
Indeed, the second is simply a corollary of the first, for the loss of the distinction between Scripture and the church's dogmas and doctrines is predicated on a prior loss of distinction between Christ and the church. And here
again, ordered relations give way to distinct and even independent areas of
divine activity. For once more, if we are speaking of the Spirit's embodiment,
are we speaking here of a second incarnation? Can we really speak of "embodiment" without implying such? How can one speak of a critical principle

---

[76]*BTBF*, p. 39.
[77]*CD* I/2, p. 799.
[78]See *BTBF*, pp. 50-51.
[79]*CD* IV/1, p. 626.
[80]*BTBF*, p. 15.

against the Spirit's own body? This seems to take the language of the church as an extension of the incarnation (problematic in itself) to another level—namely, to imply a second incarnation of the divine life.[81] Do we thus have two divine salvific histories, two incarnations of two divine subjects? Hütter's talk of the Spirit having "a salvific economy in his own right, to which the church's constitutive practices are central" does not help matters but clouds them further.[82] Are there now two salvific economies? Is the church itself an agent of salvation? The questions continue. This is how language of "mediatrix" and "co-redemptrix" gets started, and it is perhaps best to stop it at the source.

Further difficulties come to light when we turn from matters of Christology and pneumatology to a focus on the church and ecclesiology proper. First, is it really best to depict the church primarily in terms of sociological and political understandings of what constitutes a "public"? Does this not turn the church into a member of a class? Is it not, rather, that the political and social entities of the world should be understood against the backdrop of the church, rather than vice versa? Hütter certainly does not want to see the church simply as a member of a larger species—he wants to stress its uniqueness in its "very particular and concrete designation."[83] But of what really does this uniqueness consist? Is it not, in the end, a uniqueness of beliefs and practices within a particular form of life, rather than the church's very source?[84] Here at the decisive point Hütter seems to have turned from pneumatology, where it really is needed, to social and political theory.

Finally, and along related lines, Hütter states the church can exist only as a public, but one wonders if he has not traded what he takes to be mistaken

---

[81]Hütter as previously noted has no difficulty in asserting that church doctrine is "the prolongation of the body of Christ" in a pneumatological and eschatological sense (*BTBF*, p. 34).

[82]*BTBF*, p. 92. We are then also left with the question of whether there are now two Words of God rather than one, the first of Christ, the second of the Spirit. Thus the question of a second incarnation implies a second Word of revelation (in dogma), and a second work of salvation (in the Spirit's, and thus the church's, economy, these being indistinguishable for Hütter); see *SDT*, pp. 107-8. Hütter may not want to end up at such a place, yet it is unclear what precautions are in place to prevent these conclusions, for we are here not seemingly talking about one salvific event of revelation in a threefold (or twofold) form, but of two entirely distinct (and independent?) economies, of Christ and Spirit, and with regard to the latter, of a confusion of Spirit and church.

[83]*BTBF*, p. 34; cf. *SDT*, pp. 158-59.

[84]These matters have been well addressed by Nicholas Healy, so I will not belabor them here. See Healy, "Karl Barth's Ecclesiology Reconsidered," *Scottish Journal of Theology* 57 (2003): 287-99.

transcendental and invisible understandings of the church for a straightforward visible one, such that in the end the church seems directly equated
with its visibility. As he writes, "there is no public without clear visibility,
without a defining and constituting set of binding convictions, rules, and
core practices."[85] It is unclear why Hütter thinks Barth would disagree with
this requirement of visibility, as if Barth wanted to take flight from the
visible into the invisible. Indeed, "platonic" was never an ecclesial descriptor
that Barth found appealing.[86] Yet the difference is that for Hütter, concreteness is not sufficient—such concreteness must take the form of binding
and seemingly irreformable dogma because in his estimation the only alternative to binding doctrine and practices is private subjectivism.[87] Yet once
again, one can only wonder if this itself is not simply a false dilemma, for
Barth also had no affinity for subjective individualism. Where he differs,
rather, is on the point of how such binding doctrine should be understood.
For Barth, it can only be provisional, particular and open to revision. This
might be seen as undermining its absolute status, yet such absoluteness
perhaps must be undermined if it is accepted that God is in heaven and
humanity is on earth and that the church's articulation of its teaching is
moving toward an eschatological perfection that is not captured in present,
imperfect articulations.

The crucial difference is therefore not that of embracing or rejecting the
church's visibility, much less of choosing between institution or charisma,
another flat and false alternative.[88] It is, rather, a quite stark difference in
construing how the invisibility and visibility of the church are in fact related,
and thus a disagreement as to what the concreteness of the church should
entail. At its most refined point, and despite some occasional yet important
reservations, Hütter stresses that the church's reality and visibility are identical, and such identity for him ensures the church's concreteness and stability, the church itself a "nexus of core practices that at once both constitute

---

[85]*BTBF*, p. 31.
[86]Barth, *Unterricht in der christlichen Religion*, 3:363-64.
[87]*BTBF*, pp. 39-40. Hütter's appeal to Acts 15:28 is itself not a felicitous one, for even that agreement has been subject to revision, insofar as the eating of meat sacrificed to idols was handled
with more nuance by Paul, and the restriction on careful avoidance of blood has fallen by the
wayside in the Gentile mission.
[88]*SDT*, p. 108.

and characterize the church."[89] Pneumatology and ecclesiology thus are portrayed as co-extensive if not identical in character and reality. Barth, in contrast, refuses to equate the reality of the church solely with its visibility, as if the difference between it and other publics was only the difference of belief and practice, rather than the difference of origin, source and power. For Barth also the church is visible. But it is more than its visibility. At points, it is unclear that it is more than this for Hütter, and unclear also whether he truly avoids the temptation of reification he seeks to overcome, though his strong notion of pneumatology certainly would seem to offset such a criticism.[90] In the end, there may be a need to go beyond Barth in a number of ecclesiological areas, yet it is not at all clear that Hütter's proposal will get us there. Nevertheless, he is well within his right to ask whether Protestantism has preserved a reality substantial enough to warrant its own survival, or whether, to borrow Tillich's phrase, the "Protestant era" is at an end.

GETTING DOWN TO BRASS TACKS

At its heart, Hütter's argument is not with Barth. It is with Protestantism and the Reformation. What he has proposed is, in reality, a significant argument of and for Catholic substance, a unique and enduring vision for ecclesial life.[91] It is based on a few key premises at its heart, some very explicitly stated, others more implicit yet logically implied: that the church is a prolongation of the incarnation; that its dogma and practices are thus extensions of Christ's own voice and life, and its offices an extension of Christ's own agency, such that its ministers serve as vicars in his absence; that Scripture thus stands at the beginning of, and in uninterrupted continuity with, a larger source of apostolic tradition, such that it is placed on a spectrum of authority rather than over all others; and that the organic flow of such a tradition, as Scripture and dogma and liturgy and practice, is itself

---

[89]Ibid., p. 133.

[90]*BTBF*, p. 54.

[91]Hütter sees himself as seeking to transcend the conflict between Catholic and Protestant positions (see *SDT*, pp. 115-16, 237-38), but insofar he sees the first as emphasizing institution and the second as emphasizing event, he flattens out the real distinction between them, which is the ordering of event and institution, of invisible and visible church, and of the understanding of the relation between the Spirit and the church in each position. His preference, as should be now clear, is for an understanding of these that falls more along Catholic than Protestant lines.

the direct work of the presence of the Spirit in the church, and therefore as the Spirit's direct work this tradition remains binding and irreformable at its heart, if nonetheless malleable at its periphery. This is a coherent and compelling picture and vision for ecclesial life. It is not, however, one that Protestants (including Barth) have been able readily to embrace, for at least as many reasons as the questions presented above. It is one where distinctions between Christ and the church are fluid and their relation reversible; where the relation of the Spirit and the church's doctrinal teaching and sacramental life is quite direct such that revelation and grace are naturalized and historicized in the church's words and sacraments; where Scripture and later tradition stand on a chronological spectrum of continuity with no principled qualitative distinction between them; and where the church's task is to participate in an ongoing redemptive economy rather than to witness to a redemption accomplished. At times, the incarnation itself is portrayed as simply the highest illustration of a more general sacramental ontology, the highest, but not sole, sign and mediator of grace.[92]

This description is not intended to be polemical. As noted, the Catholic vision Hütter has presented is an enduring and coherent one and, as Barth himself came to realize, the only truly substantive alternative to Protestantism. Moreover, these visions are not simply construed along confessional boundaries, for there are Protestants who adhere (whether implicitly or explicitly, in whole or in part) to the Catholic vision, and Roman Catholics who adhere to the Protestant one, however ironic this may seem.[93] Indeed, Barth's criticisms of Roman Catholic ecclesiology were of a piece with those he made

---

[92]An illustration of such thinking is evident in Avery Dulles's discussion of the church as sacrament in his *Models of the Church* (New York: Image Books/Doubleday, 2002), chap. 4.

[93]As but one example of a Protestant work that embraces this Catholic vision (besides Hütter's own under discussion here), see Carl E. Braaten, *Mother Church: Ecclesiology and Ecumenism* (Minneapolis: Fortress, 1998). Braaten begins by seeing the Reformation almost solely as a tragedy. The Reformation provided not a coherent and alternative vision that sought to rediscover Scripture's pattern but simply a provisional correction that in reality led to ecclesiological exile (p. 4). Braaten seeks to broach the divide, to provide an "evangelical catholic" vision that returns to the Eucharist, rather than preaching, as grounding the church (p. 7), and where the canon is but one part of a larger tradition, comprised of (along with the canon) creeds, liturgy and (hierarchial) ministerial offices, all of them of binding validity (pp. 80-81). Braaten's work is nonetheless best thought of not as an abandonment of the Reformation vision for a Catholic one but a work of mediation between them. For an example of a Roman Catholic writer who echoes much of an alternative Protestant ecclesial vision, see Hans Küng, *The Church* (London: Burns & Oates, 1967).

of Schleiermacher. Yet this description of Catholic substance is nonetheless representative of a major trajectory within historic Roman Catholic thought, an enduring picture through the significant changes from Tridentine ecclesiological formulations up to those of the post–Second Vatican period with its welcome adoption of a newly articulated eschatological reservation.[94] One need only consider that some of the most august writers of the past fifty years in Catholic theology have provided similar descriptions. All hinge on a view of the ascension such that Christ is present only as actualized in and by the agency of the church. This is evident for instance in Henri de Lubac when he writes: "If Christ is the sacrament of God, the Church is for us the sacrament of Christ; she represents him, in the full and ancient meaning of the term; she really makes him present. She not only carries on his work, but she is his very continuation, in a sense far more real than that in which it can be said that any human institution is its founder's continuation."[95]

Such a position is witnessed also in Karl Rahner's description of the church: "As the people of God socially and juridically organized, the Church is not a mere eternal welfare institute, but the continuation, the perpetual presence of the task and function of Christ in the economy of redemption, his contemporaneous presence in history, his life, the Church in the full and proper sense."[96] He later writes: "Now the Church is the continuance, the contemporary presence, of that real, eschatologically triumphant and irrevocably established presence in the world, in Christ, of God's salvific will."[97]

---

[94]Congar, *Diversity and Communion*, p. 42.

[95]Henri de Lubac, *Catholicism: Christ and the Common Destiny of Man*, trans. Lancelot Sheppard and Elizabeth Englund (San Francisco: Ignatius Press, 1988), p. 76.

[96]Karl Rahner, *The Church and the Sacraments*, trans. W. J. O'Hara (New York: Herder and Herder, 1963), p. 13.

[97]Ibid., p. 18. Rahner continues: "The Church is the official presence of the grace of Christ in the public history of the one human race. In its socially organized form the people of God as in fact redeemed by Christ, receive his permanent presence through history. And when we examine what this one reality implies, it means a presence, as it were an incarnation, of the truth of Christ in the Church through Scripture, tradition and magisterium; a similar embodiment and presence of Christ's will in the Church's teaching when it announces Christ's precepts in her pastoral office and her constitution; and a presence and embodiment, again analogous to the incarnation, of the grace of Christ, for the individual as such, through the sacraments. Viewed in relation to Christ, the Church is the abiding promulgation of his grace-giving presence in the world. Viewed in relation to the sacraments, the Church is the primal and fundamental sacrament" (p. 19). One wonders, if all of this is true, how Christ and the church can ever really be distinguished, and if his agency and life and voice have not been at the very least subsumed into, and perhaps replaced by, that of the church.

A similar conception of the church is even echoed by such a figure of careful theological articulation and empathy toward Barth's position as Hans urs von Balthasar, as witnessed when he states: "The Church remains at every period what she was: the bulwark and the steward of all truth, for all the treasures of wisdom and knowledge are hidden in Christ, and no one has access to these treasures of Christ except through the Church."[98]

Yet one cannot be a steward of what one does not truly possess, but only a servant of what must be given each day anew. And herein lies the difference between Catholic substance and the Protestant principle. For there is an irrevocable insistence by the latter that the gift never be seen as a transferable entity entrusted to a steward who possesses it, that the church can be a servant but not a steward of grace, and that a permanent distinction be made between Giver and recipient, between Christ and his bride, between the Spirit and his temple. In effect, this insistence is made because a Protestant vision is predicated on a refusal to grant that the church is, itself, an extension of the incarnation. This refusal is in turn joined to a basic recognition that Jesus Christ is present, and not absent, and is so through the power of the Spirit. The church therefore does not "make" Christ present, but Christ makes himself present through the power of his Spirit through his own self-attestation. Once that distinction is made, the other Protestant convictions—of Christ alone as the mediator of grace (and, in Barth's estimation, thus the singular sacrament); of Scripture's unique place within but also standing over the stream of tradition as Christ's own appointed apostolic testimony to himself confirmed through the testimony of the Spirit; of the centrality of grace and faith as pointing alone to God's unique work in Christ—all of these begin to take shape. Barth provided his own description of such a vision. It could in fact include elements of Catholic substance. For instance, his understanding of the relation of the uniqueness of the incarnation did not entail that he could not speak of the *totus Christus*, Christ in his earthly form of existence in the church. But Barth ordered this relation so carefully as to avoid all talk of either a second incarnation or an extension of the unique and unsubstitutable one in Christ, as well as to avoid all con-

---

[98]Hans Urs von Balthasar, *Razing the Bastions: On the Church in This Age*, trans. Brian McNeil (San Francisco: Communio/Ignatius Press, 1993), p. 71.

fusion of the Spirit's own work with the church's witness to it.[99] For Barth, the relation of Christ and the church, and thus of the Spirit and the church, was one of a unity in permanent distinction and irreversible order.[100]

Barth's doctrine of the church is thus no less concrete than Hütter's, but it is a different and more humble concreteness.[101] All of these basic convictions are already present in Barth's lecture on Catholicism in 1928:

> Now if the Reformation was the restoration of the Church, it was such because it accepted and underscored that "Thou alone" (*Tu solus!*) and made it specifically concrete (as in the Catholic Church it never had been and never will be) by consistently fighting against all direct identifications with God in the visible Church. The Reformation applied the "Thou alone!" (*Tu solus!*) to Jesus Christ as the Lord in his immutable unlikeness to all his servants, as the Word in ineluctable antithesis to all which we ourselves say, as the Spirit in unalterable contrast to all material things. The Reformation restored the reality of this "Thou alone" with the contrapuntal accompaniment of the "by faith alone" (*sola fide*), by which it consciously willed to recognize and proclaim the presence of God in the Church.[102]

And lest this be taken as an evisceration of the mystery of the church resulting in a naturalization of it so that it is taken to be simply a sociological entity, Barth continues on to presuppose and answer such an objection:

> Therefore the purpose of the Reformation was to make this Thou greater not smaller, not dissipating him into symbolism but fixing him solidly as the centre of the Church. And therefore the Reformation was determined to

---

[99]For the inner logic of Barth's position on this point, see Bender, *Karl Barth's Christological Ecclesiology*, pp. 198-205.

[100]What is too often overlooked is that the intractability of the differences between these two visions of theological and ecclesiological life lies not simply in soteriology (over disagreements over justification) but in different understandings of Christology. This entails that the comparison of Catholic substance and the Protestant principle by Tillich and a number of evangelical catholics is too superficial, it being thought that if agreement on justification can be achieved, the two visions have effectively been reconciled, for the Protestant vision is nothing more than a critical principle and thus dependent on a richer Catholic substance (as, for example, Hütter takes it to be). Such a view fails to see the depth of the Reformation protest. See Paul Tillich, *Systematic Theology*, vol. 3 (Chicago: University of Chicago Press, 1963), pp. 223-24; see also Carl E. Braaten and Robert W. Jenson, eds., *The Catholicity of the Reformation* (Grand Rapids: Eerdmans, 1996), pp. ix-x.

[101]Barth eschewed a concreteness of deep divisions of clergy and laity and of irreformable dogmas declared from a centralized hierarchy.

[102]Barth, "Roman Catholicism," pp. 315-16.

affirm the Trinitarian and christological dogma of the old Church more strongly, not less; and with deeper meaning and greater consistency. Such affirmation was a strengthened and sharpened witness to the unalterable truth that God who is present in his Church is subject not object. It was a more precise witness to the essential deity of Christ and of the Holy Spirit.[103]

Barth once stated, in his reflections on Peterson's argument for a concrete and non-dialectical catholicity, that "only one who could say Jesus Christ, that is could say God become flesh, God and man in one word, and that word a true word, could pride himself on not being a 'dialectical theologian.'"[104] And if that is the case with Jesus Christ, how much the more is it true that "Spirit" and "church" cannot be said in one word, or the activity of the first directly equated with the action of the second. That the divine work of the first cannot be equated with the visible work of the second entails nothing less than that the confession of the church's reality must remain a matter of faith, that even with regard to the church, as with all else, including the mysteries of ourselves as both outwardly weak yet inwardly renewed, we must look beyond the visible church to the one who sustains it in its visibility. So here too, "we look not at what can be seen but at what cannot be seen; for what can be seen is temporary, but what cannot be seen is eternal" (2 Cor 4:18). This may not be the kind of concreteness we desire, for it is marked more by provisionality and pilgrimage than stability and permanence. Moreover, to long for a stable visibility might be forgiven when we honestly admit that it is very difficult and moreover quite disconcerting to live by faith and not by sight. Yet whatever glimpse of glory we see now in our mortal bodies, or the body that Christ has called to himself, such does not allow us simply to equate the Spirit's quiet work with our own. Insofar as we continue to refuse such a collapse of the two into one, or to speak of Spirit and church in one word, the Reformation vision continues to testify in our time.

CHRISTIAN CONFESSING TODAY

For Barth, confessing, like prayer, was best thought of as an activity, a verb, rather than a noun. Barth once stated that he read prayers of the past not in

---

[103]Ibid., p. 316.
[104]Barth, "Church and Theology," p. 301.

order to pray them again but rather to be instructed to pray for himself.[105] Along the same lines, Barth was more focused on the act of confessing than on the creeds and confessions per se. This fact in no way entailed that he had no place for the authority of the tradition of the church in its dogma, creeds and confessions. The confessions, Barth often said, should help us with our own theological task, our own dogmatic work in our time and preaching for our day. He could look, for instance, with deep respect particularly on the Nicene and Chalcedonian definitions and their enduring normativity, as well as those that set the canonical boundaries. He also, moreover, had a deep respect for prior Reformed confessions in his own tradition. But none of these, including the ancient creeds, existed simply for the sake of recitation within a church service or as objects of cognitive or verbal adherence.

For Barth, there must indeed be direction from and authority in the past decisions and pronouncements of the church that provides guidance for us, yet such direction and authority cannot replace or overshadow the freedom and indeed the responsibility to pray and confess in the present in light of a fresh hearing of the Word of God. Tradition must not become traditionalism, in Jaroslav Pelikan's famous distinction, for traditionalism puts forth binding dogma in the worst sense of the term, a form of ossification that hinders, rather than helps, the free responsibility, and responsible freedom, of confession. To focus solely on the authority of past confessions rather than the act of confessing can lure us into believing that our responsibility and call to confess the gospel can be fulfilled when we say in our day the same as what was said in the past. This repetition of the past was for Barth, however, never an option. And this was the case not because Barth denigrated the past or dismissed its real authority (for in truth, Barth esteemed the church's past as having an authority worthy of honor, as that of our spiritual fathers and mothers, witnessed in Barth's frequent appropriation

---

[105]Karl Barth, "Brechen und Bauen: Eine Diskussion," in *"Der Götze Wackelt": Zeitkritische Aufsätze, Reden und Briefe von 1930 bis 1960*, ed. Karl Kupisch (Berlin: Käthe Vogt Verlag, 1961), p. 117. One cannot help but think that what Kierkegaard had done for the individual Christian, Barth was doing for the church on this point—to treat the creeds not simply as accumulations of objective truths (though they were these, too) but as guides for the active subjective appropriation of faith in the confession of and obedience to the gospel in the present. In other words, the focus is placed on the present act of Christian confessing and not only the passive acceptance of past content.

of Exodus 20:12 for making this point). Repetition was not an option, rather, because he was convinced that such honor is never captured or given by mere mimicry. Simply to repeat the past is to obey its letter rather than its spirit, to abscond from our responsibility to confess in our own day, and, in the worst cases, to submit the first commandment of divine obedience to the fifth regarding our earthly parents and thus to do justice to neither.[106] What we are called to do is not to revere binding dogmas. What we are to do is to confess the gospel in our day for our day, and to do this in light of, and with a respectful listening to, the witness of the past confession of the church (a witness that is true only insofar as it is a reflection of Christ in Scripture and thus itself requiring testing, such that its binding nature can never be absolute).[107] The most important thing for the church is therefore not a fascination with the church's public but with the gospel of Christ, for this public will take shape as the church witnesses to its Lord. The church cannot be equated with, though it takes its form from, the gospel.[108] This admission in no way lessens, however, the importance of the church to commit itself to its own concrete faithfulness as this is expressed in its life, practices and doctrine.

Barth provided a description of this concrete form of the church in 1938 when faced with the Nazi crisis: "The Church is a people consisting of those who have found in Jesus Christ their own comfort and hope and the comfort and hope of the whole world, and who therefore have discovered their service in bearing witness before the world, which without Him is lost, to Jesus Christ in His office of Prophet, Priest, and King." He then continued, "the Church is at all events a people. It is a congregation, an assembly, a community, as Luther loved to say and rightly said."[109]

---

[106]Or fourth commandment, depending on the enumeration of the commandments.

[107]In addition to the extensive sections on authority in the first volume of the CD, one can get a sense for how this is understood in Barth's thought by looking at his brief response to a question on Scripture and tradition in Credo (Eugene, OR: Wipf & Stock, 2005), pp. 179-83. Barth's mature answer in the CD is present in nuce there.

[108]As Luther stated: "the church is the creature of the gospel, incomparably less than the gospel" (Weimar Ausgabe 2, 430, pp. 6-7, quoted in Bernhard Lohse, Martin Luther's Theology: Its Historical and Systematic Development, trans. and ed. Roy A. Harrisville [Minneapolis: Fortress, 1999], p. 280).

[109]Karl Barth, The Church and the Political Problem of Our Day (New York: Charles Scribner's Sons, 1939), p. 5. Originally published as "Die kirche und die politische Frage von heute," in Eine Schweitzer Stimme: 1938–1945 (Zollikon-Zürich: Evangelischer Verlag, 1945).

Troubled times call from such a people not simply a recitation of the church's earlier creeds and confessions but a faithful rendition of the truth that must indeed be informed by the past but must also be newly spoken, a truth not simply recited but actualized in concrete faith and obedience in a particular place and time:

> The actualization of the confession is its concrete form as an act of confessing, as a definite confession made here and now. In its actualization the confession necessarily touches those contemporary problems which are agitating the Church and the world. It does not do this for the sake of these questions themselves or for the sake of answering them, but for the sake of bearing witness to Jesus Christ, as it must, at the present moment.[110]

Whatever the significant differences of their understandings of the church's confessions and practices in the past, no doubt on this point Hütter and Barth, and the adherents of their representative visions, share much in common. If so, then perhaps an ecumenical future may lie ironically not as much in a shared retrieval and reception of the (or a) church's past as in all churches taking up and joining together in a common task in the present. This task may itself play a part in revealing what from the past is of enduring value and can and should be shared, and what must be left behind or at the very least considered as provincial and limited to a particular tributary of the Christian tradition. Such testing need not be the judgment of crass pragmatism but may itself be part of prayerful and humble ecumenical confession.

---

[110]Ibid., pp. 14-15.

4

The End of the Reformation?

✟

Mark Noll and Carolyn Nystrom's *Is the Reformation Over? An Evangelical Assessment of Contemporary Roman Catholicism*[1] is a remarkable achievement in ecumenical analysis, though one may wonder if it is perhaps mistitled, or more accurately, mis-subtitled. For while the book does examine contemporary Roman Catholicism from an evangelical perspective, it is in point of fact more concerned with the relation between these two Christian traditions than with an assessment of Catholicism itself. This relation between evangelicalism and Roman Catholicism is one that has greatly changed over time, as Noll and Nystrom ably document, and one that has direct influence on significant streams of contemporary ecclesial and cultural life, evidenced in growing cooperation between evangelicals and Catholics across a wide spectrum of social engagements.[2] To examine the relation itself there must be clarity regarding the identity of both traditions. Contemporary Catholicism is incredibly diverse, though it lends itself to bounded definition. It is the identity of evangelicalism that provides the more difficult problem.

In his own brief piece assessing the recent dialogue between evangelicals and Roman Catholics in his edited work, *Pilgrims on the Sawdust Trail:*

This chapter appeared in an earlier form as "The End of the Reformation: Has News of Its Demise Been Greatly Exaggerated?" *Cultural Encounters* 4 (2008): 23-36, and draws on material earlier published in *Horizons* 34 (2007): 342-47. Reprinted by permission.
[1]Mark A. Noll and Carolyn Nystrom, *Is the Reformation Over? An Evangelical Assessment of Contemporary Roman Catholicism* (Grand Rapids: Baker Academic; Bletchley: Paternoster, 2005).
[2]In addition to their work, see William M. Shea, *The Lion and the Lamb: Evangelicals and Catholics in America* (New York: Oxford University Press, 2004). Shea writes from the Catholic side of the evangelical and Catholic divide.

Evangelical Ecumenism and the Quest for Christian Identity, theologian Timothy George notes that defining Roman Catholicism is not difficult, or at least, it is not difficult to define what makes one a Roman Catholic. As George writes: "A Roman Catholic is a person affiliated with a church whose bishop is in communion with the Bishop of Rome."[3] When George turns from this concise definition to the task of providing a similar definition for evangelicalism, the waters become more muddied. To provide a definition, George relies on the four elemental characteristics of evangelicalism outlined by David Bebbington: an emphasis on "personal conversion to Christ, an activist approach to evangelism and promotion of the faith, a high view of the Bible, and the centrality of the cross." It is these elements of conversionism, activism, biblicism and crucicentrism that define evangelicalism. As George notes, Bebbington's evangelical quadrilateral has gained broad acceptance as an accurate summation of the evangelical faith.[4] It is this definition that Noll and Nystrom themselves borrow for their own identification of evangelicalism.[5] Yet evangelicalism itself is a tradition within the larger variegated tradition of Protestantism, and to assess the relation between Roman Catholicism and the former entails a recognition that it is greatly shaped by the more inclusive one between Roman Catholicism and Protestantism, a relationship complex and difficult not only because of its turbulent history but also because of the current pluralistic nature of the traditions themselves, such that some members of both camps, Catholic and Protestant, find themselves today at times more closely allied in belief and action with some across the Reformation divide than with members within their own tradition.[6] It is this relation, between Roman Catholicism and Protestantism, that has undergone remarkable change in the past few decades, and, as a result, that between evangeli-

---

[3]Timothy George, "Between the Pope and Billy Graham: Evangelicals and Catholics in Dialogue," in *Pilgrims on the Sawdust Trail: Evangelical Ecumenism and the Quest for Christian Identity*, ed. Timothy George (Grand Rapids: Baker Academic, 2004), p. 125.

[4]Ibid., p. 126. For the source of these four, see David W. Bebbington, "British and American Evangelicalism Since 1940," in *Evangelicalism*, ed. Mark A. Noll, David W. Bebbington and George A. Rawlyk (Oxford: Oxford University Press, 1994), p. 367; Bebbington, *Evangelicalism in Modern Britain* (London: Unwin Hyman, 1989), pp. 2-17.

[5]Noll and Nystrom, *Is the Reformation Over?* pp. 12-13.

[6]"The time is long past when responsible analysts could speak of either Catholics or evangelicals as a homogenous unit" (ibid., p. 225; see also pp. 225-27).

calism (as a distinct form of Protestantism) and Roman Catholicism has followed suit.

Certainly we are today far removed from the retributive actions of the Reformation, such as Luther's invectives against the medieval papacy, and Rome's answer to Luther in the papal bull *Exsurge Domine* (15 June 1520) and his eventual excommunication by Rome in January of 1521 (*Decet Romanum Pontificem*).[7] Of course, one need not travel back so far to that well-known history to witness chilly relations between Protestants and Roman Catholics. In the early twentieth century Karl Barth attempted to engage Roman Catholicism in a serious manner after his move from the university in predominantly Protestant Göttingen to that of Catholic-dominated Münster. Barth began a serious study of Catholicism, making the first book of Thomas's *Summa* the topic of his winter seminar in 1928-1929 and even inviting the Jesuit Erich Przywara to present and debate in that seminar. In doing so, Barth was swimming hard against the stream at a time when Protestant and Catholic theological faculties were almost entirely insulated from one another, the Protestant members looking at Roman Catholicism with disdain, and the Roman Catholic theologians looking at Protestants with condescension and dismissal.[8] Barth, who rejected such Protestant approaches in a number of appreciative yet guardedly critical essays examining Roman Catholicism in the late 1920s, could illustrate Roman Catholic condescension and triumphalism with a quote from the famous Hugo Lang: "The Catholic, as the old (!), as the mother Church is still in possession (*in possessione*). . . . Protestantism is accountable to her, stands before her tribunal and her seat of judgment; let us say rather, before her motherly, cherishing and demanding eye, to be tested, to justify itself."[9] Barth himself was not impressed with such a patronizing tone. Many Prot-

---

[7]For a brief synopsis of these events, see Carter Lindberg, *The European Reformations* (Oxford: Blackwell, 1996/1997), pp. 82-88.

[8]For an introduction to the interaction of Barth with Roman Catholicism during this period, see Eberhard Busch, *Karl Barth: His Life from Letters and Autobiographical Texts*, trans. John Bowden (Grand Rapids: Eerdmans, 1994), pp. 164-89; Bruce McCormack, *Karl Barth's Critically Realistic Dialectical Theology: Its Genesis and Development* (Oxford: Clarendon Press, 1995), pp. 376-91; and Kimlyn J. Bender, *Karl Barth's Christological Ecclesiology* (Aldershot, UK: Ashgate, 2005), pp. 45-58, 82-92.

[9]Quoted in Karl Barth, "Roman Catholicism: A Question to the Protestant Church," in *Theology and Church: Shorter Writings 1920–1928*, trans. Louise Pettibone Smith (New York: Harper & Row, 1962), p. 311 n 1.

estants were unimpressed with Barth simply for taking Catholicism so seriously as a dialogue partner.

With regard to the relation between Roman Catholicism and evangelicalism itself, we need not even go back as far as that. As Noll and Nystrom ably and at times painfully illustrate, the relation between evangelicals and Roman Catholics could as late as the latter part of the twentieth century be marked predominantly by antagonistic conflict, and, as they also note, this conflict has not altogether disappeared but continues to fester, both in the United States (evident in light of Frank Beckwith's conversion to Rome and resignation from the Evangelical Theological Society), and in other parts of the world, especially, it seems, in Latin America.[10]

Yet the dismissal and triumphalism of the past have given way in North America in recent decades to a new openness and dialogue between evangelicals and Roman Catholics, and for that we can be grateful. We live in a better day, if only because Catholics and evangelicals are more respectful in their disagreements with one another, and more willing to listen to one another and to recognize a common confession of Christ from those across the divide. Of course, there have been positive encounters before the recent decades. Yet Noll and Nystrom are justified in concluding: "Beyond question, disengagement and polemic were the prevailing moods of evangelical-Catholic relationship in the four centuries before 1960."[11]

As earlier mentioned, today we are a long way removed from Luther's *Open Letter to Pope Leo X* (prefacing *The Freedom of a Christian*) and Leo X's *Exsurge Domine*, from the initial thawing of the long chill with the conversations of Barth and Przywara and from the almost uniformly negative stereotyping of the Catholic Church by evangelicalism and the blanket Catholic dismissal of evangelical Christians in return. Although such antagonism has not altogether disappeared, no longer is antagonism the only response of evangelicals toward Roman Catholicism, for now responses range from antagonism and criticism to partnership and even conversion.[12]

---

[10]Noll and Nystrom, *Is the Reformation Over?* p. 27.

[11]Ibid., p. 55; see also p. 58.

[12]Ibid., pp. 185ff. For an example of contemporary antagonism and criticism, see many of the essays in *Roman Catholicism: Evangelical Protestants Analyze What Divides and Unites Us*, ed. John Armstrong (Chicago: Moody Press, 1994). From the Catholic side, one need look no further than the slight against Protestant "ecclesial communities" in the Congregation of the Faith's

Such conversion itself can occur for various reasons, often related to matters of certainty, history, unity and authority.[13] Many evangelicals have been tempted to cross the Tiber for reasons great and small (what Noll and Nystrom do not investigate is why many swim over from Rome to the other side). To introduce a bit of levity in the midst of this topic of such gravity, I might note that as a Protestant I felt this tug a bit while repeatedly listening in my office to Franz Biebl's magnificent and ethereal *Ave Maria* as I wrote this piece (in a similar way as in college I was fascinated by Rachmaninov's own wondrous *Troparion for the Virgin Mary* in the Eastern tradition). Such temptations are perhaps best staved off with a healthy dose of Bach.

Since the Second Vatican Council, and in large part because of it, a growing number of ecumenical encounters have occurred between Catholics and Protestants in general (such as between the Vatican and the Baptist World Alliance, one of many such examples) and Catholics and evangelicals in particular. In this burgeoning dialogue between the two groups there has been a growing recognition of what is truly held in common, as well as a sharpened awareness of what still divides. Noll and Nystrom see this new positive relationship as, in their words, a "moment of grace in the long history of the church."[14]

Noll and Nystrom's work is an attempt to trace what has brought us to this moment of grace. They begin in the opening chapters by outlining key developments that led to a hardening of relations between Catholics and Protestants since the Reformation, including the unique circumstances in America that led to an early anti-Catholicism which turned on a fear and superstition of papal authority and its supposed ability to undermine democracy and freedom. The authors then turn to the events since the mid-twentieth century that reversed that trajectory and which led evangelicals and Catholics today to partner in various ways, especially in North America. It is no surprise that this recent cooperation came not in the theological arena but in the cultural and political ones, as Catholics and evangelicals joined forces in the areas of social action, civic and political freedom and

---

"*Dominus Iesus*—Declaration on the Unicity and Salvific Universality of Jesus Christ and the Church," issued in 2000.
[13]Noll and Nystrom, *Is the Reformation Over?* pp. 205-7.
[14]Ibid., p. 31.

public morality, especially with regard to issues surrounding the dignity of human life.[15] Noll and Nystrom do not oversimplify this narrative but allow the exceptions of notable cooperation during times of general antagonism in the past, and of fervent opposition during the generally collegial cooperation of the present, to nuance and inform the picture presented.

When turning in later chapters from narrative to analysis of why this change from general ambivalence or even antagonism to cooperation took place, Noll and Nystrom present no great surprises. They point to the significance of the Second Vatican Council and the numerous ecumenical discussions that followed in its wake between the Catholic Church and various Protestant communions, as well as the burgeoning charismatic movement that crossed and bridged Catholic and Protestant churches with its new music and affective worship and spirituality. They also point to changes in the American political climate, including the election of John F. Kennedy as the first Catholic president, as well as a cultural shift toward secularism which caused Catholics and evangelicals to join in what Timothy George has called an "ecumenism of the trenches" to battle for traditional values against cultural realities such as abortion on demand and pornography.[16]

This shift in cultural and political cooperation was also, however, mirrored in a slower-moving theological shift. As evangelicals came to appreciate tradition in the latter part of the twentieth century, more attention was paid to the resources of the Catholic Church. From the Catholic side, Noll and Nystrom recount how Martin Luther was no longer openly anathematized but rather appreciated and studied.[17] When seen in tandem with the publication of *Ut Unum Sint* in 1995, these and other related developments point to the Roman Catholic Church's new openness to dialogue with Protestants in its setting aside of a great deal of its historic triumphalism.[18] One of the high points of Catholic and evangelical consensus on theological matters is "The Christian Mission in the Third Millennium," published in 1994 by Evangelicals and Catholics Together (ECT). Noll and Nystrom provide a judicious and fair evaluation of not only that document and the

---

[15]Ibid., p. 20.
[16]Ibid., p. 68.
[17]Ibid., pp. 25-26.
[18]Ibid., p. 28.

subsequent ones issued by ECT but also an especially enlightening discussion of the recent *Catechism of the Catholic Church*. Throughout the book, they present a balanced view regarding both real agreement and remaining disagreement between Catholics and evangelicals, and one informed by the evangelical response, both positive and negative, toward recent ecumenical endeavors such as ECT, as well as by an appreciation of the diversity within both the Roman Catholic Church and evangelicalism and this diversity's effect upon their relationship.

Noll and Nystrom conclude that while numerous serious differences on theological matters remain between Roman Catholicism and evangelicalism, at least some of these differences can be seen not as a division of the body of Christ but as a valid expression of its diversity.[19] They thus do not declare the Reformation over, but they are hopeful that the vituperative nature of its polemics are a thing of the past, replaced by a new spirit of respect and cooperation, even if full fellowship remains elusive. For the authors, the basis for this hope is the work of God, who draws his people into one body.

Noll and Nystrom's work is the most important on the subject yet from the evangelical side, mirrored by the excellent work by William Shea from the Catholic one.[20] While the recent achievements of dialogue and cooperation that Noll and Nystrom outline are welcome, there are questions that can be posed after reading their work. These questions do not trivialize real accomplishments, but they may raise some discomfort nonetheless. As Noll and Nystrom rightly and judiciously conclude: "No realistic reading of the reports of these [ecumenical] dialogues can possibly miss the serious matters of doctrine and practice that continue to divide Catholic Christians and Protestant Christians. Yet no charitable reading can possibly miss the unexpectedly broad range of agreements that participants were able to reach."[21]

First, one of the troubling questions that remains after reading Noll and Nystrom's book pertains to the nature of agreement: how much of the current cooperation comes from hard-won doctrinal consensus between evangelicals and Catholics, and how much is the result of pragmatic co-

---

[19]Ibid., pp. 246-47.
[20]See note 2 above.
[21]Noll and Nystrom, *Is the Reformation Over?* p. 114.

belligerency? Is much contemporary agreement and alliance between Roman Catholics and evangelicals pragmatic, founded on political and moral issues in which the "enemy of my enemy is my friend"?[22] Now perhaps we should not make too much of this. Such co-belligerency itself can be doctrinally grounded as well as pragmatically necessary, as members of Evangelicals and Catholics Together have themselves emphasized. For example, evangelicals have increasingly come to recognize that they hold much more in common with traditional Roman Catholics in terms of orthodox trinitarian and christological doctrine (and not only social morality) than they do with many mainline Protestants. Indeed, Billy Graham is not the first Protestant to claim that he felt "much closer to Roman Catholic tradition than to some of the more liberal Protestants."[23] Barth had made the same point already in 1928.[24] Nevertheless, the nagging question of pragmatism cannot be entirely dismissed.

The second question, then, that follows from the first, is whether this doctrinal agreement, though in itself commendable, is nonetheless in some ways made possible because of a lack of concern for doctrine today among many evangelicals. In another now famous book, Noll began with the now infamous sentence, "The scandal of the evangelical mind is that there is not much of an evangelical mind."[25] Evangelicalism has struggled to develop a rich intellectual tradition, and this struggle is mirrored in a parallel struggle to develop a theological tradition worthy of its Reformation forebears and comparable even to more recent European Protestant giants such as Barth, Moltmann and Pannenberg. This is not to deny that there are many able evangelical theologians at work in Catholic and evangelical discussions that worthily represent the Protestant heritage. Yet many evangelicals have been drawn to Catholic and Orthodox forms of spirituality and soteriology not because of real deficiencies within the classical Protestant vision but because of deficiencies within an evangelicalism

---

[22]So, for example, the comments of Jeffrey Gros: "Should it not be Jesus Christ that draws his disciples together, and not just a common enemy?" (quoted in ibid., p. 193).

[23]Ibid., p. 18.

[24]See Barth, "Roman Catholicism," p. 314 n. 1.

[25]Mark Noll, *The Scandal of the Evangelical Mind* (Grand Rapids: Eerdmans; Leicester, UK: Inter-Varsity Press, 1994), p. 3. Others have made the same point, perhaps none so famously and vociferously as David F. Wells in *No Place for Truth: Or Whatever Happened to Evangelical Theology?* (Grand Rapids: Eerdmans, 1993).

that is but an attenuated and popularized Protestantism not even conscious of the riches of the classical Reformation heritage. In a study attempting to correct such misperceptions regarding forensic understandings of justification, Bruce McCormack of Princeton Theological Seminary put the matter pointedly and succinctly by concluding:

> It could be . . . that after all the testing that needs to be done is completed, it will have been shown that the Reformation was in many respects a mistake. I don't believe that, but it is at least a theoretical possibility. My hope in the meantime is that the Reformation will not be brought to a premature conclusion by those whose power to affect the outcome is equaled only by their ignorance of the unexploited potential of their own tradition.[26]

Let us be clear: to take this warning seriously is *not* to denigrate real, hard-won agreement between evangelicals and Roman Catholics. Yet it is a sober reminder that it will serve neither evangelicals nor Catholics well if the historic Protestant tradition is abandoned because of ignorance and neglect rather than significant testing. To fail in this regard could only be to answer the question of the title of the book now under review in the affirmative prematurely and irresponsibly.

A third question, also related: Is this newfound agreement based on an equivocation of terms? In other words, is it substantive? For example, on the question of justification by grace through faith, that doctrine on which the Reformation swings, Noll and Nystrom provide evidence that in some cases the dialogue participants may agree more on form than substance. So we might ask: is there an agreement on the *meaning* of the terms, or just on the grammar or use of the formulas? Has agreement really been reached, for example, on the definition of grace? Past disputes reveal a Protestant commitment to understand grace in relational rather than substantial terms. Furthermore, as Noll and Nystrom state, the sharp precision between justification and sanctification in Protestant theology is not reflected in Roman Catholic theology, which often blends these into one.[27] Yet Protestantism sees this distinction as crucial (even while, it must be said in fairness,

---

[26]Bruce L. McCormack, "What's at Stake in Current Debates over Justification? The Crisis of Protestantism in the West," in *Justification: What's at Stake in the Current Debates*, ed. Mark Husbands and Daniel J. Treier (Downers Grove, IL: InterVarsity Press, 2004), p. 117.

[27]Noll and Nystrom, *Is the Reformation Over?* p. 140.

Protestants themselves have disagreed on specific questions regarding justification and sanctification).

Again, without in any way denigrating recent significant and ground-breaking agreement on the matter of justification, Noll and Nystrom report that the related and significant questions of indulgences, penance and purgatory remain unresolved corollaries of the doctrine of justification by faith alone. Certainly many Protestants will take issue with the language of merit (even if receding in use since the Second Vatican Council and as heavily qualified as in the current *Catechism of the Catholic Church*) as an appropriate and felicitous way to speak of the mystery of God's grace and salvation.[28] At this point, material agreement seems quite elusive. Finally, even on the matter of existing formal agreement at an official level on such questions, how can this agreement be fostered to seep down into the classrooms of seminaries, universities and colleges, as well as the churches?[29]

In the end, how we answer these questions may not rest solely on weighing evidence but may be a matter of perspective in our approach to the questions themselves. For instance, Noll and Nystrom state with regard to the *Catechism*: "We estimate that evangelicals can embrace at least two-thirds of the Catechism."[30] So it may be a matter of whether one sees the ecumenical glass as one-third empty or two-thirds full. Do we allow the significant agreements to temper remaining disagreements and put them into perspective? Or do we allow the significant remaining disagreements to temper and qualify our estimation of the recent staked-out agreements?

This brings me to a final attempt to put perhaps one of the most significant remaining disagreements into perspective. A recurring theme throughout *Is the Reformation Over?* is the recognition that questions pertaining to the church and ecclesiology are those that continue to mark the most trenchant differences between Catholics and Protestants.[31] Here, I think Noll and Nystrom are less helpful than they might be in outlining what these differences entail. At times, they state that such differences are those between Catholic corporate understandings of the Christian life and Prot-

---

[28]*Catechism of the Catholic Church*, 2nd ed. (New York: Doubleday, 1995), pp. 541-42.
[29]Noll and Nystrom, *Is the Reformation Over?* pp. 111-12.
[30]Ibid., p. 119.
[31]Ibid., pp. 82, 113, 182, passim.

estant individual approaches.[32] That may be an issue, but it is not insurmountable, nor is it the main sticking point. No, the issue is not between Protestant individualism versus Catholic communalism, nor is the main issue that of a spiritual versus an institutional church, nor even of the local over against the universal church. If the Reformation comes down to nothing more than a defense of individualism, then we might wonder if it should not be over. In my own Baptist tradition, it was not first a commitment to the freedom of the individual, but to the freedom of God, that committed the early Baptists to reject the enforcement of orthodoxy with temporal authority, later expressed in the principle of the separation of church and state.[33] It is one of the tragic ironies of history that one of the Baptists' most important contributions to the church universal in its witness to God's lordship, sovereignty and freedom over all earthly powers and authorities has been replaced in much of Baptist thought today with an emphasis on the authority of the individual and its freedom from the communal ties that bind, and certainly this trend is reflected in broader evangelicalism as well. This is not to say that the individual should be replaced by the communal, the spiritual and invisible by the institutional and visible, or the local by the universal. The New Testament is much too nuanced and dialectical in its portrayal of the relation between these such that they can be understood by a simple either/or decision, though it may be true that both Catholic and Protestant sides do stereotypically emphasize one over the other.

Yet a choice between these is not the way to get to the heart of the Protestant and Catholic divide on ecclesiology. To get at it, we might consider an excursus on Karl Barth, the Protestant theologian of the twentieth century par excellence.

When Barth takes up the subjective reality of revelation in the *Church Dogmatics*, one would expect him to begin with the work of the Holy Spirit, and he does. Next, one might expect Barth to turn to how faith is instilled in the believer, but he does not. He makes the faith of the believer de-

---

[32]Ibid., p. 84.

[33]See Paul M. Harrison, *Authority and Power in the Free Church Tradition: A Social Case Study of the American Baptist Convention* (Princeton, NJ: Princeton University Press, 1959), pp. 11-12, 18-37.

pendent on the prior witness of the church. Barth states that "God himself and God alone turns man into a recipient of His revelation—but He does so in a definite area, and this area . . . is the area of the Church."[34] Barth then continues:

> Put pointedly . . . , there exist over against Jesus Christ, not in the first instance believers, and then composed of them, the Church; but first of all the Church and then, through it and in it, believers. While God is as little bound to the Church as to the Synagogue, the recipients of His revelation are. They are what they are because the Church is what it is, and because they are in the Church, not apart from the Church and not outside the Church. And when we say "Church," we do not mean merely the inward and invisible coherence of those whom God in Christ calls His own, but also the outward and visible coherence of those who have heard in time, and have confessed to their hearing, that in Christ they are God's. The reception of revelation occurs within, not without, this twofold coherence.[35]

Now in light of this quotation, if we take Friedrich Schleiermacher's thesis that the difference between Protestantism and Catholicism is that "the former makes the individual's relation to the Church dependent on his relation to Christ, while the latter contrariwise makes the individual's relation to Christ dependent on his relation to the Church," might we not say that Barth is at least as Catholic as he is Protestant?[36] Yet Barth remains a quintessential Protestant. Why? Not because Barth is an individualist who gives the church only a peripheral role in God's economy of salvation. Nor because Barth's view of the church is insufficiently concrete. The passage I just recited specifically states that the church is not simply an invisible entity but is also the "outward and visible coherence of those who have heard in time," and so forth. And Barth can spend extensive sections of the *Church Dogmatics* speaking of such concrete issues as church law and church practices.[37] So what is it that makes Barth a Protestant?

The heart of the matter lies in the fact that Barth refuses to acknowledge

---

[34]*CD* I/2, p. 210.

[35]*CD* I/2, p. 211.

[36]Friedrich Schleiermacher, *Der Christliche Glaube*, ed. Martin Redeker, 2 vols. (Berlin: de Gruyter, 1960); ET: *The Christian Faith*, trans. and ed. H. R. Mackintosh and J. S. Stwart (Edinburgh: T & T Clark, 1989), p. 103, hereafter cited as *CF*.

[37]*CD* IV/3.2, pp. 865ff.; see also *CD* IV/2, pp. 676ff.

that Christ is absent from the world and that the church has taken his place. Now this should not be misunderstood. Barth does not deny the ascension. But he does deny that the ascension means that the authority of Christ has passed from him to the church, so that the authority of Christ now becomes the church's own. Barth refuses to concede that the time of Christ has ended and the time of the church has begun as if these were two successive stages in salvation history. This is clear in Barth's response to Erik Peterson (a later convert to Catholicism) in his essay of 1925, "Church and Theology." Barth there states that Christ's ascension and bestowal of a real authority and power on the church cannot mean that Christ has given up his own authority and power and passed it on to the church so that it ceases to be his own.[38] For Barth, this is to confuse the church and its Lord, making them successive partners in the economy of salvation, rather than preserving the rightful and irreversible distinction between them, in which Christ remains the eternal Lord and Head of the church, and the church remains his body and obedient servant whose authority is not the absolute authority of the Lord himself but is rather a "temporal, relative, and formal" authority.[39] Barth's eschatology will not allow them to be simply equated, and he denies that the authority of the church stands on the same plane as that of its Lord. For Barth, Christ must remain the center of the church's proclamation; it cannot proclaim itself. It is precisely this proclamation of itself which Barth sees in Catholicism. And it is this refusal to merge Christ and the church that makes Barth a Protestant.[40] What divides the Roman Catholic and Protestant understandings of the church, and what Noll and Nystrom themselves realize in their most perceptive moments, is that the relationship of Christ to the church, the Head to the body, is a major, if not the major, divide between evangelicals and Roman Catholics.

And so, when the *Catechism of the Catholic Church* (following *Lumen*

---

[38]Karl Barth, "Church and Theology," in *Theology and Church: Shorter Writings 1920–1928*, trans. Louise Pettibone Smith (New York: Harper & Row, 1962), p. 293.

[39]Ibid., pp. 294-95.

[40]Barth also stands on quite different ground in his ecclesiology from that of the evangelical catholic line of thinking today, and that makes what he says quite different from what is often heard in current ecumenical discussions. For examples of this thinking, see Carl E. Braaten, "The Special Ministry of the Ordained," in *Marks of the Body of Christ*, ed. Carl E. Braaten and Robert W. Jenson (Grand Rapids: Eerdmans, 1999), pp. 123-36, as well as Braaten's *Mother Church: Ecclesiology and Ecumenism* (Minneapolis: Fortress, 1998).

Gentium) states: "The Roman Pontiff, by reason of his office as Vicar of Christ, and as pastor of the entire Church has full, supreme, and universal power over the whole Church, a power which he can always exercise unhindered,"[41] well—I don't have to spell out for anyone on either side the disagreement that is going to arise here. A famous old Baptist commentary on the book of Acts makes much of the fact that the last word of that book in the Greek New Testament is "unhindered."[42] Yet for Baptists, as for other Protestants, it is not the power of the papacy but that of Christ and his gospel that alone can take that adjective to itself, for at the end of Acts Paul himself is in chains, in prison, powerless. But the gospel is free and Christ reigns.

Certainly it must also be said that these words of *Lumen Gentium* and the *Catechism* must be seen in the broader context of the nuanced discussion of the authority and relationship of the magisterium, tradition and Scripture outlined in *Dei Verbum*. Nevertheless, *Dei Verbum* may carefully qualify, but it does not undermine, *Lumen Gentium*. Even with the recognition of such qualification (and it should be recognized), there remains a significantly different way of seeing the relation between Christ and the church between Roman Catholicism and historic Protestantism.

It is the asymmetrical and irreversible relation between Christ and the church in Protestantism, with its insistence on seeing the church as a witness to the incarnation rather than its extension, that is at the root of the Protestant principle that there can be no absolutizing of the church and its dogma, a principle articulated by theologians as diverse as Luther and Barth, Calvin and Tillich, though at times inconsistently maintained within the Protestant communions themselves.[43] Protestantism, and evangelicals in particular, have struggled to see the intricate relation and unity between Christ and his church, to which the Catholic Church provides such a witness and Protestants must learn from and not ignore. Indeed, in much of evangelicalism, a theological understanding of the church does not seem to exist.[44] Yet while

---

[41]*Catechism of the Catholic Church*, p. 254, quoted in Noll and Nystrom, *Is the Reformation Over?* p. 233; see also *Lumen Gentium*, chap. 3, subsection 22.

[42]Frank Stagg, *The Book of Acts: The Early Struggle for an Unhindered Gospel* (Nashville: Broadman, 1955).

[43]The term "Protestant principle" is explicitly used by Paul Tillich in *The Protestant Era* (Chicago: University of Chicago Press, 1948), p. 163.

[44]Yet Alister McGrath's words are worth including here: "Those who accuse evangelicals of having 'immature' or 'underdeveloped' theories of the church might care to ask themselves whether

readily acknowledging this fact, it still must be said that in Protestantism, the union of the *totus Christus*, Christ with his church, must remain ever a unity in distinction, never a simple one. This distinction is not meant to entail a denigration of the church but exists in order to provide the church a true hope beyond itself. Perhaps this pointed difference between Catholic and Protestant forms of faith can be better illustrated than explained.

Richard John Neuhaus, one of the most famous of recent converts to Catholicism, related that he was deeply impressed when then Cardinal Ratzinger of the Congregation of the Doctrine of the Faith once said, "You know the difference between the Protestant and the Catholic faith is that for a Catholic, the act of faith in Jesus Christ and the act of faith in the church is one act of faith. For the Protestant, it is two acts of faith."[45] And with all due respect to the emeritus pope, I think that is exactly right. It is why a Protestant, to be a Protestant, must reject what is extolled by the *Catholic Catechism* as "the good sense of the believer," namely, when Joan of Arc states: "About Jesus Christ and the Church, I simply know they're just one thing, and we shouldn't complicate the matter."[46] Protestants *cannot* cease to complicate the matter, if only because from their perspective such an identification of Christ and the church dangerously confuses the rightful lordship of the first with the service of the latter. Noll and Nystrom do glimpse this point in a central portion of the book. As they conclude: "If Christ and his church are one, then a great deal of Catholic doctrine simply follows naturally. In a word, ecclesiology represents the crucial difference between evangelicals and Catholics."[47] What they do not say is that when this distinction is understood in the Protestant way, then a great deal of Protestant doctrine simply follows just as naturally. Indeed, the formal and material principles of Protestantism, the five *solas* rightly understood (*sola Christus, sola fide, sola gratia, sola Scriptura, sola Deo gloria*), the Protestant understanding of apostolic succession emphasizing apostolic teaching more than office, the

---

they might not have hopelessly overdeveloped theories" (in Armstrong, *Roman Catholicism*, p. 214).

[45]Richard John Neuhaus, "Why Evangelicals and Catholics Belong Together," in George, *Pilgrims on the Sawdust Trail*, pp. 103-4.

[46]*Catechism of the Catholic Church*, p. 229, quoted in Noll and Nystrom, *Is the Reformation Over?* p. 146.

[47]Noll and Nystrom, *Is the Reformation Over?* pp. 146-47; see also pp. 149, 182-83.

rejection of a vicarious priesthood, and on and on—none of these make sense if this ecclesiological distinction, which really is a christological one, is not understood.

Protestantism is not simply an ad hoc reaction to Renaissance papal abuses. If it was, the Reformation would certainly have long since been over. But the Reformation is not so much a historical epoch as an intentional confession of faith based on a principled discovery, no matter how imperfectly embodied or carried out. It is an attempt to recover and confess the right relationship between Christ and the church, and all other elements, that is, justification by grace alone through faith alone, Scripture as the living voice of Christ over against and not only within the church and its tradition, and so forth—all are intricately tied to this.

This is also why a Protestant understanding of this relation may be reflected in a difference in how it interacts with culture, for while a Protestant church may in certain instances be even more strongly opposed to elements of culture than its Catholic partner, it can never speak a final word of judgment from on high but must itself remain open to future correction, for the voice of the church and that of Christ cannot be simply equated. Judgment must begin with the household of God. This admission is not to trivialize or denigrate the real need for prophetic witness by the people of God to the world. Certainly both the Roman Catholic Church and Protestant communions must wrestle with the balance of speaking forcefully and authoritatively, but also humbly, to culture. Yet Protestantism may at times wish to, but cannot, make claims for its teaching office like those made by and for the magisterium in the opening paragraphs of *Humane Vitae* on the interpretation of the moral law. Certainly part of this is the unfortunate reality that the Protestant churches do not always speak in accord. But there is also the fact that the power of Protestantism's prophetic voice and the power of conviction for its message must come from a different source than by appeal to a historic possession of authority. This is the great outward deficiency of Protestantism. It is also a witness to its hidden strength.

In the end, it is the cohesiveness of the Catholic and the Protestant visions that makes unity so difficult to achieve (even while readily granting that this overarching vision in Protestantism exists in so many often fragmented forms). This is why, when Roman Catholic and evangelical interlocutors turn to the question of the church, there seems to be an ecumenical law of diminishing returns that mirrors the economic one. For at its heart, this is not only an ecclesiological distinction but also a christological and moreover an eschatological one, for the church is not Christ, nor is it the kingdom come. And this Protestant eschatological sensibility (like the christological one, and in fact its counterpart) is shared by Protestants as diverse as Karl Barth and C. S. Lewis, that icon of evangelicalism. For Lewis, no fan of Barth, from what he knew of him, nevertheless like him held a disdain for a temporary earthly shanty that presented itself as a finished castle.[48] For both Barth and Lewis, the things on the other side of the mirror, through which we can but dimly see, are more splendid, enduring and real than whatever ecclesiastical splendor, however theatrically or even aesthetically compelling, the church might array itself in on this side.

Yet though Protestants and Catholics are most removed on this ecclesiological point, here too there is hope for discussion, because against comments of identification of Christ and church such as those of Joan of Arc and Cardinal Ratzinger, the *Catechism* preserves statements of distinction, such as when it states that the Light of Christ is not paralleled, but simply reflected, by the church.[49] And in light of evangelicalism's own ecclesiological deficiencies, there are new attempts from its side to struggle with the unity of Christ and his church as it learns from the Catholic side.[50] It is on such

---

[48]Lewis's Protestant sensibilities have been succinctly and pointedly summarized by S. M. Hutchens, "C. S. Lewis and Mother Kirk: Why Lewis Was a Protestant," *Books and Culture*, www.booksandculture.com/articles/2004/novdec/12.30.html. Hutchens writes of Lewis's "eschatological displacement" in which there is a "deep suspicion of realized eschatology, precluding identification of the True Church . . . with any of its present, earthly forms. This conviction is also at the heart of Protestant ecclesiology, which in its purer form does not arise from mere anti-Catholicism, but from a positive vision of the nature of reality and our manner of comprehending it, a vision far older than the Reformation-era confessions on the nature and identity of the Church in which it came forward with such force." Hutchens's piece is a poignant and unapologetic attempt to present the Protestant mindset. For Barth's thoughts along similar succinct and pointed lines, see "The Concept of the Church," in *Theology and Church*, pp. 272-85. For Lewis's early negative impressions of Barth's theology, see C. S. Lewis, *The Collected Letters of C. S. Lewis*, vol. 2 (San Francisco: HarperCollins, 2004), p. 351. One difference between their eschatological reservations remains, however, in that Lewis's was abidingly Platonic and dualistic in form, whereas Barth's became ever more Chalcedonian even as it remained dialectical from first to last.

[49]*Catechism of the Catholic Church*, p. 214, quoted in Noll and Nystrom, *Is the Reformation Over?* p. 150.

[50]For example, see Kevin Vanhoozer, "Evangelicalism and the Church: The Company of the Gospel," in *The Futures of Evangelicalism: Issues and Prospects*, ed. Craig Bartholomew, Robin Perry and Andrew West (Grand Rapids: Kregel, 2004), pp. 40-99.

statements and attempts that future discussion can build. And as long as the living voice of Christ is heard in the churches each week in the reading of the Word of God, Roman Catholic and Protestant, there is hope that these communions can be re-formed to grow closer in unity to their Lord, and thus to one another. In this sense, one can hope that the Reformation has not ended.

PART TWO

✠

Canon and Confession

5

Scripture and Canon in
Karl Barth's Early Theology

✠

No theologian of the twentieth century was as responsible for restoring Scripture to the center of the theological enterprise as Karl Barth. From his early sermons as a young pastor, through his lectures and commentaries on New Testament books produced during his professorships in Göttingen, Münster and Bonn, to his massive unfinished *Church Dogmatics*, containing more than fifteen thousand biblical references and two thousand in-depth exegetical investigations of specific passages, Barth's theology was grounded in the Bible to a degree rarely seen since the Protestant Reformers of the sixteenth century.[1] Yet Barth's commitment to Holy Scripture as the source and norm for the critical and constructive task of theology was the

---

This chapter appeared in an earlier form as "Scripture and Canon in Karl Barth's Early Theology," in *From Biblical Criticism to Biblical Faith: Essays in Honor of Lee Martin McDonald*, ed. William H. Brackney and Craig A. Evans (Macon, GA: Mercer University Press, 2007), pp. 164-98. Reprinted by permission.

[1]Richard Burnett, *Karl Barth's Theological Exegesis: The Hermeneutical Principles of the* Römerbrief *Period* (Grand Rapids: Eerdmans, 2004), p. 9. At the time of Barth's seventieth birthday, his longtime friend Eduard Thurneysen commented on Barth's lifelong engagement with the Bible from his early years as a pastor onward: "Karl Barth stands before us already in this early period as a reader and expositor of Scripture. The tablets of Holy Scripture are erected before him and the books of the expositors from Calvin through the biblicists and all the way to the modern critical biblical interpretation lie open in his hands. Both then and now this has been the source from which his whole theology has come. It has grown out of the work of preaching, and it serves the proclamation of the church. And so it has remained. . . . He does not project theological speculations out of his own mind; he is not concerned about a system; he is and he remains a student and teacher of Holy Scriptures. Whoever tries to understand him as other than this will not understand him at all" (Eduard Thurneysen, "Die Anfänge," in *Antwort: Karl Barth zum siebzigsten Geburtstag*, ed. Rudolf Frey et al. [Zürich: Evangelischer Verlag Zürich, 1956], p. 832, quoted in Burnett, *Karl Barth's Theological Exegesis*, p. 23).

result of a significant conflict with the theological inheritance he had received during his university years, and this conflict was to shape all of Barth's later thought on Scripture and canon. Out of this conflict came a view of Scripture that is rich, complex and not given to facile analysis or brief summary. With this reality in mind, this chapter examines Barth's understanding of Scripture not in an exhaustive manner but through the aperture of a twofold delimitation of period and topic, so that the investigation is restricted to examining the early development of Barth's doctrine of Scripture culminating in his first dogmatic lecture cycle during the Göttingen period, and directed toward the question of the biblical canon in particular and its related concerns.

BARTH'S EARLY DOCTRINE OF SCRIPTURE—ITS NATURE AND IMPLICATIONS

Barth's view of Scripture was profoundly shaped by his break from liberalism and his rediscovery of the Bible during his pastorate in Safenwil, Switzerland.[2] On his joyful discovery of "a new world within the Bible," Barth turned to a redoubled study of Scripture and an attempt to understand its character.[3] Barth's view of Scripture witnessed in his early theological writings is highly nuanced and dialectical in character, not lending

---

[2]The story of Barth's break with liberalism has been often told. For Barth's early education, development and eventual break with liberalism, see Eberhard Busch, *Karl Barth: His Life from Letters and Autobiographical Texts*, trans. John Bowden (Grand Rapids: Eerdmans, 1994), chaps. 2 and 3; Busch, *The Great Passion: An Introduction to Karl Barth's Theology*, trans. Geoffrey W. Bromiley (Grand Rapids: Eerdmans, 2004), section 1, chaps. 1 and 2; Gary Dorrien, *The Barthian Revolt in Modern Theology* (Louisville, KY: Westminster John Knox, 2000), chaps. 1 and 2; Eberhard Jüngel, *Karl Barth: A Theological Legacy*, trans. Garrett E. Paul (Philadelphia: Westminster Press, 1986), chaps. 1 and 2; Bruce L. McCormack, *Karl Barth's Critically Realistic Dialectical Theology: Its Genesis and Development 1909-1936* (Oxford: Clarendon Press, 1995), chaps. 1 and 2, hereafter cited as *Barth's Theology*; and John Webster, *Karl Barth* (New York: Continuum, 2000), chaps. 1 and 2.

[3]See Barth, "Die neue Welt in der Bibel," in *Das Wort Gottes und die Theologie* (München: Chr. Kaiser Verlag, 1929), pp. 18-32; ET: "The Strange New World Within the Bible," in *The Word of God and the Word of Man*, trans. Douglas Horton (Gloucester: Peter Smith, 1978), pp. 28-50. Barth would extend these themes in his 1920 essay "Biblische Fragen, Einsichten und Ausblicke," in *Das Wort Gottes und die Theologie*, pp. 70-98; ET: "Biblical Questions, Insights and Vistas," in *The Word of God and the Word of Man*, pp. 51-96. For a detailed discussion of Barth's turn to the Bible and his exegetical and hermeneutical principles, see Burnett, *Karl Barth's Theological Exegesis*. Burnett writes: "To read the Bible in a way that is '*sachlicher, inhaltlicher, wesentlicher*,' that is, 'more in accordance with its subject matter, content, and substance,' represents Karl Barth's most important hermeneutical principle" (p. 65; cf. p. 95).

itself well to flat-footed or wooden description. At the heart of Barth's understanding of Scripture is his insistence that the Bible can be understood only if it is read as a unity, for the subject matter (*die Sache*) of the Bible is the unity of God's revelation in Jesus Christ.[4] This unity binds the Old Testament and the New Testament into one Scripture, for both witness to the same revelation, though in different forms—the former as promise, the latter as fulfillment. In point of fact, Barth relativizes these distinctions when he states that both promise and fulfillment can be found in the Old Testament as they both can be found in the New, for the writers of the former as well as the latter are confronted with God's revelation, the revelation of the triune God in Jesus Christ.[5] Such a statement does not mean, Barth is very aware, that all temporal distinctions between the time of the prophets and the apostles are erased into nonsense, "as though the people of the OT could see Jesus of Nazareth walking the fields of Galilee as if with telescopes hundreds of years ahead."[6] Yet Barth is striving to articulate a truth that is elusive though integral to any Christian, rather than Marcionite, reading of the church's canon, namely, that the Bible is not merely the record of numerous revelations, and certainly not the record of revelations of differing deities, but the record of the one revelation of a single divine Subject. It is the unity of this one God, the God of Abraham and Isaac and Jacob who is also the God and Father of the Lord Jesus Christ, that binds every book of Scripture to the others, and the Old Testament to the New: "The witnesses of the old covenant confront the same God as those of the new, namely, the hidden God who is also the revealed God."[7] The unity of God's revelation assures that the Old Testament never becomes

---

[4]See Burnett, *Karl Barth's Theological Exegesis*, pp. 74-78. He writes: "God is the 'object' of the Bible only to the extent that He is a Subject who must give Himself to us as object if He is to be known. The *Sache* of the Bible is not therefore an object which gives itself to us without reservation or qualification such that it is ever 'at our disposal' as it were. He is an object which always remains Subject even as He gives Himself as object" (p. 75).

[5]*GD*, p. 145; cf. p. 213. That for Barth the distinction between promise and fulfillment cannot be simply identified with the division between the Old Testament and the New mirrors the manner of Luther's distinction of law and gospel which also cannot be simply equated with the biblical division of Testaments.

[6]Ibid., p. 145; cf. pp. 145-52. "The prophets and the apostles" is Barth's idiosyncratic way of referring to the writings of the Old Testament and the New Testament, respectively, which of course recalls Ephesians 2:20.

[7]Ibid., p. 146. Barth then immediately states: "I do not see why a cautious OT scholar should have any objection to this formula."

merely a prologue to the New that may be left behind but establishes the latter as an indispensable witness alongside an earlier indispensable witness, both testifying to a common *Sache*.[8]

While there is no ultimate division between the Old Testament and the New Testament in Barth's view, there is a duality in Scripture that must be appreciated. This duality pertains to the dialectical relationship between the divine and human word. Barth consistently maintained that the revelation of God that comes to us in Scripture could not be directly equated with the human words on the page, but neither could it be separated from them. This insistence in relation to the Bible was analogous to and predicated on Barth's Chalcedonian tendencies and Reformed sensibilities that maintained the integrity of the Creator-creature distinction even within the unity of the incarnation.[9] Just as Christ's humanity was not deified in the incarnation but remained creaturely flesh, so also the words of the prophets and apostles remained their own, even as they were the vehicle of God's own Word. Against either a simple identification or separation, Barth posited that God's divine Word, the revelation of God's very self, is revealed in Christ as Christ comes to us in the promises of the Old Testament and the testimony of the New. The divine Word of revelation is thus indirectly identified with the words of Scripture and a Word that comes to us by grace; it is not grasped solely by means of perfecting an exegetical or hermeneutical program. The fundamental issue of hermeneutics thus lies in the reality and priority of God's act, rather than in human questioning and a determination of correct method.[10]

This recognition does not in any way entail that grammatical and historical exegetical study and hermeneutical principles are unimportant for Barth, however, because the divine Word is truly indirectly identified with the words of Scripture, and therefore critical study and attention to method provide the preparation for such hearing of this Word and understanding

---

[8]"The OT does not end in the NT but continues in it, just as the NT is already present in the OT. . . . The NT is not a second step above the OT, albeit at a higher stage of development. It is later witness alongside earlier witness" (ibid., p. 149; see also p. 213).

[9]For a discussion of this theme beyond what can here be provided, see Bruce L. McCormack, "The Being of Holy Scripture Is in Becoming: Karl Barth in Conversation with American Evangelical Criticism," in *Evangelicals and Scripture: Tradition, Authority and Hermeneutics* (Downers Grove, IL: InterVarsity Press, 2004), pp. 55-75.

[10]Burnett, *Karl Barth's Theological Exegesis*, pp. 41-42.

to take place.[11] Nevertheless, for Barth, the fact that humans hear God's own voice in Scripture is ultimately realized not through our own critical study but by God's own act. Critical study can at most be a preparation for such a hearing—as such it has a real value and irreplaceable task. This point, that it is ultimately the Spirit of God rather than critical science that makes our knowledge of revelation possible, lies at the heart of Barth's disagreement with his former teacher Adolf von Harnack, expressed in a famous exchange of letters in 1923 published in *Die Christliche Welt*.[12] For Barth, modern theological schools are marked by a "chaotic activity" precisely because for them "the concept of an authoritative *object* [*Gegenstand*] has become foreign and monstrous because of the sheer authoritativeness of *method* [*Methode*]."[13] If the true content of Scripture is nothing less than God's own self-giving, then this can never be grasped from our side as an accomplishment, but only given as a gift by God's own Spirit, for "it cannot be proper to reverse this order and make out of 'thus saith the Lord' a 'thus heareth man.'"[14]

Here the question of Scripture's unity returns. Because the God who speaks through Scripture is one, Barth maintains that the entire Scripture is a unified whole, for Scripture is a witness to this one God. Scripture cannot be rightly understood if considered solely as a repository of various historical, cultural and literary materials from antiquity, but it is only truly understood if seen as a united witness to a single Lord. Scripture therefore possesses a unity that transcends its real and undeniable diversity not because we can discern within it or synthesize from it an overarching idea or concept, but because of the unity and singularity of the one Lord to whom it witnesses and who speaks through it. It is the unity of this Lord for Barth

---

[11]Ibid., pp. 42, 49-50, 56-64. For an extended discussion of Barth's understanding of the role of historical criticism as a preparation for understanding, see pp. 230-40.

[12]This exchange between Barth and Harnack may be found in Karl Barth, *Offene Briefe 1909–1935*, ed. Diether Koch (Zürich: Theologischer Verlag Zürich, 2001), pp. 55-88; ET in *The Beginnings of Dialectical Theology*, ed. James M. Robinson, trans. Louis De Grazia and Keith R. Crim (Richmond: John Knox Press, 1968), pp. 165-87. For the point at issue, see pp. 59-60, 62-63; ET pp. 165, 167. For a commentary on this debate, see H. Martin Rumscheidt, *Revelation and Theology: An Analysis of the Barth-Harnack Correspondence of 1925* (Cambridge: Cambridge University Press, 1972); George Hunsinger, *Disruptive Grace: Studies in the Theology of Karl Barth* (Grand Rapids: Eerdmans, 2000), pp. 319-37; and chapter six below.

[13]*Offene Briefe 1909–1935*, p. 74; ET p. 176.

[14]Ibid., p. 76; ET p. 178.

that grounds the unity of Scripture and makes it a unified witness.[15]

Starting with the conviction of the Bible's unity has significant ramifications for how we must read Scripture, according to Barth. First, the whole of Scripture must be read in light of its parts, for every part of the Bible testifies to the same Lord, and therefore every part must be taken into account for an understanding of Scripture as a whole. No part can be summarily dismissed, and it was this dismissal and attribution of difficult and exotic material to foreign spirits and outmoded cultural accretions that Barth felt was problematic not only in his strongest critics such as Paul Wernle and Rudolf Jülicher, but also in an appreciative one such as Rudolf Bultmann.[16] Barth's dialectical understanding of Scripture entailed, as he stated, that *all* the words of Scripture were human words, all were the voice of foreign spirits, and that the divine Word could not be equated or separated from any of them.[17]

The second ramification is that the parts must themselves be read in light of the theme of the Bible as a whole. For Barth, to fail in this regard is to fail in the task of interpretation, for, once again, the Bible cannot be rightly understood if it is simply considered as a collection of various fragments of historical, literary and cultural data. Rather it must be appreciated as a unified witness to a single Lord.[18] While Barth praised modern historical criticism for its significant contributions to the first task (gaining further

---

[15]Burnett, *Karl Barth's Theological Exegesis*, p. 77.

[16]Barth addresses this issue with regard to Wernle and Jülicher in the preface to the second edition of the commentary on Romans, and with regard to Bultmann in the preface to the third. See Barth, *Der Römerbrief: Zweite Fassung 1922* (Zürich: Theologischer Verlag Zürich, 1922/1999), pp. xviii-xxiii and pp. xxvii-xxviii, respectively; the English translation of the prefaces here discussed may be found in *Beginnings of Dialectical Theology*, pp. 92-96 and p. 127, respectively. In the preface to the second edition he writes: "In contrast to this agreeably ignoring disagreeable points, my Biblicism consists in my having thought through these 'offenses to the modern consciousness' until I feel in part that I have discovered in them the most excellent insights; and in any case am able to speak of them and explain them to some extent" (p. xxii; ET p. 96). In addressing Bultmann's criticisms, he writes in the preface to the third edition: "The *pneuma Christou* is not a position on which one can take a stand, and then from there more or less play the schoolmaster to Paul. Let it suffice us, not entirely forsaken by him, to place ourselves, learning and teaching, beside Paul, despite the 'other' spirits, ready to grasp spiritually things that are meant spiritually, and ready to recognize that even our own voice, with which we pass on what we have perceived, is from the first entirely the voice of 'other' spirits" (p. xx; ET p. 129).

[17]*Der Römerbrief*, pp. xxvii-xxviii; ET p. 127. Barth's approach to Scripture thus obviously differs from Bultmann's *Sachkritik*.

[18]Burnett, *Karl Barth's Theological Exegesis*, pp. 78-84.

understanding into the various parts of Scripture), he contended that it had fallen short in the second task (understanding the diversity of the parts in light of a unified whole, the content [*Inhalt*] of Scripture). In Barth's estimation, this latter failure cast a pall over the first, for no true interpretation of Scripture is possible, even of the parts, without an interpretation in light of the theme of Scripture as a whole, and both parts and whole must be understood in light of Scripture's truth.[19]

The introduction of the theme of truth entails a further corollary regarding our reading of Scripture. Not only must the theological sense of Scripture be determined through an examination of the grammatical, historical and literary elements of Scripture, but also the latter can only be understood in light of the former. Scripture therefore must be read in light of its parts, and all of its parts in light of the whole, and all with an eye toward its truth, all themes that will be explored further in the next chapter.

It should come as no surprise that Barth's approach to Scripture placed him greatly at odds with the prevailing scientific critical scholarship of his day and some of its most esteemed practitioners, many of whom believed that Barth in the *Römerbrief* had substituted a subjective pneumatic exegesis for careful scientific scholarship, thereby illuminating Barth's own thought more than that of Paul, a charge that has never really disappeared and that requires serious consideration.[20] Barth himself knew that he was steering a very different course than that of the predominant biblical scholarship with which he was well acquainted. Yet it must be noted that contrary to much opinion past and present, Barth was not a well-intentioned but naive exegete who failed to understand the complexities of critical interpretation, but one who had in fact been thoroughly introduced and inducted into the historical-critical method of his day through his studies in Berne and later in Berlin.[21] He had himself studied under Jülicher and Johannes Weiss at

---

[19]Ibid., pp. 83-84, 90.

[20]Ibid., pp. 14-18.

[21]Barth produced various studies examining both biblical and historical topics in light of the historical-critical method of his day during his student years, including a paper on the Capernaum centurion pericopes of Matthew 8:5-13 and Luke 7:1-10 in 1905, and on the Lord's Prayer in the Gospels in 1906. See Karl Barth, *Vorträge und kleinere Arbeiten 1905–1909* (Zürich: Theologischer Verlag Zürich, 1992), pp. 46-60, 126-47. Within this latter study on the Lord's Prayer, Barth could say at the end: "Today we have taken a look into the workshop of historical criticism which—rightly—cannot call a halt even before the highest and the holiest!" (p. 146; ET in Busch,

Marburg. Nonetheless, Barth was never fully at peace with historical criticism as a sufficient method for biblical interpretation.

Such misgivings were not late developments, for Barth had already realized the problem of Scripture acutely in his student days. In a paper on Zwingli written when Barth was only a young student of nineteen, Barth stated that the current debate regarding Scripture involved two polarities: the orthodox position, for which the wording of Scripture was timeless and binding (*verbindlich*) for the Christian faith and the church for all time, and the *religionsgeschichtliche* understanding, for which the Bible is considered, like other writings of antiquity, a historical product with only historical and thus finite significance and relative binding authority (*Verbindlichkeit*).[22] Barth's later understanding of Scripture was an attempt to overcome this dilemma, refusing to side with one position over against the other in what Barth in time came to maintain was a false choice between two unacceptable positions.

Barth was too well trained in historical criticism to fall back on a premodern viewpoint regarding Scripture, though this should not be mistaken to mean that his doctrine of Scripture was formulated as a defensive doctrine against the inroads of historical criticism. Rather, his own developing principles guiding his understanding of Scripture were rooted in classical Reformed convictions that undergirded a newly formulated dynamic and dialectical view of Scripture, rather than a static and orthodox one, and he had little interest in defending such notions as verbal inerrancy of original though unproducible texts, or providing an *apologia* for Scripture's truthfulness based on qualities of such lost texts. Barth may have renounced his liberal inheritance, but Wilhelm Herrmann's disdain for apologetics remained a part of his student's theological makeup; nor did he have any inclination to adopt the defenses of the Bible's veracity produced by later Reformed scholasticism.[23] Barth was, however, not unaware of the danger

---

Karl Barth, pp. 37-38). Most important for this early period in Barth's studies are the extensive paper Barth wrote in Berlin for Harnack's seminar on Acts, "Die Missionsthätigkeit des Paulus nach der Darstellung der Apostelgeschichte" (1907), and his Tübingen qualifying dissertation, "Die Vorstellung vom Descensus Christi ad inferos in der kirchlichen Literatur bis Origines" (1908)—see *Vorträge und kleinere Arbeiten 1905-1909*, pp. 148-243, 244-312.

[22]"Zwinglis '67 Schlussreden' auf das erste Religionsgespräch zu Zürich 1523" (1906), in *Vorträge und kleinere Arbeiten 1905-1909*, p. 113.

[23]For a brief look into Barth's appreciative but critical thoughts on Reformed scholasticism, see

that resided within the path that historical criticism was following. Troeltsch and the rising *religionsgeschichtliche* school had undercut the mediating position of Ritschl and Harnack that tried to isolate an enduring message of Scripture by means of critical science, and the prospect was that the uniqueness of Scripture would be lost and its character understood solely as the product of the ever-flowing river of time, not only conditioned by but also entirely explained by the contingent events of a history that allowed for no absolutes or singularities. Such a view of Scripture mirrored an understanding of Jesus in which his uniqueness was declared untenable, and Jesus himself was explained within his context as a product of accidental history and thus without absolute enduring significance. This view was, in fact, akin to the argument made by D. F. Strauss against Schleiermacher, the latter hoping to preserve the uniqueness and ultimate importance of Jesus over and beyond the historical process.[24] The results of such thoroughgoing historicism applied to Jesus Christ and Scripture, Barth came to believe, would be the death of theology altogether and the complete triumph of historical relativism. Yet, as Barth also realized, such an end only threatened a theology that had sacrificed the dialectic of an indirect identity of the Bible with revelation for a direct one that historicized revelation.[25]

Even before his break with liberalism, Barth had maintained that historical relativism, along with individualism, were the hallmarks of modern theology.[26] Though historicism was intrinsic to a liberalism that Barth did not question at the time of this observation in 1909, from Barth's perspective such historicism was deeply problematic, for whereas positive theology had provided its students with theological convictions and doctrines that were seen as authoritative across time and over rival belief systems, modern critical theology, of which Barth was a product, allowed for no such timeless doctrines and was predicated on the conviction of a historical relativism that shunned absolute doctrines. The New Testament

---

Barth's foreword to Heinrich Heppe, *Reformed Dogmatics*, trans. G. T. Thompson (London: George Allen & Unwin, 1950), pp. v-vii.

[24]D. F. Strauss, *The Christ of Faith and the Jesus of History*, trans. and ed. Leander E. Keck (Philadelphia: Fortress, 1977), pp. 4ff.

[25]*GD*, pp. 217-18.

[26]Barth, "Moderne Theologie und Reichsgottesarbeit" (1909), in *Vorträge und kleinere Arbeiten 1905–1909*, pp. 342-44; cf. pp. 341-47; also Busch, *Karl Barth*, pp. 50-52.

(like the Old) was thus subject to the same critical methods as other religious texts and then shown to be the product of its own religious environment.[27] Taken to its logical end, such radical historicism rendered any unique claims for Jesus or a dogmatic view of Scripture untenable. The Bible would no longer be a canon but a collection of various texts that may merit historical and cultural interest but hold no claim to ongoing normativity for life and faith. Nevertheless, despite its inherent difficulties and dangers, Barth did not simply renounce the products of his liberal inheritance in favor of a return to a timeless orthodoxy. This for him would have been a betrayal of character in bad faith.[28] Instead, Barth initially took refuge from the rising waters of a radical historicism in the neo-Schleiermacherian theology of his teacher Herrmann, for whom, though the torrential flood of historical criticism might flow until all was drowned in its path, the inner life of Jesus, communicated by means of Scripture and church to our own consciousness, rose above the waters and could not be touched.[29] Once Barth forsook this refuge of Herrmann, he had to find another rock on which to stand.

In seeking out such a footing, it must once again be emphasized that Barth did not return to a precritical understanding of Scripture. True, in a famous (infamous!) line from the preface to the first edition of the commentary on Romans (1919), Barth stated that if forced to choose between historical criticism, which Barth noted has its necessary place, and the esteemed doctrine of inspiration, he would choose the latter.[30] But Barth never saw this as an either-or choice, as many of the critical reviewers of *Romans* did.[31] In re-

---

[27]See "Moderne Theologie und Reichsgottesarbeit," pp. 341-47; cf. McCormack, *Barth's Theology*, pp. 68-70; also Burnett, *Karl Barth's Theological Exegesis*, pp. 171-76.

[28]"Moderne Theologie und Reichsgottesarbeit," pp. 346-47.

[29]For Herrmann's theology, see McCormack, *Barth's Theology*, pp. 49-68; also Herdrikus Berkhof, *Two Hundred Years of Theology: Report of a Personal Journey*, trans. John Vriend (Grand Rapids: Eerdmans, 1989), pp. 143-62. To be fair to Troeltsch, he himself attempted to provide a rock in the raging river of historicism by means of stressing values that arise from but transcend history, and thus preserve an ongoing place for the uniqueness of Christian faith. But in the end, he seems to have despaired even of this (see Berkhof, *Two Hundred Years*, pp. 156-62).

[30]*Römerbrief*, p. xi; ET p. 61.

[31]In his review of Barth's commentary, Adolf Jülicher announced that "Barth forced me point-blank to make a decision about the question of the significance of practical exegesis of Scripture compared to strictly scientific exegesis" (*Beginnings of Dialectical Theology*, p. 73). Jülicher concludes: "Much, perhaps even very much, may someday be learned from this book for the understanding of our age, but scarcely anything new for the understanding of the 'historical'

sponse to those (like Jülicher) who considered Barth a foe of historical criticism, Barth denied the charge itself and stated in the preface to the second edition of the commentary that the issue was not that he opposed such criticism but that he opposed the contentment of many with establishing a translation and historical commentary of the text without going on beyond historical matters of translation and context to "*understand* Paul, that is, to discover not only how what is there can somehow be repeated in Greek or German, but how it can be *rethought*, and what it may perhaps *mean*. And it is here, and not with the obvious use of historical criticism in reference to the work which must be done before, that the dissension begins."[32]

Thus, while Barth came to reject the basic trajectory of historical criticism and its adequacy as an exegetical and hermeneutical approach to Scripture, he did not reject it wholesale (a fact often lost on biblical historians critical of Barth past and present).[33] As stated earlier, Barth openly expressed deep appreciation in his *Romans* commentary prefaces for the work of historical scholarship and its necessary task. At the same time, Barth insisted that it too often fails to push beyond historical questions to questions of meaning. On this score, Barth considered older exegetes such as Calvin superior to modern critical scholars such as Jülicher.[34] Barth had no intention of turning

---

Paul" (p. 81). Barth himself would respond to these criticisms in the preface to the second edition. For a thorough discussion of the many criticisms of Barth's commentary by its reviewers and Barth's response to them, see Burnett, *Karl Barth's Theological Exegesis*, pp. 14-23.

[32]*Römerbrief*, p. xvii; ET p. 91.

[33]For one recent example of such a reading of Barth, see Richard Hays's interaction with N. T. Wright's understanding of history in *Jesus, Paul and the People of God: A Theological Dialogue with N. T. Wright*, ed. Nicholas Perrin and Richard B. Hays (Downers Grove, IL: IVP Academic, 2011), pp. 41-65, 115-60. Once again, this conversation demonstrates that questions of faith and history are played out in every generation and that echoes of Barth and Harnack (real echoes, though not identical voices) are heard in the respective words of Hays and Wright. For an earlier example of a related conversation between Hans Frei and Carl Henry, see Hunsinger, *Disruptive Grace*, pp. 338-60.

[34]"Compare Jülicher, for example, with Calvin. How energetically the latter goes to work after he has conscientiously established 'what is there' to think the thoughts of the text after it, that is, to come to terms with it until the wall between the first and sixteenth centuries becomes transparent, until Paul speaks there and the man of the sixteenth century hears here, until the conversation between document and reader is concentrated entirely on the *matter* (which *cannot* be different here and there!). Truly, anyone who thinks he can eliminate Calvin's method with the cliché, now so well worn, about the 'restriction of the doctrine of inspiration,' proves only that in *this* direction he has not yet really *worked* at all. Conversely, how near Jülicher (I mention him only as an example) stays to the runic symbols of the words, as little understood afterward as before" (*Römerbrief*, pp. xvii-xviii; ET p. 92).

away from critical historical scholarship, but he had every intention of going through and beyond it by means of a deep wrestling with the text such that the subject matter came to the fore and could be rightly understood and grasped as one came to see that the relationship in Scripture of *"this* God to *this* man, *this* man to *this* God,"* regarding Jesus Christ is "the theme of the Bible and the sum of philosophy in one."[35]

Barth's approach to Scripture and theology therefore is mislabeled as neo-orthodox if such is taken to mean a return to a premodern understanding of Scripture in terms of either composition or collection. For Barth, the solution to the paradox of Scripture was not a return to premodern under-standings of the Bible by turning one's back on historical critical science, but rather a full engagement and wrestling with historical criticism in order to discern its inadequacies and overcome them. His is a postcritical, rather than precritical, position. As Barth would exclaim in the foreword to the second edition of the *Römerbrief*, "The historical critics must be *more critical to suit me!*"[36] Barth elaborated this point in debate with Harnack:

> What I must defend myself against is not historical criticism, but rather the matter-of-course way in which one, still today, *empties* theology's task: Instead of that which our predecessors called *"the Word"* (the correlation of "Scripture" and "Spirit") one has placed this and that which have been dug up by his-torical criticism *beyond* the "Scripture" and *apart from* the "Spirit," which one calls the "simple gospel [*schlichte Evangelium*]," a gospel that can be called "word of God" only as a figure of speech, because it is in fact at best a human impression thereof.[37]

Barth therefore did not betray his firmly entrenched historical consciousness,

---

[35]Ibid., p. xx; ET p. 94. Against the charge of "biblicism," Barth states: "Taken exactly, all the 'Biblicism' which I can be shown to have consists in my having the prejudice that the Bible is a good book, and that it is worthwhile to take its thoughts at least as seriously as one takes his own" (p. xxiii; ET p. 96).

[36]Ibid., p. xviii; ET p. 93.

[37]*Offene Briefe 1909-1935*, p. 75; ET p. 177. In Barth's exchange with Harnack, historical science is presented as having a twofold purpose from Barth's perspective. Negatively, it witnesses to its own inability to move beyond historical reconstruction to confession and thus reveals its own limitations. For Barth, this negative function contributes by witnessing to the fact that a true understanding of the gospel can come only as a gift from the side of God's activity rather than human scholarly effort. What is less clear in this exchange, however, is what exactly Barth takes to be historical science's positive and preparatory function, which he can allude to and affirms but never fully explains. For a discussion of Barth's later articulation of the positive role of his-torical criticism, see Burnett, *Karl Barth's Theological Exegesis*, pp. 230-40.

nor did he seek to impose an *a priori* principle on biblical exegesis. Even well after his break with liberalism he could go so far as to acknowledge that the Bible itself is the product of an ancient people and bears such marks: "The Bible is the literary monument of an ancient racial religion and of a Hellenistic cultus religion of the Near East. A human document like any other, it can lay no *a priori* dogmatic claim to special attention and consideration. This judgment, being announced by every tongue and believed in every territory, we may take for granted today."[38] And yet, Barth's great joyful discovery was that the Bible, when read in faith, witnesses beyond itself to something (or someone) that is more than this, more than a literary work or recorded history, and thus its message is not overcome by the raging and rising torrents of historical relativism and reductionism:

> For it is too clear that intelligent and fruitful discussion of the Bible begins when the judgment as to its human, its historical and psychological character has been made and *put behind* us. Would that the teachers of our high and lower schools, and with them the progressive element among the clergy of our established churches, would forthwith resolve to have done with a battle that once had its time but has now *had* it![39]

Barth attempted not to return to the past but to go through the historical science of his day to a different future that preserved its valid concerns and achievements while overcoming its inherent problematic deficiencies. These weaknesses were revealed not initially with the outbreak of the Great War but with Barth's own steps up into the pulpit, where Jesus Christ and Scripture and the proclaimed Word all meet:

> I know what it means to have to go into the pulpit year in and year out, obliged to understand and explain, and wishing to do so, yet being unable to do it because we were given almost nothing at the university except the famous "respect for history," which despite the beautiful expression means simply the renunciation of earnest, respectful understanding and explanation.[40]

---

[38]Barth, "Biblische Fragen," in *Das Wort Gottes und die Theologie*, p. 76; ET in *The Word of God and the Word of Man*, p. 60.

[39]Ibid., p. 76; ET pp. 60-61. Barth can state: "We think of John the Baptist in Grünewald's painting of the crucifixion, with his strangely pointing hand. It is this hand which is in evidence in the Bible" (p. 79; ET p. 65). See also *GD*, pp. 217-18.

[40]*Römerbrief*, p. xix; ET pp. 93-94; see also *Karl Barth—Rudolf Bultmann Letters 1922–1966*, trans. Geoffrey W. Bromiley (Edinburgh: T & T Clark, 1982), p. 154.

Barth's understanding of Scripture was thus nothing less than a conviction that God's Word must be heard and proclaimed. In his early theology, Barth was quite content to claim that this Word was heard in Scripture, the witness to this revelation. Barth was more interested in the question *that* it was heard in the church's Scripture than the question of the determination of this Scripture as a canon in distinction from other works. In fact, Barth is quite ambivalent about questions of canonical boundaries during this early period. In speaking of Scripture in his open letter to Harnack, Barth states:

> This witness, which can never be analyzed enough by historical criticism, but which will not for that reason cease being *this* witness, is what I term in its totality the "Scripture." In this the question of the delimitation of "Scripture" in reference to other writings seems to me to be a secondary one. Should a non-canonical writing contain this (but really *this*) witness to a noteworthy degree, there can be no a priori impossibility of letting this witness also speak through *it*; on the contrary. From this conclusion to the canonization of, for instance, *Faust* is a long road, which a sensible church will *not* enter on.[41]

This brief answer sufficed for the time being. Yet Barth could not ignore the question of canonical boundaries forever. Just as he had to deal with the question of the radical particularity of revelation in relation to Christology in a debate with Paul Tillich in 1923,[42] so also he would have to deal with the scandal of particularity in the question of Scripture—namely, why these books and not others? What are the criteria for establishing such a boundary? And why is this boundary maintained by the churches? He would take up these questions in a systematic way in his first cycle of dogmatic lectures in Göttingen in 1924–1925.

THE SCRIPTURE PRINCIPLE AND THE CANON

After exchanging the pastor's pulpit in Safenwil for the professor's lectern in Göttingen in 1921, Barth's interest in Scripture from a theological perspective focused upon his new discovery of the Reformed Scripture prin-

---

[41]*Offene Briefe 1909–1935*, p. 77; ET pp. 178-79.
[42]See Barth, "Von der Paradoxie des 'Positiven Paradoxes': Antworten und Fragen an Paul Tillich 1923," in *Vorträge und kleinere Arbeiten 1922–1925*, pp. 349-80; ET *Beginnings of Dialectical Theology*, pp. 134-58.

ciple.[43] This principle, which Barth describes in his early lectures on Calvin and the Reformed confessions and in his initial dogmatic lectures, entails an understanding of Scripture as the locus where God's Word is heard and revealed. Scripture is therefore set over against the tradition and dogma of the church, and over against the church itself, as their critical norm.[44] All other theological constructions, whether creeds, confessions or the writings of individual church figures of the past, are thus relativized insofar as they point beyond themselves to the revelation that comes in Scripture, and to which such works can only attest. They do possess an authority for the church, but theirs is a relative rather than absolute authority. As Barth articulates the Scripture principle: "*The church recognizes the rule of its proclamation solely in the Word of God and finds the Word of God solely in Holy Scripture.*"[45] Put negatively, Barth can claim that "to say that scripture is God's Word is to say that we do not know Christ outside or alongside scripture but only in scripture."[46]

Scripture thus serves positively as the locus of the spoken voice of Christ through the Spirit and thereby the basis for the hearing church's own proclamation and confession, and critically as the norm by which all proclamation and confession are tested. Barth could even proclaim that the Scripture principle is the "article upon which the church stands and falls."[47] According to Barth, it is the Scripture principle that distinguishes Protestantism from Roman Catholicism, for the latter's church principle sees Scripture as the source of later tradition but as itself standing within tradition's stream, so that Scripture and later tradition stand as two sources of authority, whereas for the former, Scripture stands over against later tra-

---

[43]For Barth's discovery of this principle, see Matthias Freudenberg, *Karl Barth und die reformierte Theologie: Die Auseinandersetzung mit Calvin, Zwingli und den reformierten Bekenntnisschriften während seiner Göttinger Lehrtätigkeit* (Neukirchen: Neukirchener Verlag, 1997), pp. 238-45; cf. McCormack, *Barth's Theology*, pp. 305-7, 317-18. For Barth's theological development in Göttingen, see (in addition to Freudenberg) John Webster, *Barth's Earlier Theology: Four Studies* (London: T & T Clark, 2005).

[44]*GD*, pp. 201-62. Barth later distilled and developed this material in the 1925 essay "Das Schriftprinzip der reformierten Kirche." See *Vorträge und kleinere Arbeiten 1922-1925*, pp. 500-544.

[45]*TRC*, p. 41; see also pp. 54, 55; cf. "Schriftprinzip," p. 504.

[46]*GD*, p. 215.

[47]*TRC*, p. 41; cf. p. 64. Barth can elsewhere say: "The Reformation stands or falls with its scripture principle. If we really draw back here, I do not see why tomorrow we should not become Roman Catholics again" (*GD*, p. 212).

dition as over against a great divide, different from it in quality, and not only in chronological priority.[48] Barth is certainly aware that Scripture itself is the product of a tradition, but as written text it serves as a witness to revelation in a way that later tradition does not, and thus it stands on the side of Christ and his time over against the church. Without this separation and distinction between Scripture and later tradition, Barth insists, Christ and church are conflated and identified, and insofar as this occurs, the "church is simply affirming itself when it affirms Christ, and it is simply talking to itself when it pretends to be listening to the Spirit or speaking in Christ's name."[49] Such a church can never hear the voice of Christ as a word of judgment—but neither can it hear a true word of grace. Such a word can be heard only where the church acknowledges that it hears the voice of its Lord, and not its own voice, through the words of Scripture, and thus Scripture must stand over the church as a canon, that is, as a rule and norm for its faith, a "ruler or plumb line or rule."[50] To fail in this acknowledgment is for the church not to know the Bible as Holy Scripture (in "infinite qualitative distinction from other writings").[51] It is to fail to see the limitation of its own real earthly authority and to acknowledge such authority as circumscribed by and placed under a higher one.[52]

Scripture therefore stands between the incarnate Word of God, Jesus Christ, and the Word of God proclaimed by the church, as the Word of God written, the witness to Christ and to God's revelation in him.[53] Barth contends that insofar as this distinction is made, Scripture plays a role in the Reformed tradition (and Protestantism generally) that it does not play in Catholicism where the church is an extension of the incarnation and revelation itself. For the Reformers, Christ and church are distinct and irreversibly related, and Scripture stands over the church as the voice of Christ in the present. It is the bridge needed between revelation and the church; for

---

[48]See *GD*, pp. 204-11. Whether Barth's criticism of Roman Catholicism can directly apply to Roman Catholicism after Vatican II is a valid question to ask, but there can be no question that it did apply to the Tridentine Catholicism of his day when he wrote these words. That it remains a question for today is witnessed in the prior chapter.

[49]Ibid., p. 209.

[50]Ibid., p. 212.

[51]Ibid., p. 210.

[52]Ibid., pp. 245-46.

[53]"Schriftprinzip," p. 520.

Catholicism, there is no bridge because there is no chasm. Instead of an insuperable ditch between Christ and the church, there is rather a continuity.[54] The recognition of this chasm is yet another way to speak of the Scripture principle.

This chasm between Scripture and all other theological works is why Reformed theology rejects any Catholic notion of "continuous succession," such that Scripture is simply the first source, or the primary source, of a larger revelatory body.[55] It is in fact better thought of as a witness than a source.[56] And it is not first and foremost a witness to the historic cultural thought forms of ancient times and inner thought of its authors (though it is this, too), but to the reality of God himself.[57] Historical considerations must be addressed, for the Bible is a product of history, and as previously seen Barth has no time for a static dictation theory of Scripture that flattens out the very distinctions between the divine and the human he has sought so hard to distinguish and preserve.[58] Yet because the Bible is not only a historical artifact but also a testimony to God's revelation in Christ and thus a vehicle for revelation to us through the Holy Spirit, Scripture itself is rightly called the Word of God:

> The Word of God is the witness of the *revelation* of God, of the *new* relation with humans created by God, special, direct, unique, actual, conquering the chasm of the fall. It is not the revelation of the *relationship to infinity* of *human* consciousness but of *God's thoughts become finite*, of Jesus Christ. The Word of God to us who are neither prophets nor apostles is the witness of the old and new covenant of this Jesus Christ, the Holy Scriptures. In this form, as prophetic and apostolic word, the eternal Word of God penetrates into our world.[59]

If this is true, however, the Scripture principle itself cannot be established

---

[54]See ibid., pp. 520-22, 525; also *GD*, pp. 202-4.

[55]*TRC*, p. 46. Barth sees this as fundamental in Reformed thought of the sixteenth and seventeenth centuries in contrast to both Catholic and Lutheran understandings of Scripture: "According to the Reformed view, the Word of God is the plan of the entire house and not merely its lowest floor" (p. 45).

[56]"Schriftprinzip," p. 516. In relation to the church's own life, Barth can state that Scripture is not a source but law (*Gesetz*) (p. 525).

[57]*GD*, pp. 215-16.

[58]Ibid., pp. 216-17. Such a theory of Scripture truly makes it a "paper pope," according to Barth, "from which we get oracles as we get shoes from a shoemaker" (p. 217).

[59]*TRC*, p. 46.

a priori by appealing to a more fundamental criterion external to Scripture but is itself established *a posteriori* only insofar as it is the recognition and formal acknowledgment of the church's actual hearing of the Word of God in Scripture. There is on this account an inescapable circularity to the church's claims regarding Scripture as the Word of God. Yet such circularity is not vicious, for God breaks into it and establishes Scripture as his chosen word of self-communication that the church can only confess. The Scripture principle is thus better thought of as resting on an acknowledgment than on an argument. It is a discovery, not a deduction, regarding Scripture.[60]

Therefore, the authority of Scripture for Barth rests not in external criteria of either reason or tradition, but, as it did for Calvin, on the internal testimony of the Holy Spirit. This is what is meant by saying that Scripture is self authenticating—that knowledge of God, like salvation, comes through God alone, so that the Spirit who speaks through Scripture is the Spirit who works in us to hear and understand its truth.[61] This revelation of God is distinguished from the words of Scripture but not separated from them, so that the union of divine and human word entails that Scripture itself is rightly called the Word of God and is this before it becomes so in our reading.[62] "The reality of revelation is indirectly identical

---

[60]See ibid., pp. 46, 55, 56-57, 59. "With the statement, 'It is God's Word!' we have arrived apparently at the point where the scriptural principle seems to be grounded on its groundlessness, or better, it is grounded in God alone. For *only* in God, and on no other grounds, can it be established that there is Word of God, and that this or that word is a Word of God" (pp. 56-57; cf. *GD*, p. 222). For Barth, this conviction is the greatest weakness, and greatest strength, of the Reformed understanding of Scripture, and he sees it as a loss, rather than a gain, when other criteria (fulfillment of prophecies, superiority of style, factual inerrancy, literary uniqueness, moral refinement, et al.) came to be used in Protestant scholasticism as establishing Scripture's truth and authority. See *TRC*, pp. 58-64; *GD*, pp. 220-22; see also note 35 above.

[61]*TRC*, pp. 59, 62-64; *GD*, pp. 222-26; "Schriftprinzip," p. 508.

[62]All misreadings (and there are many) of Barth's view of Scripture that criticize it as inherently subjective, that take Barth to teach that we make the Bible God's Word in our reading of it, fail precisely in overlooking Barth's clear answer on this score: "Let us begin at once with the unavoidable insight that the Bible cannot come to be God's Word if it is not this already" (*GD*, p. 219). Barth would consistently hold to this conviction from this point onward ("Scripture is recognized as the Word of God by the fact that it *is* the Word of God"; see *CD* I/2, p. 537). This criticism of subjectivity, so often repeated in American conservative circles past and present, misses Barth's central affirmations regarding Scripture. Barth's doctrine of Scripture, like any doctrine of any theologian, certainly should fall under critical scrutiny. But while some arguments of it may be incisive, this one will not wash, and perhaps most similar criticisms would be dispelled if the following were kept in view and rightfully understood: "The Word of God is

with the reality of the Bible"—indirectly, because the Bible is one thing
and revelation another, but identical, because revelation appears and
occurs for us not in itself but in the words and sentences of the Bible.
Revelation is always an embodied event.[63] This embodiment is actualized
by the Holy Spirit, so that the humanity of Christ, the words of Scripture
and the spoken words of the church's proclamation are taken up to
become the means of God's revelation, yet they are joined with revelation
without confusion and without change but also without division and
without separation.[64]

Such a view of Scripture raises numerous questions and difficulties, and
not only because of its highly dialectical character. Though we are here re-
signed to let most pass by without comment, one in particular exercises us
at this point. If the canon of Scripture stands over all extracanonical confessions and ecclesial decisions, this entails that the church's decision of the past
that determined the extent of the canon cannot be the ultimate criterion for
the canon itself. The boundaries of the canon on this view cannot be set for
all time by means of such a past decision. The bifurcation of Scripture and
tradition entails that the canon is not solely to be thought of as the product
of tradition (though of course it is this too) but is itself a decision reaffirmed
by each generation as it reads Scripture and hears God's Word in it. The
canon is then, according to Barth's view, not only the result of a past decision
but also is the confession by the church in the present that these books, and
not others, truly bear to us the voice of God in Christ. Barth can therefore
conclude after considering the Reformed confessions and their listing of the
books of the canon (which do not diverge from the traditional list) that this

---

the witness of the *revelation* of God, of the *new* relation with humans created by God, special,
direct, unique, actual, conquering the chasm of the fall. . . . The Word of God to us who are
neither prophets nor apostles is the witness of the old and new covenant of this Jesus Christ, the
Holy Scriptures. In this form, as prophetic and apostolic word, the eternal Word of God pene-
trates into our world" (*TRC*, p. 46).

[63]See "Schriftprinzip," pp. 515, 517; also *GD*, pp. 215-16.

[64]See "Schriftprinzip," p. 538. Once again, not withstanding the critical scrutiny of Barth's doctrine
of Scripture that is warranted, conservative critics of Barth's dialectical understanding of Scripture will have to articulate their own manner of distinguishing God and Scripture, Christ and
the Bible. Perhaps this need can be manifested by asking (even if simplistically) why we worship
God and not the Bible, the Christ of Scripture but not Scripture itself. If such distinctions *should*
be made, then we are not far from understanding the necessity of Barth's concerns even if some
may disagree with his conclusions, and this itself could only lead to a more open stance toward
evaluating his project.

"express or silent confirmation of the biblical canon may perhaps be called the fundamental act of Reformed confessing."[65]

Yet this answer itself raises a further question. We might ask, "Can this voice of God be heard in other books outside of the traditional canon?" Here Barth's answer may surprise us, for Barth's answer, in brief, is that the canon is in fact open rather than closed in principle, even if such openness is qualified in such a way to effect its closure in practice. This answer brings us to the heart of Barth's systematic teaching on the canon in his first dogmatic lectures.

First, Barth states that theoretically the canon could be extended, and he provides hypothetical examples of this, such as if a lost letter to the Corinthians would be found or if an ecumenical council formally adopted the *Didache*. Nevertheless, Barth argues, such would be an enlargement of the canon of the past according to its own criteria, not an extension of it by an inclusion of later works of the church (a point that is perhaps more apparent with Barth's first rather than second example).[66]

More serious is the question of including entirely other works in the category of revelation on a par with Scripture, if not within the Christian canon itself. Barth here mentions Socrates as an example of such a prophet or apostle who some, like Zwingli, saw as a witness to the true God. Barth is circumspect on this point and does not close off this avenue *tout court* but states that caution must be exercised on both sides, for the canon itself draws attention to *witnessing* pagans and not just witness *to* pagans (for example, Melchizedek of Salem and the wise men).[67] Yet these are witnesses to the true revelation—and, Barth asks, is this really true of Socrates (or Lao-Tse or Buddha)? This for Barth is the crucial dividing line:

> We have properly no reason to maintain the absoluteness of Christianity. It is revelation that is absolute. Who is to say that it could not come as well to those whose voices we do not hear in the canon? The canon, the witness to revelation, cannot be thought of as closed in principle. Nevertheless, before we extend it even hypothetically, we must remember what we must find in such nonbiblical witnesses to revelation—if they are indeed genuine witnesses to

---

[65]*TRC*, p. 50.
[66]*GD*, pp. 15-16.
[67]Ibid., pp. 149-50.

> *revelation*—the one revelation at all events, that is, indirect communication
> of the hidden God who is as such the revealed God, God's encounter with us,
> and hence the cross and the resurrection, offense and faith. This is the issue
> of the canon, in the OT and the NT. This is what the witness to revelation, to
> the incarnation, to Christ, is all about.[68]

When we put the question this way, Barth believes, the fogginess rolls away
and canonical boundaries become more clear and distinct. It is not impossible that there may be other witnesses to this revelation ("for nothing is
impossible with God," we must remember). But where there are, "then what
we have, as in the OT and the NT, will have to be hoping, knowing, and
promising references to the incarnation. . . . Revelation in the Bible, and
whatever might be identical with it elsewhere, differs radically from all else
that might be called revelation in religious history by reason of the fact that
it is indirect communication. And indirect communication means God's
incarnation."[69] And to recognize these other persons or writings as themselves witnesses to revelation entails that we already know this revelation,
because this revelation has already occurred: "All reflection on how God *can*
reveal himself is in truth only a 'thinking after' of the fact that God *has* revealed himself."[70] Canon, Christ and revelation are thus intricately interwoven in Barth's account of Scripture, and it is evident that for Barth all
judgments about the scope of the canon are ultimately revealed as christological judgments. It is evident that Barth is more concerned with the
question of the content *of* Scripture than with canonical boundaries, and
that the first determines the second, rather than vice versa. Canonicity is for
Barth a dynamic, rather than static, quality.

   This becomes ever more clear as the Göttingen dogmatic lectures progress.
What sets the prophets and apostles apart as witnesses to revelation from
later writings is not their genius or simply their historical or physical proximity to Jesus, for one could imagine a contemporary who portrayed Jesus
as a deluded messianic figure. What makes them stand on the side of Christ
over against all later church history is, rather, their divinely appointed vocation as contemporary witnesses to the truth of the revelation of God that

---

[68]Ibid., p. 150.
[69]Ibid., pp. 150-51.
[70]Ibid., p. 151.

has come in Israel and Jesus Christ, and through whose witness the church continues to receive Christ in its midst. It is this that is the ultimate explanation of their canonicity, and the decision of church councils in determining the canon is the penultimate explanation of their status as such. For this reason, the theological divide between those who do and those who do not realize Christ's true identity is greater and more significant than any temporal divide between either the prophets' and Jesus' time or between his time and ours.[71] Even though Christ is present to the apostles in a way that he was not to the prophets of the Old Testament, this does not lessen the miracle of their faith. Many saw Jesus in his day, and most did not believe. Faith is not a matter of physical or temporal proximity, though the apostles' status as special witnesses is not divorced from this proximity and their knowledge of God's revelation through the earthly history of Jesus. Barth is well aware that seeing in not believing, and that historical reconstruction, no matter how necessary, valuable and successful, is inadequate for confession.

So the prophets and apostles do stand in a special proximity to Christ, though this proximity rests more on divine vocation and faith than simple contemporaneity. As special and unrivaled witnesses, we need not insist that they are the only witnesses, however. Indeed, it may even be the case that we might learn more from other witnesses to the gospel, or be brought to faith by reading later Christian authors rather than the Bible itself. Barth fully concedes as much in a passage worthy of extended quotation:

> In terms of experience there are few among us who do not have to confess in all honesty that we have been placed before the reality of revelation much more impressively and clearly by some such later witness, for example, Luther, or it may be a little, unknown witness, than by Paul or John, not to speak of Jude or the Apocalyptist, or one of the in some ways very odd witnesses of the OT. A professor of theology once told me that he had learned much more from his devout mother than from the whole Bible. To this our reply must be that recognition of the special dignity of the biblical witnesses is not a matter of one experience among others. It is all very well to realize, perhaps, that one may learn more from all kinds of greater or lesser prophets or apostles of a later period, or even of our own time, than from reading the Bible. Yet the issue is not where we learn most, but where we learn the one thing, the truth.

---

[71]Ibid., p. 147.

> It is not a matter of arguing that the Bible is the finest book, but that it is the standard of all fine books.[72]

The Bible is this standard precisely because it is the canon, the witness by which all other witnesses are judged as to their truth in light of the revelation of Christ which comes to us in this witness as in no other and which grants these latter witnesses their authority. There is an unfolding of authority in Barth's thought, from the absolute authority of Christ, to the canon which stands with him as the second form of the Word of God, to these later witnesses, whose authority is relative and rests on their fidelity to Scripture. Should one ask, then, whether one might not appeal directly to Christ, the source of all authority, Barth maintains that such is an appeal for what is not given, that is, an *immediate* authority. No, for us who come after the prophets and the apostles, Christ is in heaven, and we are on earth. The church cannot seize him across this divide (which is eschatological, not temporal) in a bid for an immediate revelation, and thus the dissolution of revelation itself. But Christ himself does bridge this divide and lives in the church, and he does so through the Spirit who speaks through the words of his witnesses who form a united witness, Holy Scripture. If we understand this, Barth states, then we understand the canon as not only the first witness in time, but the first witness in principle.[73] This is yet another form of the Scripture principle itself.

Further questions remain, however. Is it not the church that has established the boundary of this witness, and thus established what is to be included within the canon of Scripture? This must certainly be admitted, Barth concedes.[74] The determination of the canon is not the domain of private judgment. In point of fact, individuals and even individual Christians may have all manner of thoughts as to the contents of Scripture as it stands or what it should include.[75] But though the canon is in fact "not

---

[72]Ibid., p. 213.

[73]Ibid., pp. 214-15.

[74]Ibid., pp. 232ff. Barth states that the church determines both the boundaries of Scripture and the text of Scripture (textual criticism); see pp. 234-37.

[75]"We may regret it that the *Didache* or Luther's *Freedom of a Christian Man* or various other good works that the church may profitably read are *not* holy scripture. We need not regard the verdict that pronounces Yes and No in this matter as God's verdict. We may even have divergent private opinions and prefer them to this verdict. Nevertheless, we have to realize that all divergent opinions in this matter are in fact private opinions and do not have authority as such. The Word

assembled privately by individuals but collected by the church as such, by the historical fellowship of all those who receive God's Word in this literature,"[76] its boundaries are nonetheless the result of decision, albeit an ecclesial rather than private one, and Barth does not deny this. Nevertheless, invoking an old Protestant point in a new manner, Barth insists that it is the Holy Spirit who leads the church to recognize Holy Scripture, not to establish it as such. Canonization is a matter not so much of decision and authority but of faith and obedience. That the canon is a matter of faith and obedience is precisely why the affirmation of the canon rests on a recognition that must be made by each new generation, and why the authority of the canon cannot rest on a past ecclesiastical conciliar decision, no matter how old or ecumenical in scope. It is also why an extension of the canon cannot be ruled out in principle, for the delimitation of the canon rests ultimately on the free work of the Spirit and not on a past council. Nevertheless, for the canon to be enlarged would require not a private judgment, even if it is a judgment by a trained, knowledgeable historian, or even a bevy of expert historians. It would, rather, "have to be an act of the church as such, an act of faith."[77] Any such decision to modify the canon would be predicated on the church's having come to an understanding of a work not only as contemporary with the time of Jesus but also as apostolic:

> The mark of canonicity for the NT works was obviously the concept of apostolicity. It was not that of antiquity, of historical credibility, or of the closest proximity to Jesus. The name of Paul, which governs much of the NT, makes the latter qualifications of apostolicity quite impossible, not to speak of such disciples of the apostles as Mark and Luke. A person is an apostle, and can qualify for the canon, as a witness of the risen Lord, not as a historical eyewitness. Hence the church needs the Spirit and faith, and not historical research, to decide what is canonical and what is not.[78]

---

of God comes to us with historical authority within the confines of the canon, *this* canon" (ibid., p. 234). In the later *Church Dogmatics*, Barth would give even more weight to the necessity of appealing to the decisions of the church over private judgment (see Barth's discussion of the canon in *CD* I/2, pp. 597-660).

[76]*GD*, p. 233.

[77]Ibid. See note 85 below.

[78]Ibid. Elsewhere Barth writes: "What made the NT a *holy* book in the eyes of the church, alongside the OT, was not its relation to the period A.D. 1-30 but its relation to the content of this period, to the reality of revelation, to God's encounter with us, to the concrete event of the in-

With this we come to the end of this historical investigation and discover the unity of Barth's thought regarding questions of Scripture and canon. For Barth, the question of Scripture's meaning and that of the canon's boundaries fall under a common form of thought. While historical criticism can allow us to approach both, and both are dependent on historical investigation, the ultimate judgments of Scripture's meaning as well as its canonical boundaries are not made by the disinterested historian but by the confessing church. Certainly the church must listen to the historian (and, of course, the historian may stand within the church and profess its faith) and even be open to correction of its historical reconstruction of the past. Yet regardless of this indispensable role in reconstructing the history of both text and canon, the historian cannot establish such texts as witnesses or establish the revelation they proclaim and confess. This is something the church can recognize only in faith. While the canon cannot be divorced from the history that produced it, the question of the canon is for Barth ultimately a question of confession and theological discernment, rather than historical inquiry.

In the end, the canon is nothing more than the church's judgment that in these books (and really in these, and in these unlike in others), the Word of God has been heard, Christ has become present and the Spirit's truth has become known. This judgment of the canon is not final. It is not absolute. It must be made again and again. But it is nothing less than the church's judgment as it rests on the Spirit and faith, and as such it

> is an authority with all the weight which accrues historically to such a unanimous and universal act of faith on the church's part, with all the weight of that which preceded our own faith and that of those who were before us. In calling us to faith, the church sets the canon before us as a reflection of the loneliness and isolation of God himself: This is holy scripture, not all kinds of things, but this in particular.[79]

So while the canon is not closed in principle, for *all* ecclesial decisions (even pertaining to the canon itself) stand under Scripture and remain open to revision, some are settled for all practicality. When the nature of the canon is rightly understood, it is seen to be closed in practice, and it may indeed

---

carnation at the center, not the relation to the historical Jesus as such but the relation to the crucified and risen Jesus" (p. 149).

[79]Ibid., p. 234.

be closed in reality, for even the ancient church's decision, as weighty as it stands with its universal consensus, is not the final arbiter of the matter:

> To work through our definitions once again, a criticism of the canon, an angry call to reduce or increase what we now call holy scripture, is by no means an inconceivable possibility. The canon did not fall from heaven. The church and the church alone fixed it. But the church is not a final court. Above it stands scripture as the Word of God by which the church is established. . . . The canon will stand for long enough yet against the "it seems to me" of some agitators.[80]

With this, Barth's understanding of the canon was in place. It would undergo further development and enrichment, but Barth would not retract the basic principles that undergirded it and which were developed in these early years of his teaching career.[81]

CONCLUSION: THINKING WITH AND AFTER . . .

To evaluate Barth's rich understanding of Scripture and canon developed during his first professorate demands more than a brief conclusion. Yet we can make provisional judgments with an eye on his understanding of the canon in particular.

No doubt Barth's early doctrine of Scripture and canon is marked by a theological understanding that is remarkably set above historical details, details that betray a messy process of canon formation, and a process much better understood today than when Barth developed his understanding of Scripture nearly a century ago. The formation of the canon is not as neat and tidy as one might believe having read only Barth's discussion in his early dogmatics.[82]

It is important to note, though, that an increasing knowledge of the messiness of the historical process by which the church's canon was formed does not undermine Barth's understanding of the canon itself, for Barth's dialec-

---

[80]Ibid., pp. 246-47.

[81]For Barth's later development of these questions, see *Die christliche Dogmatik im Entwurf: Die Lehre vom Worte Gottes*, ed. Gerhard Sauter (Zürich: Theologischer Verlag Zürich, 1982); *CD* I/2: *The Doctrine of the Word of God*.

[82]For the complex history of the formation of the biblical canon, see Lee M. McDonald, *The Biblical Canon: Its Origin, Transmission and Authority* (Peabody, MA: Hendrickson, 2007); also the essays in *The Canon Debate*, ed. Lee M. McDonald and James A. Sanders (Peabody, MA: Hendrickson, 2002).

tical understanding of Scripture as the product of divine action and human history pertains not only to its composition but also to its collection, and if Barth was not threatened by radical criticism in regard to the former, it is hard to imagine that he would be threatened by it with regard to the latter. The collecting of the books of the Bible, like their earlier composition, is without question the result of a long and extremely complicated history. The ancient church's canonical selection process was the result of human action and decision, marked and marred by human limitations. The canon did not, Barth states, fall ready from the sky. In fact, the problems of tracing the history of collection and canonization are in all likelihood as complex as the problems related to tracing the history of the biblical texts' composition and redaction. Yet Scripture's authority is not undermined by such historical disorderliness but comes to the church precisely through it.[83] As Barth often remarked regarding a host of issues, *"Hominum confusione et Dei providentia."* The more enduring question is how historical investigation and theological formulation are to relate to one another, an answer addressed but not fully answered by Barth.

A second issue is that the canonical boundaries may appear to us to be less clear than in Barth's time, especially in relation to recent work in canon studies and discoveries such as the influence of extrabiblical sources on the biblical writers. It is a far way, however, from recognizing this influence and allowing it to inform our understanding of Scripture, to canonizing such sources themselves. Without facetiousness of any kind, we might say that it has long been recognized that Paul (or Luke, or whomever wrote Acts, it matters not) draws on Epimenides and Aratus in the Mars Hill address of Acts 17, but only someone lacking any sense of proportion would see this as calling for the church's canonization of Stoicism. This itself may cast light on more difficult cases, such as Jude's use of *Enoch*.

---

[83]What should also be said is that tracing the historical development of the canon was in Barth's view the domain of biblical, rather than dogmatic, theology. In the Göttingen dogmatic lectures, Barth saw himself as providing a doctrine, not a history, of Scripture. Barth's neglect of historical details regarding the development of the canon is better understood as a division of labor within church theology, rather than as a disdain for such historical work altogether. Such historical reconstruction is presupposed by dogmatics. Yet it must be added that Barth would no doubt see the conclusions of such historical investigation regarding the canon's development as at best an abstraction that fails to understand the true nature of the canon when such investigation is separated from larger theological concerns.

More importantly, what truly is unfortunately missing from Barth's early discussion of the canon is a serious appraisal of the disagreements between Christian communions themselves as regards the scope of the canon (for example, the inclusion within Roman Catholicism and exclusion within Protestantism of the Apocrypha).[84]

Third, the process of canonization is now known to have been marked by a decision-making process of sifting and not by tidy and uncomplicated recognition, as Barth's exposition in his first dogmatics at times seems to imply. Books like Hebrews, 2 Peter, 2 and 3 John and Revelation (among others) were disputed and were not simply recognized without comment by all of the churches. Yet without smoothing over difficulties in Barth's viewpoint or overlooking the difficult exceptions of such books at the boundaries, we can say that Barth's understanding of the canon coincides with those who conclude that the canonization process was not so much the church deciding for a canon, as its recognition of books already considered Scripture and included within its worship and liturgy.[85] The exceptions should not overshadow the rule, which was that the Gospels, Paul's letters, and most books of our current New Testament were recognized by the churches as Scripture and used within the liturgy from the second century onward. Barth himself states that not all books are of equal character and perspicacity, though all point in various ways to a common theme.

Fourth, Barth's view of the canon as open may be seen by some as undermining the very notion of canon itself.[86] Barth maintains that the canon being open entails that the exclusion of current books, as well as the inclusion of new books, is a possibility. Such an inclusion, however, would require a universal consensus of the church, and in the case of exclusion, a recognition by the church that the Spirit no longer speaks in the book under consideration. Barth states that when the history of the church is in

---

[84]For a discussion of this question in relation to Barth's understanding of the canon and in contemporary New Testament scholarship, see chapter six below. See also the very insightful discussion in Brevard Childs, *Biblical Theology of the Old and New Testaments: Theological Reflection on the Christian Bible* (Minneapolis: Fortress, 1993), pp. 66-68.

[85]McDonald, *Formation of the Biblical Canon*, pp. 64-65; see also Bruce Metzger, *The Canon of the New Testament: Its Origin, Development and Significance* (Oxford: Clarendon Press, 1987), pp. 237-38.

[86]See Eugene Ulrich, "The Notion and Definition of Canon," in McDonald and Sanders, *Canon Debate*, pp. 21-35.

view, a history in which these books, and these books like no others, have nourished the church's faith, momentary disputes become just that, and inclusion and exclusion become for all intents and purposes an impossibility, so that the canon is effectively closed, though it cannot be closed in principle.[87] What is important to see is why Barth speaks of an open canon. It is open solely and simply because ultimately it is the Spirit, and not a church decision, which determines what is and is not Scripture and thus what is to be included in the canon. Such is a radical *ecclesia semper reformanda* upheld even in regard to canonicity itself. The ultimate determination of the canon is revelation, not tradition. Yet Barth recognizes the weight of the ancient church's decision and confession regarding discernment in this matter (and its subsequent confirmation by all succeeding generations), and he finds it difficult to imagine circumstances that would mandate a change of the canon and an overturning of the church's past decision. For this reason, for all intents and purposes the canon is closed, though it remains open in principle.

Finally, what may be most controversial is Barth's christological understanding of the canon. Such a position may seem readily apparent with the New Testament, but less so with the Old, and most difficult with regard to the Wisdom literature. Yet it could be argued that despite difficulties, Barth's weakness is in fact his greatest strength, for it is precisely by locating the unity of the canon in God's revelation in Christ rather than in any specific unifying concept or theme that Barth is able to prevent the schism of the Old and the New Testament. Anyone who believes that Barth's christological orientation regarding the canon rends the unity of the Old and New Testaments asunder should be reminded that not only does Barth himself refuse such a division, but also that he was kept from this and not insignificantly from the rampant anti-Semitism of his time (evident even among many of his colleagues) by his ceaseless proclamation that the Christ of the New Testament is the Christ of the Old, and that (as he put this point in a famous sermon of 1933 in which a large part of the congregation in Germany stood up and left in disgust) "Jesus Christ was a Jew."[88] It was precisely this understanding of Jesus as both God's Son and

---

[87]*GD*, p. 247.
[88]Busch, *Karl Barth*, pp. 234-35.

Israel's Son, as both divine and human that entailed that Barth could see no wedge however narrow between the Old Testament and the New, and why he accepted the judgment of Judaism regarding its Scriptures, which became for the church its Old Testament, and which, Barth argued, the church rightly received from the synagogue.[89] To divide the Testaments is for Barth tantamount to committing a christological heresy, and history here is on the side of Barth. In his time, Jülicher judged Barth to be a Marcionite, yet it was Harnack the scientific historian, not Barth the pneumatic exegete, who ultimately tipped his hand in this direction.[90] On this question as well, Barth's position seems to coincide and concur with what historical investigation has discovered: that Jesus Christ was the early church's canon, and the Old and New Testament became the canon as a witness to him.[91]

It is in fact reasonable to conclude that, regardless of any necessary criticisms of Barth, his approach to Scripture remains compelling and is gaining rather than losing ground among many in North America. Many within biblical studies in the United States and elsewhere are moving toward rather than away from Barth's position on the unity of Scripture, and his criticisms of Harnack's arguments (or others like his) have become so forceful in their reverberation in the course of time that their echo can be heard among

---

[89]GD, p. 233.

[90]"The rejection of the Old Testament during the second century A.D. would have been a mistake, which the great Church rightly refused to make. Its retention in the sixteenth century was a fate from which the Reformation was not yet able to extricate itself. Its conservation as a canonical document for Protestantism since the nineteenth century is the consequence of a religious and ecclesiastical paralysis" (Harnack, *Marcion* [Leipzig: J. C. Hinrichs Verlag, 1924], p. 217, quoted in Rumscheidt, *Revelation and Theology*, p. 98). Unfortunately for Harnack, some of his later heirs took him seriously. Martin Hengel rightly pronounces judgment on this trajectory: "The Marcionitism of neo-Protestantism since the Enlightenment and German Idealism were a pernicious wrong turning" ("'Salvation History': The Truth of Scripture and Modern Theology," in *Reading Texts, Seeking Wisdom: Scripture and Theology*, ed. David F. Ford and Graham Stanton [Grand Rapids: Eerdmans, 2003], p. 242). For an expansion on these reflections, see chapter six below.

[91]McDonald argues that "during the formative years of the early church Jesus was the church's primary canon par excellence and that the biblical tradition (the OT scriptures) gave witness to that canon" (*The Formation of the Christian Biblical Canon*, rev. ed. [Peabody, MA: Hendrickson, 1995], p. 95; see also pp. 153, 189). The larger point here made is in no way negated even should we adopt a more narrow definition of "canon" as a closed list of sacred books; see Ulrich, "Notion and Definition of Canon," pp. 34-35. For a judgment similar to that of McDonald and which coincides with this discussion, see James D. G. Dunn, "Has the Canon a Continuing Function?" in McDonald and Sanders, *Canon Debate*, pp. 560-62.

others looking for a new way forward for biblical interpretation.[92] Moreover, a case can be made that the trajectory from Barth's own hermeneutical program of *Nachdenken* and *Mitdenken* in the *Romans* prefaces (set over against the *Sachkritik* of Bultmann and others like him) to Richard Hays's "hermeneutics of trust" (set over against those practitioners of a "hermeneutics of suspicion") is a strikingly straight line.[93] Hays is appealing for a renewed consideration, as Barth did in the preface to the second edition of *Romans*, that the Bible be seen as a good book, and that it be taken at least as seriously as we take our own experience and cultural assumptions.

It is the fruitfulness of Barth's approach for challenging our own oftentimes narrow understandings of Scripture and canon that is his enduring legacy, regardless of any perceived or real historical deficiencies. What Barth draws our attention to is that biblical questions, whether regarding historical composition or collection, or regarding questions of interpretation or canonical authority, can be separated from neither the larger context of the church's proclamation nor the claims regarding its center in Jesus Christ. Questions of canon are thus questions not only of history and authority but also of an authoritative center that binds these discrete and various books into a unity rather than a ragtag collection. In addition, for the canon to be more than of historical interest, this unity must be more than an accident of ecclesiastical whim or power politics. Questions of canon are always related to claims about Christ and the church's proclamation, as well as the understanding of these in terms of an ongoing tradition of interpretation and development.

The concept of the canon is therefore theological rather than solely historical. It implies a unity, authority and function as the basis and guide for the proclamation, confession and belief of the Christian community.

---

[92]See, for example, the essays in *The Art of Reading Scripture*, ed. Ellen F. Davis and Richard B. Hays (Grand Rapids: Eerdmans, 2003), as well as those in *Reading Texts, Seeking Wisdom*. For a brief introduction to recent trends in scriptural interpretation along parallel lines, see Daniel J. Treier, *Introducing Theological Interpretation of Scripture: Recovering a Christian Practice* (Grand Rapids: Baker Academic, 2008). See also Francis Watson, *Text, Church and World: Biblical Interpretation in Theological Perspective* (Grand Rapids: Eerdmans, 1994); Watson, *Text and Truth: Redefining Biblical Theology* (Grand Rapids: Eerdmans, 1997).

[93]See Richard B. Hays, *The Conversion of the Imagination: Paul as Interpreter of Israel's Scripture* (Grand Rapids: Eerdmans, 2005), pp. 190-201. When one reads these pages, one hears in this debate of today a new and vibrant echo of Barth's early debates with Harnack and Bultmann transposed into a new and different, but nevertheless related, key.

Without such a theological understanding, the canon itself is separated from the church that reads it and its intrinsic unity is sacrificed, a unity not found in a particular doctrinal perspective or viewpoint. In fact, quite the opposite is true, for it is the diversity of Scripture that strikes us on a first reading. It is the church that confesses that, in spite of all of the trials of interpretation and understanding in the midst of this real and irreducible variety, through the cacophony of voices we come to hear one voice, a voice that kills and makes alive, a voice the church believes and obeys in the midst of its own struggles, doubts and fears.

In the end, the question of the canon is intrinsically related to the contingency of revelation and the inescapable scandal of particularity: that God's revelation comes to us in a particular medium—in Jesus Christ, in these particular books, in this particular proclamation. This necessitates that the Christian question of canon is not confined to an investigation of its historical development. Nor is the question of the canon exhausted by discerning its moral usefulness (Bennett) or aristocratic aesthetic quality (Bloom).[94] It is, rather, the question of where God has spoken and does speak. It points not to a possibility but to the reality of having heard God in *this* community through *this* Scripture attesting *this* Lord, Jesus Christ. Attempting to present the historic Reformed viewpoint and simultaneously articulating his own position, though one that so much needs to be rediscovered and reproclaimed by the church in this day of vague, amorphous, effervescent yet everywhere-present spirituality, Barth states that

> The isolatedness of God generates the isolatedness of his revelation. *Revelation* is not this and that, not everything and anything, but rather this definitive, incomparable one thing. Therefore, legitimate witness to revelation cannot be any random human word about God but rather this definite human word about God, which the prophets and apostles were called by God and equipped to say.[95]

The scandal of the particularity of the canon is therefore defined not so

---

[94]William J. Bennett, *The Book of Virtues: A Treasury of Great Moral Stories* (New York: Simon and Schuster, 1993); Harold Bloom, *The Western Canon: The Books and School of the Ages* (New York: Harcourt Brace, 1994).

[95]*TRC*, pp. 48-49. Or elsewhere: "The claim that scripture is God's Word implies a selection from among all the words that are spoken around us" (*GD*, p. 231; cf. p. 60).

much by its boundaries as by its subject matter. And this subject matter, God's revelation in Christ, calls for decision. The most important decision posed by the canon, then, is not regarding its definition and contents but regarding the truth of its subject matter that calls for our faith, and this decision imposes itself on us in the twenty-first century as on those of Jesus' own day:

> No matter what our attitude to the words and the historical aspect of the witness may be, we have to regard them as transparencies through which a light shines. It shines with varying degrees of brightness and clarity—no one need argue that Jude is as powerful a witness as Romans—yet it is always a light, *the* light. Everything relates to this light, everything that we might view as a transparent medium pointing us in this direction. Even Jude is in its own way a witness to Jesus Christ and not to someone or something else. In this sense—and again the understanding of the historical element is a secondary concern—everything is truth. There is no possibility of regarding scripture as merely historical. There is no possibility of folding our arms and adopting the stance of onlookers or spectators. The only possibility is that of seriousness, of decision, of being taken captive, of faithfulness, of an act of supreme spontaneity.[96]

Any theology that attempts to remain faithful in our own time and place among so many competing voices could do worse than to begin its reflection here.

---

[96]*GD*, p. 254.

6

Christ and Canon,
Theology and History

The Barth–Harnack Dialogue Revisited

✝

We live in an age in which the boundaries of the canon are questioned within the academy and the reverberation of these questions are felt within the church.[1] In order to comment on these developments, I wish to revisit the exchange between Adolf von Harnack and Karl Barth of the early twentieth century that is most often discussed regarding matters of exegesis and hermeneutics, but which I will examine with an eye toward the question of the biblical canon.[2] This conversation sheds light not only on issues regarding the content and interpretation of Scripture, but also upon its form and parameters in historical and theological conversation.

THE HARNACK-BARTH CORRESPONDENCE OF 1923

During Barth's time, there was no historian with the credentials or the achievements of Adolf von Harnack. Harnack's erudition was and remains

---

This chapter appeared in an earlier form as "Christ and Canon, Theology and History: The Barth-Harnack Dialogue Revisited," in *Theology as Conversation: The Significance of Dialogue in Historical and Contemporary Theology*, ed. Bruce L. McCormack and Kimlyn J. Bender (Grand Rapids: Eerdmans, 2009), pp. 3-29. Reprinted by permission.

[1]For two recent examples of such questioning, see Bart D. Ehrman, *Lost Christianities: The Battles for Scripture and the Faiths We Never Knew* (Oxford: Oxford University Press, 2003); and Robert W. Funk, "The Once and Future New Testament," in *The Canon Debate*, ed. Lee Martin McDonald and James A. Sanders (Peabody, MA: Hendrickson, 2002), pp. 541-57.

[2]This chapter draws from the material of the previous one.

famous, and in spite of critical evaluations of his work that have appeared with the passing of time, he continues to stand as a giant of historical studies.[3] In a similar manner, no theologian of the twentieth century was as influential as Karl Barth in restoring Scripture to the center of the theological enterprise.[4] In 1923, following tensions brought about by Barth's criticisms and renunciation of the liberal inheritance he had received from his former teachers such as Harnack, what had been for the most part private tension became public debate as Harnack critically questioned the dialectical movement, and thus Barth, in the pages of the *Christlichen Welt*, and Barth returned the favor in what became a spirited and extended exchange.[5]

This published conversation ranged widely in the number of issues addressed, but no small part of the debate concerned the matter of Scripture and how it should be approached and understood. Harnack's position on Scripture was shaped by and influential in shaping the liberal school of historical-critical exegesis, and in the opening salvo Harnack's primary criticism of the dialectical theologians is that they have abandoned scientific and historical exegesis for a naive biblicism. As he states in his first of fifteen questions:

> Is the religion of the Bible, or are the revelations in the Bible, something so unequivocal that in reference to faith, worship, and life it is permissible to speak simply of the "Bible"? But if they are not, can the determining of the content of the gospel be left entirely to subjective "experience," or to the "experiences" of the individual, or are not historical knowledge and critical reflection necessary here?[6]

---

[3]For an introduction into Harnack's life and work, see *Adolf von Harnack: Liberal Theology at its Height*, ed. H. Martin Rumscheidt (London: Collins, 1989), as well as G. Wayne Glick, *The Reality of Christianity: A Study of Adolf von Harnack as Historian and Theologian* (New York: Harper & Row, 1967).

[4]Richard Burnett, *Karl Barth's Theological Exegesis: The Hermeneutical Principles of the* Römerbrief *Period* (Grand Rapids: Eerdmans, 2004), p. 9; see also p. 23.

[5]This exchange between Barth and Harnack may be found in Karl Barth, *Offene Briefe 1909–1935*, ed. Diether Koch (Zürich: Theologischer Verlag Zürich, 2001), pp. 55-88; ET: *The Beginnings of Dialectical Theology*, ed. James M. Robinson, trans. Louis De Grazia and Keith R. Crim (Richmond: John Knox, 1968), pp. 165-87. For perceptive commentary on this debate, see H. Martin Rumscheidt, *Revelation and Theology: An Analysis of the Barth-Harnack Correspondence of 1925* (Cambridge: Cambridge University Press, 1972); George Hunsinger, *Disruptive Grace: Studies in the Theology of Karl Barth* (Grand Rapids: Eerdmans, 2000), pp. 319-37.

[6]Barth, *Offene Briefe 1909–1935*, p. 62; ET p. 166.

For Harnack, the content of the Bible is rightly determined and understood only by means of "historical knowledge and critical reflection."[7] The need for such historical knowledge and critical reflection (*geschichtliches Wissen und kritisches Nachdenken*) is hammered home by Harnack over and again in his questions. In the dialectical school, Harnack believed that he was witnessing a flight from history and science into the dangers of fanaticism and a resurgent gnosticism. Such a flight threatened the heart of Christian faith itself. If Christ stands at the "center of the gospel," Harnack asked, then "how can the basis for a reliable and common knowledge of this person be gained other than through critical historical study, lest we exchange the real Christ for one we have imagined? But how else can this study be accomplished than by scientific theology?"[8]

Barth responded to Harnack's fifteen questions one by one, and his answers demonstrate how far he had moved during his Safenwil pastorate from the position of his former teacher and the liberal tradition.[9] On his joyful discovery of "a new world within the Bible" during that period, Barth had turned to a redoubled study of Scripture and an attempt to understand its character.[10] Barth's new outlook is readily evident in his answers to Harnack's questions.

In response to Harnack's charge that the diversity of the Bible makes "historical knowledge and critical reflection" necessary to understand its

---

[7]Ibid, p. 60; ET p. 165.

[8]Ibid, p. 62; ET p. 166.

[9]The story of Barth's break with liberalism has been often told. See Eberhard Busch, *Karl Barth: His Life from Letters and Autobiographical Texts*, trans. John Bowden (Grand Rapids: Eerdmans, 1994), chaps. 2 and 3; Busch, *The Great Passion: An Introduction to Karl Barth's Theology*, trans. Geoffrey W. Bromiley (Grand Rapids: Eerdmans, 2004), section 1, chaps. 1 and 2; Gary Dorrien, *The Barthian Revolt in Modern Theology* (Louisville, KY: Westminster John Knox, 2000), chaps. 1 and 2; Eberhard Jüngel, *Karl Barth: A Theological Legacy*, trans. Garrett E. Paul (Philadelphia: Westminster Press, 1986), chaps. 1 and 2; Bruce L. McCormack, *Karl Barth's Critically Realistic Dialectical Theology: Its Genesis and Development 1909–1936* (Oxford: Clarendon Press, 1995), chaps. 1 and 2; and John Webster, *Karl Barth* (New York: Continuum, 2000), chaps. 1 and 2.

[10]See Barth, "Die neue Welt in der Bibel," in *Das Wort Gottes und die Theologie* (München: Chr. Kaiser Verlag, 1929), pp. 18-32; ET: "The Strange New World Within the Bible," in *The Word of God and the Word of Man*, trans. Douglas Horton (Gloucester: Peter Smith, 1978), pp. 28-50. Barth would extend these themes in his 1920 essay "Biblische Fragen, Einsichten und Ausblicke," in *Das Wort Gottes und die Theologie*, pp. 70-98; ET: "Biblical Questions, Insights and Vistas," in *Word of God and the Word of Man*, pp. 51-96. Burnett writes: "To read the Bible in a way that is '*sachlicher, inhaltlicher, wesentlicher*,' that is, 'more in accordance with its subject matter, content, and substance,' represents Karl Barth's most important hermeneutical principle" (*Karl Barth's Theological Exegesis*, p. 65; cf. p. 95).

content in the midst of its heterogeneity, Barth unflinchingly responded by saying: "Beyond the 'religion' and the 'revelations' of the Bible, the *one revelation of God* should be taken into consideration as the theme of theology."[11] For Barth, the unity of the Bible's content is not a message distilled by means of critical science, and is certainly not the reductionistic moralism that Harnack espoused but is instead grounded in the *Deus dixit*, so that theology is scientific insofar as it remembers that "its object had *previously* been the subject, and must become this again and again."[12] What becomes clear in Barth's responses to Harnack is Barth's insistence that it is not historical knowledge and critical reflection, but the power of the Spirit and the corresponding faith it establishes, that provides the true understanding of the content of Scripture, which is God's own self-revelation in Christ.[13] Historical criticism may play a part in preparation for the task of theology, which is to communicate the "word of Christ," but it is nonetheless a divine act, rather than a human achievement, that is the basis for a proper understanding of Scripture. The center of Scripture, therefore, is none other than the one to whom it testifies, and this one can properly be known for who he truly is only by an acknowledgement of his lordship, which is a true recognition of the unique objectivity of revelation that supersedes claims of a scientific method and its own abstract objectivity. As Barth writes:

> The reliability and common nature of the knowledge of the person of Jesus Christ as the midpoint of the gospel can be no other than that of a *faith* awakened by God. Critical historical study signifies the deserved and necessary end of the "bases" of this knowledge, which are not really bases, because they were not laid by God himself. He who still does not know (and we all still do not know it) that we no longer know Christ according to the flesh may let himself be told this by critical biblical science; the more radically he is terrified the better it is for him and for the subject matter. And this may well be the service which "historical knowledge" can render to the real task of theology.[14]

Harnack was not appeased by these answers. In an open letter to Barth that was published following their appearance in print, Harnack stated that

---

[11]Barth, *Offene Briefe 1909–1935*, p. 62; ET p. 167.
[12]Ibid., p. 62; ET p. 167.
[13]Ibid., p. 63; ET p. 167.
[14]Ibid., pp. 66-67; ET p. 170.

he found Barth's position flummoxing. Where Barth saw scientific theology as a recent development, Harnack asserted that it was the only means forward for "mastering an object through knowledge." By sacrificing this means, Barth was guilty of transforming the professor's chair into a pulpit and confusing the scientific task of theology with that of spiritual edification.[15] Furthermore, reiterating his initial criticisms, Harnack maintained that Barth was losing his grip on history for an ahistorical faith that would in the end prove to be nothing more than pure subjectivism. In response to Barth's prior statement that we do not know Christ "according to the flesh," Harnack trenchantly asked: "Thus we no longer know the Jesus Christ of the Gospels, the historical Jesus Christ? How am I to understand that? On the basis of the theory of the exclusive inner word? Or on the basis of one of the many other subjective theories?"[16] The only way forward if true knowledge is the goal is that of historical science; the alternative to science and reason is not faith but occultism.[17] Barth's disdain for historical science would in the end be evidenced in an absolute division of the Christ of faith from the Jesus of history. Without historical science to place parameters on our claims of this Christ and give true knowledge of the historical person of Jesus, such a faith as that of Barth's would at best give rise to unchecked speculative fantasy and at worst to a theological dictatorship that "seeks to torture the consciences of others with its own experience."[18] For Barth's theology to gain ascendancy over that of historical science would lead to nothing less, Harnack concluded, than the handing over of the gospel to revival preachers who are unhindered in their idiosyncratic understandings of the Bible.

Barth responded to this open letter with one of his own. Though initially somewhat more conciliatory in tone in this letter than in his prior answers, Barth's response displayed an unwillingness to back down in the face of Harnack's charges. Three themes of relevance for our investigation emerge: the identity of the Jesus of history with the Christ of faith; the unity of Scripture in light of this identity; and the need for an ordered unity between what Barth deems the wider task of theology (with regard to discerning the

---

[15]Ibid., p. 68; ET p. 171.
[16]Ibid., p. 69; ET p. 172.
[17]Ibid., p. 71; ET p. 174.
[18]Ibid., pp. 71-72; ET p. 174.

identity of Christ and the unity of Scripture) and historical science itself. In Barth's response the question of unity becomes a prominent theme. Where Harnack was most inclined to draw simple distinctions, such as that between the task of preaching and that of historical science, and to note simple unities, such as that between revelation and history, as well as that between the accomplishments of religion and culture, Barth's dialectical position intimated complex unities of ordered relations between permanently distinct realities even while at other times falling into simple disjunctions that his later theology would eventually move beyond. The unity of revelation and history in the person of Jesus Christ without their confusion; the unity of Scripture among its undeniable diversity of voices, such that divine Word and human word are united yet distinct; and the unity and ordered relation of theology and historical science in which the latter is taken up into the service of the former were all important, if inadequately developed, themes in Barth's response.

First, Barth turned the accusation that he had bifurcated the Jesus of history and the Christ of faith back against Harnack himself. Barth rejected Harnack's distinction between the confessed Christ of the church and the historical person of Jesus as discerned by the professional academy, a distinction that played no small part in Harnack's entire historiography and sharp inviolable division between professor's lectern and pastor's pulpit. For Barth, the Jesus of Nazareth known by historical science fails to display Jesus' true identity if abstracted from the confession of him as the risen Lord:

> The historical reality of Christ (as reality of revelation, or of the "central point of the gospel") is not the "historical Jesus," whom an all too zealous historical research had wanted to lay hold of while bypassing those warnings erected in the sources themselves (only to come upon a banality which is now and will continue to be vainly proclaimed as something precious), of course not, as you said, an "imagined" Christ, but rather the *Risen One*, or let us say—holding back because of our little faith—the Christ witnessed to as risen. *That* is the "evangelical, the historic Jesus Christ," and otherwise, that is, apart from this testimony to him, apart from the revelation which must here be believed, "we know him no longer."[19]

---

[19]Ibid., p. 79; ET p. 180.

The recognition of this Jesus as the risen Lord, which is his true identity, cannot be gleaned by historical study alone but is a gift of the Spirit and a confession of faith. This is the content of the scriptural witness: "The witness relates that the word became *flesh*, God himself became human, historical *reality*, and that this occurred in the *person of Jesus Christ*."[20] Jesus of Nazareth *is* the Christ and Lord of history, and therefore any historical reconstruction of his earthly life that ignores his lordship can at best be an abstraction. What Barth insisted on was that there was no "Jesus of history" that was more true, more real, than the risen Jesus Christ the Gospels attested, and that there was no accessibility to this Jesus behind the text but only within and through it.

This reality of God's revelation in Christ is the true identity of Jesus' historical existence, such that the Jesus of history and the Christ of faith cannot be divided or played against one another. This unity itself is then mirrored in the fact that this revelation of God in Christ is the center of Scripture, and the unity of this God with his revelation entails that Scripture itself possesses a unity in the midst of its diversity. Because the God who speaks through Scripture is one and is to be identified with the one who has been revealed in Jesus, Barth maintains that the entire Scripture (as Old and New Testaments) is a unified whole, for Scripture is a witness to this one God. The writings of Scripture are not the products of detached observers of various religious phenomena, or of subjective recorders of their own idiosyncratic religious experiences, but of diverse witnesses to an objective revelation, and thus are better understood as testimonies to a single revelation to be accepted by faith than as religious sources understood by means of historical science. It is the central reality of God's revelation in Christ that lies at the heart of Scripture and provides its unity, even while Barth himself at this point could remain quite ambivalent about the parameters of the canon itself.[21]

Therefore, Scripture cannot be rightly understood if considered solely as a repository of various historical, cultural and literary materials from antiquity (while it is certainly that, too), but is truly understood only if seen as

---

[20]Ibid., p. 78; ET p. 179.

[21]As Barth states: "This witness, which can never be analyzed enough by historical criticism, but which will not for that reason cease being *this* witness, is what I term in its totality the 'Scripture.' In this the question of the delimitation of 'Scripture' in reference to other writings seems to me to be a secondary one" (ibid., p. 77; ET pp. 178-79).

a united witness to a single Lord. Scripture possesses a unity that transcends its real and undeniable diversity not because we can discern within it or synthesize from it an overarching idea or concept, such as Harnack's own "simple gospel," but because of the unity and singularity of the one Lord to whom it witnesses and who speaks through it. It is the unity of this Lord for Barth that grounds the unity of Scripture and makes it a unified witness.[22] What is clear in Barth's debate with Harnack is Harnack's uneasiness with Barth's readiness to speak of the Bible as a unity, and Barth's own undaunted insistence that this unity is at the heart of Scripture's identity, and his own uneasiness in turn with Harnack's historicism, positivism, reductionism and scientism that prioritized method over subject matter (*Sache*) and content (*Inhalt*) and whittled Scripture down to a central core.[23]

Finally, the unity of God's revelation in Christ, witnessed in the unity of Scripture's content, entails that the reality and recognition of this revelation and this unity are the requirements for, rather than the conclusions reached from, a valid interpretation of Scripture such that the content, or object, of Scripture, must shape the method by which we approach it. With regard to Harnack's overarching theme of the need for historical science as the proper method for determining knowledge of the gospel of Jesus, Barth reasserted that for modern theological schools "the concept of an authoritative *object* [*Gegenstand*] has become foreign and monstrous because of the sheer authoritativeness of *method* [*Methode*]."[24] If the true content of Scripture is nothing less than God's own self-giving, then this can never be grasped from our side as an accomplishment but only given as a gift by God's own Spirit, for "it cannot be proper to reverse this order and make out of 'thus saith the Lord' a 'thus heareth man.'"[25] A theology which took such divine disclosure as its starting point, a theology which Barth remarked was that of Luther and Calvin, was to be embraced not in slavish imitation of revered Reformers, or as a mindless repristination of theology past that ignored the recent accomplishments of historical science, but as a way of rightfully acknowledging the proper objectivity of theology itself.

---

[22]Burnett, *Karl Barth's Theological Exegesis*, p. 77.
[23]Barth, *Offene Briefe 1909-1035*, pp. 59-60, 62-63, 77; ET pp. 165, 167, 178-79.
[24]Ibid., p. 74; ET p. 176.
[25]Ibid., p. 76; ET p. 178.

Therefore, the unity of revelation of the one Lord of Scripture, and the unity of Scripture itself, entails that there be a unity, albeit an ordered one, between theology and historical science. Against a priority given to historical science, Barth states that historical criticism itself must be taken up into the larger aim of theology, which is nothing less than putting forth the reality of God's revelation in thought and speech for understanding in the present. As Barth wrote to Harnack, "it is really not specifically a question of removing from theological study the critical historical method of biblical and historical research developed in recent centuries, but of a meaningful way of incorporating it into theology and of sharpening the questions which result from it."[26] For Barth, a correct understanding of Scripture can therefore only be a theological one that incorporates the historical into itself.[27]

A proper examination of Scripture must therefore squarely face the question of the truth of the message of Scripture and cannot simply rest content with objective description of past events, thought forms and literary conventions. Indeed, long before it became *avant-garde* to decry the myth of pure objectivity, Barth called into question the very notion of impartiality in exegesis devoid of all presuppositions.[28] For Barth, Harnack's historicism is therefore not so much objective as self-deceived. To understand Scripture rightly entails that one read it as a participant in its truth, or at least as one open to such participation, and not with a cool and passive affectation and detachment.[29] This different approach to the task of reading Scripture lies at the heart of Barth's disagreement with Harnack, for whom such participation, when incorporated within the historical task, entailed a loss of scientific objectivity and responsibility. Barth's commitment to a different kind of objectivity and responsibility is also, in large part, what lies behind his insistence in the preface to the third edition of the commentary on Romans that we must think not so much *about* Paul but *after* and *with* Paul toward

---

[26]Ibid., pp. 74-75; ET p. 176.

[27]"Strictly speaking, for Barth, there was no such thing as a genuine theological understanding of the Bible apart from a historical understanding, just as apart from a theological understanding there was nothing but the most trivial, banal sort of historical understanding of the Bible" (Burnett, *Karl Barth's Theological Exegesis*, p. 85).

[28]See GD, pp. 257-60.

[29]GD, pp. 254-55; see also Burnett, *Karl Barth's Theological Exegesis*, pp. 95-100, 111, 125-27, 192-97.

the subject matter with which he himself was concerned, what Barth so famously coined as *Nachdenken* and *Mitdenken*. Barth elaborated this point
in debate with Harnack:

> What I must defend myself against is not historical criticism, but rather the
> matter-of-course way in which one, still today, *empties* theology's task: Instead
> of that which our predecessors called "*the Word*" (the correlation of "Scripture"
> and "Spirit") one has placed this and that which have been dug up by his-
> torical criticism *beyond* the "Scripture" and *apart from* the "Spirit," which one
> calls the "simple gospel [*schlichte Evangelium*]," a gospel that can be called
> "word of God" only as a figure of speech, because it is in fact at best a human
> impression thereof.[30]

Therefore, if Scripture's content can be truly understood only theologically,
and if this content is a unity, then there can be no dichotomy of method between "scientific" and "edifying" exegesis, Barth insisted that the object of
investigation must determine the method, rather than a single scientific
method superimposed on the object, and he rejected the common view of his
day regarding the uniformity of a single scientific method (so fundamental to
Harnack) with its attendant reductionism, historicism and scientism.[31] In response to Harnack's charge that he had replaced the professor's lectern with a
pulpit, Barth maintains that there cannot be different truths for each:

---

[30]Barth, *Offene Briefe 1909–1935*, p. 75; ET p. 177.

[31]Hunsinger, *Disruptive Grace*, pp. 331-33. Burnett states that scientific objectivity "had come to
mean something different to Barth than it did to the majority of his contemporaries. They understood scientific objectivity in terms of impartiality and unprejudiced observation; he understood it in terms of being faithful to the object of investigation. To be scientific to him meant
fidelity to the object" (*Karl Barth's Theological Exegesis*, p. 97). It should also be noted that contrary to much opinion past and present, Barth was not a well-intentioned but naive exegete who
failed to understand the complexities of critical interpretation, but one who had in fact been
thoroughly introduced and inducted into the historical-critical method of his day through his
studies in Berne and later in Berlin. He had studied under Adolf Jülicher and Johannes Weiss at
Marburg. Barth produced various studies examining both biblical and historical topics in light
of the critical method of his day during his student years, including a paper in 1905 examining
the Capernaum centurion pericopes of Matthew 8:5-13 and Luke 7:1-10, and one on the Lord's
Prayer in the Gospels in 1906; see Karl Barth, *Vorträge und kleinere Arbeiten 1905–1909* (Zürich:
Theologischer Verlag Zürich, 1992), pp. 46-60, 126-47. Most important for this early period in
Barth's studies are the extensive paper Barth wrote in Berlin for Harnack himself on Acts, "Die
Missionsthätigkeit des Paulus nach der Darstellung der Apostelgeschichte" (1907), and his
Tübingen qualifying dissertation, "Die Vorstellung vom Descensus Christi ad inferos in der
kirchlichen Literatur bis Origenes" (1908); see *Vorträge und kleinere Arbeiten 1905–1909*, pp.
148-243, 244-312.

> The *theme* of the theologian . . . which he *investigates* in history, and which he
> must strive to express in a manner relevant to his own situation, cannot be a
> second truth distinct from the truth which he is obliged to present as a
> preacher. . . . I cannot see . . . how the subsequent abstract separation of
> "scholarly" [*gelehrten*] and "edifying" [*erbaulichen*] thinking and speaking can
> be based on the nature of the subject matter [*Sache*].[32]

Consequently, while there are real and practical differences between the
purposes of critical theology and preaching, there is no difference in terms
of their subject matter. Indeed, to posit two different subjects for each would
imply that the "Jesus of history" and the "Christ of faith" were in fact two
different realities.[33] Barth single-mindedly refused any such dichotomy and
bifurcation. As noted earlier, because Jesus of Nazareth is Christ the Lord,
there can be no absolute separation of historical and theological claims or
methods. Jesus Christ must be known for who he is—any purely "historical"
reconstruction that fails to see him in this light can only be an abstraction
that fails to address his true identity.[34]

Historical science thus has a twofold purpose from Barth's perspective.
Negatively, it witnesses to its own inability to move beyond historical reconstruction to confession, and thus betrays its own limitations. For Barth,
this negative function contributes by witnessing to the reality that a true
understanding of the gospel can come only as a gift from the side of God's
activity rather than human scholarly effort.[35] What is less clear in this exchange, however, is what exactly Barth takes to be historical science's positive and preparatory function, which he can allude to and affirms but never
fully explains.[36]

---

[32]Barth, *Offene Briefe 1909–1935*, pp. 75-76; ET p. 177.

[33]Ibid., pp. 78-80; ET 179-80.

[34]T. F. Torrance rightly states that while Barth has no interest in a construct and adheres to the historical Jesus, he holds that "the attempt to find a 'Jesus' apart from his Gospel, a Jesus apart from the concrete act of God in him, a 'Jesus' that can be constructed out of the historical records by means of criteria derived from secular sources alone, is a failure to understand the New Testament. The real, objective, historical Jesus is the Jesus Christ who cannot be separated from his self-revelation or from his Gospel, for that Revelation and Gospel are part of the one historical Jesus Christ who is to be understood out of himself, and in accordance with his own being and nature" (Torrance, *Karl Barth: An Introduction to His Early Theology* [London: SCM Press, 1962], p. 208). See also *GD*, p. 91.

[35]Barth, *Offene Briefe 1909–1935*, p. 80; ET p. 180.

[36]For a discussion of Barth's later articulation of the positive role of historical criticism, see Burnett, *Karl Barth's Theological Exegesis*, pp. 230-40.

The public debate in the *Christlichen Welt* came to an end with Harnack's brief postscript in response to Barth's lengthy letter, in which he once again reiterated the sharp division between historical-critical science and that of theology's witnessing to revelation. The boundaries between these were irrevocable for Harnack.[37] Concluding the correspondence, he again stressed the diversity of the biblical texts and the irreducibly human character of them, such that to speak of an objective and united "revelation" is futile when accompanied by a conviction that the "influence of human speech, hearing, perception, and understanding can be eliminated."[38] Harnack's response to Barth's adamancy regarding the unity of Scripture was a reiteration of the priority of Scripture's diversity only partly overcome by means of critical science. As we shall see, when such diversity was intractable, Harnack's solution was to abridge the canon itself and dissolve the very notion of canonical authority.[39]

THE QUESTION OF THE CANON

In the present chapter, it is impossible to evaluate and adjudicate between the rival viewpoints of Harnack and Barth with the attention their positions deserve, nor is it my intention here to attempt as much. I more modestly want to address the question of Scripture and canon in light of three themes that have emerged above, namely, the center of Scripture as canon, the unity of Scripture as canon and the relationship of theological and historical understandings of the canon with an eye toward how such matters might inform the church's response to challenges to its canon in the present.[40] I will take these themes in reverse order.

The conversation between Harnack and Barth is indeed a particular instance of a more general one affecting church and academy regarding the

---

[37]Barth, *Offene Briefe 1909–1935*, pp. 87-88; ET p. 186.

[38]Ibid., p. 88; ET p. 186.

[39]See Glick, *Reality of Christianity*, pp. 245, 247; cf. pp. 242-55.

[40]Scripture and canon are not, necessarily, coterminous in meaning. It is possible to distinguish between the authority attributed to scriptural books in the early church apart from the later definitive lists of such texts. For a brief discussion of this matter within the context of current studies of the history of the Jewish and Christian canons, see Lee McDonald and James A. Sanders, "Introduction," in McDonald and Sanders, *Canon Debate*, pp. 8-15; Harry Y. Gamble, "The New Testament Canon: Recent Research and the Status Quaestionis," in McDonald and Sanders, *Canon Debate*, pp. 267-94.

relationship of a theological and historical understanding of the biblical canon and its bearing on our understanding of revelation, faith and the person of Jesus Christ. In light of the positions of Barth and Harnack outlined above, I want to propose a number of theses, not as definitive or exhaustive, but in order to provoke further thought. They are not meant so much to settle questions as to help sharpen the ones we might ask when we consider the canon as a central reality of Christian faith and life, and thus, of the church.

Thesis 1: Questions about the canon are ultimately theological in nature and penultimately historical, for the definition of the canon finally rests in the acknowledgment of it as testimony and norm rather than as source and cultural artifact.

While the content and development of both Scripture and the canon are worthy objects of historical investigation, the question of the truth of Scripture's content and the reality underlying its development are matters of confession that lie beyond the reach of what biblical criticism can establish. The ultimate question to be asked of both particular books within the canon, as well as of the canon itself, is not the precise determination of their development, much of which seems, even after the excellent historical investigations of the recent past, lost to history, but the question of its subject matter which is nothing less than the God to whom the canon witnesses, and the contemporary confession of faith in this God. This confession is the sole proper response of the church in light of ascertaining Scripture's true content within its particular boundaries, echoed in Barth's later statement that "the fixing of the Canon is the basic act of church confession."[41] It is the question of truth rather than historical development that is primary, for to take the Scriptures in their objectivity is to treat them not only as ancient sources of historical, cultural and religious interest but also as testimonies that demand a verdict. For this reason, the ultimate significance of the canon hangs on ongoing recognition rather than past establishment.

At the same time, this theological definition of the canon cannot ignore questions of historical development or be indifferent to them. How such

---

[41]*CD* I/2, p. 597; Barth had made a related observation earlier in his lectures collected in *TRC*. He there says that "the express or silent confirmation of the biblical canon may perhaps be called the fundamental act of Reformed confessing" (p. 50).

historical findings are to be incorporated into a broader theological under-standing of the canon is an unavoidable and perennial question and one scarcely settled by Barth and Harnack in their exchange. Barth was certainly justified to reaffirm the theological center of Scripture that hinged on the work of the Spirit against Harnack's reductive positivism, yet Barth's indif-ference at the time to matters of Scripture's periphery and its form could not be sustained. Questions of the latter are affected by historical realities and investigation, and in this, Harnack poses a valid question to Barth's side.

As but one example, while the exact genetic history of canonical devel-opment may ultimately be unanswerable, we are still left with the canonical question that arises from the historical fact that the canon of the Old Tes-tament of the patristic period and the following medieval world of the West (against the recommendations of Jerome, who drew the distinction be-tween canonical and what he termed apocryphal writings) was not what later came to be determined as the Hebrew Bible but was in fact the Sep-tuagint with its more inclusive listing of books.[42] Should the contemporary church side with Jerome or Augustine on this issue, and thus respectively with Luther or with Trent? To put the question perhaps more pointedly—should we side in solidarity with Judaism in determining the canon, or with the ancient church? Both arguments for historical continuity with Judaism and for the catholicity of the churches and their respective Scriptures had their proponents in the early church with regard to the question of the

---

[42]For the role of the Old Testament apocrypha in the New Testament and patristic period, see Daniel J. Harrington, S.J., "The Old Testament Apocrypha in the Early Church and Today," in McDonald and Sanders, *Canon Debate*, pp. 196-210; and Martin Hengel, *The Septuagint as Christian Scripture: Its Prehistory and the Problem of Its Canon*, trans. Mark E. Biddle (Grand Rapids: Baker Academic, 2002). As noted, historical criticism itself can only draw provisional judgments due to off-setting evidence regarding the boundaries of Jewish Scripture during the New Testament era, for while the New Testament never directly quotes from the Apocrypha (though some do dispute this), it is deeply stamped by its use of the Septuagint. Harrington concludes: "The historical evidence is not adequate to justify the conclusion that the apocrypha were always part of the Christian Old Testament. Neither does it prove that they were never part of the Christian canon" (pp. 205-6). See also Hengel, who argues that in terms of the limited number of books cited within the New Testament, one would actually expect a smaller Old Testament canon in Christianity, though in terms of actual reference (such as Jude's use of *Enoch*) one sees a more fluid and inclusive approach to texts as authorities (pp. 110-12). That the church accepted the apocryphal books in the West, and eventually in the East, is for Hengel ultimately explained by Luther's assessment, namely, that such writings were useful if secondary (pp. 122-27). It might also be noted that the Apocrypha was included in the Geneva Bible until its 1559 edition, as well as in the first edition of the King James Bible.

canon. While most Protestants, following the Reformers, side with the former, and most Catholics with the latter, no straightforward answer is provided by an acknowledgment of Scripture's theological nature and christological center. For instance, Brevard Childs firmly attests to the theological nature of Scripture when he states that the canon is predicated on its witness to Christ: "The scriptures of the Old and New Testament were authoritative in so far as they pointed to God's redemptive intervention for the world in Jesus Christ."[43] But such a firm and unqualified christological affirmation does not entail that Childs finds the peripheral questions of the canon's boundaries and determination (in light of the aforementioned historical developments) easily answered, for such an affirmation does not finally resolve the question regarding the choice for a narrower or more inclusive canon, but indeed exacerbates it and rightly makes the question of the canon not a past accomplishment discerned by historical science but a matter of present-day and perennial confession.[44] Thus this question of history continues to have contemporary theological significance for the Christian churches insofar as the canons of the churches inherited from the past are not conterminous in form.[45]

---

[43]Brevard Childs, *Biblical Theology of the Old and New Testaments: Theological Reflection on the Christian Bible* (Minneapolis: Fortress, 1993), p. 64.

[44]Childs does not despair in such indetermination but rather concludes: "Perhaps the basic theological issue at stake can be best formulated in terms of the church's ongoing *search* for the Christian Bible. The church struggles with the task of continually discerning the truth of God being revealed in scripture and at the same time she stands within a fully human, ecclesiastical tradition which remains the trident of the Word. The hearing of God's Word is repeatedly confirmed by the Holy Spirit through its resonance with the church's Christological rule-of-faith. At the same time the church confesses the inadequacy of its reception while rejoicing over the sheer wonder of the divine accommodation to limited human capacity" (p. 67). Childs's own discussion of the strengths and weaknesses of the Protestant and Catholic canonical decisions is extremely insightful; see pp. 66-68.

[45]James A. Sanders states: "Relevance or adaptability has always been the primary trait of a canon, early and late. When one speaks of canon, in fact, one has to ask which canon of which community is meant, whether in antiquity or today. The Protestant canon is the smallest and the Ethiopian Orthodox canon the largest. While canons differ, all believing communities agree that their canon is relevant to their ongoing life. The concept of canon cannot be limited to a final stage in the history of the formation of a Bible, as it has been until recently. It must, on the contrary, be understood as part of the history of transmission of the text. Even the issue of its closure must be so understood" ("The Issue of Closure in the Canonical Process," in McDonald and Sanders, *Canon Debate*, p. 259). However much one might object to Sanders's central criterion of relevance or adaptability as an understanding of the canon *kata sarka* (and one can), the questions of canonical boundaries and diversity among the Christian churches that he points to remain.

Therefore, while the ultimate definition of the canon must be theological and christological in nature, the question of its composition and parameters are not straightforwardly answered by such a definition. If one states that the guiding criterion for the determination of the contents of the canon is that which testifies to Christ, one must remember that Luther's adoption of precisely such a principle led him negatively to judge, though not ultimately exclude, such books as James and Jude that are broadly accepted books of the New Testament canon.[46] Moreover, such a principle could also be appealed to as a justification to expand the canon, or at least imply such an expansion. In antiquity, Tertullian could defend the authority of pseudapigraphal *Enoch* by stating that it is to be accepted as authoritative precisely because it was rejected by the Jews who, "just as they also rejected other things which proclaim Christ" (*sicut et caetera fere quae Christum sonant*), also reject it and other works as well.[47] Such a radically expansive view of the Old Testament canon was opposed by Augustine, and, of course, Jerome, though they differed on other canonical questions.[48] Yet even today a christological principle can be used not to narrow the canon but to commend that the Apocryphal books be included within all Christian canons.[49] Barth himself would later defend their exclusion but admit that such a decision by the Protestant church can be only provisional rather than final because it is based on human rather than divine authority.[50] Like Childs, Barth sees the

---

[46]Harrington, "Old Testament Apocrypha in the Early Church and Today," pp. 204-5.

[47]Tertullian continues: "Nor is it remarkable if they have not received other scriptures which speak of him, just as they would not receive him when he spoke openly," quoted in William Adler, "The Pseudepigrapha in the Early Church," in McDonald and Sanders, *Canon Debate*, p. 224. Even here, however, matters are more complicated, for Tertullian may be arguing not for a revision of the Old Testament canon so much as for a justification and defense of his own use and reliance on *Enoch*, though this book and *4 Esdras* did obtain canonical status in the Ethiopian Orthodox Church, and the latter is also included in the Vulgate. See Adler, p. 227.

[48]Adler, "Pseudepigrapha in the Early Church," p. 224.

[49]See Harrington, "Old Testament Apocrypha in the Early Church," p. 206. He argues that such texts help us take Jesus' identity in Judaism seriously. What is unclear, however, is where such canonical expansion will end, for he lists Josephus and Philo, the Dead Sea scrolls and the Old Testament Pseudepigrapha as doing the same thing, yet it is quite doubtful he would want to see these included in the canon itself. Here, again, we may be witnessing an inability to distinguish apostolic texts from simply illuminating historical ones. Hengel, however, entertains a more radical thought: "Does the church still need a clearly demarcated, strictly closed Old Testament canon, since the New Testament is, after all, the 'conclusion,' the goal and the fulfillment of the Old?" (*Septuagint as Christian Scripture*, pp. 125-26).

[50]*CD* I/2, p. 598.

determination of the canon as a current ecclesial confession of an imperfectly discerned eschatological reality.

It is not surprising in light of the historical messiness of canonical development and contested boundaries that Barth in his mature reflections on the canon appealed not only to its theological center in revelation but also to the historical judgment of the church in determining its parameters, even while refusing the latter any final authority on the question. The latter did not supersede the superiority of the former. For Barth, the revelation of God which comes through Scripture is the ultimate basis and criterion for the canon itself, and the freedom of God in this address overrules even historic usage and the past decisions of councils regarding canonical lists, such that the canon does and must remain open in principle. Yet the church's long-standing recognition of these past ecclesial decisions, itself predicated on recognition of the Spirit's speaking through these particular books, ensures that the canon is effectively closed in practice, even if with regard to the Old Testament it is closed differently between the Catholic and Protestant (and Eastern) churches.[51]

Barth's emphasis in the *Church Dogmatics* on the relative authority of the early church's acceptance of these books, later ratified in ecclesial decisions regarding the canon, once again demonstrates the inalienable, if not determinative, place of historiography in the church's contemporary task of confession, though in Barth's case, and this is quite important, one that respects the past decisions of the church perhaps more than the viewpoints of individual historians and even the findings of contemporary biblical scholarship. In face of those who today might challenge particular books of the canon due to their pseudapigraphal origins, or, more seriously, by questioning whether God's revelation is indeed heard in them in the present (or ever was), Barth gives precedence not to the contemporary discernment of individuals but to a measured reservation and corresponding preservation of such books in light of the church's judgment of having heard God's Word in them in the past.[52] So while the canon does remain open in principle, for

---

[51]Ibid., pp. 597-603; see also pp. 473-537. Barth writes: "When we adopt the Canon of the Church we do not say that the Church itself, but that the revelation which underlies and controls the Church, attests these witnesses and not others as the witnesses of revelation and therefore as canonical for the Church" (p. 474).

[52]Ibid., pp. 597-601.

the Spirit is not bound, it is closed in practice, and Barth seems quite skeptical regarding the possibility of future revisions to the canon the church has received, for it has been through these books that the church has heard the voice of God in the past and can hope to again in the future in light of God's faithfulness. Such divine faithfulness over time entails that it is the long-standing decision and practice of the church continually reaffirmed through history, rather than of an individual or individuals in the transitory present, that truly matters.

However much Barth rebelled against the liberalism of Harnack in the early years of his professional life, it was in the years of the *Church Dogmatics*, and precisely as a theologian of the church, that he most testifies to his overcoming of its individualism, which, along with historical relativism, he discerned to be the hallmarks of modern theology's identity, and did so even before his break with liberalism.[53] It is the church, rather than the academy, that confesses the Word of God in the canon, and therefore the final arbiter of the canon's parameters remains the church itself, though whether the church of today (in its manifold forms) should rethink the decisions of the church of the past in light of the historical and critical knowledge of the canon possessed in the present remains a question the church must answer, and can only answer, by a reaffirmation of what it understands the canon to be. It must at least remember in its considerations that "there is no more dangerous subjectivism than that which is based on the arrogance of a false objectivity,"[54] and thus take care not to fall into the hubris of chronological snobbery. There is good reason to believe, however, that the "canon will stand for long enough yet against the 'it seems to me' of some agitators."[55]

Thesis 2: An acknowledgment of the canon is ultimately an acknowledgment of its unity and only penultimately one of its diversity, for to speak of Scripture as canon entails more than speaking of it as a collection of texts.

Questions of unity with regard to the canon can be addressed from two perspectives: the functional and pragmatic unity that a canon of texts serves

---

[53]Barth, "Moderne Theologie und Reichsgottesarbeit" (1909), in *Vorträge und kleinere Arbeiten 1905–1909*, pp. 342-44; cf. pp. 341-47; see also Busch, *Karl Barth*, pp. 50-52.

[54]*CD* I/2, p. 553.

[55]*GD*, p. 247.

in shaping a communal tradition over time, and the question of the intrinsic unity of the canon itself. While the first is an essential outcome of the concept of canon, the second is determinative for the definition of canon itself. When unity in the second sense is not recognized, then questions of pragmatic usefulness come to the fore and eventually lead to problematic reevaluations of the received canon and dissolution of its authority.

As noted above, the question of the unity of Scripture was a central element in the correspondence between Barth and Harnack. Harnack's reticence to speak of Scripture as a unity was shaped by his own particular conviction that whatsoever unity existed was to be discerned and derived by means of historical science. For Harnack, such is the particular achievement made possible by a true scientific objectivity. Yet it was such objectivity itself that time has revealed to be a chimera, for the presuppositions of Harnack's scientism ruled out a serious consideration of the unity of the canon and in fact denied the validity of the question. Thus supposed objectivity could readily give way to pragmatism and axiology.[56]

It is not difficult to determine that Harnack was struck much more by the diversity of the canon than by its unity and saw Barth's appeal to a unity grounded in a unified revelation as both naive and unscientific. Harnack saw not so much a unity but an essence in Scripture, defined as a spiritual-moral norm, and the criterion for this norm was not simply read out of the New Testament but read into it, not so much a canon within the canon as a canon outside of it.[57] Moreover, whatever failed to fit this norm was considered the husk of the kernel and thus expendable. Nowhere is this more evident than in Harnack's rejection of the Old Testament.[58] When the emphasis is placed on the irreconcilable diversity of Scripture, it should not be sur-

---

[56]Glick, *Reality of Christianity*, p. 14; for the presuppositions behind Harnack's supposed objectivity, and his implicit utilitarianism with regard to the question of Scripture in mediating religion and culture, see Glick, pp. 3-15, 65-67, 68-84, 94-95, 105-11, 117-18, 158-61, 161-76, 202, 213-15, 230, 240, et al.

[57]I borrow this latter phrase from James D. G. Dunn, "Has the Canon a Continuing Function?" in McDonald and Sanders, *Canon Debate*, p. 569.

[58]"The rejection of the Old Testament during the second century A.D. would have been a mistake, which the great Church rightly refused to make. Its retention in the sixteenth century was a fate from which the Reformation was not yet able to extricate itself. Its conservation as a canonical document for Protestantism since the nineteenth century is the consequence of a religious and ecclesiastical paralysis" (Harnack, *Marcion, das Evangelium vom fremden Gott* [Leipzig: J. C. Hinrichs Verlag, 1924], p. 217, quoted in Rumscheidt, *Revelation and Theology*, p. 98).

prising that unity is not discovered within it but imposed on it, and imposed by means of subtraction, a subtraction itself determined by an external principle, and one that ultimately dissolves canonicity into canonical essence.[59] Objective scientific rigor thus bows to pragmatic cultural apologetics.[60]

In his own later reflections on the canon, Barth went a very different direction, emphasizing the unity of Scripture and the inalienable canonical status of the Old Testament. Such was due to a number of factors, but no doubt the central one was that Barth saw Scripture as the witness to a single Lord and saw Scripture as a testimony to a united revelation, and thus through the single lens of Christology, whereas Harnack approached Scripture through multiple lenses, most notably those of a spiritual moralism that was predicated on a Kantian universal rationalism modified in light of Schleiermacher, as well as through a modern Lutheran law and gospel dichotomy (both via and modified by Ritschl).[61] When these lenses focused, they focused together on an essential message which Harnack deemed the "simple gospel."[62] This gospel, when once understood, Harnack believed, entailed that the Old Testament had to be discarded in Marcionite fashion not only because of this gospel's opposition to law (in spite of its own moralism) but also because of the Old Testament's intractable parochialism, or, put differently, because of the scandal of its particularity.[63] In the end, Barth was perhaps more true to history if for no other reason than that he refused to divide in *any* way the person of Jesus from the content of his message and

---

[59]Glick, *Reality of Christianity*, p. 249.

[60]As Glick perceptively asks: "Was the Old Testament adjudged noncanonical by Harnack simply because he did not believe it contributed to the needs of his time? Does this not mean, then, that the central category of interpretation must always be 'worthfulness'?" (*Reality of Christianity*, p. 13).

[61]Ibid., pp. 77-78; cf. pp. 161-76, 240.

[62]Perhaps most famously put forward in Harnack's *What Is Christianity?*, trans. Thomas B. Saunders (New York: Harper & Brothers, 1957). For Harnack, the gospel can be summarized in three propositions: "*Firstly, the kingdom of God and its coming; Secondly, God the Father and the infinite value of the human soul; Thirdly, the higher righteousness and the commandment of love*" (p. 51). The kingdom is thus supernatural, purely religious and the most important experience a person can have (p. 62). The gospel is itself an ethical message of love for humanity (p. 70).

[63]Harnack's definitive study of Marcion is *Marcion, das Evangelium vom fremden Gott*. For Harnack, Marcion achieved what Paul intimated and what Luther attempted but ultimately could not accomplish, namely, definitively to overcome the law with the gospel. See Glick's discussion, *Reality of Christianity*, pp. 117-20. He later writes that "it becomes quite evident that for all his emphasis on historical event, Harnack is really quite contemptuous of historical particularity" (p. 253).

just as resolutely refused to separate him from his context in Judaism. Thus he was more true to the particularity of Jesus and accepted the scandal rather than attempting to overcome it. Barth's primary concern was not the gospel's relevance but its truth, and he had little or no interest in serving as a mediating theologian or in such apologetic tasks, whereas Harnack, like Schleiermacher, saw the mediation between Christian faith and culture as a, if not the, central task of a theologian.[64] Such mediation entailed a jettisoning of particularity for universal or contemporary concerns.

What we must consider, then, is that a recognition of Scripture's unity as a canon is dependent on the acceptance of revelation's scandal of particularity. A rejection of the latter always leads to a reductive program, moral or otherwise. It has often led to a jettisoning of the Old Testament. Harnack has been criticized for such, but he was not the first to question the place of the Old Testament in the Christian canon, and he will not be the last. Once again, such an acknowledgment does not alleviate questions regarding the boundaries of the canon, and historical considerations cannot be ignored when such questions are considered. Indeed, Barth's own disdain for apologetics (inherited from Herrmann) may be unhelpfully extended to exclude valid historical arguments that need to be made today, such as that against recent appeals even by some within the churches for an inclusion of the *Gospel of Thomas* within the canon because of its early date and supposed authenticity, when in reality, it is demonstrably late and typically gnostic in its rejection of the scandal of Jesus' particularity and its indifference to his rootedness in first-century Palestine (thus akin to other late gnostic gospels and their modern-day proponents).[65] As Barth had to admit in his other famous debate

---

[64]Glick, *Reality of Christianity*, pp. 83-84.

[65]See Nicholas Perrin, *Thomas: The Other Gospel* (Louisville, KY: Westminster John Knox, 2007); as well as his *Thomas and Tatian* (Atlanta: Society of Biblical Literature, 2002). An accessible evaluation of *Thomas* is provided by Craig A. Evans, *Fabricating Jesus* (Downers Grove, IL: InterVarsity Press, 2006), pp. 52-77. Recently Perrin's claims have been questioned as regarding the Gospel's original language and origin but not as to call into question Thomas's later date and reliance on the Synoptics themselves. See Simon Gathercole, *The Composition of the Gospel of Thomas: Original Language and Influences* (Cambridge: Cambridge University Press, 2012). For the decontextualizing of Jesus from Judaism among some prominent members of the Jesus Seminar, see Philip Jenkins, *Hidden Gospels: How the Search for Jesus Lost Its Way* (Oxford: Oxford University Press, 2001), pp. 99-100, et al. For the importance of historical study to correct such misperceptions and domestications, see Dunn, "Has the Canon a Continuing Function?" pp. 574-75.

of 1923, that with Paul Tillich, the particularity of God's revelation entails a particular history.[66] This fact entails that historiographical concerns and biblical criticism are integral for Christian faith, even while they also need to be taken up into larger theological frameworks, and can indeed serve them in no small way by correcting these frameworks themselves.[67]

Thesis 3: Judgments about the canon are ultimately christological judgments, for the central question of the canon pertains to its center rather than its periphery and constituent membership, as important as these are.

The question of the canon is to be addressed from its center, rather than its periphery, and when this is done, it is not cynicism and skepticism but a deep impression of its overarching narrative unity that has impressed itself on the church. However contentious such a claim might be from the standpoint of an exacting historiography, it is nonetheless true that for Christian faith it is the center, rather than the periphery—its content rather than its boundaries—which is the primary question of the canon. When this is kept in mind, the matter of discerning boundaries itself gains in clarity, both with respect to the Old Testament and New Testament canons.

First, while the exact scope of the Old Testament canon was and remains a question for the church, the Old Testament itself was not questioned as Scripture but central to the church's very definition of it. The contested

---

[66]This published debate is found in *Beginnings of Dialectical Theology*, pp. 133-58. While Barth was facing an entrenched historicism in Harnack, in Tillich he faced a true flight from history altogether into the transcendence of the "unconditioned" (pp. 147-48). Whereas against Harnack Barth asserted the distinctiveness of revelation from history, such that the former could not simply be subsumed into the latter and be directly ascertained by means of historical criticism, against Tillich Barth now had to assert that revelation and history were not to be torn asunder and that God has bound himself to a particular history in his self-revelation. As Barth writes, "Christ is *the* salvation history, the salvation history *itself*," whereas for Tillich, Christ is "the presentation of a salvation history which more or less occurs always and everywhere with completely symbolic power" (p. 150). The decisive difference between Tillich and himself, Barth concluded, was a difference of Christology. Both Barth and Tillich opposed the idolatry of the "man-god," but where they parted company was on the reality of the "God-man." For Barth, the pride of humanity that must be opposed in the former should not be used to negate the freedom and love of God in choosing to be the latter, and who does so in a history which is "*the* site of *the* salvation history" (p. 151).

[67]For a strong and provocative defense of the need for biblical criticism against its contemporary detractors, see John Barton, *The Nature of Biblical Criticism* (Louisville, KY: Westminster John Knox, 2007); and Dunn, "Has the Canon a Continuing Function?" pp. 574-575. With regard to the question of the canon, Jenkins writes: "Contrary to recent claims, the more access we have to ancient 'alternative gospels,' the more we must respect the choices made by the early church in forming its canon" (*Hidden Gospels*, p. 106).

nature of the Old Testament canon mentioned earlier should not distract from the larger affirmation to be made regarding the ongoing normativity of the First Testament along with that of the Second in the church's history.[68] That the early church retained the Old Testament and saw the New Testament as a commentary on it, rather than a replacement for it, entails a very particular understanding of the God the church confessed and the Christ it worshiped.[69] And it is undeniable that Barth came to see the Old Testament more in terms of the first, and Harnack in terms of the second.[70] Furthermore, Barth's increasing appreciation for classical Chalcedonian Christology, and Harnack's disavowal of it (along with a rejection of the resurrection), could only stem from and in turn entail hermeneutical and canonical judgments. Barth would emphasize Jesus as the risen Messiah of Israel, the fulfillment of the promises to Abraham, whereas Harnack, in true nineteenth-century fashion, saw him primarily as the founding personality of a new faith, even while acknowledging the usefulness of the Old Testament for the early church, if not for today. So while it is true that both Harnack and Barth can rightly be deemed christocentric theologians, their Christologies differed dramatically, and such Christologies inescapably had canonical implications.[71]

One implication directly affects the question of canonical unity. Indeed, another way to say that Barth focused on the unity of Scripture is to say that Barth saw all of Scripture as ultimately about Christ. The same could not be said of Harnack. Where Barth saw Scripture as grounded in a particular

---

[68]Childs, *Biblical Theology*, pp. 66.

[69]As Glick perceptively notes regarding Harnack's understanding of the history of dogma: "The fact that the Church from the beginning laid claim to the Old Testament, interpreting it, to be sure, in most unusual ways, is of crucial importance here. For whatever the mode of interpretation, it was still to this content that it was applied. And the indisputable fact that the New Testament, when written by the Church, placed itself within the framework of Jewish thought ("the God of Abraham, Isaac, and Jacob," "God spoke of old to our fathers by the prophets,") is certainly presumptive evidence that the situation from which the dogma developed was by no means as 'Hellenic' as Harnack assumes" (*Reality of Christianity*, p. 173).

[70]For Barth's mature reflections on the Old Testament within the Christian canon, see *CD* I/2, pp. 70-101.

[71]For Harnack's Christology, see the selections in *Adolf von Harnack: Liberal Theology at Its Height*, pp. 63-77; cf. pp. 155-66, 303-12; also the summary in Glick, *Reality of Christianity*, pp. 181-215. It was in view of the nineteenth century's view of Jesus, culminating in Ritschl and Harnack, that Barth surprisingly claimed in his first dogmatic cycle that theology must be less christocentric (*GD*, pp. 90-91). The end result for Barth was of course not a theology less christocentric but a radically different theology and Christology altogether.

revelation in Christ, foreshadowed in the Old and attested in the New, Harnack was enamored by a universal message that could be extracted ultimately from both. One must be fair to Harnack here, for he resolutely refused to dispense with the person of Jesus in favor of his message and would not give up on the uniqueness of Jesus against the later objections of the *Religionsgeschichtliche Schule*.[72] Nevertheless, he was inclined to separate Jesus from his own history. Barth could not follow this path, because in his view, to divide the Testaments is tantamount to committing a christological heresy.[73] His emphasis on the unity of revelation entailed that he emphasize the unity of the Testaments. The canon of Scripture was thus not the source of a message but a testimony to a Lord and a testimony throughout. Barth would never refrain from treating the Old Testament as an extended infancy narrative, and this has been and remains perhaps one of the most controversial aspects of his understanding of the canon.

Barth's christological understanding of the canon is, nevertheless, in line with that of the historic church. While Barth's approach to the Old Testament has been challenged on various fronts for its failure to take the Old Testament on its own terms, it is very difficult to see the Old Testament and New Testament as one canon if not by means of Christ hidden in the Old and revealed in the New. It is no doubt more difficult to see this unity with a dialectic of law and gospel as the primary hermeneutic, and perhaps impossible for a reductive moralism. Certainly it became impossible for Harnack in light of his "simple gospel." We should not expect it to be any less difficult for contemporary moral programs with their own axiological judgments and mediating agendas that call for canonical revision. As but one example, consider the lament of Robert Funk: "To retain the traditional New Testament and understand it as a canon is to condemn it to progressive irrelevance with each passing century."[74] His answer? "My own solution to the problem is to issue a revised canon, a new New Testament, by both

---

[72]Harnack thus attempted to preserve the uniqueness of Jesus against those like D. F. Strauss and Ernst Troeltsch who insisted on a more consistent historicism, though Troeltsch himself would later attempt to find a way to preserve the "absoluteness of Christianity."

[73]"Whether we like it or not, the Christ of the New Testament is the Christ of the Old Testament, the Christ of Israel. The man who will not accept this merely shows that in fact he has already substituted another Christ for the Christ of the New Testament" (*CD* I/2, pp. 488-89).

[74]Funk, "Once and Future New Testament," p. 544.

shrinking and expanding the texts to be included."[75] Let us make no mistake: Funk's argument is not just canonical, it is christological, again hidden behind the veil of (dubious) scientific respectability. He asks: "Shall we continue to affirm the picture of Jesus provided by the four canonical gospels, or shall we heed the findings of historical research?"[76] We have heard this before.

In his time, Harnack (as well as Jülicher) judged Barth to be a Marcionite, yet it was Harnack the scientific historian, not Barth the pneumatic exegete, who ultimately tipped his hand in this direction. On the question of the canon, Barth's position seems to coincide with what historical investigation has itself discovered: that Jesus Christ was the early church's canon, and the Old and New Testament became the canon of the church as a witness to him.[77] It remains the canon of the church today for the same reason.

Moreover, Barth's position on Scripture makes his own theology more amenable to later judgments of biblical criticism than Harnack's and with reference to two in particular. The first is that New Testament studies have not been kind to Harnack's reductive moralism, for if there is one thing that contemporary biblical scholarship has grown increasingly to affirm in the past century, it is the Jewishness of Jesus and his place in the context of rabbinic Judaism and the eschatology of his day, no matter how contested the precise nature of this relationship may be among New Testament scholars.[78]

---

[75]Ibid., pp. 549, 542. The Old Testament does not make out so well in Funk's proposal, either.

[76]Ibid., p. 541. It should not be surprising that Funk is enamored only with the diversity of Scripture and sees historical criticism as entirely undermining any sense of its unity (pp. 542-44).

[77]Lee McDonald argues that "during the formative years of the early church Jesus was the church's primary canon par excellence and . . . the biblical tradition (the OT scriptures) gave witness to that canon" (*The Formation of the Christian Biblical Canon*, rev. and expanded ed. [Peabody, MA: Hendrickson, 1995], p. 95; see also pp. 153, 189). The larger point here made is in no way negated, even if we should adopt a more narrow definition of "canon" as a closed list of sacred books; see Eugene Ulrich, "The Notion and Definition of Canon," in McDonald and Sanders, *Canon Debate*, pp. 34-35. For a judgment similar to that of McDonald, see Dunn, "Has the Canon a Continuing Function?" pp. 560-62, as well as William R. Farmer, "Reflections on Jesus and the New Testament Canon," in McDonald and Sanders, *Canon Debate*, pp. 322-23. Dunn judges that "the canon of the New Testament still has a continuing function in that *the New Testament in all its diversity still bears consistent testimony to the unifying center*. Its unity canonizes Jesus-the-man-now-exalted as the canon within the canon" (p. 561).

[78]And this is the consensus of biblical scholars who are more akin to the presuppositions of Harnack, treating the Jesus of history as a person behind the Gospels, as well as to those who may be more sympathetic to the presuppositions of Barth. For an example of the former, see E. P. Sanders, *The Historical Figure of Jesus* (London: Penguin/Allen Lane, 1993), esp. pp. 78-97, 169-88. For a writer more amenable to the latter, see N. T. Wright, *Jesus and the Victory of God*

Harnack's isolation of Jesus from his Jewish environment is nothing less than a subtle gnosticism, and there is no more subtle form of gnosticism than an ahistorical moralism.[79] Barth avoided this temptation. Yet in his struggle with how the New Covenant not only completes but also supersedes the Old one, Harnack rightly wrestled with a question that Barth was less interested to answer, yet one the church must perennially face in the challenge of relating old and new wineskins.

Second, the increasing appreciation in biblical studies for the intertextuality of the Bible affirms the deeply woven unity of the New Testament with the Old, further demonstrating the problems with Harnack's canonical judgment. It is precisely an appreciation for the unity of the subject matter that is mirrored in an appreciation for the contemporaneity of the Old in the New in the light of Christ, for, as Robert Wall presciently notes: "The intertextual character of Scripture—the constant repetition of one text alluding to or citing an earlier text—reflects the simultaneity of its subject matter."[80]

In the end, the irony of the Barth and Harnack debate is that it was the scientific historian who strove for objectivity who was the most unknowingly captive to passing presuppositions of his own time and its intrinsic gnosticism, and it was the openly confessional position of the theologian accused of gnosticism that has proved more rooted in history and able to weather the changes of time in biblical studies. If Barth indeed had a fault in this regard, it was in his too ready acceptance of the findings of radical

---

(Minneapolis: Fortress, 1996), esp. pp. 91-98. Wright concludes that in light of the Third Quest, what is emerging is a position in which Jesus can neither be separated from the Judaism of his day nor simply be subsumed into it so that his critique of it disappears (p. 98).

[79]As Harnack writes: "Since Christianity is the only true religion and is not a national religion, but belongs to all mankind and pertains to our inmost life, it follows that it can have no special alliance with the Jewish people, or with their peculiar cult. The Jewish people of today, at least, stand in no favored relationship with the God whom Jesus has revealed; whether they formerly did is doubtful; this, however, is certain, that God has cast them off, and that the whole Divine revelation, so far as there was any revelation prior to Christ . . . had as its end the calling of a 'new nation' and the spreading of the revelation of God through his Son" (*Outlines of the History of Dogma*, trans. Edwin K. Mitchell [Boston: Beacon Press, 1957], p. 42). Such a quote reveals that a rejection of the scandal of the gospel is the flip side of gnosticism, and indeed recent history has not judged Harnack's position lightly.

[80]Robert W. Wall, "The Significance of a Canonical Perspective of the Church's Scripture," in McDonald and Sanders, *Canon Debate*, p. 531. Later he writes: "The current reductionism of interpreting the Old Testament or New Testament in isolation from the other, thereby undermining the New Testament's relationship to the 'Hebrew Bible,' is subverted by the New Testament's appeal to and exegesis of the Old Testament" (p. 537).

biblical criticism, failing to question not only its presuppositions but also its findings. This was in no small part due to Barth's own liberal inheritance from Herrmann and his early ambivalence toward history, as well as to a dialectic of contradiction that had in time to be taken up and overcome in a richer dialectic of correspondence. Nevertheless, from the very first, and evident in his debate with Harnack, it is his hermeneutic of trust and canonical richness, rather than suspicion and canonical reductionism, that continues to intrigue many.

EPILOGUE

Readers of this chapter will no doubt note the treacherous and tenuous dialogue between theology and biblical studies within it. Practitioners of both may find fault with such egregious discipline-crossing. Yet, without excusing any shortcomings of content, no apology from my side will be forthcoming.

One of the greatly unfortunate realities of contemporary Christian scholarship is the parting of the ways of biblical studies and systematic theology, although there are now some significant attempts to bring them back into vibrant dialogue with one another. Yet if both of these are to be Christian, and thus servants of the church, and not simply professional avocations of a guild, such a division can only be ad hoc, provisional and practical, not systematic, permanent and principled.

7

The Canon as
Theological Category

Bart Ehrman's Questions to Scripture

✠

In the history that has followed the appearance of Jesus and the founding of the church, there have been no small number of skeptics who have built a reputation on questioning the truth of Christian faith by raising doubts about the historical claims that accompany its theological doctrines. From Celsus and Hume to Lessing and Strauss, questions of faith and history, and the undermining of the former by calling into question claims of the latter, have led to responses from the church and the historians and theologians within its ranks. Such responses have varied greatly, from an intentional apologetic program defending traditional positions on the historicity of biblical events, to a staunch separation by theologians of faith and history altogether, thus protecting the first by cutting it loose from its moorings in the second. Both of these responses find their most impressive articulations in light of the historical consciousness and criticism that arose in the modern period which both sharpened and intensified such questioning.[1] I have no intention here of tracing the initiation and development of historical criticism itself and its wedding by some to a powerful agnosticism or skepticism regarding Christian convictions.[2] That history is lined with names such as

---

[1]For one example of a recent sophisticated attempt at the first, see N. T. Wright, *The Resurrection of the Son of God* (Minneapolis: Fortress, 2003); for the second, one can think of the existentialist programs of Rudolf Bultmann and Paul Tillich.

[2]For summaries of this history, see Henning Graf Reventlow, *History of Biblical Interpretation,* vol. 4:

Semler, Reimarus, Bauer, Strauss and Wrede, among many others. I want, rather, to address the question of the canon in its theological and historical aspects by examining one modern critic of its composition and collection.

While there have been numerous skeptics of faith and Scripture, few have been able to make such a cottage industry of it as Bart Ehrman. Ehrman's many scholarly gifts have of late been applied to creating a popular barrage on traditional faith via historical cynicism. That statement is not meant to stir provocation. If anything is deemed provocative, it must be the collection of titles that Ehrman's more popular books bear: *Misquoting Jesus: The Story Behind Who Changed the Bible and Why*; *Jesus, Interrupted: Revealing the Hidden Contradictions in the Bible (And Why We Don't Know About Them)*; *Forged: Writing in the Name of God—Why the Bible's Authors Are Not Who We Think They Are*; and perhaps only slightly less sensational, having been written for a scholarly rather than a popular audience, *The Orthodox Corruption of Scripture: The Effect of Early Christological Controversies on the Text of the New Testament*, and *Forgery and Counterforgery: The Use of Literary Deceit in Early Christian Polemics*.[3]

One of the greatest myths of the Enlightenment period that lingered on into the era of historical criticism of the late nineteenth and early twentieth centuries was that of an absolute objectivity, a kind of cool and chastened if nevertheless ambitious, and occasionally even smug, claim to scientific impartiality aspiring to the ideal of encyclopedic omniscience. That myth has

---

From the Enlightenment to the Twentieth Century, Society of Biblical Literature Resources for Biblical Study (Atlanta: Society of Biblical Literature, 2010); also Reventlow, *The Authority of the Bible and the Rise of the Modern World* (Minneapolis: Fortress, 1985); William Baird, *History of New Testament Research*, 3 vols. (Minneapolis: Fortress, 1992–2013); and Gerald Bray, *Biblical Interpretation: Past and Present* (Downers Grove, IL: InterVarsity Press, 1996).

[3]Bart D. Ehrman, *Misquoting Jesus: The Story Behind Who Changed the Bible and Why* (reprint; San Franciso: HarperOne, 2007); Ehrman, *Jesus, Interrupted: Revealing the Hidden Contradictions in the Bible* (reprint; San Francisco: HarperOne, 2010); Ehrman, *Forged: Writing in the Name of God—Why the Bible's Authors Are Not Who We Think They Are* (reprint; San Francisco: HarperOne, 2012); and, though more academic and technical, Ehrman, *Forgery and Counterforgery: The Use of Literary Deceit in Early Christian Polemics*, 1st ed. (New York: Oxford University Press, 2012); Ehrman, *The Orthodox Corruption of Scripture: The Effect of Early Christological Controversies on the Text of the New Testament* (Oxford: Oxford University Press, 2011). Most recently, and too late for inclusion in this chapter, is Ehrman, *How Jesus Became God: The Exaltation of a Jewish Preacher from Galilee* (New York: HarperOne, 2014). For a response to this work, see Michael F. Bird, Craig A. Evans, Simon J. Gathercole, Charles E. Hill and Chris Tilling, *How God Became Jesus: The Real Origin of Belief in Jesus' Divine Nature—A Response to Bart D. Ehrman* (Grand Rapids: Zondervan, 2014).

had its day. Nevertheless, Ehrman's books can draw on the myth when needed, producing and defending critical judgments on historical claims behind a wall of historical objectivity, stating that to read the New Testament critically rather than devotionally leads to a right understanding of its true nature as a fully human document, an understanding that Ehrman states is shared as a consensus among New Testament scholars who are not caught up in the church's theological concerns. Yet such an appeal to historical objectivity is a bit strained, for book titles like Ehrman's are not about conveying a cool academic objectivity—they are about a particular type of critique and even evangelization. Ehrman is not simply a gifted historian and textual critic—he is an atheologian of Gospel cynicism.[4] This fact is not refuted simply by Ehrman's appeals to historical criticism as an impartial discipline, for as we have seen earlier, one need not abandon oneself to a relativism of all historical judgments to see that historical criticism has oftentimes been in truth the means by which we argue for our convictions behind a veneer of objectivity.

Rather than focus on a detailed response to Ehrman's claims made in books with salacious titles that, one must admit, are brilliantly conceived to move paper (such a response is a task best left to historians better trained in textual criticism and the New Testament world), I want to focus on a book with a more serious title and attempt to display the theological and philosophical presuppositions that may be lurking in the background, although historical considerations will not be excluded (and there I will borrow from the New Testament historians aforementioned).[5] I then hope to show that a full consideration of Scripture, and specifically of Scripture as canon, can never be about only the canon itself, nor can it be circumscribed in tightly

---

[4]Clearly evident in another provocatively titled work that has little or nothing to do with historical scholarship (Ehrman's area of expertise) but one replete with theological judgments: *God's Problem: How the Bible Fails to Answer Our Most Important Question—Why We Suffer* (San Francisco: HarperOne, 2009).

[5]For accessible responses to Ehrman, see Craig A. Evans, *Fabricating Jesus: How Modern Scholars Distort the Gospels* (Downers Grove, IL: InterVarsity Press, 2006); Timothy Paul Jones, *Misquoting Truth: A Guide to the Fallacies of Bart Ehrman's* Misquoting Jesus (Downers Grove, IL: InterVarsity Press, 2007); J. Ed Komoszewski, M. James Sawyer and Daniel B. Wallace, *Reinventing Jesus: What* The Da Vinci Code *and Other Novel Speculations Don't Tell You* (Grand Rapids: Kregel, 2006); see also Craig A. Evans, "Textual Criticism and Textual Confidence: How Reliable Is Scripture?" in *The Reliability of the New Testament: Bart D. Ehrman and Daniel B. Wallace in Dialogue*, ed. Robert B. Stewart (Minneapolis: Fortress, 2011), pp. 161-72.

historical categories. For both those who accept and those who reject its broad claims, canonical judgments are theological, and not only historical, for the term "canon" is a theological concept as well as an object of historical interest. Moreover, and more important still, such judgments are always christological at their heart.

A Plethora of Christianities

In *Lost Christianities: The Battles for Scripture and the Faiths We Never Knew*, Ehrman displays in the title the central convictions that guide his understanding of the biblical canon and its constitutive books in matters of origin, transmission, collection and eventual canonization.[6] In the canon, as well as the history that lies behind its formation, Ehrman sees only diversity, rather than unity; he sees relativism of religious perspectives, rather than a reality to which the canon attests; he sees ecclesiastical power and popularity wielded to eliminate rival understandings, rather than prudent and apt ecclesial judgments; and he sees what was lost, rather than what was gained, in ecclesial and conciliar decisions regarding canonization. One should not begin by faulting him for this type of vision, even if his first example of diversity begins not with the canon itself but the modern-day plethora of groups under a Christian banner ("New England Presbyterians and Appalachian snake handlers. . . . Greek Orthodox priests. . . . liberal Methodist political activists . . . Pentecostals who think that society will soon come to a crashing halt with the return of Jesus").[7] Ehrman is entirely in the right to highlight such pluralism. Such diversity today is irrefutable and simply a given. But diversity itself is never the issue, but rather what one makes of it. For Ehrman, such diversity means that one may be best served to speak of Christianities, rather than Christianity, and that normative canonical and conciliar judgments are suspect. Moreover, such diversity for Ehrman is not found simply among the seemingly innumerable groups of readers of the biblical canon in the present, but within Christianity in its very earliest centuries. And here Ehrman throws the floodgates open as wide as possible: "In the second and third centuries there were, of course, Christians who be-

---

[6]Bart D. Ehrman, *Lost Christianities: The Battles for Scripture and the Faiths We Never Knew* (Oxford: Oxford University Press, 2003).
[7]Ibid., p. 1.

lieved in one God. But there were others who insisted that there were two. Some said there were thirty. Others claimed there were 365."[8] Such a collection of sentences would be well served with at least one footnote. But alas.

Of course, diversity did in fact exist in the ancient world among groups making claims about Jesus.[9] *That* significant diversity existed is unquestionable for anyone with even a passing familiarity with the early church of the second and third centuries. Such diversity itself, however, was not unquestioned. Beginning within the texts of the New Testament themselves, those found within the first century, certain positions were rejected in the very act of making positive claims—diversities seen as beyond the pale (1 Jn 2:22 and 1 Jn 4:1-3 are but two pertinent christological examples). Later in the second century, larger and more developed ways of thinking about Christ were likewise rejected and disappeared from history (e.g., Docetism, Ebionism and Gnosticism), and in time some grand attempts at articulating a common faith were formulated by the churches—attempts that not only provided positive articulation but also excluded rejected positions (the Nicene Creed and Chalcedonian Definition being perhaps the most important examples). Moreover, a biblical canon was formed which, despite the ongoing diversity of its Old Testament component among ecclesial traditions, existed in a New Testament collection of twenty-seven books that gained broad consensus as canonical Scripture and that is read across Catholic, Orthodox and Protestant lines.

---

[8]Ibid., p. 2.

[9]That Ehrman draws his examples only from the second century and later is telling, however. Ehrman's examples of the Ebionites, the Gnostics and Marcion are all second-century examples; the only first-century example of such diversity is that between Paul and his opponents regarding the Gentiles and the law, and it could be argued that he exaggerates these differences in order to buttress his claim of many different "Christianities" of equal worth and validity in the early centuries. While these differences between Paul and certain Jewish Christians who demanded that Gentiles follow the law were serious and divisive, no evidence is forthcoming that any early Christians proposed a different understanding of the death and resurrection of Jesus and thus a radically different Christology such as we see in the second century (see *Lost Christianities*, pp. 95-112). To speak of "lost Christianities" may be judged an anachronistic importation of later debates into the first century, seeing plurality where it does not exist, and confusing plurality, where it does exist in the later centuries, with relativism and claims for equal authenticity and authority among the rival parties. Ehrman's conviction that the Ebionites may be closest to the first-century disciples is not convincing (p. 253). Craig Evans concludes: "In short, Ehrman and others who speak of 'lost Christianities' are talking about individuals and groups who moved away from the earlier, widely attested teaching of Jesus and the first generation of his followers. These hypothetical Christianities did not exist in the middle of the first century" (Evans, *Fabricating Jesus*, p. 203; see also pp. 180-203).

Ehrman is of course fully aware of this emerging consensus. But this movement to canonical and theological uniformity was, he contends, the result of a power play, or rather, a number of them. The canon itself was the product of the exclusion of other textual voices by means of those in ecclesial predominance. The canon was not only a late development (fourth century and later) but also the result of a powerful and successful attempt to exclude other books with, in his words, "equally impressive pedigrees— other Gospels, Acts, Epistles, and Apocalypses claiming to be written by the earthly apostles of Jesus."[10]

Now, from a purely historical standpoint, such a claim is itself not compelling and is far from a settled conclusion of historical scholarship. To state that these other books possess "equally impressive pedigrees" is misleading at best. As but the most important example, the Synoptic Gospels of the New Testament are nearly universally regarded to have been written by the close of the first century and had a wide circulation by the second, and indeed were never challenged after their appearance. To provide a Gospel of an equal stature, Ehrman puts forward the *Gospel of Thomas*, a Gospel that he states is "arguably the single most important Christian archaeological discovery of the twentieth century."[11] Later he writes that the *Gospel of Thomas* is "the single most important noncanonical book yet to be uncovered, a collection of the sayings of Jesus, some of which may be authentic, many of which were previously unknown."[12] He states that many of its sayings are "pithier and more succinct than their canonical counterparts" and intriguingly asks: "Is it possible that Thomas presents a more accurate version of the sayings [of Jesus] than, say, Matthew, Mark, and Luke . . . that is, a closer approximation to the way that Jesus actually said them?"[13] This possibility is especially intriguing to Ehrman because the *Gospel of Thomas* presents a

---

[10]Ehrman, *Lost Christianities*, p. 3. In this, Ehrman's views of canonization seem to align with the general conclusion of Robert Funk when he states: "Canonization, in fact, was an integral part of the bureaucratization and politicization of the tradition" which itself served to "flatten and crystallize the tradition." See Funk, "The Once and Future New Testament," in *The Canon Debate*, ed. Lee M. McDonald and James A. Sanders (Peabody, MA: Hendrickson, 2002), p. 545. Like Ehrman, Funk equates canonization with the process whereby the strong seek to preserve their authority and power (p. 545).

[11]Ibid., p. 14. One could be forgiven for thinking this was actually the Dead Sea Scrolls.

[12]Ibid., p. 51.

[13]Ibid., pp. 55-56.

Christ very different from the Christ of the Synoptic Gospels and that of the Gospel of John, a picture not of a risen Lord but of a cryptic sage. In *Thomas's* frame of reference, salvation comes not from Christ's death and resurrection but from his secret sayings.[14]

Once again, however, there are problems with this interpretation. A preliminary problem is that Ehrman has no basis for judging between the Synoptic picture of Jesus and that of the *Gospel of Thomas* on purely historical grounds if the *Gospel of Thomas* is only of "equally impressive" pedigree with that of the Synoptics and John. In order to be given at least equal if not superior weight as Ehrman himself seems to imply and maintain, it must actually be a Gospel that presents a "more accurate version" of Jesus' sayings and thus stands closer to him in time.[15] Let us here engage in some arguments *kata sarka*, "according to the flesh" (on purely historical grounds) which, for Ehrman, are the only kind of arguments that matter.

Even limited to historical considerations, without appealing to overt theological conviction, Ehrman's is a position that many will find underwhelming. First, contrary to claims that the *Gospel of Thomas* represents an early and widespread tradition, it is difficult to imagine such a Gospel gaining any wide acceptance in the early church, which by the end of the first century had widely accepted the Synoptic Gospels and Paul's letters such that collections of both were widely circulating among the churches, and for which the death and resurrection of Christ form the heart of the gospel in its earliest and nascent form and present a very different picture of Jesus (for instance, Paul's texts of 1 Cor 15:1-11 and Phil 2:1-11). Moreover— and yet again *kata sarka*—perhaps just as damaging to Ehrman's thesis is the fact that, rather than reflecting the early traditions of Jesus' sayings, the *Gospel of Thomas* is, in light of recent scholarship, most certainly late in composition, itself the product of a gnostic sect. Contrary to Ehrman's assertion that in *Thomas* we have another independent source of the oral tradition going back to Jesus, and one perhaps as early and reliable as that of the Synoptics, what we really seem to have is a work of the mid-to-late second century that relied not on an early tradition predating the Synoptics but on the Synoptics themselves, and according to one historical reconstructive

---

[14]Ibid., pp. 57-58.
[15]Ibid., pp. 57-59.

account, as dependent on them as they were transformed and indeed corrupted in Tatian's *Diatessaron*.[16] Therefore, rather than getting closer to Jesus,
we are now one step, and perhaps two steps, removed in time. *Thomas* is not
only itself reliant on the earlier Synoptics but perhaps on a harmony of them,
and it seems to be a distortion of both at that.

It would be a mistake, however, to think that Ehrman's objections to the
present canon of the church are simply based on historical miscalculations.
He writes: "We now know that at one time or another, in one place or another, all of these noncanonical books and many others were revered as
sacred, inspired, scriptural."[17] But, apart from this statement's glossing over
the difference between a book's being read, being "revered" and being
"scriptural," much less "canonical," and without defining these carefully, why
does Ehrman believe that the churches rejected the vast majority of these
texts and quite quickly abandoned them all in favor of what became the
core of the New Testament? His answer hinges on power politics: one of a
vast array of interpretations of Jesus Christ and its adherents gained the
upper hand and won the day, and thus one form of Christianity excluded
all other (valid?) forms. He does not consider the possibility that these
books were rejected because they failed to express Jesus as he was remembered by the disciples, and more or less faithfully rendered through a reliable oral and then written tradition. Nor does he seem to entertain the
notion that perhaps not only for modern historians but also for the original
disciples and their successors, Jesus was not an infinitely malleable object
but a subject who impressed himself on his disciples and for whom they
were witnesses, and whose collective witness, handed down orally and
then collated and written, thus became the basis for a normative understanding of his person inchoately yet nonetheless faithfully reflected in
what came to be regarded as, however anachronistically termed, orthodoxy

---

[16]See Nicholas Perrin, *Thomas: The Other Gospel* (Louisville, KY: Westminster John Knox, 2007),
as well as his *Thomas and Tatian* (Atlanta: Society of Biblical Literature, 2002). An accessible
discussion of *Thomas* is provided by Evans, *Fabricating Jesus*, pp. 52-77. Recently, however, Perrin's claims have been questioned as regarding the Gospel's original language and origin, but not
so as to call into question *Thomas's* later date and reliance on the Synoptics themselves. See
Simon Gathercole, *The Composition of the Gospel of Thomas: Original Language and Influences*
(Cambridge: Cambridge University Press, 2012).

[17]Ehrman, *Lost Christianities*, p. 4.

(or proto-orthodoxy).[18] For Ehrman, rather, following the general path and position if not the details of the historian of dogma Walter Bauer, the term "orthodox" has nothing to do with truth at all but is simply a label the winners of a conflict of power gave to themselves to justify their villianizing of their defeated opponents, the "heretics." Thus Ehrman consistently places "orthodoxy" and "heresy" in quotation marks, as if to give us a wink, that we really know that these are categories only of power and popularity, not truth.

As such, heresy and orthodoxy have little or no meaning for Ehrman apart from "the losers of a conflict" and "the winners of a conflict," respectively.[19] On one level, there is truth to this, but when put forward as the only position of interest to historians, it can itself become distorting. The question of truth seems not to arise for Ehrman, except ironically when the im-

---

[18]Ehrman is consistently skeptical of the oral tradition (both its content and its transmission) lying behind the Synoptic Gospels. For a sober yet contrary assessment of this oral tradition and transmission, see James D. G. Dunn, *A New Perspective on Jesus: What the Quest for the Historical Jesus Missed* (Grand Rapids: Baker, 2005). Relevant for the matters under consideration is Dunn's conclusion that "*variation in tradition does not of itself either indicate contradiction or denote editorial manipulation*. Variation is simply the hallmark of oral tradition, how the Jesus tradition functioned" (p. 123).

[19]Ehrman, *Lost Christianites*, pp. 13, 163-80. For Ehrman's reflections on the terms "orthodoxy" and "heresy" in addition to the discussion in *Lost Christianities*, see Ehrman, *Orthodox Corruption of Scripture*, pp. 3-17; also Ehrman, *The Lost Gospel of Judas Iscariot* (Oxford: Oxford University Press, 2006), pp. 174-79; and Ehrman, *Jesus, Interrupted*, pp. 212-16. He notes that these terms are not useful for historians because they imply value judgments regarding which group was right and which wrong (*Lost Gospel*, p. 175). Ehrman then notes: "Historians have gotten around that problem by redefining what these terms mean. Rather than using the term *orthodoxy* to say that one group was right in what it believed about God, historians today use it to refer to the group that won the disputes over what was right. One group overcame all its opposition and became the dominant form of the religion; it then decided what creeds Christians should recite and what books they ought to consider authoritative. From a historian's perspective, this dominant group is labeled 'orthodox' not because it was necessarily right but because it was the one that decided what would be right" (*Lost Gospel*, p. 175). If this exhausts the matter, however, we are left with the unspoken assumption that the one who must in the end decide if something was "necessarily right" is the modern impartial historian. Indeed, historical judgments themselves then seem to submit to ones that dictate that all past historical judgments of acceptance and rejection could only have been arbitrary and predicated on matters of power: "The Gospel of John was preserved throughout the Middle Ages because it was accepted by the orthodox party; the Gospel of Judas was not preserved because it was deemed heretical" (*Lost Gospel*, p. 175). But perhaps this acceptance and rejection was due to matters of truth (even historical truth) as much as power? Is this a possibility that could be *historically* considered? Perhaps this attempt to navigate theological understandings of Jesus goes beyond historical criticism's jurisdiction. But if so, then also beyond its scope of jurisdiction, it would seem, are Ehrman's implicit and sometimes quite explicit judgments of theological relativity between such books.

pression is consistently given that whatever hints at Nicene orthodoxy is suspect and whatever hints at Gnostic thought is promising. Ehrman's method of analyzing what was lost is to engage in hypothetical "if . . . then" thought experiments, such that *if* a different "form" of Christianity had won, *then* this would have changed the nature of the canon (which would now be composed of other books), and thus the nature of confession itself (for instance, the confession of two gods, rather than one, and no confession of the divinity of Christ as displayed in the Nicene and Chalcedonian formulas).[20]

On the surface, this seems trivial: had historical outcomes been different, so would other historical outcomes have been, as best we can imagine. But more seriously, it is a curious way to go about historical scholarship—a bit akin to investigating American history by asking: What would have happened had Columbus and the Europeans never come to America? These may be intriguing questions, and certainly are entertained by everyone from time to time, but it is a strange thing to relegate almost unilaterally all historical decisions to arbitrary contingencies. For Christians of a traditional stripe (and not just of a fundamentalist bent), the question of the canon can never be one fully captured in terms of historical contingency and relativity but is more like the question, "What if alchemy had succeeded over chemistry?" An interesting question—even a real one in history, at least for a time, but less so in the light of a wider historical lens. There were reasons why the first disappeared and the latter continued, and the category of power politics seems quite inadequate to capture their scope. For Ehrman, however, canonical decisions are best and rightly understood as the product of historical accident, while for the Christians who were actually involved in such decisions and those who affirm them today, canonical judgments were matters of discerning a real truth, of the confession of what can only be said in the light of a reality revealed in a particular historical appearance. Of course this itself is a judgment with its own presuppositions. Certainly canonical questions are not entirely settled, nor is the canon's history a straight and smooth path of ratification and acceptance. Nevertheless, for the early church there was a truth to pursue. The matter of truth seems to play little role in Ehrman's approach in estimating these historical disputes and deci-

---

[20]Ehrman, *Lost Christianities*, pp. 6, 247, et al.

sions, with all attention and emphasis given instead to the explanations of power and contingency. Now to be fair, Ehrman deems such questions as touching on the matter of theological judgments, and such judgments are for him outside the scope of what a historian can speak.[21] But this firmly stated principle is not consistently followed. Ehrman does not in fact limit himself strictly to historical observations, for he not only recognizes theological plurality but also moves beyond its mere recognition to argue for the relativism of the various views held, explaining the predominance of one view as due only to the contingencies of power. This is a curious way to make an argument, for certainly there could be many rival claims within modern science, but plurality of positions need not make all equally valid. Sometimes positions are rejected because they are, quite simply, wrong-headed, misinformed and inaccurate, even historically so.

The danger that we have been dancing around is whether Ehrman confuses pluralism with relativism, which in itself is as much a philosophical problem as a historical one. That there were rival accounts of Christianity during the early centuries of its existence does not entail that all were equally faithful to the teachings of Jesus or rightful interpretations of his person. Ehrman knows this, yet in the end he seems committed to a pluralism that rolls over such questions of truth, eschewing normative Christianity for matters of relativism. This in turn causes one to wonder if he has furthermore confused popularity with normativity, as when he states that the *Gospel of Peter* was more popular than that of Mark based on the number of surviving manuscripts.[22] Because

---

[21]Ehrman, *Forgery and Counter-Forgery*, p. 7.

[22]Ehrman, *Lost Christianities*, p. 23. This is perhaps especially distorting because within early extant lists of canonical books, Mark appears in all of them, whereas the *Gospel of Peter* appears in none except to be repudiated. See Lee Martin McDonald, *The Biblical Canon: Its Origin, Transmission and Authority* (Peabody, MA: Hendrickson, 2007), appendix C, pp. 445-51. Everett Ferguson writes in a related vein: "The continuity of these gospels [the canonical Gospels] with the Old Testament story contrasts with the apocryphal gospels, notably the *Gospel of Thomas*. This finding coincides with the fact that there is no time in Christian history after the writing of the four gospels when one can find evidence of their not being accepted as scripture" (Ferguson, "Factors Leading to the Selection and Closure of the New Testament Canon," in McDonald and Sanders, *Canon Debate*, p. 30); see, however, the somewhat more complex and untidy picture painted by Harry Y. Gamble, "The New Testament Canon: Recent Research and the Status Quaestionis," in McDonald and Sanders, *Canon Debate*, pp. 267-94. Nevertheless, Ferguson is sound in his conclusion: "If other gospels such as the *Gospel of Thomas* and *The Gospel of Peter* were as early as the canonical gospels, then the need for differentiation between what was authentic and correct and what was not was equally early; if those works are later, they represent alternatives produced in part under the influence of the canonical gospels" (Ferguson, "Factors

the theme of truth is excluded, only the themes of popularity and power remain. These philosophical and theological judgments lead Ehrman to make questionable historical ones. For instance, we might ask, when did history relegate questions of truth to the simple counting of witnesses or manuscripts? Suppose (simply for sake of argument) that years from now archeologists dig up large numbers of young earth creationist tracts and but few scientific text-books in a world after an apocalyptic, catastrophic event—not entirely im-plausible, because more people currently reject evolutionary theory than accept it.[23] Yet, this dearth of manuscript evidence does nothing to undermine evolutionary theory or its claims, nor does it determine their truth. There is an analogy here that holds however different the areas of science and history. In canonical judgments no less than in textual ones, matters must be weighed and not simply counted.

This realization thus points to the possibility that there may be philo-sophical problems as well as historical ones with Ehrman's approach. I wonder, for instance, if the "diversity equals relativity" argument really has any ongoing normativity or usefulness when Ehrman leaves the confines of his scholarly office and flips on the evening news. There is a plurality of opinions in the world today about women and their access to education, a diversity of beliefs about racism, a superfluity of beliefs about a host of moral issues. Does such diversity mean that one position is "right" and one "wrong" simply because of the imposition of a view by the strong on the weak? (See how easy it is to play with scare quotes?) Certainly if we are simply counting the various views of women and their place in society, the Western egalitarian ideal fares poorly in terms of global popularity and may be seen by some as either implicitly and sometimes explicitly imposed by America's powerful hegemony. So while fully acknowledging with Ehrman the question of the Bible's very human pedigree, the moral ambiguity of many passages within it (whether regarding women, slaves, or others) and the politics that unquestionably surrounded the early church's conciliar decisions, we are still left with questions regarding Ehrman's scholarly

---

Leading to the Selection and Closure," p. 304). It should be clear by now that the latter seems almost certainly closer to the truth.

[23]Here I draw on a scenario similar to the hypothetical one that begins Alasdair MacIntyre's *After Virtue*, 2nd ed. (Notre Dame, IN: University of Notre Dame Press, 1984), pp. 1-5.

method, in which diversity entails relativity and popularity entails normativity, and which, if carried through to today, seems to make moral prophets unintelligible.

THE REAL SCANDAL OF THE BIBLICAL CANON

In the end it is inevitable, however, that the question of the canon cannot be limited to its historical development but must include a serious appraisal of its theological claims, and thus its truth, if one is to evaluate and set forth the "gains" and "losses" of its final determination as Ehrman proposes. To fail to consider such claims openly and sweep them aside by pointing instead to the historical phenomena surrounding the formation of the texts in which they arise is to make the oft-repeated mistake of the genetic fallacy—in this case, the implicit claim that by exposing the complexity of the canon's development and ascertaining its variegated and even messy formation we can relativize and thus implicitly dispose of its claims to truth. Such dubious reasoning is not restricted to textual matters, of course, but seems to be a mark of our age. As but one example, the attempt to ascertain an evolutionary development of religion is used by some in turn to dismiss its claims. One need not be sympathetic to natural theology or a generic religiosity to acknowledge the problems of such thinking. While in a similar worldview it is also true that mathematical thought is dependent on the evolutionary development of the cerebral cortex, this fact tells us nothing much about the truth of "$2 + 2 = 4$"—nor, one would guess, would such a truth be used as an argument to dismiss the relevance or validity of mathematics.

In a similar manner, drawing attention to the complex and indeed contentious history of canonization does not, in the end, undermine the seriousness of the theological claims the canon puts forward, claims that must be judged in the end on their own merits. To deny this is to embrace an implicit principle that Ehrman himself seems to espouse, one classically expressed by D. F. Strauss: "The true criticism of a dogma is its history."[24] Yet Karl Barth may in the end have had a more steady and sure grip on both the

---

[24] Attributed to Strauss in Martin Hengel, *The Son of God: The Origin of Christology and the History of Jewish-Hellenistic Religion*, trans. John Bowden (London: SCM Press; Philadelphia: Fortress, 1976), p. 6; quoted also in Larry W. Hurtado, *Lord Jesus Christ: Devotion to Jesus in Earliest Christianity* (Grand Rapids: Eerdmans, 2003), p. 8.

realities of such messy historical development and the dangers of slipping from an acknowledgment of this untidiness to a false conclusion, for as Barth once said with an eye on the politics and intrigue of Nicaea as well as that of any such council: "There is no confession whose authority might not seem endangered by the history of its origination. But there is none whose authority might not have the testimony of the Holy Spirit in spite of that history."[25] This divine affirmation may go beyond the historian's interest but belongs inescapably to the church's confession and is a matter of concern if only implicitly for all those who reject such a confession entirely. At the very least, Barth's dictum does not commit the fallacy of dismissing the truth claims of an ecclesial judgment and position on the grounds of its complex and perhaps even contentious origin and circumstances. Such cannot be said of Strauss's dictum, or of Ehrman's implicit principle of relative plurality.

That the church itself sees such questions of the canon in the light of discerning and confessing truth should therefore not lead one to dismiss the church's determination of the canon as hopelessly biased from the start. For in the end, all final judgments about the canon range beyond observations of its formation to questions of its character and indeed the veracity of its claims which at their heart are about God and Christ. Some confession, inevitably, must be made by all who approach the canon and examine it with seriousness and attention. This is why it is impossible in the end for the church's response to such attacks on the canon (whether old or new) to restrict itself to arguments on foreign soil, whether historical or philosophical. The church cannot in the end argue solely "according to the flesh," nor should it; to do so would not only be insincere in its reply to critics who pose to it serious questions but also cause it to be untrue to itself. The most important question of the canon is not one of an exhaustive historical reconstruction of its formation, nor even one of determining the closest and earliest historical proximity of books to Jesus in the first century. Both Kierkegaard and Barth realized that the apostles and the books written by them (or in the tradition they generated, it matters not—see Lk 1:1-2) were not accounts *only* valid and thus canonical because of their historical proximity to him, though this proximity did count for something important in

---

[25]*CD* I/2, p. 639.

arguments of antiquity and apostolicity. To be a witness to Christ, rather, was more than being a contemporary of his, for while to be a witness to Christ requires historical proximity, historical proximity does not of itself entail that one is an apostolic witness. Such arguments from proximity alone would be not only a theological mistake, but perhaps even historically questionable. One can imagine, for instance, a biography of Jesus written by a Jewish or Roman contemporary of him that treated him from the stance of cynicism and as a would-be messianic and/or magical pretender, or a first-century treatise written by a contemporary of Jesus filled with false polemical propaganda and spurious stories about him. That this claim that contemporaneity is not equal to canonicity *simpliciter* is not simply speculation is demonstrated by the fact that even some of the *first-century writings of authors such as Paul were not preserved.* That the others were preserved points to their almost immediate recognition as authoritative and of scriptural value and estimation.[26] Once again, contemporaneity does not equal apostolicity—not even, ironically, for the apostles themselves. James Dunn thus comes at the end of a long historical path of investigation to a quite traditional conclusion: "In short, the New Testament canon was not so much decreed as *acknowledged*."[27] Historical study can take us but so far, to the edge of a decision, but it does not force such a decision itself.

With this in view, we must conclude that the formation of the canon may indeed have taken into account the age of its constitutive books, though it was not solely determined by this account but ultimately by the nature of the witness that comprises them, for it is, after all, a canon and not simply a collection of texts, even the earliest ones. It points to a normative and accepted witness to a revelation and reality that the church confessed to have heard and encountered in Jesus Christ as it heard and read *these* books (and not others). And when this fact is taken into account, one begins to understand why the church had and continues to have a

---

[26]See James D. G. Dunn, "Has the Canon a Continuing Function?" in McDonald and Sanders, *Canon Debate*, pp. 566-68. Hence the historical conclusion of Dunn echoes that of Luther, perhaps a bit ironically: "The New Testament writings were hailed as canonical in recognition of the authority they had been exercising from the first and in steadily widening circles since then. It is not the church that determines the gospel, but the gospel which determines the church" (p. 568).

[27]Ibid., p. 568.

healthy skepticism with regard to those who would propose to revise the canon under the guise of a false scientific objectivity.[28] Make no mistake. When another canonical cynic of our time recommends a drastic revision of the canon and asks whether we shall "continue to affirm the picture of Jesus provided by the four canonical gospels" or whether we should rather "heed the findings of historical research," this has in fact only little to do with historical research but rather more with the presuppositions behind it that are nothing if not predicated on theological and christological judgments every bit as foundational as "objective" and "scientific" ones.[29] And it is generally recognized that the earliest Gospel, that of Mark, whose status as Scripture and whose canonical inclusion were universally unquestioned, mysteriously pointed at its conclusion not to a human sage but a risen Lord.[30]

In the end, the church felt compelled not only to accept books as canonical but also to reject others, and to do so because these others presented

---

[28]As seen in the prior chapter.

[29]Funk, "Once and Future New Testament," p. 541; see also p. 548. Commenting on the Jesus Seminar and such judgments, Darrell Bock perceptively concludes that what causes certain judgments to be made is in reality "the hidden Christological standard of the Seminar that is applied even when the source evidence goes the other direction. In fact, one can suggest that Christology is the *real* issue in the debate over many sayings, much more so than history or the objective application of abstract criteria. In an almost circular kind of way, a saying is accepted because it reflects a certain circumscribed Christology formed on an impression not created by the consistent application of the criteria, but by the preconceived, limited Christology. This Christology is affirmed because Jesus was only, it is argued on the basis of the accepted sayings, a sage and teller of parables" (Bock, "The Words of Jesus in the Gospels: Live, Jive or Memorex?" in *Jesus Under Fire: Modern Scholarship Reinvents the Historical Jesus*, ed. Michael J. Wilkins and J. P. Moreland [Grand Rapids: Zondervan, 1995], pp. 92-93), quoted in Komoszewski, Sawyer and Wallace, *Reinventing Jesus*, pp. 45-46.

[30]If true, then a rejection of the resurrection cannot be done purely on historical grounds (for *all* of the first-century Gospels mention and indeed presuppose it in framing their narratives), but on other theological or philosophical ones, including the latter ones that shape modern historicism, for it is these philosophical convictions that shape the historical ones, and not simply the historical discipline that shapes the philosophical commitments. Ehrman himself recognizes that the oldest Gospel not only was uniformly recognized as canonical but also that "the text is completely unambiguous that Jesus has been raised from the dead." See Bart Ehrman, *Did Jesus Exist? The Historical Argument for Jesus of Nazareth* (San Francisco: HarperOne, 2012), p. 29. Thus if historical proximity and authenticity were truly the only important criteria for claims about Jesus, the resurrection would seem to be a necessary element of whatever reconstruction of the historical Jesus was presented and, even if the resurrection were nonetheless rejected as in any sense historical, the attempt to find a "historical" Jesus behind the resurrected Christ of faith would need be abandoned, for it appears that, from the very beginning of the church's existence, these are not two persons but one. Yet it is of course only too true that historical considerations are never the only ones in play.

a different Christ than the one that the church heard, knew, confessed, worshiped and obeyed. What Ehrman and the average pious person in the pew may well agree on is that the Jesus of the *Gospel of Thomas* is a different Jesus than the Jesus of the New Testament Gospels.[31] Here the church rejected a Gospel which was not an openly proclaimed good news of salvation to be received by faith but an invitation to secret knowledge cleverly discerned, where Jesus is not the Good News itself in his person but the bearer of an esoteric message, and thus not the content but simply the deliverer of the message of salvation. This is a different Jesus than the one the church confessed from its earliest days. It is therefore not a stretch of the imagination but a sound historical judgment to conclude that for this reason, and this reason before all others, the church rightly rejected this Gospel as foreign to its earliest and most basic conviction that this Jesus is worthy not only of respect but also of worship "as to a god" (a conviction readily confirmed by both Pliny the Younger without and Athanasius within the Christian fold and evident already in the first-century Gospels).[32] Indeed, rather than affirming an evolutionary development of a high Christology that comes into fruition only in the fourth century with the events of the Nicene decision, as Ehrman and others maintain, recent historical study has in fact pushed such a Christology back deep into the first century as evidenced within the very earliest New Testament documents themselves.[33]

In light of this development, Ehrman's statement that the earliest Gospels knew nothing of Jesus as divine does not seem to pass muster.[34] For if we

---

[31]This is readily admitted by Ehrman himself as well as those who oppose his reading of the history of the canon. See Evans, *Fabricating Jesus*, p. 64.

[32]As witnessed in Mt 28:17; Jn 20:28.

[33]Ehrman's evolutionary view of Christology is evident when he writes: "Within three hundred years Jesus went from being a Jewish apocalyptic prophet to being God himself, a member of the Trinity," something Ehrman attributes to the creativity and power of the "proto-orthodox" (Ehrman, *Jesus, Interrupted*, p. 260). He does acknowledge, however, that even if the church "invented" this view, it is not necessarily untrue (see p. 292 n. 12).

[34]When, then, Ehrman states that "the view that Jesus was himself God is not a view shared by most of the writers of the New Testament" and "is, in fact, a theological view that developed rather late in the early Christian movement: it is not to be found, for example, in the Gospels of Matthew, Mark or Luke," we have a view that is not only theologically but also historically suspect, and in the end, a questionable interpretation of both (*God's Problem*, p. 273; cf. *Jesus, Interrupted*, pp. 16, 247, 249). For a quite different way to understand devotion to Christ in the very earliest centuries of Christianity, see Hurtado, *Lord Jesus Christ*; also Hurtado, *How on Earth Did Jesus Become a God? Historical Questions About Earliest Devotion to Jesus* (Grand Rapids: Eerdmans, 2005); see also Richard Bauckham, *Jesus and the God of Israel: God Crucified and Other*

take the Gospel of Mark, the earliest Gospel as admitted by all of critical scholarship today, and look at its portrayal of Jesus, we see an understated yet unmistakable pattern of correlation between Jesus' person and activity (and these intrinsically related) with the identity and activity of God. For important examples related to Jesus and the created order, we can briefly consider two familiar stories of Jesus on the Sea of Galilee. In Mark 4, Jesus rebukes the wind and the waves while in a storm that draws intentionally from the portrayal of God's power over the storm in Psalm 107 and the worship of God after the storm in Jonah 1, as well as the general Old Testament belief that God alone commands the weather. In Mark 6, Jesus walks on the waters of the sea, evincing God's portrayal in the Old Testament as walking on the waves, and then pronounces to the disciples that "It is I" (in the Greek equivalent of God's "I AM" revelation to Moses in Ex 3:14). He pronounces these words as he was about to "pass them by" as they were in the boat, words directly reminiscent of God passing by Moses long ago in a divine theophany. Both of these stories unmistakably point to a picture of Jesus that goes far beyond that of mere admiration or even reverence. In his commentary on Mark, James Edwards, having considered such passages, comes to a very different conclusion than Ehrman: "In this respect Mark's Christology is no less sublime than is John's, although John has Jesus *declaring* that he is the Son of God (John 10:36), whereas Mark has him *showing* that he is the Son of God."[35] Yet as Ludwig Wittgenstein has himself shown us, showing is a particular and powerful form of pronouncement.[36]

Here we come to the end of what historical or even exegetical study itself

---

Studies on the New Testament's Christology of Divine Identity (Grand Rapids: Eerdmans, 2008); Simon J. Gathercole, *The Preexistent Son: Recovering the Christologies of Matthew, Mark and Luke* (Grand Rapids: Eerdmans, 2006); and the essays esp. by Darrell Bock, E. Earle Ellis and James Dunn in *Jesus of Nazareth Lord and Christ: Essays on the Historical Jesus and New Testament Christology*, ed. Joel B. Green and Max Turner (Grand Rapids: Eerdmans, 1994).

[35]James R. Edwards, *The Gospel According to Mark* (Grand Rapids: Eerdmans, 2002), p. 199; for discussions of the passages mentioned in light of the Old Testament background and significance for understanding Mark's Christology, see pp. 147-52, 196-201. That Mark's Christology is more narrative than abstract or conceptual does not undermine its distinctive and even high character. For a balanced if perhaps overly guarded discussion in this vein, see R. T. France, *The Gospel of Mark* (Grand Rapids: Eerdmans, 2002), pp. 20-27.

[36]One could indeed argue that for the Gospel writers more than for any others before or since it is true that, in Wittgenstein's words, "the *meaning* of a name is sometimes explained by pointing to its *bearer*" (Ludwig Wittgenstein, *Philosophical Investigations* [Englewood Cliffs, NJ: Prentice-Hall/Simon Schuster, 1958]), p. 21.

can deliver. Ehrman, with skepticism and cynicism no longer masked behind a veil of objectivity, writes: "Someone decided that four of these early Gospels, and no others, should be accepted as part of the canon—the collection of sacred books of Scripture. But how did they make their decisions? When? How can we be sure they were right? And whatever happened to the other books?"[37] Later he continues:

> Where did we get our New Testament Gospels in the first place, and how do we know that *they*, rather than the dozens of Gospels that did *not* become a part of the New Testament, reveal the truth about what Jesus taught? What if the canon had ended up containing the Gospels of Peter, Thomas, and Mary rather than Matthew, Mark, and Luke?[38]

Returning to these questions at the end of the study, he writes:

> But why were these twenty-seven books included, and not any others? Who decided which books to include? On what basis? And when? It is one thing for believers to affirm, on the theological grounds, that the decisions about

---

[37]Ehrman, *Lost Christianities*, p. 3. Elsewhere he writes: "There were lots of early Christian groups. They all claimed to be right. They all had books to back up their claims, books allegedly written by the apostles and therefore representing the views of Jesus and his first disciples. The group that won out did not represent the teachings of Jesus or of his apostles. For example, none of the apostles claimed that Jesus was 'fully God and fully man,' or that he was 'begotten not made, of one substance with the Father,' as the fourth-century Nicene Creed maintained. The victorious group called itself orthodox. But it was not the original form of Christianity, and it won its victory only after many hard-fought battles" (Ehrman, *Jesus, Interrupted*, p. 215). Again, we may conclude that Ehrman has overlooked the power of showing versus declaring something, as well as confusing the full and expanded explication of a conviction with its earliest and nascent, nevertheless present and incipient, form. The absence of the first in the documents that present the second does not undermine their continuity of thought. In other words, just because the Nicene Creed is not in the New Testament does not entail that the creed is a betrayal or perversion of Gospel claims. It *may* be, but need not be. It may, in fact, be an elaboration of the ramifications of a truth to which the New Testament itself seems to point. In any event, Ehrman's skeptical questioning should at least be balanced with Bauckham's rather different conclusion about the New Testament and its claims for Christ, even while acknowledging New Testament differences from later conciliar formulas: "The earliest Christology was already the highest Christology" (Bauckham, *Jesus and the God of Israel*, p. x).

[38]Ehrman, *Lost Christianities*, p. 93; see also p. 248. "But where did this book [the New Testament canon] come from? It came from the victory of the proto-orthodox. What if another group had won? What if the New Testament contained not Jesus' Sermon on the Mount but the Gnostic teachings Jesus delivered to his disciples after his resurrection? What if it contained not the letters of Paul and Peter but the letters of Ptolemy and Barnabas? What if it contained not the Gospels of Matthew, Mark, Luke, and John but the Gospels of Thomas, Philip, Mary, and Nicodemus? Or what if it did not exist at all?" (p. 248). Certainly Ehrman does not underestimate the historical influence of Christianity as it came to be: "All things considered, it is difficult to imagine a more significant event than the victory of proto-orthodox Christianity" (p. 251).

the canon, like the books themselves, were divinely inspired, but it is another thing to look at the actual history of the process and to ponder the long, drawn-out arguments over which books to include and which to reject. The process did not take a few months or years. It took centuries. And even then there was no unanimity.[39]

Lying behind such words is of course Strauss's dictum. Nevertheless in fairness to these questions, we must admit that such cannot finally be answered by historical judgment alone. We might bring forth arguments as to the historical precedence of the Synoptic Gospels to that of the *Gospel of Thomas* or others as we have done. Certainly from a historical standpoint, such arguments can bear a particular and certainly quite important weight. But they cannot in the end answer why these books (and not others) *should* be in the canon, or why they should function as a unified authority, for such a normative authority cannot simply rely on historical antiquity or ecclesial precedent, even of the most august variety, but must remain a matter of contemporary confession that can only honestly and without pretense or embarrassment, humbly yet no less confidently, state that in these books the church has heard nothing less than the echo of a divine voice, but through that echo the divine voice itself. For this reason alone, Barth wrote, the acknowledgment of the canon's contents is the first act of Reformed confession. The canon comes first in this act of confession because the canon is first in the order of knowing, yet it is so only because it follows in truth and reality the confession *Iēsou Kuriou* in the order of being. For Barth, reflecting an ancient consensus, we have access to Christ only through his witnesses, and to these through Scripture.[40] The scandal of the gospel is thus the scandal of

---

[39]Ibid., p. 230. Though this claim itself again masks a historical reality: the center of the canon of the four Gospels and Paul's letters were very early accepted and widely dispersed. That the final form of the canon is not witnessed in its current configuration until Athanasius's *Festal Letter* (A.D. 367) does not mean that these books were not read as Scripture or collected in sacred groupings until this time.

[40]*CD* I/2, p. 583; also pp. 580-85, 552. Again Dunn reverberates this christological and theological point in his own historical way, yet in a way quite similar to Barth's own: "Here we must revert to our earlier talk of canon *within* the canon . . . and define the concept more carefully, for in fact Jesus-the-man-now-exalted is *the Jesus of the New Testament*: he is not separable from the New Testament; the diverse New Testament witness to him cannot be peeled away like a husk leaving an easily detachable Jesus-kernel. In other words, in Jesus as the center we have not so much a canon *within* the canon, as a canon *through* the canon, a canon embodied in and only accessible through the New Testament. *It is not possible to hold to Jesus the center without also holding to the New Testament witness to the center*" (Dunn, "Has the Canon a Continuing Func-

particularity, which is itself both christological and canonical, and these aspects are inseparable, though they exist in an irreversible order, for Christ does not exist for the sake of the canon, but the canon exists for the sake of Christ.[41] The particularity of God's revelation in Christ is echoed in the particularity of the books that witness to him.

Historical questions regarding the content and determination of the canon are thus peripheral questions that encircle an acknowledged or unacknowledged center, but a center, nonetheless. One can truly ask if the contents of a collection are the oldest texts that might be included in the collection. But the question of the canon is not simply one of historical age but of truth, not solely one of contemporaneity but of appointed and authoritative witness.[42] For this reason, Ehrman's picking at the edges of the

---

tion?" p. 572). Moreover, this is why the canon must stand not only within but also above all later church tradition, for as Dunn states, "with *only* the New Testament, and without all the rest of Christian history and documentation, we should have more than enough to serve as chart and compass as Christianity presses into the unknown future. On the other hand, with *all* the confessions, dogmas, traditions, and liturgies of church history, but without the New Testament, we would be lost, with no clear idea of what Christianity should be or of where it should be going" (p. 573; see also pp. 572-75).

[41]For this reason, the confession of Jesus as Lord, and the understanding of this confession, is not only shaped by the biblical canon but also in turn influences how it is viewed and understood. For the Christian who confesses Christ as Lord, the canon opens to reveal a unity that transcends its diverse themes and concepts. It is to be read in a particular light, a light that, it must be admitted, shines from its own pages. There is an implicit circularity here that for some appears lethal, yet for others witnesses to the fact that the Bible (through the Spirit) not only causes us to confess that "Jesus is Lord" (1 Cor 12:3) but that the confession in turn shapes our reading of Scripture as canon. The preeminent Christian question of the canon thus differs from that of Judaism from which it emerged, for as Brevard Childs writes: "Although the church adopted from the synagogue a concept of scripture as an authoritative collection of sacred writings, its basic stance toward its canon was shaped by christology" (Childs, *Biblical Theology of the Old and New Testaments* [Minneapolis: Fortress, 1992], p. 64, quoted by Lee McDonald and James A. Sanders, "Introduction," in McDonald and Sanders, *Canon Debate*, p. 14). Moreover, this entailed a relative indifference to interpretive methods among the New Testament writers, for a number of methods were employed and interwoven by authors who differed in method but agreed on one thing: "What they were conscious of, however, was interpreting the Scriptures from a Christocentric perspective, in conformity with the exegetical teaching and example of Jesus, and along Christological lines" (Richard Longenecker, *Biblical Exegesis in the Apostolic Period* [Grand Rapids: Eerdmans, 1975], p. 103, quoted in Bray, *Biblical Interpretation*, p. 65). For Ehrman, this intricate circle is a broken one wherein the history of Christianity (or Christianities) is one of competing theological convictions devoid of intrinsic truth that are victorious only because of decisions of propaganda and power. He thus reverses the question: whereas the church's self-understanding is that it acknowledged books as canonical that represented its faith and confession in the risen Lord, for Ehrman, the powerful chose books (and rejected others) which then in turn shaped the church's confession (see *Lost Christianities*, p. 11).

[42]For recent noteworthy theological accounts of the canon along such lines, see John Webster,

canon (books that were included, but may well have been left out; books that may have been left out, but perhaps should have been included) is, from a historical point of view, interesting and indeed not unimportant, yet it masks and indeed evades a larger question. For while there is indeed a diversity within the canon and its voices, the church confesses that God speaks through a canon that while questioned at the periphery is settled at the center.[43] Such peripheral questions, however abiding, should not be casually dismissed, yet also need not cause extraordinary anxiety for a church that remembers that canonical judgments like all other theological ones are seen through a glass darkly and await an eschatological future.[44] While there is indeed a plurality of voices, the canon implies, despite this plurality, a normativity of its truth and message, and in the case of the New Testament, the churches have in fact a broadly shared agreement as to the confession of the canon's constituency and authority. To speak of a canon implies a rule or standard in discerning a reality to which it attests as well as an exclusivity to its witness, rather than a relativism of competing voices that point to nothing besides their own cacophony of claims, each voice gaining ca-

---

Holy Scripture: A Dogmatic Sketch (Cambridge: Cambridge University Press, 2003), as well as his essays in *Word and Church* (Edinburgh: T & T Clark, 2001), pp. 9-46; for a different but related theological account that provides an alternative to Ehrman's own journey with Scripture, see Telford Work, *Living and Active: Scripture in the Economy of Salvation* (Grand Rapids: Eerdmans, 2001).

[43]Thus Christ is seen at the intersection that closes the era of promises and that marks the arrival of the era of fulfillment (Acts 2). The central concern of the early church regarding the Old Testament was therefore not the determination of a definitive canonical list of its contents but of a growing appreciation of its stereoscopic witness to the promises to Israel now fulfilled in Christ. Thus the later Christians simply accepted the consensus of Judaism on its canon even while differing on whether its Hebrew or Greek (Septuagint) form was to be accepted. To distinguish the periphery and the center goes beyond, however, the question of a stable collection of books (the Gospels and Pauline letters) surrounded by those that were more questioned in the early century (2 Peter, 2-3 John and Revelation, especially). To speak of a center is to speak of the canon as not only a matter of historical interest but also of theological significance. To abstract the historical questions from the theological ones can only lead to a misshapen understanding of what the canon is and how it functions. For an argument along similar lines, see Webster, *Holy Scripture*, pp. 5-6.

[44]As Childs concludes: "Perhaps the basic theological issue at stake can be best formulated in terms of the church's ongoing *search* for the Christian Bible. The church struggles with the task of continually discerning the truth of God being revealed in scripture and at the same time she stands within a fully human, ecclesiastical tradition which remains the trident of the Word. The hearing of God's Word is repeatedly confirmed by the Holy Spirit through its resonance with the church's Christological rule-of-faith. At the same time the church confesses the inadequacy of its reception while rejoicing over the sheer wonder of the divine accommodation to limited human capacity" (*Biblical Theology*, p. 67).

nonical entrance only because of an advocate's ability to wield and harness power and popularity, rather than prevailing because of its own truth discerned through prudent reflection, measured judgment and, from the church's confession as most important, hidden providence and divine action. If what was lost with the canon's determination is the *célébration de la différence*, and Ehrman does have a point in noting its loss, what was gained was the clarity and truth to which all scholarly endeavors at their heart subscribe. Or at least did so, before the adoption of the new bedrock of academic pursuit: *célébration de la diversité*.

Such should not be taken as a flippant or even absolute negative judgment against diversity itself. For the canon itself recognizes both a diversity of witnesses and a unity of subject, just as the church itself is, in the Pauline and Petrine traditions of the New Testament, a celebration of diversity in unity, of unity in diversity, of Jews and Gentiles together as God's new people.[45] Such canonical judgments were, of course, never flattened out into peons to diversity for diversity's sake if gutted of the scandal of the exclusive and central christological claims of Jesus as "the way, the truth, and the life" (Jn 14:6), or, in James Dunn's term for such canonical unity that may itself be overly modest and cautious, "Jesus-the-man-now-exalted."[46] Canonical judgments are and in fact always were ultimately about this christological and theological center, and not simply the historical periphery. The canon is a question of a norm, and not only a source, for Christian faith and life. It points to the confession of a single Lord among its unquestioned and readily acknowledged diversity of voices, and to the apprehension, to borrow a modern philosophical idiom, that while the various senses of the New

---

[45] 1 Cor 14:12-31; Gal 3:26-29; Eph 2:11-22; 4:1-16; 1 Pet 2:4-10; cf. Rev 7:9.

[46] Dunn, "Has the Canon a Continuing Function?" p. 561. Dunn's article is a brief but insightful entry point for considering both the unifying center of the New Testament as well as forms of acceptable and yet delimited diversity to which it witnesses. Dunn follows a similar pattern of thought as Barth when he states that it is the [christological] center that "*determined the circumference*" of the church's confession and life (p. 566). For this reason, Dunn argues that there are discernible boundaries beyond which the term "Christian" no longer applies (*pace* Ehrman): "Of course, to accept the New Testament as canon is not simply a matter of restricting the adjective 'Christian' only to the actual Christianity witnessed to by the New Testament. . . . But it does mean that any claimants to the title 'Christian' who cannot demonstrate their substantial dependence on and continuity with the New Testament (in its unity as well as its diversity) thereby forfeit their claim" (p. 566). Dunn adds: "There is nothing, beyond scholarly imagination and contrivance, to indicate that first-century diversity stretched much further than what is indicated by the New Testament writings themselves" (p. 567; cf. note 9 above).

Testament contents and christological titles differ, they share the same referent at their heart.[47] It is the church's acknowledgment of Scripture's unity in the midst of its diversity that is so different from Ehrman's stark conclusion: "The Bible is not a unity, it is a massive plurality."[48] Yet the acknowledgment and confession of Scripture's unity, however, is what it means to say that it is a canon and not simply a collection of texts.[49] It is the particular and exclusive esteem given to the canon by the church that lies at the heart of all objections to it and of calls (whether hidden behind a veil of supposed scientific objectivity or not) for its abnegation, augmentation or revision. For in the end, the most important question the New Testament canon poses to us is not whether or not we agree with its make-up but how we might answer the question at its center that looms behind all others on the circumference: "Who do you say that I am?"[50] When all of our questions are asked to Scripture, it is this one put to us that still remains. Such a question can be set aside, sublimated, all but ignored in favor of historical questions of dating, redaction, collection and transmission, and even brushed aside in the criticism of its historical authenticity. Nevertheless, it is inevitable for

---

[47]The relation of sense and referent pertains in the New Testament not only to the various christological titles attributed to Jesus but also to narrative descriptions, and extends outward to descriptions of Christian existence in the light of God's revelation of divine purposes in Christ insofar as all of the New Testament centers around the person of Jesus. The early church thus could accommodate the descriptions of Jesus in the four Gospels as, however diverse in sense, nonetheless presenting the truth of a single referent, the risen and exalted Lord Jesus Christ to whom the church gave worship and devotion and whom it understood to share in the creative and sovereign powers of YHWH. It did not, however, see the later apocryphal and pseudepigraphal Gospels as speaking of the same Jesus, and thus they were excluded from canonical status, readily evidenced in all extant canonical lists. Such narrative descriptions were the same not only in the Gospels themselves but also in the New Testament letters, regardless of their apostolic dispute found therein. In other words, the identity of Jesus as the crucified and risen Messiah was presumed by all of the writers of the New Testament documents. From a slightly different angle, we may say that the church sees the New Testament as a unity because "the interlocking character of so many of its component parts holds the whole together in the unity of a diversity which acknowledges a common loyalty" (Dunn, "Has the Canon a Continuing Function?" p. 579). This diversity includes that not only of material but also of function, according to Dunn. Intriguingly, the canonical structure itself of Gospels and Epistles "is the logical outgrowth and materialization of a revelation that articulates an event and the proclamation that follows, that is, Jesus and his disciples." See François Bovon, "The Canonical Structure of Gospel and Apostle," in McDonald and Sanders, *Canon Debate*, p. 516.

[48]Ehrman, *Jesus, Interrupted*, p. 279.

[49]As discussed in the prior chapter.

[50]Mk 8:29; also Mt 16:15; Lk 9:20; cf. Jn 6:67-69. With this inquiry we see that to give an answer to this question regarding Jesus' identity inescapably leads one also to give an answer, however implicitly, to the question of God's own identity and existence (Ex 3:14).

any who confront the New Testament as a canon rather than ill-conceived collection as one thing at the heart of many for any who would approach it with real seriousness. Questions of textual transmission and discrepancy, questions of canonical constituency, questions of Christian diversity, can mask the ultimate question, but they cannot replace it. We cannot live forever at the periphery.

Even here, Ehrman understands that this is what ultimately is at stake. When all is said and done, Ehrman is not a relativist in his judgments about early Christianity or Jesus himself. While for Ehrman all canonical and non-canonical books are limited and thus equally problematic for leading us to a true picture of who Jesus really is (and this knowledge, in the end, is the true holy grail Ehrman seeks), there is happily for him a more trustworthy way to find it. It is, in fact, by means of a quintessentially typical move of the modern period: one must get behind the propaganda of the texts of the ancient world about Jesus to reconstruct a true picture of him by means of historical criticism. It should not be overlooked that when Ehrman moves on to this task in a later study, he focuses on the Synoptic Gospels, not the *Gospel of Thomas*. What does Ehrman find? He finds a Jesus not entirely unlike the one found by Albert Schweitzer before him—Jesus as an apocalyptic prophet who died hoping for an immanent in-breaking of the kingdom of God.[51] Some type of answer must be given. Yet it is one that itself

---

[51]For Ehrman's thoughts on Jesus in this regard, see *Jesus: Apocalyptic Prophet of the New Millennium* (Oxford: Oxford University Press, 1999); also Ehrman, *Did Jesus Exist?* pp. 14, 37. Though this view of Jesus as apocalyptic prophet is central to his understanding of Jesus, Ehrman can describe Jesus as a religious genius as well. In either case, Jesus is a figure of the past, and thus the offense he gives remains for those of the past. Perhaps no one grasped the significance of this general relegation of Jesus to the past via historical criticism better than Kierkegaard: "The possibility of the offence with relation to Christ about which we have spoken [as a single individual in history] is a vanishing historical possibility which actually vanished with His death; it existed only for His contemporaries in relation to Him as this individual man. On the other hand, the possibility of offence at Christ *qua* God-Man will last to the end of time. If you take away the possibility of this offence, it means that you also take Christ away, that you have made Him something different from what He was, the sign of offence and the object of faith" (Kierkegaard, *Training in Christianity*, trans. Walter Lowrie [Princeton, NJ: Princeton University Press, 1952], pp. 94-95). Thus for Kierkegaard, and for Barth after him, a reconstructed historical Jesus can only be an abstraction that does not capture but evades the question of his true identity. All attempts to reconstruct his identity "behind" the texts of the New Testament are themselves *already predicated* on certain theological and christological presuppositions (and ones that often preclude the incarnation and the resurrection from the start), and ones that thus distort, rather than illuminate, his person. For the church, it is to know Christ "according to the flesh." But, as Paul states, "we know him thus no longer" (2 Cor 5:16, author's translation).

is more constructed against rather than with the grain of the earliest Gospels, all of which end with a risen Lord. While we can answer the question of Jesus' identity by constructing a historical picture of Jesus as an apocalyptic prophet and thus write our own ending to the gospel tale, the more we know, historically, of that tale, the more we realize (as we have seen) that the ending seems to have been already written. Perhaps the only thing on which all historians, as well as believers and cynics, seem to agree with regard to Jesus is that from the very first, and during his very life, he was a divisive figure, such that the immediate outcome of his life was a divergent and dichotomous set of viewpoints about him, some of which during his life brought him to his death.[52] From the days of Jesus' life until now, he has been the cause of dissention and inescapable decision. "Do you think that I have come to bring peace to the earth? No, I tell you, but rather division!"[53] Such words ring true regardless of the color we might decide to print them in our Bibles.

Turning the Tables

In the end, everyone has a perspective—even, perhaps, an agenda. Certainly the New Testament writers did, though that neither confirms nor abnegates their historical claims. The author of the Gospel of John, often maligned and distrusted in such details, is pretty clear as to why his theological treatise and historical account (both the one and the other in a single narrative) was written (see Jn 20:30-31). Paul is also quite open with his own perspective that could not ever be mistaken for cool detached objectivity (see 1 Cor 1–2). Ehrman must have his convictions, too. His criticisms, indeed, are easiest to take when he acknowledges his underlying convictions and approaches them with openness. Historical judgments are, as should be evident by now, never entirely shorn of underlying philosophical and indeed theological

---

[52]Hurtado, *Lord Jesus Christ*, pp. 63-64; Hurtado, *How on Earth Did Jesus Become a God?* pp. 2-3. This is as true today as when Jesus walked the earth, and is as true of New Testament historians as of the general populace. Lee McDonald writes: "Those who have experienced faith in Jesus as Lord generally have fewer problems acknowledging the message of the New Testament about him. This experience often is a distinguishing factor among biblical scholars today, though it is almost never discussed." See Lee M. McDonald, *The Story of Jesus in Faith and History: An Introduction* (Grand Rapids: Baker Academic, 2013), p. 45.
[53]Lk 12:51.

convictions.[54] Is there an agenda for Ehrman? I think the cards are laid on the table toward the end of the book, though a few perhaps are held back. Foremost on the table is the principle of tolerance, that most quintessentially (post)modern of all virtues.

For a contemporary academic committed to tolerance, there are few things more off-putting than an exclusive particularity. Ehrman rightly recognizes that this obstinate refusal to let a thousand flowers bloom was indeed what was at the very heart of early orthodox Christianity—that is, its exclusivity in worship and rejection of all syncretism. This was an exclusivity that, Ehrman rightly judges, "bred an intolerance toward religious diversity." These orthodox Christians were not sentimental or simply sincere but serious. For the proto-orthodox, "Faith was *in* something; it had *content*."[55]

Against such stark exclusivity, Ehrman presents the voice of tolerance, diversity and difference. It may indeed be the most cultured among the despisers who are most scandalized by the exclusive claims of the gospel, and he looks back with a sense of melancholy wistfulness at the "Christianities" that were lost, specifically "upon realizing just how many perspectives once endorsed by well-meaning, intelligent, and sincere believers came to be abandoned, destroyed, and forgotten—as were the texts that these believers produced, read, and revered." Yet sadness gives way to hope, for Ehrman states that a rediscovery of these once rejected ancient texts and their alternative religious visions might not only serve antiquarian interests but also provide a genuine retrieval of live options for today: "There is instead a sense that alternative understandings of Christianity from the past can be cherished yet today, that they can provide insights even now for those of us who are concerned about the world and our place in it."[56]

It is difficult not to be drawn to such an open and empathetic tolerance. Nonetheless, it is self-sacrificial love even of the enemy and hospitality of the stranger, not tolerance, that are Christian virtues (however imperfectly exemplified in history), and the former two cannot be identified with the latter. For the early Christians of the third and fourth centuries until those

---

[54]For a discussion of this element of New Testament historical study, see McDonald, *Story of Jesus in Faith and History*, pp. 3-45.

[55]Ehrman, *Lost Christianities*, pp. 255-56.

[56]Ibid., p. 257.

of today who maintain any semblance of embracing the scandal of the gospel's exclusive particularity, tolerance cannot become a cheap appeal to evade hard questions of truth. The only answer that the church can only give to its continuing exclusion of other books from its canon is that these other gospels present a different Jesus than that proclaimed in those found in Holy Scripture. The church has no other basis for its faith than such a statement, and certainly not a retreat to canonical boundaries upheld simply for the sake of tradition. And yet it is no betrayal of its faith, no cheap apologetic maneuver, no stooping to a need for external validation, to point out the lack of seriousness in Ehrman's questions, as if the early witnesses of the Synoptics, all of them written in the first century, could be compared with those of later centuries which in turn not only draw from them but also attempt to invoke authority by copying their form, such that imitation truly is the most sincere form of flattery. Ehrman lines these Gospels up with the Synoptics as if the choice between them could only be one of arbitrariness. For its part, the church's choice was anything but arbitrary, and there is not only no theological reason but also no historical reason to believe that any of these other Gospels (whether of Thomas, Peter, Mary, or others, all of which came at least one hundred years after the death of Christ) give us any more reliable, or even remotely reliable, witness to Jesus as he lived, taught and died (and was raised) than the canonical ones.[57] Nor is there a significant witness in the first century to another Jesus than the one the Synoptics present to us.[58]

---

[57]Perhaps the only exception to this would be the hypothetical source Q itself which lies behind the Synoptic text. Yet there is perhaps a very good reason that Q has not survived: it may have been a pre-Easter collection of sayings finding its initial form during Jesus' historical ministry. Therefore, rather than providing a rival "teaching" tradition over against the Gospels that stressed Jesus' death and resurrection, it is entirely possible that Q rather represented a preresurrection tradition that was later taken up into the larger picture of Jesus's postresurrection identity, and thus passed out of existence as it was superseded by that larger picture. Q then, too, is a remnant of knowing Jesus "according the flesh," and, in light of Easter, the apostles and the church "know him thus no longer" and faithfully included yet subsumed this source into its resurrection testimony. For an argument along similar lines, see James D. G. Dunn, A New Perspective on Jesus (Grand Rapids: Baker Academic, 2005), pp. 120-25.

[58]Evans, Fabricating Jesus, p. 189. He writes: "Christian faith began with the resurrection of Jesus, whose death was interpreted (in Jewish terms) as atoning and saving and in fulfillment of prophecy. There was no disagreement on this point. All who believed in Jesus and were numbered among his followers concurred on these essential beliefs. There was no other 'Christianity' that thought otherwise. The Gospels written in the first century, that is, the New Testament Gospels (Matthew, Mark, Luke and John), narrate the discovery of the empty tomb and appear-

Recently the tables seem to be turned on Ehrman, the skeptic now the target of the skeptical, the tolerant now becoming the intolerant. For despite Ehrman's critical positions, he firmly believes that there was a person named Jesus of Nazareth who actually lived. Yet to his acknowledged surprise, there is a whole body of literature that has appeared in recent years that denies that Jesus ever existed at all. Ehrman has not greeted this view with an open embrace in the spirit of broad-minded acceptance, nor does he think the truth or falsity of such a claim simply a matter of who can strong-arm an argument. Ehrman, on the contrary, seems perplexed and even a bit agitated by this novel idea of Jesus as total myth, and his recent book is an attempt to provide historical arguments for Jesus' existence and reasoned responses against those skeptics who deny that Jesus ever existed.[59] Hence the skeptic Ehrman now must take a very different tack.

In light of his earlier popular books and their own skeptical and at times quite cynical trajectories, there is something a bit jarring in reading this work, one in which the reader of his earlier books has the distinct impression of an author throwing the transmission hard into reverse. Is Ehrman now simply the "orthodox" who has labeled his own "heretics"? I suppose time will tell. No doubt, the new heretics will see his arguments as telling plays of power by one whose privilege (for are not university research professors the most privileged of all?) gives him a formidable publishing platform that in turn suppresses the *real* truth from coming forward.

In some timeless coffee shop, perhaps Irenaeus and Ehrman would have something to commiserate together about after all, because, despite their seemingly irreconcilable differences on religious tolerance, Irenaeus's argument for apostolic succession, and Ehrman's for academic expertise, while of course not identical, nevertheless bear a family resemblance.[60] Both argue for a received and established historical tradition of acceptance and acquaintance marked by reflective and careful transmission against the

---

ances of the risen Jesus to his followers. The resurrection of Jesus and its saving power become the central truth of Christian preaching and missionary activity, to which Peter and Paul give emphatic witness. There simply is no evidence of any other Christian movement in the first generation following Easter that preached something else" (p. 191).

[59]Ehrman, *Did Jesus Exist?*

[60]See ibid., pp. 4-5. To presume that modern historians are intrinsically better able to speak truthfully of Jesus of Nazareth than the ancient church with its received tradition seems to be nothing less than a case of chronological snobbery.

novel, new and not the least fecund views of those who espouse the strange, the esoteric and the ahistorical. Reading Irenaeus, and then Ehrman in this recent book, one senses in both a palpable frustration with this plethora of silliness. One wonders if it has ever crossed Ehrman's mind that this consternation is perhaps what Irenaeus—with his rule of faith and apostolic succession standing behind him, with a universally accepted quartet of Gospels in his hand, not to mention with a firm and ancient commitment to monotheism inherited from and stretching back to ancient Judaism—felt when confronted by seemingly intractable gnostic speculation and an unchecked proliferation of deities. *Célébration de la diversité* indeed.

THE MAKING OF A SKEPTIC

It would be a colossal mistake to think, however, that Ehrman's questions are not important. Nor should he be attacked as a particular kind of threat to Christian faith. Indeed, if anything, he reveals just how the church has failed honestly and straightforwardly to address difficult historical questions, and thus even his critical judgments serve a constructive and important service, not least for calling Christians out for their hypocrisy regarding the Bible.[61] Ehrman is, by all accounts (and his popular writings, which are refreshingly accessible and unpretentious, seem to reveal this), a critic who is often charitable to faith and who recognizes that his critical questions need not lead to agnosticism.[62] In short, he is someone with whom a Christian could enjoy having an ongoing conversation. This admission does not negate the strong statements previously made about some of his deeply problematic historical (and other) claims. Just as Harnack's historicism was itself shaped by numerous theological judgments and convictions, so also Ehrman's work is not simply one of "objective" history but of a theological manifesto. Facts are read in one way, rather than another. Such must be said regardless of the winsome way such claims are made.

And truth be told, the problems are not only on Ehrman's side of the ledger. Those who would take strong issue with his theological conclusions from the right side of the theological spectrum need recognize that skeptics like Ehrman are made, not born (and Ehrman has been quite open about

---

[61]Ehrman, *Jesus, Interrupted*, pp. 225-26.
[62]Ibid., pp. 269-83.

his Christian evangelical past and path to agnosticism). Ehrman's cynicism is the legacy of fundamentalism, and as has often been noted, there is no liberal fury so great as that of a fundamentalist scorned, though as far as such things go, Ehrman's rejection of his former faith often comes across as more reflective and wistful than reactionary.[63] For when Jesus Christ, risen and living as Lord, the revelation of God through his Spirit, is not the center but is replaced by elements along the periphery, and quite problematic ones at that—that is, a rigid inerrancy of fact and autograph (and who defines how much exactness must hold for such facts, and who has such autographs?); or scientific accuracy (and according to which science?); or even, though less common, the aesthetic literary qualities of Scripture (and according to whose tastes?)—then we should not be surprised that problems at the periphery become problems that take their place at the center. For any deeply reflective and observant Christian whose faith is made to rest on such a center—one who takes notice of textual variants and even knows what such are; one who recognizes Synoptic (and other) differences and even inconsistencies; one who learns that the history of the church's canonization is not unlike the messiness of a church business meeting today, for we should not hide the ecclesial fact that *plus ça change, plus c'est la même chose*—such questions become eventually unbearable. The center cannot hold. The vortex begins pulling faith in on itself.

Ehrman is adamant that it was *not* such historical questions, but ultimately the problem of evil, that evaporated what was left of his faith.[64] But such textual doubts could not help. Yet despite his move from faith to agnosticism, Ehrman has, interestingly, never really left the fundamentalist mindset behind—and a fundamentalist mindset is not easily shaken off even when intentionally repudiated. For fundamentalism, one factual error in the Bible means the entire structure crashes down, and the Bible becomes nothing but a human book. Ehrman still thinks this way, but he gave up propping the structure and stands amid the ruins of the crash.[65] These are

---

[63]Ehrman, *Misquoting Jesus*, pp. 1-15; Ehrman, *Jesus, Interrupted*, pp. 1-18. For a more embittered rejection of a former fundamentalist faith, see Funk, "Once and Future New Testament," pp. 548-49; also Funk, *Honest to Jesus* (San Francisco: HarperCollins, 1996); cf. Evans's discussion of such liberal conversions in *Fabricating Jesus*, pp. 19-33.

[64]Ehrman, *Jesus, Interrupted*, pp. 17, 277.

[65]Ehrman, *Misquoting Jesus*, pp. 1-15, 211-18.

the telling remains of a rigid fundamentalism that is, at its heart, and like
every type of legalism of which it is a modern variant, the placement of
matters along the periphery at the center. How many times the rooster
crowed before Peter's denial in the Gospels thus becomes a matter of faith's
life and death. This is why it may appear commendable for its biblical seriousness but is in fact theologically barren and pastorally disastrous.[66] At its
heart, liberalism of Ehrman's type is but the flip side of fundamentalism. It
is the phoenix that rises from the ashes of a burned faith. Yet considering
both of these twins is useful and necessary, for they remind us that Christians have faith in Christ, not in a particular theory of inspiration, or of interpretation or even of canonization, though that faith must take up historical study itself in order to rule out certain naive forms of each.

As noted, Ehrman has been quite open about his journey from evangelical
faith to liberal agnosticism. It would thus be grossly unfair to commit the genetic fallacy with regard to his own arguments, to dismiss his serious questions
by pointing back to their origin in his own journey to and away from faith. The
questions remain serious ones and remain so regardless of who asks them, and
the truth that is needed to answer them cares not for their origin. But we might
be forgiven for an indulgence to ask the type of hypothetical question that
Ehrman himself relishes: What might Ehrman have concluded had he not been
converted into such a narrow fundamentalist view of Scripture?[67] Ehrman
himself moved to the other side of the mirror, from (in those tired terms) fundamentalist to liberal. Yet in his views of Scripture, he is but a mirror image of
his former self—the central convictions about Scripture have, ironically, remained the same; only the conclusions have changed.

Karl Barth had another famous conversion from the faith of his youth,
but he moved in a very different direction. Barth never had a real interest in

---

[66]For a discussion of this point, see James D. G. Dunn, *The Living Word* (Philadelphia: Fortress,
    1988), pp. 106-7; also pp. 89-140. For the general problems of strict inerrancy, see pp. 89-140;
    and Paul J. Achtemeier, *Inspiration and Authority: Nature and Function of Christian Scripture*
    (Peabody, MA: Hendrickson, 1999), pp. 36-63.

[67]In fairness, this type of question can be turned on anyone. For my part, I have played that game
    with myself as well, wondering what my views of Scripture would be had I not had the great
    good fortune to encounter Donald Bloesch in the evangelical world during my undergraduate
    days rather than the rationalism of the modern inerrantists. It saved me greatly from the pain
    I witnessed in my seminary roommate, who had to navigate the vortex himself yet did not,
    thankfully, succumb to it.

strict Protestant views of inerrancy, but he moved away from the liberalism of his early years with his own kind of fervor. This move was not to a polar opposite side but to a different plane altogether, moving from a focus on our questions of Scripture to a new rediscovery of Scripture's own questions to us and the "strange new world within the Bible." In an essay in which he considered this new world of the Bible, Barth stated that the really important questions arise only after we have put the historical-critical ones behind us, not ignoring them, but with all seriousness considering them, acknowledging them, and yet then pushing on through them to consider the subject matter to which the books of the Bible, in their vastly different ways, seem to point.[68] Having passed through the higher critical camp, he well knew that in terms of its origination and composition, Scripture was human, all too human—in other words, human all the way down.[69] He did not deny the very human complexity and contingency Ehrman seems to have made a living pointing out—the textual variants of the surviving manuscripts; the complex and perhaps forever hidden path of their composition and transmission; the messy process of their acceptance, inscripturation and canonization. Barth was indeed on a different side of a historical brook that divides the premodern and modern periods; there was no going back to a timeless biblical naiveté, a textual innocence of easy harmonization, a simple view of pristine autographs, *leider*, lost to history. Barth faced the full complexity and diversity, and even in places moral ambiguity, of Scripture and its stories with no sense of theological or textual wistfulness for simpler times or apologetic defensiveness in facing his own.

---

[68]"It is all too clear that a rational and fruitful discussion about the Bible begins when we've admitted to and *gotten beyond* its human, historical-psychological character." Barth, "Biblical Questions, Insights and Vistas," in *The Word of God and Theology*, trans. Amy Marga (London: T & T Clark; New York: Continuum, 2011), p. 79. For an insightful discussion of how Scripture is abstracted from such rich theological understandings in the modern (and postmodern?) period, see Webster, *Holy Scripture*, pp. 17-41, as well as the often-overlooked yet brilliant discussion of biblical authority in James Wm. McClendon Jr., *Doctrine: Systematic Theology* (Nashville: Abingdon, 1994), pp. 454-88. He writes: "The Bible is for us the word of God written; it is that text in which the One who lays claim to our lives by the act of his life makes that claim afresh in acts of speech; it is for us God speaking; it is the word of God" (p. 464).

[69]"The Bible contains the literary monuments of an Ancient Near Eastern religion and of a religious cult of the Hellenistic epoch. As a human document like any other, it can lay no *a priori* dogmatic claim for special attention or consideration" (Barth, "Biblical Questions," p. 79). See also Barth, "The Authority and Significance of the Bible: Twelve Theses," in *God Here and Now*, trans. Paul M. van Buren (New York: Routledge, 2003), pp. 55-74.

And yet . . . and yet. What Oliver Wendell Holmes memorably longed for, Barth seemingly gained, namely, a simplicity on the far side of complexity, a unity on the far side of diversity.[70] In the midst of this acknowledged canonical diversity and complexity and even ambiguity, Barth saw a unity and a subject matter that the church could only confess, a unity that even brought the Old Testament and the New Testament with their respective array of voices into juxtaposition as a single story, joined not only in the proximity of a collection but also in the inseparable unity of a single canon. That discovery, the discovery of a seemingly infinite variety of voices and themes now joined into a united canonical witness to one theme, indeed to one Subject—this was Barth's discovery about the Bible. This question of unity does not deny real diversity—of the ups and downs of an elect people brought out of Egypt and into a new home; of stories of disciples who risked their lives for what they believed was more than a sentimental vision of remembrance; of a persecutor of the church who became its greatest evangelist; of a church that grew and expanded despite initial insignificance and continuing challenges without and within. All of these stories are ripples from a hidden center that continue to spread beyond the pages of Scripture throughout history, though historical criticism itself cannot say much about the rock that fell crashing into the middle of the pool and can only proffer improbable scenarios for the ripples, scenarios some take to be less improbable than the one scenario all of the early Gospels themselves openly attested and proclaimed. The question of this center, however, remains precisely at the canon's heart. And perhaps one of the greatest mysteries is that the distance of time that separates us today from those earliest witnesses and contemporaries of Jesus is less significant than that distance which separates the contemporaries Peter and Pilate, or of the church that confesses faith in Christ today from those who cannot confess it or are disinterested in or even put off by the very idea. It may be not our questions to the Bible, but the Bible's questions to us, that are in the end the most significant, the most intractable, even perhaps the most troubling. As Barth put this: "It is precisely not the right human thoughts about God that form the content of the

---

[70]"I would not give a fig for the simplicity this side of complexity; I would give my right arm for the simplicity on the far side of complexity" (attributed to Oliver Wendell Holmes).

Bible, but rather the right thoughts of God about humans."[71]

In considering those who would highlight the human, so very human, nature of the church's book, Christians of a traditional sort are not best served by beginning with a reactionary defensiveness. This is true even when a defense itself must be given, when skeptical claims require a straightforward and perhaps even pedantic dismantling of questionable historical judgments made by historical cynics. Nonetheless, perhaps it is best remembered that the church must first begin, even before this responsive task, with the humble but confident acknowledgment that it has had to embrace and confess from its very beginning: that for everything on this side of the line separating time and eternity, for the church's people and pastors, and even for its apostles and the writings that came from them (however indirectly), the same holds true, but really holds true: "We have this treasure in clay jars" (2 Cor 4:7). And this is perhaps mysteriously as true for the book of Christ as for his body, the church, and all those within. In the end, the church has no greater defense than confessing with Paul in that Corinthian letter that it really has no defense to give that is greater than its own proclamation of the Word it confesses to have heard and believed.[72] For while it is easy for humans to prove the humanity of Scripture in both its history and transmission, its reality as Word of God cannot be proven from this side of the line; it can only be witnessed to and proclaimed. The divine question regarding Scripture, as Barth stated in the *Church Dogmatics* in reference to Protestant doctrine, is a question that must be left unanswered, "because there at its weakest point, where it can only acknowledge and confess, it has all its indestructible strength."[73]

At the end of the day, the most important thing that Christians can do is point beyond the ripples in the pool to the one who has broken into history and explains their existence, the one who stands at the center of the canon. In this, the church of today follows the pointing hands of those who saw and heard and believed long ago, and thus we point with hands of our own:

---

[71]Barth, "The New World in the Bible," p. 25.

[72]"But we have this treasure in clay jars, so that it may be made clear that this extraordinary power belongs to God and does not come from us" (2 Cor 4:7). The church thus lives in faith and hope—for it lives by looking at what cannot be seen (2 Cor 4:18).

[73]*CD* I/2, p. 537.

We all know the uneasiness that comes over us when we look out our window and see the people on the street suddenly stop, turn their heads, shade their eyes with their hands and look straight into the sky at something that is hidden from us by the roof. The unease is not necessary; it is probably an airplane. But in the face of the sudden stopping, focused gazing, and tense listening that is characteristic of individuals in the Bible, we are not so quickly put at ease.[74]

---

[74]Barth, "Biblical Questions," p. 80.

8

Barth and Baptists

A Fellowship of Kindred Minds

✠

Next to Roman Catholics, the largest contingent of Christians in our world today belong to traditions that can be broadly defined as Free Church in order and conviction. Indeed, depending how one counts heads, this group may rival Catholic numbers in terms of actual regular church participation and attendance. Nevertheless, this group has been as difficult to categorize as to count. Troeltsch's term "sect" as a label has never been a particularly helpful one, and others have sought to provide more fitting descriptions. In recent years, James McClendon attempted to corral this contentious band of Christians under the term "baptist" (small-b Baptist) to signify those who shared a common hermeneutical strategy, theological vision and ecclesial form of life amid great outer diversity.[1] For McClendon, this group is neither Catholic nor Protestant but belongs to a third type of Christian existence altogether. While McClendon's placing of this type as equidistant from the magisterial Protestant tradition as from the Catholic one may be questioned, his larger purpose was to unite the variety of "baptist" groups under a common appellation within a meaningful typology for Western Christianity, that is, Catholic, Protestant and baptist. This baptist type for McClendon includes the descendants of the Radical Reformation, as well as other Baptist,

---

An earlier form of this chapter was given as the Willson-Addis Endowed Lecture at George W. Truett Theological Seminary, Baylor University, on April 27, 2012.

[1]James Wm. McClendon Jr., *Ethics: Systematic Theology* (Nashville: Abingdon, 2002), pp. 17-44.

Holiness, Pentecostal and evangelical traditions.[2] This elusiveness of identity holds not only for the type but also for the actual constituent churches categorized by it. For my purposes, and as a test case, if you will, I will focus on the churches within this type that belong to the self-identified Baptist tradition, particularly Baptists in North America, though what is here investigated I hope to be of interest for all Free Church traditions and others as well. Yet even by limiting the center of focus to Baptists proper, determining Baptist identity itself is perhaps more elusive than we may sometimes like to admit. Nevertheless, in this chapter I will put the thought of Karl Barth into conversation with contemporary Baptist life. Such a juxtaposition of a famous twentieth-century theologian with a particular church tradition could be taken in a number of directions. Let me begin by setting aside what I will not be examining here.

First, I will not be addressing the history of the reception of Barth's theology by Baptists in general or Baptist theologians in particular, whether in North America or elsewhere. This could be a story unto itself, for since Barth's time his influence can be seen not only on those who embraced or at least appreciatively if critically engaged his thought but also on those who spent significant time and energy refuting and rejecting it. In the first group we might mention a range of thinkers such as Bernard Ramm, George Eldon Ladd, David Mueller, and in their own way Walter Conner and Dale Moody, as well as more recent persons such as McClendon himself, Elizabeth Barnes and Steven Harmon. In the second group are those much more critical of Barth's entire project, perhaps most preeminently Carl F. H. Henry and most recently Albert Mohler. While the history of Barth's reception among Baptist theologians might warrant its own study, it must be said that the diversity of such thinkers and their varied evaluations of Barth would undoubtedly make for a quite fragmented story, and I do not believe that what might be discovered in Barth for benefit to Baptist theology today is best grasped by such a study. Which leads to the next topic which I will address briefly but in the end set aside.

Most interest in Barth's theology on the side of Baptists has revolved around Barth's rejection of infant baptism and his embrace of believer's

---

[2]Ibid., p. 19.

baptism. In a short monograph of 1943, as well as in a more developed piece comprising the final and unfinished fragment of the *Church Dogmatics*, Barth, working against the grain of his Reformed heritage, put forward an argument which opposed the practice of infant baptism and espoused and defended the practice of believer's baptism.[3] Unsurprisingly, Baptist interest in Barth has largely focused on this aspect of his theology, but I am not sure that this has been entirely beneficial, and for two reasons.

First, Barth's theology of baptism was developed only within the context of a much larger theological framework, and any attempt to pluck his writings on baptism, and especially his final fragment, out of this framework can lead to a partial, or even distorted, view of his doctrine. As I would argue, it is important that Barth be read with an eye following along the development of his thought, both before and within the *Church Dogmatics*, for Barth's theology is best understood in light of this development. Barth, I would argue, is helpfully read according to the practice of historical theology. Moreover, the doctrines Barth discusses within the *Church Dogmatics* themselves are best understood in light of other doctrines, so that Barth must also be read as a constructive, or systematic, theologian, for when we do not examine each doctrine in light of the others, we open ourselves to the risk of theological distortions both benign and more costly.[4]

The first, more benign distortion that comes from a singular and isolated focus on the doctrine of baptism is that it keeps us from seeing that Barth's theology should be of interest to Baptists for many more reasons than the question of baptism, if only because Barth's doctrine of baptism is itself placed in a larger matrix of theological thought that Baptists might find quite amenable. Let me illustrate by providing a number of strands within the rich tapestry of his thought that are akin to Free Church thinking.

While his doctrine of baptism might be the most famous of these strands, there are in fact a significant number of others. His understanding of baptism itself is placed within a larger framework of an ethics of discipleship, a word near and dear to Baptists. Barth developed a rich description of

---

[3]Published in English as Karl Barth, *The Teaching of the Church Regarding Baptism*, trans. Ernest Payne (London: SCM Press, 1948). Barth's unfinished fragment was published as *CD* IV/4.

[4]Barth favored the term "dogmatic" rather than "systematic" as an appellation for the theology he carried out. Nevertheless, such a term has not been widely embraced by Free Church traditions and thus here the terms "constructive" and "systematic" are used.

discipleship in the latter part-volumes of the *Church Dogmatics*, but already in the first volume Barth could write that the goal and purpose of Christ's action is such that "out of man's life there should come a repetition, an analogy, a parallel to His own being—that he should be conformable to Christ."[5] Barth's conception of discipleship, which he distinguished from imitation, is closely tied to his rich notion of correspondence (*Entsprechung*) that can be traced throughout the *Church Dogmatics*. This understanding of correspondence as it finds its place in Barth's discussion of discipleship is itself a part of what might be called Barth's rich ecclesial and moral ontology in which, as I have said elsewhere, "God's free call is echoed in humanity's free response, a response that does not deny the sociality of Christian faith but that recognizes the constituency of the people of God as comprised of confession rather than biology."[6]

Barth's descriptions of baptism and discipleship are themselves found in a yet larger context of ecclesiology, and here too we find discoveries that may pique Baptist interest. Barth's understanding of the church, formally explicated in the final volumes of the *Church Dogmatics* but intimated and presupposed throughout, is one that holds the local gathering of believers as the primary site of God's activity, witnessed in Barth's proclivity to use the words "community" (*Gemeinschaft*) or "congregation" (*Gemeinde*) in reference to the church. As Barth could state in his postwar lectures in Bonn in reference to the church, and in a way entirely consonant with the rest of the corpus of his writings: "When I say congregation, I am thinking primarily of the concrete form of the congregation in a particular place."[7]

This concrete ecclesial identity is coupled with other ecclesial strands, including Barth's rejection of strong distinctions between what some traditions refer to as clergy and laity, a rejection of overly hierarchical forms of church order and an embrace of the Reformation principle of the priesthood of all believers in practice and not only in principle, so much so that Barth charges that not only pastors but also all baptized Christians are responsible for the tasks of the church, including that of serious theological reflection. There can be no hard demarcation beyond that of particular calling and

---

[5]*CD* I/2, p. 277.
[6]Kimlyn J. Bender, *Karl Barth's Christological Ecclesiology* (Aldershot: Ashgate, 2005), p. 285.
[7]Karl Barth, *Dogmatics in Outline*, trans. G. T. Thomson (New York: Harper & Row, 1959), p. 142.

function between ordained pastors and "ordinary" church members, for "the community is not divided by this ordering into an active part and a passive, a teaching Church and a listening, Christians who have office and those who have not."[8] Barth can thereby sharply write: "The statement: 'I am a mere layman and not a theologian,' is evidence not of humility but of indolence."[9] The church is a place for instruction in which every individual member need participate as a theologian among theologians, a witness among witnesses, a member among members.[10] Such strands are themselves then enjoined to Barth's later appreciation for congregationalism, evident in his address to the Amsterdam Assembly of the World Council of Churches in 1948.[11]

Moreover, Barth's understanding of the church's identity was intricately tied to its activity of mission, and Barth stated that he discovered this integral connection not in the magisterial Reformers but in the Free Churches and among the pietists.[12] This identity found in mission is woven with an exemplary understanding of the church in relation to the world and its political orders, discussed in detail and depth in his *Dogmatics*, but which Barth summarized in his response to a question pertaining to their relation at a press conference in New York City in 1962 with a Baptist motto, "A free church in a free state."[13] Though I will not discuss these strands further, make no mistake—they are deeply enmeshed one within the other and cannot be separated without misunderstanding their place in Barth's theology.

If the first distortion is then one where the riches of Barth's theology for Baptist life are overlooked due to a narrow and myopic vision on a single doctrinal thread, the second, more serious distortion occurs when we not only take Barth's doctrines out of their historical and theological context but also mine Barth's theology of baptism simply to undergird a settled argument on a single doctrinal or ethical topic. For whenever we mine the-

---

[8]*CD* III/4, p. 490.

[9]*CD* IV/3.2, p. 871.

[10]*CD* III/4, pp. 497-99.

[11]For the text of this address, see Karl Barth, "The Church—The Living Congregation of the Living Lord Jesus Christ," in *God Here and Now*, trans. Paul M. van Buren (London: Routledge, 2003), pp. 75-104.

[12]*CD* IV/3.1, pp. 25-38.

[13]Karl Barth, *Gespräche 1959–1962* (Zürich: Theologischer Verlag Zürich, 1995), p. 492; also p. 284.

ology, any theology, to underwrite our own convictions rather than to allow
them to be challenged, and do so in tandem with a focus only on one doctrine rather than on the whole scope of theological topics, we run the great
risk not only of misreading Barth but also, more seriously, of misshaping the
doctrine under consideration due to our investing it with our own ideo-
logical or polemical baggage. If Barth can aid Baptists, part of that aid consists of his warning that no theological tradition can truly thrive if tempted
to build an entire edifice on a selectively chosen and narrowly defined range
of theological topics that serve a predominantly apologetic or polemical
rather than constructive purpose.

While all of these themes in Barth that I have mentioned display affinity
to Baptist thought—Barth's emphasis on the concrete congregation and his
growing appreciation of congregationalism; his rejection of strong distinctions between ordained and non-ordained Christians; his strong avowal for
the responsibility of all church members in light of a robust doctrine of the
priesthood of all believers; his separation and yet dialectical ordering of the
church and civil society; and his advocacy of believers' baptism—and while
all are worthy of further exploration, these themes are not what I want to
place at the heart of this chapter.

What I want to focus on is not these areas of overlap with Baptist thought
but rather on the challenges Barth presents to Baptists. What will be more
interesting and in the end more fruitful for Baptist theology and thought, I
believe, is to read Barth as an amenable but also critical partner in dialogue
from outside of the Baptist family, challenging Baptists to think carefully
about their own tradition. The great benefit to reading Barth, then, is that
his work provides a quiet and reflective place to stand outside of the fray that
is, as Alasdair MacIntyre says, a "socially embodied and historically extended argument," or, in a word, a tradition, and in this case, an extended
argument that is the Baptist tradition.[14] By standing outside of the tradition,
particularly that within this country, Barth provides a particular kind of
objectivity, not a naively construed neutral standpoint but an alternative
point from which to view the Baptist tradition and its conflicts. Barth may
thus serve as a disinterested correspondent to a foreign country (and at

---

[14]Alasdair MacIntyre, *After Virtue*, 2nd ed. (Notre Dame, IN: University of Notre Dame Press,
1984), p. 222.

times, a foreign war). Barth's own theological context provides a template that perhaps could distort, but might in fact better illuminate, the field of Baptist life, and that may help to organize the disagreements into different configurations for the purpose of envisioning other possibilities for a way ahead. Such, I would argue, is one of the greatest gifts of a comparative historical theology. Such is also the proposal for a large project. But here I will focus on but one aspect of it. It begins with a recognition that Barth's theology provides a hill on which to stand and survey from a distance both large and small skirmishes over the identity of what makes Baptists who and what they are.

But before climbing up the hill, one last comment on Barth's affinity to Baptist thought. I have often thought that if a truly great Baptist theologian emerged and produced a massive systematic theology that was widely recognized as of enduring importance, such a work would look very much in formal ordering and shape (if not in all material content, commitment or detail) like Barth's *Church Dogmatics*. In Barth we see a truly unparalleled focus on Jesus Christ, a truly christocentric theology at work, with a firm commitment to Holy Scripture as the unparalleled authority for the church's faith and confession, and with an emphasis on proclamation and preaching as central to the church's worship and practice, all within a theology dedicated to service to the church that focuses on themes of witness and discipleship. Barth's unquestionable commitment to Christ as the beginning and end of all of the ways and works of God with humanity, his untiring avowal of the superiority and unrivaled authority of Holy Scripture for the doctrine and practice of the church and rejection of speculation and his unapologetic emphasis on proclamation as the heart of the church's worship and life—all of these capture well convictions that Baptists share. Moreover, added to this, his sensitivity to the narrative shape and construal of both Scripture and the Christian life sits well with a tradition that next to the Bible considers Bunyan's *Pilgrim's Progress* one of its most central texts.

Now to the heart of the matter. In this chapter, I want to explore Barth's doctrine of the Word of God in this threefold form of Christ and Scripture and proclamation in light of his discussion of authority and authorities within the church. This doctrine presents a challenge to Baptist thought and practice. For while Barth and Baptists share much in their verbal commitments to these things, Barth provides a detailed theological investigation of their interrelation that Baptists often leave largely unexplored. Moreover, where Baptists often make statements of opposition and mutual exclusion, for example, pitting the Bible and tradition against one another, or where an emphasis on the dignity of the believer seems to preclude a high doctrine of the church, leading often to a purely sociological and collective understanding of it, Barth places Scripture and tradition in a dialectic of irreversible order and yet real relation in which the superiority of Scripture is unquestionably affirmed but where *sola Scriptura* never devolves into *nuda Scriptura* (or sole *Scriptura*), and where these are joined to a rich and high ecclesiology. In other words, Barth is ever aware that there is no such thing as a reader of Scripture on his or her own, and there is never a reader of Scripture all alone. It may look that way, but looks can be deceiving.

To begin: Barth's understanding of Scripture, developed over time but most fully articulated in the first volume of the *Church Dogmatics*, is set between an understanding of Christ and that of the church's own proclamation. Scripture is thus the bridge between Christ and the church, and for Barth, it is the recognition of this bridge that makes Protestantism what it is, the recognition of Christ's proper and true lordship over and not only within the church. In 1925 Barth could expound on the Protestant Scripture principle of the Reformers, which he interpreted to understand all other authorities,[15] and which he could define already in 1923 this way: "*The church recognizes the rule of its proclamation solely in the Word of God and finds the Word of God solely in Holy Scripture.*"[16] Because the revelation of God in Christ was unique and could never be directly identified with or subsumed into the teaching of the church, just as this stood in analogous fashion to how the divinity and the humanity of Christ could not be directly identified, so Scripture was needed as the means by which the voice of Christ was mediated to the church. For this reason, all church proclamation, as well as all church tradition, comprised of its doctrine, creeds and confessions, must be based on Scripture which stands over them. In Catholicism, Barth main-

---

[15]Karl Barth, "Das Schriftprinzip der reformierten Kirche," in *Vorträge und kleinere Arbeiten 1922–1925*, ed. Holger Finze (Zürich: Theologischer Verlag Zürich, 1990), pp. 500-544; esp. 520-21.
[16]*TRC*, p. 41.

tained, no such bridge is needed, for the church flows out from the incarnation as the extension of revelation and is itself the bridge to the present moment.[17] It is not, Barth maintains, that Protestants have Scripture and Catholics have Scripture and tradition (though in some conversations he can put it that crassly). No, Protestants too recognize with Scripture a confessional history, that is to say, church tradition. But the understanding of the relation between Scripture and tradition differs greatly for Catholics and Protestants in Barth's estimation.

The groundwork for the formal and systematic exposition of Barth's nuanced understanding of the relation between Scripture and tradition in the *Church Dogmatics* is already laid in the mid-1920s, but surprisingly, not so much in reflection on Roman Catholicism but in relation to Lutheranism (Barth would not turn to investigate Catholicism in earnest until the later 1920s). In other words (and this is important against those who see Barth as setting his theology as a foil against Catholic conceptions), Barth's understanding of tradition, and the place of confessions specifically, was worked out in a comparison of the Reformed understanding of confessions with Lutheranism, not Catholicism, and thus as an attempt to clarify a particular positive Protestant conception. In a brilliant set of lectures of 1923, Barth states that the Lutheran understanding of its Augsburg Confession saw it as a historic restatement of an ecumenical faith akin to the ancient creeds. The Augsburg Confession was thus understood within Lutheranism as a single and final articulation of Christian faith incumbent on others for subscription, such that it could not be changed or replaced.[18] Thus, it takes the character of a symbol, which the Formula of Concord describes explicitly as "our creed for this age."[19] Barth states that while the Formula of Concord tries to preserve the distinction between Holy Scripture and all other writings, with regard to the Augsburg Confession this distinction "gets *blurred*."[20] Thus the Formula of Concord can judge which positions are correct by whether they agree with "*God's Word and the* Christian *Augsburg Confession*," placing these in parallel apposition, which, Barth avers, danger-

---

[17]See also Barth's late discussion in *Gespräche 1959–1962*, pp. 378-79.
[18]*TRC*, pp. 1-3.
[19]Ibid., p. 2.
[20]Ibid., p. 4.

ously confers the authority of the former to the latter, such that it "moves fundamentally into remarkable proximity to the Holy Scriptures."[21] So Barth then asks:

> Is there for the Lutheranism of the Formula of Concord a basic and legitimate freedom to call upon this highest authority, the Scripture, *without reference* to or even *against* the Augustana? Is the church itself fundamentally willing to review the question, Whether the understanding of Scripture preserved in the Augustana is the right one? That would be, I think, the persuasive proof that the "brilliant distinction" ["luculentum discrimen"] between the Bible and all other documents is understood to be a fundamentally *qualitative* one and not merely a *quantitative* one.[22]

Barth then turns to inquire about lower-level Lutheran confessions that serve to interpret the Augustana, that is, Augsburg Confession. Do they share in its authority? Further, can the Augustana be appealed to

> *without reference* to or even *against* the understanding of it in these documents? Is there a basic openness to revisit their interpretation of Augustana? If there is not, then do they not also participate in that dignity which is ascribed to Augustana itself as "drawn from the Word of God" . . . , if at a somewhat lower level?[23]

It seems to me that Barth has his finger on a hermeneutical problem that those who insist on the need for creeds to interpret Scripture often ignore, namely, that the hermeneutical problem goes all the way down. In other words, there must be tradition to interpret tradition, and where does the chain of authority end? We may as well end by beginning with the recognition that Scripture does, in a real sense, stand alone and over against all later tradition.[24] But in the end, Barth concludes that this recognition is

---

[21]Ibid.

[22]Ibid., p. 5.

[23]Ibid.

[24]John Howard Yoder makes the case that this must be so not only for doctrinal and moral judgment but also for the very possibility of ecumenical progress: "In such [ecumenical] conversation no community can impose its separate past path on the others. Roman Catholics cannot ask Protestants to share the decisions of Trent. Lutherans cannot expect the 'anabaptists,' whom their *Confessio Augustana* condemns five times, to share that text as an identity marker. The canonical Scriptures are, at least on pragmatic grounds, the primary court of appeal." See Yoder, "Walk and Word: The Alternatives to Methodologism," in *Theology Without Foundations: Religious Practice and the Future of Theological Truth*, ed. Stanley Hauerwas, Nancey Murphy and

foreign to the Lutheran understanding of its own tradition. In light of the ascription of even "inspiration" by later Lutheran thinkers to the Book of Concord, in which the primary author of it is said to be no human person but the Holy Spirit, Barth concludes that the difference between Holy Scripture and the Augsburg Confession is "only a quantitative one and not qualitative."[25]

Barth then turns to consider the Reformed tradition. The Reformed tradition and understanding of confessions, Barth asserts, is entirely otherwise. The Reformed, whether consciously or unconsciously, recognized that the time of the Roman Empire and an imperial church was over, and with the passing of the *corpus Christianum*, the time of a universal enforced confession had passed.[26] The universality of the church was not to be sought in a return to a past uniformity but in the future. As Barth states, this universality "is not something given but something sought."[27] Reformed confessions were thus intentionally modest in scope and intent. Barth concludes:

> Such a *particular confessing church* sought to prove and defend the truth of its confession *solely* through its connection to Holy Scripture and not through its formal connection to a universal church or a normative exposition of Scripture. And it was such churches that, on Reformed ground, were the bearers of hope for an ecumenically recognized confession; the Reformed held to that hope as firmly as they held to the confessions of the first centuries. The legitimate pathway to universality is here the pathway of particularity.[28]

In other words, for the Reformed, and this is the road Barth would take too, ecumenicity travels from the bottom up, not the top down, but it does travel, and it should.

Barth then states that for the Reformed there was not a single confession but many, and that they had no desire to create a single and final confession for all churches, so that "a certain self-confident if not defiant assertion of one's own approach is connected here in an unusual way with an equally

---

Mark Nation (Nashville: Abingdon, 1994), p. 89. For this reason, one could argue that it is agreement on the New Testament canon, even more than and prior to the Apostles' or Nicene Creed, that is the most promising point of departure for ecumenical conversations.

[25] *TRC*, pp. 5-6.
[26] Ibid., pp. 7-8.
[27] Ibid., p. 11.
[28] Ibid., pp. 11-12.

confident respect for other approaches."[29] Contrary to the Lutheran conviction that a united symbol to which all must subscribe was a precondition for church unity, the Reformed did not see things this way. Rather, as Barth writes: "That which is 'required above all else' is that the doctrine of the church everywhere and constantly be grounded upon Holy Scripture, which defines not the confessional *unity* but the confessional *freedom* of the particular churches in their relationship to each other."[30] Barth wryly notes that it was precisely this diversity and lack of concern for uniformity that led Luther to think that the doctrine of these opponents from the Alps was from Satan.[31] Of course, agreement among the Reformed, when found between confessions, was celebrated, and diversity was not boundless. But as Barth noted: "Such agreements, however, did not descend somehow from above, from some kind of central coordinating agency, nor were they an agreement of the letter but of the spirit and matter."[32]

To summarize a large swath of Barth's discussion: the confessions in the Reformed tradition were seen not as one but many; not universal but local; not symbols but precisely what they were called, confessions, and thus not final but provisional; not parallel to Scripture in apposition but always subordinate to Scripture in reality and in description, and thus always open to correction and revision in the light of Scripture but also in light of discussions with other Christians. They are not ever described as inspired or the work of the Spirit, but very human documents which themselves acknowledge their own capability of error (interestingly, Barth says the only exception is the Westminster Confession in this regard).[33] Scripture and confession thus differ qualitatively, for what is revealed must not be confused with what one confesses, for revelation comes from above, and confession comes from below, and, regardless of its origin in human witnesses, Scripture's true origin rests in the Holy Spirit, and thus it properly stands on the side of revelation.[34] As Barth can say, "the Reformed confession is, to be sure, a very particular house, but a house whose doors and windows are

---

[29]Ibid., p. 12.
[30]Ibid., pp. 12-13.
[31]Ibid., p. 13.
[32]Ibid.
[33]Ibid., p. 19.
[34]Ibid., pp. 19-20, 23.

open in all directions."[35] I must say that after I first read these lectures, I felt I had read the most Baptist articulation of confessions that may have ever been written.

But if one were to draw the conclusion based on Barth's discussion of confessions here in 1923 that he is pitting Scripture against confessions, or tradition, such that the second is set aside and no authority given to it, this would be a mistake, a misreading of Barth's highly dialectical and nuanced understanding of their relation. For besides his sustained critical engagement with the Lutheran tradition, Barth could take a swipe also at the other side of the Protestant spectrum and say curtly: "We need scarcely speak of the recklessness of the English Congregationalists (Independents), who have elevated to the level of principle the idea of freedom over against one's own ecclesial past."[36] Here Baptist ears may begin to burn. Perhaps this point is best translated in the words of one contemporary Baptist when he says: "Baptists have come to make a tradition of rejecting tradition."[37] While Barth thoroughly relativizes the confessions, he did not empty them of all authority. To find Barth's understanding of their rightful authority, one must turn from the rough though splendid lectures of 1923 to Barth's mature discussion of authority within the *Church Dogmatics*. There, Barth states that confessions are the record of the church's confessing its faith in a particular place and time, and to confess its faith in the present well, the church must pay attention to the confession of the church in the past. In other words, Barth has an important place for tradition. If Barth is careful never to equate Scripture and tradition or even place them on the same plane, he is also very careful to speak of their inseparable relation. They exist in a secondary relation of unity, differentiation and irreversible order and asymmetry as a reflection of the primary relation of revelation and humanity in the first form of the Word of God, Jesus Christ, which itself is echoed in the second form of Scripture and the third form of church proclamation. The relation of Scripture and tradition is, however, further elucidated through a number of accompanying dialectical relations, the first being that between the church and the believer.

---

[35]Ibid., p. 16.
[36]Ibid., p. 26.
[37]Philip Thomson, quoted in Roger A. Ward and Philip E. Thompson, *Tradition and the Baptist Academy* (Milton Keynes, UK: Paternoster, 2011), p. xi.

In one respect, Barth seems to prioritize the individual with relation to the Word of God over against the church. Barth quite simply will not allow for an authority within the church to override the hearing of the Word, even if this hearing is that of a single individual, and he can appeal to Luther positively as the quintessential example in this regard. But lest we take this authority of the Word over the church to imply the supremacy of private judgment in all matters of faith and in turn see this as a disregard for the church, Barth points in another direction, seen quintessentially in the believer's acceptance of the canon of Scripture itself. With regard to the acceptance of the biblical canon's contents and boundaries, Barth thus writes:

> The individual in the Church certainly cannot and ought not to accept it [the canon] as Holy Scripture just because the Church does. He can and should himself be obedient only to Holy Scripture as it reveals itself to him and in that way forces itself upon him, as it compels him to accept it. But he still has to remember that Scripture is the Word of God for and to the Church, and that therefore it is only in the Church that he can meaningfully and legitimately take up an attitude to Scripture. Whatever his private judgment may be, even his private judgment of faith, however much it may diverge, he must always listen to the Church. The so far unaltered judgment of the Church radically precedes as such the judgment of the individual, even if it is the judgment of quite a number of individuals who have to be reckoned with seriously in the Church.[38]

Here we see the intricate relationship of unity and distinction in Barth's mind between revelation, Scripture and canon. But we also see the dialectical relationship between the church and the believer, the believer and the church. This relationship contains a real though relative authority for the tradition of the church, which in this instance is the church's recognition and acknowledgment of the canon, its contents and boundaries. It is therefore not a capitulation to an external coercive authority in the church but a trustful honoring and respect for the church's historic witness to the location of revelation when one recognizes Scripture as Scripture, and this collection of these particular books as a canon. As Barth writes: "It is where the Church declares that it has found Holy Scripture that we have actually

---

[38]CD I/2, p. 479.

to expect Holy Scripture."[39] In everyday terms, when a young person receives his or her first Bible in Sunday school, that person is already receiving the results of a number of church decisions with regard to Scripture's content and form, its collection, canonization and translation.

This dialectical relation between Scripture and church is nothing other than the relation of Scripture and the church's tradition, comprised of its confession that it has heard the Word of God, and heard it in Holy Scripture. This is the question of the canon, itself a past confession, and thus a part of the church's tradition, yet a confession that the church and the individual believer must reaffirm in the present yet with a certain weight given to the church's decision of the past. And if we have a problem with this notion of tradition, it may be because we have not recognized that to listen to the church is not to listen to a magisterial authority above ourselves but a true authority that is recognized in our openness to instruction and correction from others.

After Barth has spent literally hundreds of pages showing why Scripture is unparalleled and superior and unique in its witness to God's revelation in Christ, superior to tradition and all later ecclesial creeds and confessions, he then turns the entire discussion around to consider the side of the church's response. And this response does have its own authority.

In section 20, titled "Authority in the Church," Barth provides this opening thesis:

> The Church does not claim direct and absolute and material authority for itself but for Holy Scripture as the Word of God. But actual obedience to the authoritative Word of God in Holy Scripture is objectively determined by the fact that those who in the Church mutually confess an acceptance of the witness of Holy Scripture will be ready and willing to listen to one another in expounding and applying it. By the authority of Holy Scripture on which it is founded, authority in the Church is restricted to an indirect and relative and formal authority.[40]

Now this thesis receives many pages of exposition from Barth, but here attention can be drawn to but a few things. Notice that listening begins with listening to one another. This is no coercive authority from on high.

---

[39]*CD* I/2, p. 479.
[40]*CD* I/2, p. 538.

Rather, it is a recognition of mutual instruction given to us by others within the church. If we can recognize this within our own community of faith, then beginning to listen to those in other Baptist communities should not be so difficult. And then we might extend the circle to listen to those in other Protestant traditions similar to our own, and then to those a bit further removed, and then to listen to Catholic and Orthodox traditions as well. Finally, in recognizing, as Barth did, that God is not the God of the dead but of the living, we might then listen to those from the past. Now make no mistake: none of these voices, those of our neighbors and friends that we worship with every Sunday, those of fellow Christians we work with but who belong to different communities and perhaps different traditions of worship, those we hear represented in confessions of the past, can or do rival the living voice of Christ in Holy Scripture. Christ and church stand in the end, as Barth states, in a "definite and irreversible order, united, but distinct,"[41] and so it is with the living voice of Christ found in Scripture and the church's tradition. But the hearing of this voice in Scripture is not isolated from hearing it in a community of faith which hears with us and expounds and instructs us in its meaning. In other words, we must recognize another dialectic at work that accompanies that between Scripture and tradition and that of the church and the individual. This dialectic is the relation between trust and dissent.

This dialectic is another element of the question of authority within the church. As Barth maintains, there is a real authority that tradition possesses, and a real authority of the church in relation to the individual. It is both a real and relative authority, and, Barth maintains, can be briefly expressed: "All that we have still to say about the authority of the Church itself can be understood in the light of the commandment in Ex. 20:12: 'Honor thy father and thy mother.'"[42] This verse encapsulates Barth's understanding of the real though relative authority of church tradition and is a verse that appears throughout his work. With its quotation, Barth means the following.

The fifth commandment does stand in seeming tension to the first— "Thou shalt have no other gods before me." Yet, because this commandment is included within the ten, it must have its own place. Certainly there can be no conflict with the first commandment. It cannot contradict the first com-

---

[41]CD I/2, p. 542.
[42]CD I/2, p. 585.

mandment, but neither is it abrogated by it. In its own sphere, and when qualified by the first, it has its own dignity and authority.

As the relation between the commandments goes, so goes the relation of Christ and church, Scripture and tradition. Barth puts it this way:

> Under the Word and therefore under Holy Scripture the Church does have and exercise [sic] genuine authority. It has and exercises it by being obedient, concretely obedient, by claiming for itself not a direct, but only a mediate authority, not a material but a formal, not an absolute but a relative. It has and exercises it by refraining from any direct appeal to Jesus Christ and the Holy Spirit in support of its words and attitudes and decisions, by not trying to speak out as though it were infallible and final, but by subordinating itself to Jesus Christ and the Holy Spirit in the form in which Jesus Christ and the Holy Spirit is actually present and gracious to it, that is, in His attestation by the prophets and apostles, in the differentiation from its own witness conditioned by its written nature. Therefore, it has and exercises it in the concrete humility which consists in the recognition that in Holy Scripture it has over it everywhere and always and in every respect its Lord and Judge: in the incompleteness of its own knowing and acting and speaking which that involves, in the openness to reformation through the Word of God which constantly confronts it in Holy Scripture. It is in this way, in this concrete subordination to the Word of God, that it has and exercises genuine authority.[43]

Now having heard such strong qualifications of the authority of the church and its tradition, one might be tempted to dismiss such authority as empty. And one might be especially so tempted in light of the necessity at times to dissent against a misuse of the Word of God, to emphasize that one must obey God, that is, Scripture, rather than men or women. Barth does not deny such a place for dissent; he is a Protestant, after all. The Word may need to be held by one or few against the church, and not only held within it. Yet the dialectical nature of the relation between church and individual is paralleled also in a dialectic of trust and dissent, and for Barth the occasional nature of the second should not overshadow the regular practice of the former. Again quoting Barth at length, for he puts this best:

> Therefore, in what I hear as the confession of the Church, I will certainly have

---

[43]*CD* I/2, p. 586.

to reckon with the possibility of falsehood and error. I cannot safely hear the voice of the Church without also hearing the infallible Word of God Himself. Yet this thought will not be my first thought about the Church and its confession, but a necessarily inserted corrective. My first thought in this respect can and must be a thought of trust and respect which I cannot perhaps have for the men as such who constitute the Church, but which I cannot refuse to the Word of God by which it lives and Jesus Christ rules it. How can I know Jesus Christ as the Lord who has called me by His Word if in relation to the rest of the Church I do not start from the thought that despite and in all the sin of the men who constitute it it too has been called and ruled by the same Word? Because my sins are forgiven me, I am bold to believe and, in spite of the sin of which I am conscious, to confess my faith as created in me by the Word of Christ. And if this is the case then in relation to the rest of the Church and its confession I cannot possibly begin with mistrust and rejection, just as in relation to our parents, no matter who they are or what they are like, we do not begin with mistrust and rejection or with the assertion that we must obey God rather than man, but with trust and respect and therefore, in the limits appointed to them as men, with obedience. As in and with the confession of the Church I hear the infallible Word of God, I have to reckon first and above all with the lordship of Jesus Christ in His Church and the forgiveness of sins, which is operative in the Church; not with sin and therefore with the possibility of falsehood and error which it involves. And this means that I have not primarily to criticize the confession of the Church as it confronts me as the confession of those who were before me in the Church and are with me in the Church. *There will always be time and occasion for criticism. My first duty is to love and respect it as the witness of my fathers and bretheren. And it is in the superiority posited by this fact that I shall hear it.* And as I do so, as I recognize the superiority of the Church before and beside me, it is to me an authority. This is how the authority of the Church arises. It always arises in this way, that in the community of hearing and receiving the Word of God which constitutes the Church, there is this superiority of the confession of some before others, this honour and love, this hearing of the confession of some by others, before the latter go on to make their own confession. Before both and therefore above both is the Lord of the Church with His Word. Only under His Word can some confess and others hear their confession before they confess themselves. But under His Word there does arise this priority and superiority of some over others, the necessity that in the Church we should listen to other men before we go on to speak. Under His Word there is, therefore, a genuine authority of the Church.[44]

Baptists could indeed learn much from this, and perhaps, not least of all, a sense of individual humility. Dissent needs to be done at times, and done boldly. Yet dissent is always a stance of tragic if necessary conviction, not a prideful position, and never a right claimed, just as refusing the advice of our parents and acting against their wishes is not the norm but a sad situation that displays that trust has been broken, and it is never to be done lightly. There is a respectful listening to our parents that may entail a mature judgment that, having listened, we in our own place and time must go our own way. There is another kind of proud intransigence that shows no such respect at all. As Christians we stand in relation to one another, and our general attitude to others in the church, whether present or past, must be one of trust that can turn to dissent only where the honor we would give our ecclesial parents would cause us directly to disobey the first commandment.

Beyond Slogans

Having surveyed, though briefly, Barth's nuanced understanding of the relation between Holy Scripture and the church and its tradition, between the corporate community and the individual and between trust and dissent, one sees that Barth is unsatisfied with simple oppositional statements but places seeming opposites into ordered relations that are richly narrated and contextualized. In the case of Scripture and tradition, this relation is marked by a unity, differentiation and strict and irreversible ordering. In the case of human responses to revelation, seen in the relation of the community and the individual believer and that of trust versus dissent, Barth seeks to maintain the integrity of the latter term within the pairs while establishing its meaning and significance in the larger contextual framework of the former term—in other words, individuals retain an irreducible and inviolable integrity but not an absolute autonomy when seen in the context of the church, and dissent finds a necessary place but only within a larger context of trust, the first an occasional though sad necessity, the second the normal practice.

---

[44]*CD* I/2, p. 590, emphasis added; cf. pp. 588-90.

In light of these thick descriptions, Baptists may be helped by Barth to think theologically of the relation between Scripture and tradition, Bible and creed, community and individual and conformity and dissent, in ways that go well beyond the preservation of slogans. Barth I think challenges Baptists to explicate carefully, in light of sustained and concentrated theological attention, what so often is simply taken for granted, or worse, flippantly parroted. In sum, what Baptists often set against each other as dualities (Scripture versus creeds or tradition; individual autonomy versus church authority; dissent versus conformity), Barth sees as realities in ordered relationships. If willing to consider a different way, Baptists might learn to see confessions and even the classic creeds not as timeless documents to be used to enforce conformity but as nevertheless having a descriptive and even relative prescriptive value when understood in light of Barth's injunction to honor our fathers and our mothers. In other words, oppositions of descriptive versus prescriptive understandings of confessions may themselves be far too simple, for again drawing on Alasdair MacIntyre, the debate about what a tradition is always entails an implicit argument as to what we believe a tradition is to be.

Where Barth therefore seems to challenge Baptists most in this regard is where they choose one side of the opposition against the other—namely, Scripture against tradition, the individual against the community, dissent as more central than trust and conformity. Despite discomfort, Baptists might be better served by at least contemplating his challenge rather than dismissing Barth as a foreign interloper. Barth's rejection of anything that smacked of a contextless reading of Scripture, of religious individualism or dismissive parochialism that enshrined contentiousness for its own sake may certainly test Baptist thought. But at their best, Baptists themselves have understood that Scripture is read among a company of the faithful in a setting of love and trust. This is also why Baptists have written and read and given relative authority to Bible commentaries (not to mention Sunday school curricula) and rarely questioned this practice, though Bible commentaries are themselves nothing but an engaged and extended conversation about the exegesis and interpretation of Scripture, and as Barth says, theology is nothing else than the history of exegesis, which itself is but another way of saying tradition. Confessions are thus themselves nothing but commentaries on Scripture, and their value is not lessened or attenuated simply because they are written by churches rather than individual members of the Society of Biblical Literature.

If these stated challenges are seriously considered, Barth's theology might also exhort Baptists to reflect on slogans such as "No creed but the Bible" or, even more colloquially and perhaps notoriously, "Ain't nobody but Jesus going to tell me what to believe."[45] There may have been historical periods in which such forceful slogans were needed. But slogans do not age well when simply asserted through the ages. They need careful review and explication in order to preserve the truth they attempt to articulate. Barth himself had a penchant for taking traditional theological concepts that had grown tired and, without either dismissing or repeating them, placing them in richer descriptive contexts where they were reconstituted in a way that sought to preserve their witness to a significant truth while overcoming their intrinsic or acquired deficiencies, thus giving them new meaning and form.[46] Perhaps such slogans need to be, if not rejected, nonetheless critically and innovatively rethought. There really is something true that persons are trying to articulate in saying that no one but Jesus can tell us what to do. Both Barth and Bonhoeffer, not to mention the apostles, said something akin to this as well. But context is important, as is the explication of the meaning and significance of the assertion in light of this twofold context, both theological and cultural. Without such a contextual setting, such slogans become not only simplistic mantras but also perversions of the truth to which they point. How does Jesus tell us what to do? Jesus' voice is found in Scripture, and Scripture is read in a community of persons that, like us,

---

[45]The first, ironically, serving as a creed, and the second, it seems, the evidence of individualism gone to seed, its effect perhaps classically and best expressed by the early twentieth-century Baptist Winthrop Hudson, who concluded: "The practical effect of the stress upon 'soul competency' as the cardinal doctrine of Baptists was to make every man's hat his own church." See Winthrop Hudson, "Shifting Patterns of Church Order," in *Baptist Concepts of the Church*, ed. Winthrop Hudson (Philadelphia: Judson Press, 1959), p. 216. The problem also points to a complete disregard for ecclesial parents, and more seriously, to the question of just how exactly one knows it is Jesus (and not my own conscious and unconscious desires) telling me what to do.

[46]In German, this move is called *Aufhebung*, in which concepts like nature and grace are, to borrow the description of George Hunsinger, "affirmed, negated, and reconstituted on a higher plane." See Hunsinger, *How to Read Karl Barth* (Oxford: Oxford University Press, 1991), pp. 85-86.

he has called to be one people. If at the end of this chapter one is not convinced that Barth has anything much to say of value for such things to Free Church folk, then perhaps one could be encouraged to at least return to read Paul with seriousness. For Paul reminds us that the voice of Christ comes through the voice of witnesses (1 Thess 2:13; cf. Rom 10:14-15; 1 Cor 15:1-2), and he is not nearly so hung up on individualism versus communitarianism as we sometimes are (with 1 Cor 11 as but one example). He, like Barth, was far too much a dialectical thinker for such simplistic bifurcations, and much too theological to think of the body of Christ only as, in the words of E. Y. Mullins, "a community of autonomous individuals under the immediate lordship of Christ held together by a social bond of common interest," a definition more reminiscent of the social contract theory of Locke and Rousseau than of the New Testament.[47]

One should not make mistakes as to what is here being argued. I am not saying that only Barth has thought carefully about such things, or that the challenge from Barth to Baptists goes in only one direction, though as Barth has said, listening must precede criticism. Nor am I arguing that the particular doctrinal and material positions he takes should be simply embraced. Certainly I am not arguing that the excesses of individualism be remedied with a healthy dose of ecclesial authoritarianism. That itself is a false choice. Nevertheless, I do think that he provides Baptists and other Free Church traditions with a unique and valuable voice. He sees a real authority in confessions but does not see them as absolute, nor does he espouse forced subscription. He upholds the uniqueness of Scripture against all creeds and confessions but does recognize a real authority in them and refuses to ground Christian faith in subjective personal experience. And he attempts

---

[47]E. Y. Mullins, *The Axioms of Religion: A New Interpretation of Baptist Faith* (Philadelphia: Judson Press, 1908), p. 129. One could make a strong case that while the dialectic of community and individual became greatly skewed in America during the Revolutionary period with Francis Wayland, it positively fell off the rails into cultural Protestant liberal individualism with Mullins. With this move, all nuanced New Testament dialectical understandings were lost, a judgment already confirmed by Winthrop S. Hudson, who concluded that soul competency was "derived from the general cultural and religious climate of the nineteenth century rather than from any serious study of the Bible" (Hudson, "Shifting Patterns," p. 215). There can be no doubt that had Barth been an American, he would have had great problems with Mullins, just as he had with Schleiermacher and Wilhelm Herrmann, his former teacher, and for the same reasons. At the very least, the concept of "soul competency" needs a radical *Aufhebung* of its own if it has any hope of useful service for serious Baptist theology in the future.

to engage the entire Christian tradition in a way that speaks to the entire church but does so as one firmly committed to the Protestant tradition and its convictions. In other words, Barth provides numerous areas of amenability to Baptist sensibilities but is not easily mapped onto current Baptist configurations. That itself makes him worthy of study.

The current Barth renaissance in America demonstrates that a growing number of people think so, including a contingent of younger Baptists. I am not a prophet or the son of a prophet, but I will prophesy anyway. I believe that as the distance between our time and the twentieth century grows greater, Barth's star will shine brighter among the constellation of twentieth-century theologians. I think there are a number of reasons for this, but let me name just one. In the end, Barth was a theologian's theologian, attempting to renarrate the Christian faith in a manner and on a scale similar to what Aquinas attempted in the Middle Ages, and in a way fully conversant with the church's past. Barth, though deeply involved with the issues of his time, undertook a theological task that consumed the latter half of his life.

There is thus a reason why some (not all!) young Baptists are intrigued with Barth's theology. Here we find articulated a description of the Christian universe that bears weight. It rejects the cultural pessimism and theological triumphalism of fundamentalism, as well as the cultural accommodation and theological subjectivism of liberalism. It recognizes the contextual nature of theology, including confessions, but does not dissolve theological truth into contextual relativism or human subjectivity. It does this while trying to articulate a truly Protestant vision for theology, recognizing both the indebtedness any true theology must have to the church's entire past, while maintaining that the Protestant vision still has a vital contribution to make to the church at large. It thus provides a theological and intellectual structure for those who are hopelessly Protestant in which to live, or at least augment their own ecclesial shelter, and may provide a resource for those who are loyally Baptist, while providing a way ecumenically to engage and even glean from the Catholic and Orthodox traditions. I recognize that some believe that the Reformation is over and that all that is left for us to do is to "unlearn Protestantism."[48] Yet I would

---

[48]To borrow a phrase from Gerald W. Schlabach, *Unlearning Protestantism: Sustaining Christian Community in an Unstable Age* (Grand Rapids: Brazos, 2010).

argue that it is difficult to unlearn what one never really knew. If the Protestant Reformation is to end, it will not be a good end if it comes to an end out of ignorance of its importance rather than because its true concerns have been met, answered and preserved.

In sum, Barth may help Baptists not to lose their identity but to find it in becoming even better Baptists, and in turn, better Christians, especially in regard to the unique gifts Baptists bring the larger Christian community. Baptists rightfully speak unabashedly of the priesthood of believers, but at their best they have always recognized that you cannot be a priest by yourself. Certainly each person can boldly approach the throne of grace; that is not the question. It is rather that the idea of an autonomous priest is a contraction in terms. To be a priest is to be an intercessor. And to be a priest you need someone to intercede for. And Christians are called to intercede for each other, and together, to intercede for the world.

A Path into the Future

While the exposition that has here occurred has focused on historical questions for the sake of encouraging constructive theological reflection and engagement, it is with the hope that such theological reflection may in the end serve very practical ends. For if Baptists are to serve in a substantial way the kingdom of God in coming decades, then our churches cannot turn within themselves and attempt singular self-preservation through pragmatic marketing strategies. That temptation is enormous, and as a former pastor who is often disillusioned with trends in larger Baptist life, I know it well. Yet if Baptists are to present their theology as a house in which to live, and not a specialty shop to visit for one or two doctrines, then they must themselves consider again serious constructive work. Barth provides a model for how this might be done, or at least one that can provide guidance for the task.

Moreover, he might even provide very practical assistance for Christian existence today in reminding Baptists that protection against captivity to the spirit of an age is best given by attention to different ages, for to ignore the history of the interpretation of Scripture is to become captive precisely to the current unspoken cultural presuppositions which are present if unacknowledged and unconscious to every individual. Tradition is, for Barth, ironically the means by which we can read the Bible freely, for it is in the examination of the past that the parochialism of our own current commitments are exposed and revealed. Such is not to capitulate to a relativism of the immediate or to subjugate the present hearing of the Word to the church's confession of the past. But it is to recognize that all confession, conscious or not, is always not only a word to culture but also one that is shaped, if only passively, though often actively, by culture itself. One way to reveal such cultural assumptions is therefore to compare our age with those that did not share such assumptions. In short, it is to read Scripture in light of the church's past reading of Scripture.

In closing, it is in relation to a cultural picture of ourselves that Barth might provide a final challenge to Baptists, namely, in Barth's own *Aufhebung* of the cherished concept of freedom itself. Barth's Protestant sensibilities and convictions were rooted in a doctrine of freedom. For those with eyes to see, and Baptists should, Barth's *Church Dogmatics* is filled in every corner with the theme of freedom. This is seen in the very thesis beginning Barth's discussion on the incarnation of the Word in volume one under the heading "God's Freedom for Man." There Barth writes: "According to Holy Scripture God's revelation takes place in the fact that God's Word became a man and that this man has become God's Word. The incarnation of the eternal Word, Jesus Christ, is God's revelation. In the reality of this event God proves that He is free to be our God."[49]

But this freedom of which Barth speaks was not first a political, social or cultural one. It was not a celebration of individual liberty. Indeed, Barth could speak of freedom for the churches behind the Iron Curtain to the consternation and confusion of American theologians, perhaps most famously Reinhold Niebuhr. Barth could do so because while political and religious freedom were very good things, they were and remained secondary to the freedom of the Word of God. And because Barth's understanding of freedom was always rooted in the freedom of God, and not the human person, and because it was so deeply woven into a thick description of the actuality and reality of God, it was always safeguarded against those who would turn freedom into individual license or, worse, a sedative for churches living in a free state. Such perversions of freedom were seen clearly by Barth

---

[49]CD I/2, p. 1.

long before they became the focus of fiction. For if there is a commentary on freedom today in our culture, and an iconic representation of it, it is certainly the novel by Jonathan Franzen titled *Freedom,* a portrayal of the modern concept of freedom as the uninhibited consummation of every natural desire that in the end leaves the self corrupted, disillusioned and alone.[50] To recognize this for what it is, as but a new form of captivity, requires that one know what true freedom is, which in turn allows us to know precisely what form of dissent is needed, as well as what kind of prophetic word need be spoken. In an interview with *Newsweek* in 1962, Barth was asked regarding his thoughts on the greatest failure of contemporary Protestantism: "How shall I formulate it?" he asked himself aloud. "The true thing in the original Protestantism was God's word to man, and then man's response to it. Modern Protestantism has lost its character as a response. If Protestantism is only a fight for individual liberties—freedom of the soul— then its cause is lost. Man is left alone with himself."[51]

The fiftieth anniversary of Barth's one and only visit to the United States was marked in 2012. It was the coming together of a theologian of freedom with a land that prided itself and was so shaped by religious and political liberty. Barth had the following to say at the end of a talk in that quintessential American city, Chicago:

> Now a concluding word: If I myself were an American citizen and a Christian and a theologian, then I would try to elaborate a theology of freedom—a theology of freedom from, let us say, from any inferiority complex over against good old Europe from whence you all came, or your fathers. You do not need to have such an inferiority complex. That is what I have learned these weeks. You may also have freedom from a superiority complex, let us say, over against Asia and Africa. That's a complex without reason. Then I may add— your theology should also be marked by freedom from fear of communism, Russia, inevitable nuclear warfare and generally speaking, from all the aforementioned principalities and powers. Freedom for which you would stand

---

[50]Jonathan Franzen, *Freedom: A Novel* (New York: Farrar, Straus and Giroux, 2010). Franzen's novel may be read (in spite of itself) as a theological commentary on human freedom gone awry.

[51]Barth, *Gespräche 1959–1962,* pp. 446-47. Baptists in America could do worse than to inscribe these words on their hearts and perhaps the doorposts of their houses, for Barth's words are nothing less than a call back to the first commandment, which gives meaning and context to all of the others.

would be the freedom for—I like to say a single word—humanity. Being an American theologian, I would then look at the Statue of Liberty in the New York Harbor. I have not seen that lady, except in pictures. Next week I shall see her in person. That lady needs a little or, perhaps, a good bit of demythologization. Nevertheless, maybe she may also be seen and interpreted and understood as a symbol of a true theology, not of liberty, but of freedom. Well, it would be necessarily, a theology of freedom. Of that freedom to which the Son frees us [cf. Jn 8:36], and which as His gift, is the one real human freedom. My last question for this evening is this: Will such a specific American theology one day arise? I hope so.[52]

May we all.

---

[52]Barth, *Gespräche 1959–1962*, p. 489.

9

Karl Barth and the
Question of Atheism

✠

Recent years have witnessed the ascendancy of a vibrant atheism in the West. Such atheism is perhaps new not so much in content as in form, for the highbrow atheism arising out of the Enlightenment and ever present in academic and intellectual circles thereafter has more recently been matched with a populist one with evangelical aspirations. Writers such as Richard Dawkins, Daniel Dennett, Christopher Hitchens and Sam Harris, among others, have changed the debate of God's existence from being one primarily carried out in ivory towers and French salons to one of passionate conversations among persons who may only be familiar in passing with the bestseller lists of the *New York Times*.[1] Indeed, if one wonders if the term "evangelical" is an appropriate descriptor for such atheism, one need only consider the Atheist Bus Campaign in Britain of a few years past. Plastered on the side of buses was the good news according to atheism, captured in a slogan as trite as that of any bumper sticker on a car sporting a fish decal: "There is probably no God. Now stop worrying and enjoy your life." Thus the good news according to Saint Epicurus and his modern-day disciples is proclaimed.

Responses to such atheism from the Christian community have varied,

---

This chapter appeared earlier as "Karl Barth and the Question of Atheism," *Theology Today* 70 (2013): 269-80. Reprinted by permission.

[1]Richard Dawkins, *The God Delusion* (Boston: Houghton Mifflin, 2006); Daniel C. Dennett, *Breaking the Spell: Religion as a Natural Phenomenon* (New York: Penguin, 2006); Christopher Hitchens, *God Is Not Great: How Religion Poisons Everything* (New York: Twelve, 2007); Sam Harris, *The End of Faith: Religion, Terror and the Future of Reason* (New York: Norton, 2005); and Harris, *Letter to a Christian Nation* (New York: Knopf, 2006).

though many have viewed it as a new threat that requires a robust philosophical response by means of a revived natural theology in order to stave off a growing secularism. Yet it may be helpful to remember what we have noted earlier, namely, that while atheism is demonstrably on the rise, it is not new, for it is a distinctive element of the modern era from the Enlightenment onward and one that has arisen in light of and not despite the era's natural religion, as Michael Buckley has incisively argued in his magisterial study *At the Origins of Modern Atheism*.[2] So it is worthwhile to consider how a very different and idiosyncratic response to atheism from one of the twentieth century's most noteworthy theologians might inform a contemporary Christian response to the New Atheism. This unique and distinctive response was that of Karl Barth to the atheism of Europe in the nineteenth and twentieth centuries.

Barth was, as is well known, an extraordinarily prolific theologian, and it is therefore impossible within the space of a few pages to provide an exhaustive overview of his reflections on modern atheism. Nevertheless, we are on solid ground if we tend to three overarching themes in Barth's response to it that remain consistent throughout his life and work.

THE FIRST RESPONSE: THE WORD OF GOD IN JESUS CHRIST

First, Barth does not address atheism with a resurgent philosophical theology but a robust Christology. This is seen formally in that Barth's most vigorous interaction with atheism in his magisterial *Church Dogmatics* occurs not under the doctrine of God, where most theologians take it up in the dogmatic *loci*, but within the Christology of the latter volumes of the *Church Dogmatics*, a point well attested below. This is not to say that Barth does not address it elsewhere. One must consider, for example, his important discussion of atheism in the provocative section on religion in the first volume of the *Dogmatics*. Nevertheless, his response even there is christologically grounded. In this, he stands in the tradition of Pascal, rather than that of the natural theologians such as Paley and more recent philosophical apologists. Like Pascal, he looks to God's par-

---

[2]Michael J. Buckley, *At the Origins of Modern Atheism* (New Haven, CT: Yale University Press, 1987); see also Buckley, *Denying and Disclosing God: The Ambiguous Progress of Modern Atheism* (New Haven, CT: Yale University Press, 2004).

ticular action in history, rather than to philosophy, as the means of addressing atheism.[3]

In addition to Barth's formal placement of the question of atheism within his *Church Dogmatics*, there is a very concrete and practical example of this commitment to particularity. Barth opposed Nazism in the years leading up to World War II not with a generic theism but with a rich Christology set within a trinitarian framework, witnessed perhaps most famously in the Barmen Declaration, though not only there, for Barth's mind was on such matters in Germany as he worked on the first two volumes of his *Church Dogmatics*. Theism may appear as a proper response to a growing atheistic secularism, but for Barth, such was fool's gold. Theism may be an appealing alternative to a generic secularism for those who lament the loss of a so-called Christian culture, but generic theism is helpless before a true idolatry, and for Barth, this is what the church was facing in National Socialism. The proper response to such idolatry is not to present philosophical arguments for theism but to present an image truly worthy of worship and capable of evoking not only allegiance but the courage to resist evil and even suffer at its hand, the image of God found in the revelation of Jesus Christ to be proclaimed and confessed by the churches. This observation leads to Barth's second response to atheism.

THE SECOND RESPONSE: A WORD OF JUDGMENT

If Barth's first approach to addressing atheism was one of positive affirmation, setting against it not an apologetics for philosophical theism but a rich confessional Christology, Barth's second approach to atheism was one of critical negation, and was nothing less than a negation not only of atheism's argumentation but also its very existence. Barth's audacious conviction was that, in truth, it was atheism, not God, which truly did not exist, for what appeared to be atheism was but a new way to hide our idolatries behind the veneer of a rational objectivity. Barth thus turned atheism's deconstruction of religion back on itself, embracing its critical appraisal of religion while expanding it to include atheism as but a new form of religion, which is itself a very old form of idolatry.

---

[3]See *CD* I/2, p. 7; see also pp. 3-8.

In a move not altogether surprising to those familiar with Barth's argumentation, Barth did not set atheism and religion against one another as two polar opposites but united them as two variations of one rebellion against God. Religion is in this account not seen as the solution to atheism, but atheism as but a new form of religion, with mysticism and atheism as two sides of one coin, and a coin collected within the coffers of the more general category of religion.[4]

Barth outlined this position in his section on religion in the first volume of the *Church Dogmatics* titled "The Revelation of God As the Abolition of Religion,"[5] and this understanding of religion is a particularly intriguing if controversial element of his thought. Yet his work here arose out of a fundamental commitment forged in his earliest theology and readily evidenced in the commentary on Romans, a commitment that he never abandoned. Barth was from first to last dedicated to preserve the distinction between and to reject the reversal of theology and anthropology.[6] Concretely, this entailed a sharp distinction between revelation, God coming to humanity in an act of grace, the true subject of theology's investigation and reflection, and religion, humanity's ongoing quest to arrive at transcendence.[7] As Barth stated, religion is not the complement, but the contradiction, of revelation.[8] This position is seen not only in Barth's extended discussion of religion in the first volume of the *Church Dogmatics* but also in his introductory essay to the English edition of Feuerbach's *The Essence of Christianity*, where, contrary to what would be expected of a theologian, Barth fully accepted the veracity of Feuerbach's critical analysis of religion

---

[4]See *CD* I/2, pp. 318-25; see also Barth's comparison of atheism and superstition in *CD* IV/3, pp. 807-8.

[5]*CD* I/2, pp. 280-361. A recent translation of this section by Garrett Green has retitled this section to be more faithful to the German original—see *On Religion: The Revelation of God as the Sublimation of Religion* (London: T & T Clark, 2007).

[6]As Barth could write on this subject: "Thus to understand God from man is either an impossibility or something one can do only in the form of Christology and not of anthropology (not even a Christology translated into anthropology). There is a way from Christology to anthropology, but there is no way from anthropology to Christology" (*CD* I/1, p. 131).

[7]Such a reversal had concrete consequences for Barth, for such a reversal of revelation and religion left one defenseless against the German Christians (see *CD* I/2, p. 292). The only answer would be to reject natural theology in any form and embrace a rich Christology, focusing on God's revelation in Christ, the true object of theology.

[8]*CD*, I/2, pp. 302-3.

and heartily endorsed it.[9] Barth could do so as a Reformed thinker who stood in a tradition that shared with Feuerbach a fear of anthropomorphism (something that, despite their many differences, Barth and Schleiermacher also shared in common). Even more importantly, Barth stood in the tradition of Calvin, whose ambiguous estimation of religion was rooted in his condemnation and wariness of idolatry. Barth was consequently less threatened by modern atheism than were some of his contemporaries, and this was so if for no other reason than that he considered it not a new and unique threat to Christianity in the modern era but a recent variation of a very old problem, namely, idolatry. Barth thus addressed atheism not on its own terms but placed it as a subcategory of religion, which is itself a form of self-righteous idolatry, and which is in turn a form of unbelief.[10] In the same way and along the same line of reasoning, Barth refused to see Christian revelation as simply a member of the larger species of religion, or to admit that philosophical arguments against theism have any bearing whatsoever on Christian revelation.

If this refusal is truly appreciated, then we can understand an important though often overlooked reason why Barth rejected Emil Brunner's appeal for a new theological apologetic strategy in light of the modern secular era. Barth rejected Brunner's eristic method, his particular take on a theological apologetics grounded in anthropology, first and foremost because it sacrificed the particularity of revelation which is but an epistemological commitment that reflects the soteriological one to salvation by grace alone. This reason was certainly the most important for Barth. Yet he also rejected it because, as he argued, while there may be cultural and intellectual changes in modernity, there is no theological basis for thinking our modern secular age is different from any earlier ones. In other words, Barth took a long view of history, and it was rooted in a hermeneutic derived not from the Enlight-

---

[9]Karl Barth, "An Introductory Essay," in Ludwig Feuerbach, *The Essence of Christianity*, trans. George Eliot (New York: Harper & Brothers, 1957), pp. x-xxxii. Barth endorsed Feuerbach's critique of religion precisely because of its trenchant critique of modern Protestant theology that is in fact anthropology, which Barth saw quintessentially in Schleiermacher, and rooted in the problematic Christology of Luther (see pp. xx-xxv). Barth can, however, turn the tables and criticize Feuerbach's own failures and naivety (see pp. xxvii-xxx).

[10]As Barth wrote, it is "only by the revelation of God in Jesus Christ that we can characterize religion as idolatry and self-righteousness, and in this way show it to be unbelief" (*CD* I/2, p. 314; see also p. 299).

enment but the apostle Paul. Barth adamantly insisted that the problem of atheism that faces the church today is the problem that has faced it from the beginning—namely, the problem of unbelief in God's revelation.[11] The only valid and worthy response to atheism, on this account, will be a robust dogmatics, a rich presentation and explication of revelation's content, and not a philosophical or cultural apologetics, for apologetics always takes unbelief more seriously than it takes revelation and faith.[12] Barth was less afraid of Feuerbach and D. F. Strauss than of a theology that had ceased, in his words, of "taking itself seriously as theology."[13] For Barth, atheism is not answered by, but feeds off of, natural theology.

Barth's strategy in responding to atheism was thus to refuse it the freedom to set the terms of the debate. Instead, he treated it as an example of the larger category of human sin which itself is to be understood in the context of God's revelation in Christ. It could be argued that this may be the ultimate form of condescension, but it may in fact also be viewed as a triumph of contextualization, for rather than allowing atheism to define itself as a new kind of enlightened and neutral objectivity, Barth defined it on theology's own ground and within a wider framework of history. It was, Barth argued, but a new modern instantiation of self-deceived unbelief and idolatry, and in the latter volumes of the *Church Dogmatics*, he even more strikingly categorized atheism not only as unbelief and pride[14] but also as a kind of sloth and indeed stupidity.[15] Rather than allow atheism to see itself as humanity come of age, Barth defined it as something old and mundane, indeed pedantic and uninteresting.[16] Rather than allow it to place the existence of God on the defensive, Barth placed atheism on the defensive by denying its very existence, for it was predicated on enslavement to a lie.[17] If one accepts Alasdair MacIntyre's assertion that one tradition is superior to another if it can provide a more robust narrative for its rival than its rival can of itself,

---

[11]*CD* I/1, p. 28.

[12]*CD* I/1, p. 30.

[13]*CD* I/2, p. 291.

[14]For the relation of pride and unbelief, see *CD* IV/1, p. 414. Barth defined atheism under the rubric of sin, which itself is discussed in Barth's latter christological volumes of the *Dogmatics* in the discussions of the pride, sloth and falsehood of humanity.

[15]*CD* IV/2, pp. 415-16; cf. pp. 411-21.

[16]*CD* IV/1, p. 610; cf. *CD* I/2, pp. 320-25.

[17]*CD* IV/3, pp. 449-51.

and if one also accepts Michael J. Buckley's assertion that atheism is always parasitic on a particular religious tradition, then Barth, despite the misgivings he would have with MacIntyre's natural description of Christian faith as a tradition and Buckley's affinity for religion, was nevertheless shown in great respects to be in agreement with both in terms of argumentation.[18] In the end, Barth quite simply refused to meet atheism, or secularism itself, on its own terms but attempted to out-narrate it. He wrote:

> Theology has all too often tried to seek out and conquer the consciousness of an age on its own ground. We have protested already against theology allowing adversaries to dictate its action, since this can only mean conceding to them half or more than half of what should not be conceded, namely, the Church's lack of independence of life and thought over against the world and the primacy of the questions that world has to put to the Church over the questions the Church has to put to itself.[19]

In the end, Barth contended, the church cannot take the atheism of the world too seriously.[20] He could, in fact, be quite dismissive, calling atheism "an artless and childish form" of religion.[21] He wrote of an atheism of his time but presciently of an atheism now present with us, and perhaps one that is increasingly uneasy of its inherent deficiencies, when he said:

> It hurls itself against religion in open conflict. It loves iconoclasm, the refutation of dogmas, and, of course, moral emancipation. It denies the existence of God and the validity of a divine law. And its whole interest is in the denial as such. That is its artlessness. It fails to see what mysticism does not fail to see: that absolute denial can have no meaning except against the background of a relative affirmation. A herd cannot be periodically slaughtered, unless it is continually fed and tended, or at any rate kept in being. Atheism lives in and by its negation. It can only break down and take away, and therefore it is exposed to the constant danger of finishing at a dead end.[22]

---

[18]See Alasdair MacIntyre, *After Virtue: A Study in Moral Theory*, 3rd ed. (Notre Dame, IN: University of Notre Dame Press, 2007); MacIntyre, *Whose Justice? Which Rationality?* (Notre Dame, IN: University of Notre Dame Press, 1989); MacIntyre, *Three Rival Versions of Moral Enquiry: Encyclopaedia, Genealogy and Tradition* (Notre Dame, IN: University of Notre Dame Press, 1991). For Buckley, see note 2 above.

[19]*CD* I/1, pp. 127-28.

[20]*CD* I/1, p. 155.

[21]*CD* I/2, p. 320.

[22]*CD* I/2, p. 321.

If Barth's first response to atheism was a positive declaration of the richness of God's revelation in Christ, then his second response was a withering word of judgment that seeks to expose atheism's pride in its freedom from God as but naive slavery to other unrecognized gods. He therefore sought to reveal atheism's confidence in its intellectual astuteness as naive folly and indeed stupidity, and to unmask its satisfaction in its modern enlightened and sophisticated consciousness as a mundane and uninteresting variation on a very old theme. This judgment was withering and relentless, if nonetheless brief and limited considering the scope of Barth's corpus. If apologetics finds any place in Barth's theological project, it is precisely not in the buttressing of a generic theism and construction of a Babel tower but the tearing down of false idols and the deconstruction of all such attempts to build any such tower in light of the ladder that drops from above. In other words, while Barth may have no place for an independent apologetics, he certainly had a place for it in the form of a hearty polemics within the dogmatic task.

The Third Response: A Word of Grace

Yet there is another means by which Barth responded to atheism and similarly claims that true atheism does not exist, and this by means not of a word of judgment against human idolatry but by the pronouncement of a word of divine mercy. Just as God's word of judgment for Barth served a more inclusive message of grace and promise, so also Barth echoed this pattern in following his pronouncement of judgment on atheism with a word of grace and indeed hope. Barth thereby turned his denial of atheism back on itself yet again, now denying that atheism truly exists not only because it is but a new form of idolatry, a fact that must call forth a word of judgment, but because, while humanity may yearn to be free of God, God has eternally chosen to be with humanity in Jesus Christ and thus to be God for us despite our unbelief and rebellion.

In this third as in the second response, atheism is again not allowed to determine the terms or means of the debate. Yet if earlier this took the form of the pronouncement of a word of judgment, now it takes the form of an unexpected word of grace, so that atheism is shown clemency in the very fact that it is not left to itself to decide its own ultimate meaning. For Barth, it is a divine mercy that atheism cannot provide the final word about itself, for when human rebellion has exhausted itself into nihilism, the dead end of atheism cannot ultimately be a conclusive end, because while humanity may choose to live without God, God has elected from eternity to live with and for humanity. For this reason, Barth's ultimate response to atheism was grounded in his doctrines of election and of Christ, and these themselves in Barth's mature thought become but two sides of one coin.[23] In Barth's revolutionary conception of the doctrine of election, God has chosen rejection and reprobation for himself, and salvation for us in the election of the Son. God has thus chosen to exist in no other way than as in covenant with humanity, choosing rejection for himself and election for humanity in his election to be God for us in Jesus Christ. Because Christ alone has experienced reprobation and abandonment as the Judge judged in our place, godlessness in its true form is not for anyone else an objective possibility.[24] That no man or woman can absolutely choose to be without God is due to God's choice for him or her in eternity.[25] Regardless of whatever soteriological questions this may raise, and these are of course supremely important ones that go far beyond what can here be explored, Barth's doctrine affirms that no person can truly exist apart from God, and that for a person to attempt to do so is to live falsely in the face of the reality of God's eternal election. This is a point that Barth consistently made throughout the *Church Dogmatics* from the second volume on election onward. As he stated in the doctrine of creation, set within the third volume of the *Dogmatics*:

> Man can be godless. But God—and this is the decisive point—does not become "man-less." He is always the Creator and Lord of man. And because he is not "man-less," the godlessness of man can be only a human notion, however frightful in itself and serious in its consequences. There is no ontological godlessness. Even the most rabid atheist cannot achieve this either theoretically or practically. And the ontological band which binds every man to God is the honour which God shows him, even if he is a theoretical and

---

[23]For a discussion of the relation between Barth's doctrine of election and Christology, see Bruce McCormack, "Grace and Being: The Role of God's Gracious Election in Karl Barth's Theological Ontology," in *The Cambridge Companion to Karl Barth*, ed. John Webster (Cambridge: Cambridge University Press, 2000), pp. 92-110.

[24]*CD* II/2, p. 346.

[25]*CD* II/2, p. 316.

practical atheist, in the fact that He is always his Creator and Lord, so that he for his part, however well or badly, was and is and will be His creature.[26]

Final Words on the Subject

These then are Barth's three primary responses to atheism, yet we must note one more related aspect of his thought. As Barth reframed the question of atheism, so Barth also did not see secularism so much as a threat but as a clarifying reality of postwar Europe that forced the church to confront the problems created by its having become wedded to culture and serving as its handmaiden. To appreciate this, one must understand Barth's reaction against the cultural Protestantism of his youth in light of the First World War, as well as his developed theology of the relation of the church and the state, of Christ and culture. For Barth, secularism was the shadow side of the church being the church, the lesser of two evils, the greater one being the conflation of church and culture. Therefore, as with atheism, Barth was less threatened by secularism than his contemporaries. He could indeed accept it as a by-product of a proper recognition of the distinction of the Christian community and the civil community, as well as the more basic distinction of church and world, and their rightful ordering in this time between the times of Christ's first and second advent. The great threat in Barth's estimation was not the secularization of culture but the secularization of the church, whereby the church sacrificed its unique identity in merging with the society around it.[27]

This estimation of what comprised the greatest danger to the church remained a running theme in Barth's thought. In a late cursory essay on atheism when Barth was at the end of his writing career, his approaches against atheism discussed above are all on display, as are his firm distinctions between revelation and religion, between theology and anthropology and between church and world. But there is also witnessed a prophetic edge coupled with a wizened reserve that befitted one who had lived not only to reflect from a distance on a problem but also to experience its effects not only within the surrounding culture but within himself. Atheism was thus

---

[26]*CD* III/2, p. 652; also *CD* IV/1, pp. 480-84; *CD* IV/2, pp. 409-11.

[27]For the dangers of secularization and practical atheism for the church, see *CD* IV/2, pp. 664-71; also *CD* IV/3, pp. 118-21.

something Barth realized that had to be not so much outargued as outlived. Barth was invited to respond to Max Bense, an atheist and a philosopher at the University of Stuttgart, whose essay titled "The Necessity of Atheism at the Present Day" appeared, along with Barth's response, in the *Zürcher Woche* in June of 1963. Barth's response was titled, not "The Rationality of Theism," but, rather intriguingly, "The Rationality of Discipleship."[28]

Barth stated at the beginning that he had little interest in providing a defense of Christianity against Bense, as the editors desired. As he wrote:

> Since a "Christianity" that, on being attacked by one professor, automatically required a defence by another, would not be worthy of the name, and since real Christianity has always been its own best defence against its assailants and even more against its own defenders, how am I to come to its defence?[29]

Barth was not, however, above critiquing Bense's own faith in determinism and individualism and human progress, his own particular real if unacknowledged gods, indeed his own evangelical and, might we say, religious fervor. Here Barth's ad hoc and deconstructive apologetics are once again on full display. In words borrowed from Bernard Shaw that might for us today not only conjure comparisons to Richard Dawkins but also provide him with his most fitting description, Barth compared Bense with Charles Bradlaugh, the feisty advocate of atheism in Victorian England, of whom Shaw wrote that "had he been an archbishop, he would have been the most awe-inspiring archbishop that this country has ever seen."[30]

Following such colorful cordialities, Barth was mystified that Bense was so concerned with attacking Christian faith when there are so many other gods, of sport, sex and money, or Bense's own more sophisticated ones, that are much more prevalent in modern society and near at hand. Even more intriguingly, Barth sympathized with Bense, for he maintained that a true atheism is always plagued by the unspoken fear that humanity will fail to act as its own and only redeemer, and that, if it does so act, it will become alienated by and enslaved to the very powers it conjures to save it.[31] There is much of value here in this brief essay that again displays an uncanny

---

[28]Translated and republished in Karl Barth, *Fragments Grave and Gay* (London: Collins, 1971).
[29]Ibid., p. 40.
[30]Ibid.
[31]Ibid., pp. 43-44.

ability to speak into our time. In brief and to summarize, Barth criticized atheism only in turn to show that its deepest and rightful concerns are only properly taken up in a humanity-embracing and world-affirming Christian confession, and that rather than being a slave to religious deities, humanity finds its true freedom in a God who has determined himself for us and us for him. Barth wrote: "Man belongs to this God, who is inherently not apart from man, is not against but for him; he is the God of all men, including those who give themselves out to be atheists."[32]

Barth's final word therefore was not to fear the atheism in the world but to take caution against that which is within our churches and ourselves:

> I know the rather sinister figure of the "atheist" very well, not only from books, but also because it lurks somewhere inside me too. But I believe I know even better the real God and the real man who is called Jesus Christ in the unity of both. He let the atheist depart once and for all and long ago, completely, and that goes for Max Bense as well as for me. Only in our bad dreams can we want to be "atheists."[33]

Barth ended by stating that it is not a theoretical or cultural atheism in society, but a practical one within the church itself, that is to be most feared. Such atheism is subtle and unacknowledged, so that while God's existence is affirmed, Christians act for all intents and purposes as if he did not exist, treating God as an ignored piece of furniture in a house, something that its owner would "refuse to part with in any circumstances, but for which he has nevertheless ceased to have any real use."[34] Worse even than this neglect is when God is no longer acknowledged as God but becomes but an idolatrous conception of our own making to be embraced simply for pragmatic purposes, perhaps a remnant of a "Christian Europe" or a "Christian America." In the end, Barth placed the blame for atheism at the feet of Christians. He concluded that, in response to this practical atheism, "the atheists of the other kind live on the fact that we are not better Christians." The splinter in the eye of the world's atheism is pointed out by those who have a beam in their own, and for Barth the greatest threat was an atheism that was within,

---

[32]Ibid., p. 44.
[33]Ibid., pp. 45-46.
[34]Ibid., pp. 46-47.

rather than without, the church.[35] Throughout his life, Barth was more inclined to reflect on and listen to this atheism of the world and what it might say of the churches than to dismiss it out of hand or move on too quickly to defensive argument that evades its criticisms of Christianity.

SUMMING UP

Barth's response to atheism could take the form of negative judgment, and one that began with the household of God. But the negative judgment of both church and world served a larger positive affirmation of God's faithfulness in the face of human faithlessness and unbelief. The response to a resurgent atheism was not best found in a new philosophical theism or sophisticated apologetics but a clear presentation of Christian revelation, a strong Christology that embraced rather than ignored or apologized for the scandal of particularity and, as Athanasius argued long ago, the evidence provided by the presence of a new people in the world, a Christian community that really knew what it was about and remained true to its distinctive task. For this reason, Barth could naturally move from Christology to ecclesiology and state that the response to atheism by Christians must not first be intellectual but ecclesiological, a matter of witness and not primarily of argument, for, as Ambrose noted, it is not through dialectic that God chose to save the world. Argument may have its place, but it cannot live a disembodied existence or allow judgment to be the first or last word spoken.

A few years ago, I had an undergraduate student who, sadly, turned his back on his faith. This turn took place for him during his college tenure where he began as a double major in social work and in theology. Having finished his theology classes early in his course of study, he took other classes with only one remaining in his theology program—his senior seminar. Wanting to graduate and finish the major, he knew he had to take the course, though he had quite lost interest in the subject matter in light of his conversion. I agreed to take him on for a summer independent study. He came to me, a theologian, with a visible chip on his shoulder. He was a bright student who read widely in his new atheist faith. I tried to set him at ease and told him that I was glad to have him as a student and that we would have

---

[35]Ibid., p. 47.

a good time together reading theology, and that I was not that concerned with or even particularly interested in engaging his newfound atheism. His face fell and he replied, "It's not fun if you are not threatened by it." Perhaps that response is something for all Christians to keep in mind, for certainly Barth did.

PART THREE

Christ and Creation

10

Christ, Creation and
the Drama of Redemption

"The Play's the Thing . . . "

✠

During my first year of teaching, the building where the theology department would reside was under major renovation, and the theology faculty was housed temporarily in a suite of offices in the science building. It was an interesting year, this year of exile, as we awaited our exodus. Housing a theology faculty in a science building may seem to be a cruel joke played by administration, but it was a beneficial experience, and it is perhaps good to be reminded that, while theologians have oftentimes celebrated the demise of positivism, its aroma hangs quite heavy over some working scientists' laboratories. Make no mistake—our hosts were quite hospitable. But I'm not certain that some of them always knew what to make of us.

To keep my bearings during that year, I scrawled a single phrase on the chalk board in my office: "Creation is the context of the covenant."[1] This shortened phrase of Karl Barth reminded me each day of the deep and abiding connection between my office and the office of the chemist down the hall. In some way, we were engaged in related, though assuredly differentiated, tasks, both seeking understanding in God's world, a world of mol-

---

An earlier version of this chapter appeared as "Christ, Creation and the Drama of Redemption: 'The Play's the Thing,'" *Scottish Journal of Theology* 62, no. 2 (2009): 149-74. ©2009 *Scottish Journal of Theology*. Reprinted by permission.
[1]Karl Barth entitles two subsections of §41 "Creation and Covenant" as "Creation as the External Basis of the Covenant" and "The Covenant as the Internal Basis of Creation" (*CD* III/1).

ecules and microscopes, of Moses and Mary. As Barth so carefully explains, creation and covenant are ever distinguished and not to be confused, but nor are they to be separated or divided. The creation does not stand as an autonomous entity, a brute fact, nor is it left to its own devices. Rather, while it has its own integrity and indeed purposes, it exists not only for itself but also as the context for a relation of God and humanity in Jesus Christ, established before the world's very foundation and therein for a relation between God and all creatures.[2] The world that God created is the very same world where Jesus lived and walked and died. Ever since the shunning of Marcion and the shedding of the Gnostics, the church has firmly held to its core conviction that creation and redemption belong together, that there is but one good world created and redeemed by one good God. So, while fully acknowledging that the God Christians worship and seek to know stands apart from the world and cannot be confused with the world or known through scientific instrumentation and measurement, it must also be said that the physical world in which both theologians and chemists work, as well as where both the believer and the unbeliever reside, is commonly shared, if quite differently perceived.[3]

To speak of creation is therefore implicitly yet intentionally to speak not first of a cosmology but of a relation between God and the world. As often noted, this acknowledged relation is why Christians speak of creation rather than simply of nature. For the Christian theologian, it is not only an understanding of God that one must strive to achieve, or an understanding of the created order, but of the relation between them. Indeed, one cannot understand the doctrine of God or that of creation without understanding this relation, for these are understood in light of the relation itself, even as the relation is comprehended only in light of God's revelation as this itself is known through faith.[4] In brief, to speak of creation rather than nature is

---

[2]Eph 1:3-4.

[3]Wittgenstein's comment that the believer and the unbeliever live in different worlds notwithstanding.

[4]See Robert Sokowlowski, *The God of Faith and Reason: Foundations in Christian Theology* (Washington, DC: Catholic University Press of America, 1982/1995). He writes: "Christian theology is differentiated from pagan religious and philosophical reflection primarily by the introduction of a new distinction, the distinction between the world understood as possibly not having existed and God understood as possibly being all that there is, with no diminution of goodness or greatness" (p. 23).

to speak of God, for creation implies a Creator with a logical and analytic assurance. It is the nature of this relation that I would like to examine in this chapter.

THE QUESTION OF GOD'S RELATION TO CREATION

Kathryn Tanner, in her penetrating book *God and Creation in Christian Theology: Tyranny or Empowerment?*, strives to present the logic of this relation in terms of its deep and underlying grammar.[5] Her stated purpose is to provide an investigation of theological language pertaining to God and the world, as she writes: "My direct concern is not for the object of theological discourse—e.g., God, the world, eternal life—but for theologians' talk about it." Her goal is to specify "rules for forming first order statements."[6] Some might be a bit disconcerted by such a stark separation between language and reality and such a thoroughgoing linguistic turn in which material talk about God and world is traded for formal rules that regulate discourse, or unsettled by Tanner's statement that "[t]heologians seem to know that it is appropriate to say certain things about God without quite knowing what they mean by doing so."[7] Yet she herself notes that her pragmatist method need not necessarily imply "non-referentiality" or antirealism and indeed insists on the need for a referential aspect to theological language and the place in theology for first-order claims about God and the world.[8] For our present discussion, while recognizing the complexity of issues surrounding reality and reference in regard to theological discourse and the

---

[5]Kathryn Tanner, *God and Creation in Christian Theology: Tyranny or Empowerment?* (Oxford: Basil Blackwell, 1988).

[6]Ibid., pp. 11, 27.

[7]Ibid., p. 11; see pp. 11-12. She writes: "It makes sense then to recast the 'material mode' of a theologian's statements about God and world into a 'formal mode' whereby they express recommendations for talk about these matters. Statements about God and world become rules for discourse, proposals about what should and should not be said" (p. 12).

[8]Ibid., pp. 12-13; cf. pp. 49-53. She writes: "Although the referential character of theological discourse is crucial to the whole enterprise (what would be the point of doing theology if one were not really talking about God?), the informational vacuity of such talk should shift the focus of someone investigating it away from epistemological questions of truth and meaning. Theologians simply assume that what they say about God is meaningful and true: they have no way of actually specifying what they are talking about . . . apart from the meanings of the terms they use, and it is just those meanings whose applicability to God they admit to failing to understand" (p. 12). Such statements provide assurance of reference but raise as many questions as they answer, even among those sympathetic and indeed appreciative of Tanner's holistic account that refuses to separate theology and Christian practice (see p. 13).

importance of their investigation, I want to leave such deep linguistic waters and move on to Tanner's central argument.[9]

At the heart of Tanner's work lies the explication of two convictions pertaining to and governing discourse regarding the relation between God and the world, convictions that she takes to be basic for Christian theology and practice. The first is that God is transcendent. God's transcendence is a central presupposition of various Christian practices:

> God must not be of this world if God is to act as its savior and judge. Biblical and liturgical doxologies proclaim God's "otherness" in power and mystery. Prohibitions against idolatry forbid the ascription of divine attributes to things of this world. The mystery of God's ways is a presupposition of the Christian trust that, appearances to the contrary, the world is ruled by a good, just and loving God.[10]

The second conviction is that God is active as a creative agent in the world. This conviction is readily witnessed throughout the biblical canon, wherein God is described as acting both to create and to sustain the world.[11] Reconciling these two fundamental convictions of God's transcendence and God's creative agency—these rules that determine all that may and must be said of God's relation to the world—lies at the heart of Tanner's work and is her central task. She rightly argues that only a radical transcendence that portrays the relation between divine and creaturely causation as incommensurable allows one to avoid a competitive and contrastive view of God's transcendence and creative activity in which an increase in divine agency necessarily entails a decrease in human freedom.[12]

---

[9]I would argue that, once even significantly qualified referentiality in theological discourse is accepted, any strong distinction between formal rules and material statements pertaining to the relation between God and the world becomes attenuated (rightly so, in my view, and Tanner may well agree with this claim). The formal statements themselves point to some material commitments, for example, that God is transcendent, even while we might readily admit with Tanner that we cannot comprehensively specify the exact nature of such transcendence. Another way to put this question is to ask whether the rules of theological discourse are as akin to mathematical and grammatical rules as Tanner seems to hold. The first seem to imply some implicit material commitments in a way that the latter do not.

[10]Tanner, *God and Creation in Christian Theology*, p. 38.

[11]Ibid., p. 38.

[12]Ibid., pp. 46-48. This does not mean that Tanner avoids all difficulties. By radicalizing divine action in a manner that entails that God becomes the source of all that is, she introduces the problem of evil and yet chooses not to engage it (see pp. 47-48, 174 n. 12).

Few theologians of a traditional bent would quarrel with these convictions, or with Tanner's claim that they are central to Christian theology and practice across various ecclesial traditions. Of course, it must be acknowledged that some have discarded such claims of transcendence, evident in types of process theology, for example, and illustrated in Whitehead's axiom: "It is as true to say that God creates the world as the world creates God."[13] Such approaches are exceptions, however, rather than the norm. Nevertheless, in light of such approaches, one is warranted to ask the question whether theology can rest content with elucidating the interplay between these formal rules and defending their compatibility amid seeming contradiction without specifying their ground. In other words, we might ask, from where do these formal rules come, and how are they themselves grounded for Christian belief and practice? What is distinctive about the Christian doctrine of creation so that these convictions themselves become central? And why do Christians have these specific conceptions of divine transcendence and activity rather than others?[14]

THE DISTINCTIVENESS OF THE CHRISTIAN ANSWER

These are valid questions, for such convictions regarding divine transcendence and activity were, of course, not self-apparent in the matrix of Christian faith, nor are they so today. In pagan thought, divinity stood as the highest principle within the cosmos. One could differentiate between things within the world, but only in Christian thought (as prefigured in Judaism) does the world itself become but one term within a distinction, a relation between God and the world.[15] In contrast, pagan divinities exist in

---

[13]Alfred North Whitehead, *Process and Reality: An Essay in Cosmology* (New York: Macmillan, 1929/1969), p. 405, cited in Anne M. Clifford, "Creation," in *Systematic Theology: Roman Catholic Perspectives*, ed. Francis Schüssler Fiorenza and John P. Galvin (Minneapolis: Fortress, 1991), p. 227.

[14]Therefore, while Tanner expertly outlines the use and interplay of transcendence and divine activity, the grounding of such use receives less attention. There at times seems to be an abstractness in Tanner's work because the rules of the God–world relation are not explicitly rooted in the revelation of this relation itself. This observation is not a denial that Tanner may well ground such a relation in a particular event rather than in a general metaphysics. But the question remains from where such convictions regulating the description of the God–world relation come, and why Christians have such a distinct doctrine of creation and specific understandings of divine transcendence and activity.

[15]Sokolowski, *God of Faith and Reason*, pp. 31-32. For the following, see also R. A. Norris Jr., *God and World in Early Christian Theology* (New York: Seabury, 1965), pp. 11-40; Tanner, *God and Creation in Christian Theology*, pp. 36-80; Clifford, "Creation," pp. 210-16.

relation to other things within the world, and they do so of necessity whereby their very identity and essence is dependent on this relation.[16] They cannot exist without the world.

This judgment is, moreover, as true of later Greek philosophical notions of an abstract deity as of the gods of Homer and Hesiod's anthropomorphic myths. Aristotle's Unmoved Mover stands at the pinnacle of a cosmology; it does not stand above the cosmology itself as its transcendent creator.[17] Even Plato's seemingly transcendent One, or the Good, exists only as a part of all that is, as "one over, for, and in many," never as the One or the Good only in itself.[18] And when Greek notions of divinity do emphasize a type of transcendent other-worldliness, as in Plato's understanding of the eternal forms, they do so only by making the identity and integrity of divinity dependent on its absolute removal and distance from the world's instability and becoming. The more stark the contrast between the divine world and the sensible one, the more the divine is isolated from the physical world and excluded from action within it. Greek thought is thus devoid of true transcendence, and, insofar as it begins to approach such a conception, it excludes divine participation within the world.[19] Divine transcendence and divine activity are thus mutually exclusive. In fact, it is very questionable whether we should speak of either at all. Aristotle's Unmoved Mover exists within the universe, and his exalted state within it is such that he may influence the other realities of the universe, but he neither acts within it nor exercises providence over it.[20] Furthermore, the pagan universe is itself a divinized one; as Plato relates in the *Timaeus*, the universe is "a single living thing that contains within itself all living things, mortal or immortal."[21] This

---

[16]See Sokowlowski, *God of Faith and Reason*, pp. 12-20, 33. He writes: "The being of pagan gods is to be a part, though the most important part, of what is; no matter how independent they are, the pagan gods must be with things that are not divine" (p. 12).

[17]"No matter how Aristotle's god is to be described, as the prime mover or as the self-thinking thought, he is part of the world, and it is obviously necessary that there be other things besides him, whether he is aware of them or not" (Sokowlowski, *God of Faith and Reason*, pp. 15-16).

[18]Ibid., p. 18. For Plato, as for Aristotle, the Stoics and the Epicureans, "the divine, even in its most ultimate form, is never conceived as capable of being without the world. It is divine by being differentiated from what is not divine and by having an influence on what is not divine" (p. 18).

[19]Tanner, *God and Creation in Christian Theology*, pp. 45-46.

[20]See Aristotle, *Metaphysics*, bk. 12; also Christopher Stead, *Philosophy in Christian Antiquity* (Cambridge: Cambridge University Press, 1994), p. 35.

[21]Plato, *Timaeus*, 69c. Cf. Plato, *Complete Works*, ed. John M. Cooper (Indianapolis: Hackett, 1997), p. 1270.

position leads Richard Norris to conclude that Plato presents us with a picture in which the cosmos "in virtue of the supreme Intelligence which indwells it, is a god."[22] The Greeks lived in a divinized universe, even after jettisoning the early anthropomorphisms of Homer and Hesiod's gods, and the divine was the highest principle within this universe.

The Christian conception of God's relation to creation diverges significantly from such understandings. Christians, drawing on earlier Jewish traditions, think of both the world and God differently than their pagan contemporaries.[23] First, whereas for the Greeks the world is understood basically as a natural order, an order that is eternal and constitutes a cosmology, the Jewish and Christian conception sees the world as the context of human life and human decisions occurring within temporal history and examined and evaluated in light of their correspondence to God's will and purposes.[24] The Old Testament thus portrays God's relation with the world not in metaphysical but moral terms, and the New Testament portrays this relation especially in terms of grace and mercy. As Norris notes, it is not that the world of nature is ignored, but it is not the most important thing: "It is like the stage setting for a drama: subordinate both to the actors and their movements and to the purposes of the author or producer. It finds its meaning in the developing story for which it provides a setting."[25]

Furthermore, the Christian conception of God also differs greatly from pagan understandings. For the Greeks, the word "god" denotes a kind of thing and can therefore be applied to various beings, whereas in Judaism and Christianity, God is a singular being who is known through a specific history of events.[26] As Norris concludes: "The Greek deity is the final point

---

[22]Norris, *God and World*, p. 23.

[23]For the background in Second Temple Judaism of such Christian convictions regarding the uniqueness and transcendence of God, see Richard Bauckham, *God Crucified: Monotheism and Christology in the New Testament* (Carlisle, UK: Paternoster, 1998), pp. 1-22.

[24]Norris, *God and World*, pp. 37-39. For a similar distinction between Old Testament and modern scientific understandings of the world, see Clifford, "Creation," p. 207. For patristic understandings of the material world, see David C. Lindberg, "Science and the Early Church," in *God and Nature: Historical Essays on the Encounter Between Christianity and Science*, ed. David C. Lindberg and Ronald L. Numbers (Berkeley: University of California Press, 1986), pp. 19-48. He writes: "There was, of course, no unitary Christian view of the material world. But orthodox Christianity, as it developed, emphatically rejected the extremes; nature was neither to be worshiped nor to be repudiated" (pp. 30-31; see also pp. 31-32, 41).

[25]Norris, *God and World*, p. 38.

[26]This is not to deny the complex history of the development of the conception of the divine in

of stability in a world of apparently senseless change. The Hebrew Lord is the initiator of significant change which transforms the character of historical experience."[27]

The Christian conceptions of God, of the world and of their relation are thus very different from pagan conceptions. The notion of God's creation of the world *ex nihilo* is intimated in Scripture[28] and firmly established by the time of Irenaeus, who takes it for granted. God stands apart from the world but not against it. God is defined in relation to God's own being and free decisions, not in contrast and opposition to other realities.[29] Contrastive notions of the divine and the human are pagan, not Christian, notions. Indeed, according to Tanner, it is precisely the radical transcendence of God that makes divine activity coherent, for God is not set over against the world in such a manner that his activity in it would lessen his divinity and thus make such activity problematic. Rather, God's independence from the world makes his activity possible without either lessening his deity or undermining the integrity of the created order, for divine and human causality are incommensurable and, in Tanner's words, related not in inverse but direct proportion. God's activity does not threaten human activity but establishes it.[30]

In sum, there is, quite simply, no equivalent in Greek or Roman pagan thought (or, for that matter, in ancient Near Eastern thought) to the Christian idea of a transcendent God who creates a contingent world out of free grace rather than necessity, who creates out of nothing (*ex nihilo*), a God who would exist with no loss of goodness or majesty even if the world

---

ancient Israel witnessed in its Scriptures, in which one can find both reference to "gods" (e.g., Ps 82), as well as apparent ambiguous conceptions of the relationship between Yahweh and his messengers. See, for example, David N. Freedman, ed., *The Anchor Bible Dictionary*, vol. 1 (New York: Doubleday, 1992), s.v. "Angels," by Carol A. Newsom. Yet Bauckham convincingly argues that by Second Temple Judaism such ambiguity had cleared away (*God Crucified*, pp. 3-5, 16-22).

[27]Norris, *God and World*, pp. 38-39.

[28]Some of the most important biblical and apocryphal passages in support of this doctrine being Heb 11:3; Rom 4:17; 2 Macc 7:28; and, according to some interpretations of it, Gen 1.

[29]The relation between God's triune identity and his eternal decision of election has become a matter of great controversy in recent years. While I acknowledge this difficulty here, addressing it would go far afield from the limited task at hand. Both sides in the controversy want to preserve the distinction of God and the world, and so the answer given to the question does not fundamentally alter but may have bearing on the distinction I am here trying to highlight.

[30]See Tanner, *God and Creation in Christian Theology*, chap. 3.

was not.[31] And it is important to note, as Robert Sokowlowski does, that the movement from the first (pagan) conception to the second (Christian) one has nothing to do with intelligence, nor is it a move simply along the path of reason, but it is a very different move altogether. We might inquire how this move was made.

To begin, we might remember that the origin of Israel's conviction pertaining to God's transcendence over creation and distinct activity within it did not occur as the result of contemplating creation's order. Rather than following such an examination of nature, the conviction that God was the transcendent creator and ruler of heaven and earth who transcended ethnic and national boundaries was the result of God's salvific action expressed in superiority over all rival gods, be they Egyptian in the exodus, or Canaanite or Babylonian. In the Old Testament, creation and redemption are often explicitly related, as in Isaiah 43:1:

> But now thus says the LORD,
>> he who created you, O Jacob,
>> he who formed you, O Israel:
> Do not fear, for I have redeemed you;
> I have called you by name, you are mine.[32]

The creation accounts in Scripture, including the prototypical accounts in Genesis, are not primarily cosmological explanations of the natural order but identity narratives of God and his relation to the world which were written in light of God's salvific action.[33] The understanding of creation that Christianity inherits from Judaism is one in which God and the world are distinct and in which God is superior to the world in such a way that his lordship and sovereignty exercised in his mighty acts of redemption imply his independence from the world, so that creation itself is a free, gracious and sovereign act.

---

[31]Sokowlowski, *God of Faith*, pp. 19, 31-34; see also Colin Gunton, "The Doctrine of Creation," in *The Cambridge Companion to Christian Doctrine*, ed. Colin Gunton (Cambridge: Cambridge University Press, 1997), p. 148; cf. Gerhard May, *Creatio ex Nihilo: The Doctrine of "Creation out of Nothing" in Early Christian Thought*, trans. A. S. Worrall (Edinburgh: T & T Clark, 1994).

[32]See also Is 42:5-7; 45:8-18, et al.

[33]As Clifford notes: "The Genesis creation texts were not composed to answer the scientific question of how the world came to be. On the contrary, they proclaim the relationship of God to reality, a relation of creator to creation" ("Creation," p. 198; see also pp. 203-4). Moreover, they themselves were written in light of the exodus, to which they were subservient.

It is this inheritance that Christianity receives from Judaism, an inheritance of a distinction drawn between God and the world in which God is both transcendent and active within the world. This distinction was related not only to liturgy but also to life. The Christian distinction between God and the world is not only a theoretical distinction but also a lived distinction, first lived in anticipation in the life of Israel, and fully lived and expressed in the life and teaching of Jesus.[34] Moreover, not only is it witnessed in the life and teaching of Jesus, but also, *and this is the crux of the matter*, it is revealed and established in the existence of the divine incarnate Son. Christ reveals the true relation between God and the world precisely because he *is* God with us. So not only is this relation revealed in Jesus, it is indeed established in this mystery and miracle. In other words, Jesus Christ does not merely teach the distinction and relation of God and the world; he is its very revelation, basis and ground, the Word become flesh, the singular union of God and nature on which all other relations between God and creatures are predicated and in which they exist as analogical reflections of this singular, unique and true relation. The distinction and relation between God and creation finds not only its noetic but also its ontic basis in him.

If this is true, then here one must begin to distinguish between chronological and logical priority. It is true that the distinction between the Creator and the creation is witnessed in Israel's history long before the birth of Jesus of Nazareth and the church's reflection on his life, death and resurrection. Yet the New Testament does not see Christ simply as an instance, no matter how unique, of a general relation between God and the world. Rather, Christ is portrayed as the basis for the world's very existence and the foundation on which all of God's relations with particular creatures are established, not an object or product, but the Subject and agent, of creation. What is remarkable of the vast majority of references to creation in the New Testament is that they are christologically determined and emphasize precisely this point. So, for instance, in the prologue of the Gospel of John, the Word who becomes flesh is the Word through whom all things came into being, and without whom "not one thing came into being."[35] This prologue

---

[34]Sokowlowski, *God of Faith*, pp. 23-24; also p. xiv.
[35]Jn 1:3.

is echoed in that of Hebrews, where the Son is appointed by God as the "heir of all things, through whom he also created the world."[36] Paul can state, in the very context of a discussion of meat offered to idols where he stresses that there is only one true God regardless of claims for other gods in heaven and earth, that "for us there is one God, the Father, from whom are all things and for whom we exist, and one Lord, Jesus Christ, through whom are all things and through whom we exist."[37] The context, the parallelism and the claim itself are remarkable, for central to Judaism's understanding was that God alone participated in creation.[38] Finally, perhaps the most exalted of all such texts occurs in Colossians, where after describing the redemption and forgiveness effected by the Father through the Son, the author describes this Son in glorious terms: "He is the image of the invisible God, the firstborn of all creation; for in him all things in heaven and on earth were created, things visible and invisible, whether thrones or dominions or rulers or power—all things have been created through him and for him. He himself is before all things, and in him all things hold together."[39] It is noteworthy that the very phrase that the Nicene Creed attributes to the Father, the Creator of all things "visible and invisible," is in fact attributed to the Son in this passage that displays Christ as both the origin and the goal of creation.[40]

For the New Testament, then, as for the Old, creation and redemption are closely related. In conjoining divine creative and redemptive freedom, Paul can thus assert: "For it is the God who said, 'Let light shine out of darkness,' who has shone in our hearts to give the light of the knowledge of the glory of God in the face of Jesus Christ."[41] Therefore we can conclude, as does Anne Clifford, that "just as the primary purpose of the Old Testament accounts of creation is not to report the physical beginnings of the world but

---

[36] Heb 1:2.

[37] 1 Cor 8:4-6. For the role New Testament Christology plays with regard to the identity of God and the question of creation, see Bauckham, *God Crucified*, pp. 35-40.

[38] "As the only eternal one . . . , God alone brought all other beings into existence. God had no helper, assistant or servant to assist or to implement his work of creation. God alone created, and no one else had any part in this activity. This is axiomatic for Second Temple Judaism" (Bauckham, *God Crucified*, p. 12).

[39] Col 1:15-17; cf. Eph 1:3-14.

[40] See Arthur G. Patzia, *New International Biblical Commentary: Ephesians, Colossians, Philemon* (Peabody, MA: Hendrickson, 1984/1990), p. 30.

[41] 2 Cor 4:6.

is to express faith in God, so the New Testament creation theology is a reflection of the meaning of Christ."[42]

After the close of the apostolic period, the patristic writers continued this trajectory of closely relating creation and redemption, creation and Christology, seen nowhere so clearly as in their appropriation and articulation of a Logos Christology in expounding on the created order. Drawing on the implicit though unsystematic formulations of Scripture, they came to confirm the transcendence of God as well as his activity within the world, both closely tied to an understanding of the incarnate Logos. As we have seen, these two mutual affirmations were not self-evident at the time, either individually or in tandem, and their intimate pairing is unique to Christian writers.[43]

Later, Irenaeus relates that God acts in the world through his two hands, the Son and the Spirit.[44] Regardless of the real problems created by the merging of biblical and Platonic thought in Irenaeus as well as other early thinkers, the centrality and uniqueness of the revelation in Christ is accepted, and this is the key to their understanding of creation.[45] Indeed, it is

---

[42]Clifford, "Creation," p. 209. For a further discussion of the relation of Christ and creation in Scripture, see Colin E. Gunton, *Christ and Creation* (Eugene, OR: Wipf & Stock, 1992/2005), pp. 11-34. Gunton there writes: "However remarkable the claim, whatever the origin of the words used to express it, and however incredible may appear the content, there appears to have developed soon after the death of Jesus a widespread Christian confession to the effect that the one through whom God had acted to save the world was also the agent of its creation" (p. 22).

[43]That this is the case does not entail that there are no difficulties raised by the formulations of Logos Christology among patristic authors. For example, at times the Logos can appear to be more a cosmic principle than a person, Jesus Christ. Such is certainly evident in Justin Martyr. Nevertheless, though Justin melded Christian and pagan conceptions through his understanding of Christ as the universal reason in a controversial manner, the sufficiency and uniqueness of Christ were for Justin not at issue (see Norris, *God and World*, pp. 53-54; for problematic aspects of Justin's doctrine of creation and Christology, see pp. 64-68). On a balanced reading, it is clear that Justin does not sacrifice the particularity of Christ for a Christ principle as to trade a philosophy for Christology (see Justin's *Second Apology*, chaps. 6, 13; also *First Apology*, chaps. 5, 13, 46.). The balance may be precarious, but Justin does not abandon the historical person of Jesus for an atemporal metaphysics. Further complicating this picture, the cosmic status of the Logos is not yet settled for early Christian thinkers, who often portray the Logos as a mediating principle subordinate to the Father. The full equality of the Logos (the Son) with the Father is not fully articulated until the work of Athanasius, the Cappadocians and Nicea. For a discussion of the status of the Logos in the thought of Justin, Irenaeus, Tertullian and Origen, see Norris, *God and World*, chaps. 2-6; also Stead, *Philosophy in Christian Theology*, chap. 13; J. N. D. Kelly, *Early Christian Doctrines*, rev. ed. (San Francisco: HarperSanFrancisco, 1978), chaps. 4-10.

[44]See Stead, *Philosophy in Christian Theology*, pp. 67-68; Norris, *God and World*, pp. 87-97; also Gunton, "Doctrine of Creation," p. 148.

[45]"One result, then, of the dialogue of Christian faith with Greek philosophy was the formulation

precisely the uniqueness and concreteness of the divine and creaturely union in Christ that allows Tertullian to overcome the Greek contrastive accounts of divine changelessness and worldly change. That the incarnation occurred, Tertullian argued, is precisely why one cannot claim that should God enter into a real direct relation with the world his divine nature would be compromised.[46] For Tertullian, it is the actuality of the incarnation, not a preconceived notion of divinity that precludes intimacy with the world, that must dictate one's understanding of God, the world and their relation.

Such close bonds between Christ and creation were beginning to fray, however, by the late patristic period, in which Platonic forms translated into the mind of God, rather than Christ, began to be seen as the archetype for creation.[47] Thus the christological emphasis that provided the shape for the doctrine of creation began to wane. So, for example, as Colin Gunton notes, Christology is almost entirely absent in Augustine's doctrine of creation.[48] Such an absence became the rule rather than the exception, and this would remain the case for a long stretch of church history. Creation and Christ were ever more treated as independent topics of theological discourse.

The Answer Rearticulated

Moving far ahead in time, it is in the modern period that one finds a thoroughgoing christological reshaping of the doctrine of creation, though this move is perhaps prefigured in the Reformation. Two attempts to read the doctrine of creation in light of the second article appear in the modern period with the work of Friedrich Schleiermacher and Karl Barth. At the risk of doing justice to neither in such limitations of space, I will examine each in turn.

Even though Schleiermacher's doctrine of creation proper is relegated to

---

of an idea of God which, at its very center, embraced a fundamental tension between the ideals of an immutable Perfection beyond the world and a creative Sovereignty in and over it" (Norris, *God and World*, pp. 164-65). In addition, the Neoplatonic influence on Christian thinkers created a marked tension between the Platonic notion of the inferiority of the material world and the biblical notion of the goodness of the physical creation (see Lindberg, "Science and the Early Church," pp. 30-32).

[46]Tanner, *God and Creation in Christian Theology*, pp. 56-57. Tanner here provides an analysis of Tertullian's *On the Flesh of Christ*, chap. 4.

[47]For some of the problems raised by making the forms central to the doctrine of creation, see Diogenes Allen, *Philosophy for Understanding Theology* (Atlanta: John Knox, 1985), chap. 1.

[48]Gunton, "Doctrine of Creation," p. 150.

a brief section of the *Glaubenslehre,* or *Christian Faith,* it is a very significant doctrine in that, as combined and subsumed under the doctrine of preservation, it exerts an influence on the entire work.[49] Schleiermacher's dogmatics is nothing if not systematic, and every doctrine has a reciprocal influence on every other one. For this reason, the doctrine of Christ in the second part of the *Glaubenslehre* exerts an influence on the first part in which the doctrine of creation is addressed. This judgment is corroborated when it is noted that, for Schleiermacher, every Christian doctrine must be derived from Christ's own self-proclamation which comes to be the basis for Christian piety, for all Christian piety is grounded in the appearance of Christ the Redeemer.[50]

Schleiermacher sees Christ as the culmination of both God's creative and redemptive purposes, for, as Schleiermacher states, "He alone is destined gradually to quicken the whole human race into higher life" (*CF,* §13.1). Yet the appearance of Christ in history is not an absolute miracle, a discrete divine action, but a natural fact, for regardless of how different Christ is from other persons generally, his perfect God-consciousness demonstrates an intrinsic capacity and possibility within humanity to take the divine into itself, expressed as the "highest development of its spiritual power" (*CF,* §13.1). That Christ is the highest instantiation of a human capacity for the God-consciousness does not mean for Schleiermacher that Christ's appearance and his God-consciousness are simply the actualization of latent historical possibilities. Christ's appearance is divinely determined in an eternal decision; it is not simply the product of an evolutionary development of the God-consciousness within history. Nevertheless, Christ stands as the pinnacle of a human development, even though one that is grounded in an eternal election. Christ is not the incarnation of an eternal divine subject but appears in history through an eternal divine decree.[51]

It is important to understand why Schleiermacher takes this christo-

---

[49]For the doctrine of creation, see §§36-41, §§42-45; for preservation, §§46-49. For Schleiermacher's subsuming creation into preservation, see §38.1. For the broader implications and scope of Schleiermacher's doctrine of creation beyond these sections, see Robert Sherman, *The Shift to Modernity: Christ and the Doctrine of Creation in the Theologies of Schleiermacher and Barth* (New York: T & T Clark, 2005), pp. 7-8.

[50]See *CF,* §19.4 postscript; also §28.2, §29.3.

[51]See chapter 12 in this volume.

logical route rather than a more traditional one of a true incarnation of God in history. Two reasons for this approach can be discerned. The first is explicitly stated and dogmatic in nature. The second is implicit and due to a consideration external to dogmatics proper.

The first reason that Christology is redefined as it is for Schleiermacher is apparent in light of his doctrine of preservation, which itself encapsulates the doctrine of creation. There, Schleiermacher maintains that the feeling of absolute dependence arises out of the awareness that all finite existence is determined by and contingent on the interdependence of nature (the *Naturzusammenhang*) (see *CF*, §46). The very ground for our relation to God, the feeling of absolute dependence, is thus itself dependent on and arises from the uniformity of nature which admits of no exceptions.

Such a view of the world makes miracles especially problematic. Insofar as they are defined as disturbances of the constant causal nexus, their occurrence would undermine and indeed destroy the basis for the feeling of absolute dependence. Therefore a true miracle is an impossibility, and such miracles need to be abandoned. In the end, this includes any true incarnation, if such is understood to mean a discrete and specific act of God in history. Schleiermacher does, in fact, speak of Christ's appearance as miraculous, yet this is always qualified to mean that Christ's appearance cannot be explained by his surrounding history and context but rather requires a grounding in an eternal divine law (*Gesetz*), itself established in an eternal decree (*CF*, §89.2). It does not imply a discrete activity of God in history. Again, this does not mean that Christ is simply the product of historical forces, for his appearance is grounded in an eternal election. But Christ does not exist prior to his appearance or as the creator of the stage of his own dramatic activity.[52] He may be the goal, but he is not the agent, of creation.

The second reason why Schleiermacher abandons traditional notions of incarnation and miracle needs to be pieced together. In a letter to Friedrich Lücke, Schleiermacher discusses the organization of the *Glaubenslehre* into the first and second parts and states that he could have reversed the order of these major divisions. Yet one reason he provides for not doing so is his belief that only the present organization can adequately

---

[52]See *CF*, §47, §13, §88.4, §93.3.

address the issue of reconciling Christian faith and free scientific investigation.[53] If this is so, then we might rightly point out that this external, non-dogmatic concern proves that not only internal dogmatic questions but also external ones shaped the character of Schleiermacher's doctrine of creation as well as his Christology.

In short, a concern to preserve a covenant of peace between dogmatics and natural science, joined to problematic metaphysical presuppositions regarding the relationship between God and the natural order, directly led to a problematic Christology.[54] It is one thing to abandon the notion of a literal six-day creation, as Schleiermacher feels must be done in light of modern scientific understandings of the universe. It is another thing altogether to abandon Nicene and Chalcedonian Christology, a Christology of a true incarnation. Yet Schleiermacher's understanding of the God-world relation required both.[55]

Modern scientific assumptions explicitly drive the first rejection; but they may well also implicitly drive the second. Indeed, in his letter to Lücke, Schleiermacher relates that the very notion of creation itself may need to be abandoned in light of a new scientific understanding of the world, which was that of a closed deterministic universe.[56] Schleiermacher held that scientific advancement would lead to a comprehensive view of the world, a prognostication that has not come to pass, while the conception of a closed universe that so influenced Schleiermacher has in fact passed away.

Turning to Barth, one is first struck by notable similarities to Schleiermacher. Like Schleiermacher, Barth has no desire to root a doctrine of creation in speculative principles of either a metaphysical or scientific nature.[57]

---

[53]Schleiermacher, *On the Glaubenslehre: Two Letters to Dr. Lücke*, trans. James Duke and Francis Fiorenza (Atlanta: Scholars Press, 1981), pp. 60-65; see also *CF*, §37.2; Sherman, *Shift to Modernity*, pp. 21-23.

[54]See chapter 12 in this volume.

[55]And this is true regardless of Schleiermacher's statement that attributing to Christ an absolutely potent God-consciousness is equivalent to positing an existence of God in him (*CF*, §94.1). For the problems raised by such a statement within Schleiermacher's system and its ultimate unintelligibility, see chapter twelve below.

[56]Schleiermacher, *On the Glaubenslehre*, pp. 60-61.

[57]For Schleiermacher's differentiation between speculative and dogmatic propositions, see *CF*, §16.3 postscript. Whether Schleiermacher was consistent in maintaining such a separation is questionable in light of the previous discussion. Barth's understanding of theology's method and task is spelled out in *CD* I/1, §1. Barth's doctrine of creation is presented in *CD* III/1-4.

Speculative convictions, for both Schleiermacher and Barth, are abstract, in that they are not derived from God's specific revelation, which Schleiermacher understands to be the Christian self-consciousness and which Barth understands to be the specific revelation of God in Jesus Christ. Both thereby claim to begin with dogmatic, rather than speculative, approaches to the question of creation (though, as we have just seen, Schleiermacher was not successful in this regard). But very important differences appear, for whereas Schleiermacher understands the causal order as uniform and unbroken so that Christ's own appearance is the product of a natural development grounded in an eternal election, Barth reappropriates and reformulates traditional Chalcedonian Christology in a manner in which Christ is once again seen first and foremost as God's in-breaking into the world, a true miracle, rather than as the highest point of its natural development. So while there are important formal similarities in Christology between the two that may even provide warrant for saying that both have a christological orientation in regards to their doctrines of election and creation (most notably that both see a very close relationship between election and Christology), what also needs to be said is that the nature of this orientation is quite different for each.[58]

For Schleiermacher, Christ is the goal of the created order, but he is not itself its Creator and Lord. Christ may be understood as the hermeneutical key for understanding the purpose of creation, but in reality a preconceived notion of the God-world relation greatly influences and shapes the Christology itself. For Schleiermacher, any true notion of incarnation is problematic, for any disturbance in the universal causal nexus, any true miracle, any discrete action of God, would in fact undermine the feeling of absolute dependence and thus undercut piety itself. Christ's appearance is grounded in an eternal decree, but Christ himself is the product of the natural order ordained to give rise to him. And in this, while we can speak of Christ as

---

[58]For an insightful comparison between Schleiermacher and Barth on the question of creation and Christology, see Sherman, *Shift to Modernity*. While Sherman rightly notes similar christological emphases in the doctrine of creation of both Schleiermacher and Barth, he fails to wrestle adequately with their very significant differences, especially in their respective Christologies. Barth himself states that the doctrine of creation cannot be established on a feeling of dependence (*CD* III/1, p. 9), and in this he distances himself from Schleiermacher, as he does on so many points.

central to creation, he is so in a way quite different than for Barth, for whom a general God-world relation does not determine Christology, but a specific Chalcedonian Christology is the basis for understanding all other relations between God and the world.[59]

To fully explore this Chalcedonian Christology and its effect on Barth's dogmatics would take us far afield. Yet, it can be briefly summarized with special reference to the doctrine of creation. For Barth, Christ is not only the goal but also the ground of creation, as he is the ontic and noetic basis for all relations between God and the world. As Barth states: "Jesus Christ is the Word by which the knowledge of creation is mediated to us because He is the Word by which God has fulfilled creation and continually maintains and rules it" (CD III/1, p. 28). Creation and Christology are thus intricately tied together because Christ is the Subject of both creation and incarnation.[60] Furthermore, the relation between God and creation is itself established and revealed in God's eternal election to be God for us in the person of Jesus Christ. Therefore, creation can only be understood in the light of Christ and redemption: "What is said in prospect of Him can be understood only in retrospect of Him. That is, the whole circumference of the content of Scripture including the truth and reality of the creation of the world by God, can be understood only from this centre" (CD III/1, p. 24).[61] Thus, God the Creator is only fully known as God the Redeemer, and it is the second that is the key to understanding the first, rather than the first being the key to the second, just as we know the Father through the revelation of the Son.

Without this christological grounding for understanding such notions as God's transcendence and activity, Barth contends, we can do little better than default to metaphysical and mythical speculation. In contrast to this, Christ is the hermeneutical key for both creation and Scripture. Barth's un-

---

[59]It is precisely this stark difference between Schleiermacher and Barth that Sherman does not adequately address (see Sherman, *Shift to Modernity*, pp. 2-3). I have borrowed the term "hermeneutical key" from him here.

[60]Barth can state: "In contrast to everything that we know of origination and causation, creation denotes the divine action which has a real analogy, a genuine point of comparison, only in the eternal begetting of the Son by the Father, and therefore only in the inner life of God Himself, and not at all in the life of the creature" (CD III/1, p. 14).

[61]Barth can also say that creation is understood through the analogy of grace and justification (CD III/1, p. 30).

derstanding of the scriptural narrative, and of doctrine, is better conceived as a set of concentric circles with Christ at the center than as a set of pearls on a chronological string. So Barth maintains that the creation narratives themselves can be rightfully understood only when seen in the light of Christ: "Indeed, what is the value of the rest of the biblical witness to creation without the centre? . . . It is here that God Himself has revealed the relationship between Creator and creature—its basis, norm, and meaning. At this point we are secured on all sides. And everything else that is to be learned from the Bible may be learned *in nuce* here" (*CD* III/1, p. 25).

For Barth, the incarnation is a unique and unsubstitutable event, the singular instance of incarnate unity between God and humanity. As singular, it has no true analogy.[62] And yet, it is also the basis for every other specific relation of God with his creatures, and for the general relation of God and the world. In Christ, we learn the identity of God, and not only of God but also of the creature. Christ is the revelation of both God and creation, the one who reveals that which he himself has created. Barth thus does not eliminate but reverses analogical predication.

In Christ, Creator and creature are bound together and their relation revealed. In Christ, God is shown to be superior to the world and distinct from it, yet in Christ is also revealed the truth that God will not be God without the world and that he acts within it. This relation with the world is not one of necessity but of a free divine decision made in eternity. This decision entails that the creature has its own reality, its own causality, its own self-determination, as this itself has been determined by God. God has, outside of himself, in Barth's terms, a partner, who, though subject to the divine lordship, has his or her own integrity, existence and nature (*CD* III/1, p. 25). So God is not confused with the creation, but neither is God separated from this creation. God lives in fellowship with the creature as creation's Lord and Savior. And we know this not by examining the fluctuations of the world life process or the regularity of the universe. The first may leave us shaken, the second may leave us cold, and both are at best ambiguous. Rather, we know this God and his fellowship with us in Christ through the Holy Spirit, and through Christ, we know the creation as good amidst its brutal realities and cold indifference.

---

[62]See, for example, *CD* IV/2, pp. 57-58.

Barth thus provides the most consistently christological doctrine of creation since the patristic era. In returning to such a reading of the doctrine of creation, Barth is in effect jumping over the deistic notions of the modern Enlightenment period, as well as earlier medieval ones, and in truth takes up themes not prevalent since the time of Irenaeus. Barth's dialectical relationship between creation and covenant is an attempt to reappropriate the New Testament themes of Christ as the divine agent of creation who, with the Father and the Spirit, brings the world into existence in order to save it. Regardless of the difficult theological topics this may raise (of which the old supralapsarian and infralapsarian debates are examples), for Barth the world is created to exist in a redeemed relationship with God. Such a claim denies neither the tragedy of sin nor the distinction of creation and redemption. Yet the latter provides the interpretative key to the former. For Barth, Christ is not only ordained to appear in history, but he is creation's very Creator and Lord, not only the goal, but also the ground, of creation.

In sum, though both Schleiermacher and Barth present us with christologically focused doctrines of creation, the differences between them are significant. For while Christ is central as the goal of creation for Schleiermacher, the understanding of creation itself is derived from reflection on the immediate feeling of absolute dependence, and, while this itself derives from Christ, it is apparent that a preconceived notion of an unbroken causal order exerts a determining influence on both the doctrine of creation and the doctrine of Christ in ways that are problematic for each.[63] In the end, for Schleiermacher, Christ is the product of the world process as divinely established, whereas for Barth, Christ is the Subject and Lord of the process itself.

IMPLICATIONS OF THE ANSWER

Any future doctrine of creation would do well to take this theme of the relation of Christ and creation, evidenced from the New Testament through Schleiermacher and Barth, into account. Of course, it must extend beyond these latter figures, though it is not feasible for more recent theologians and

---

[63]For a full investigation of this claim, see chapter 12 below. Richard Niebuhr states that Schleiermacher's theology is better understood as christo-morphic, rather than christocentric (Niebuhr, *Schleiermacher on Christ and Religion: A New Introduction* [New York: Charles Scribner's Sons, 1964], pp. 211-12).

trends to be examined here. This historical survey is not meant to be exhaustive in any respect. Certainly the pneumatological themes of creation require further study. Nevertheless, this investigation does highlight its intended topic, that is, the centrality of Christology for the doctrine of creation. In light of this examination, I would like to provide three final suggestions for further reflection regarding the doctrine of creation.

The first is that any Christian doctrine of creation should begin and end with a recognition that this doctrine, like all others, is an article of faith. To confess the doctrine as an article of faith entails that we recognize that it is grounded in God's revelation in Christ, and that our answering of the christological question of creation is prior to addressing any scientific ones. That question is precisely the nature of the relationship between Christ and creation and the explication of this relation. If this is so, then the most important decision one must make about the world is a christological one: is Jesus Christ the product of the cosmological process, grounded in immutable laws and an evolutionary development, or is he the Lord of both such law and development? This is the first question that must be answered in formulating a Christian doctrine of creation, and how we answer this question at the center shapes all that follows along the periphery. Moreover, I would contend that any pneumatological reflections on the Spirit's work in creation cannot be divorced from these christological concerns. It is a matter of logical order, not historical accident, that the ancient church focused on christological concerns prior to pneumatological ones. To divorce the Spirit from the Son in any doctrine of creation is to threaten not only the christological aspects of creation but also the very trinitarian nature of it. Of course the reverse is true as well, for to ignore the Spirit in creation is to ignore God's ever present work in the world and its teleological goal. But the Spirit is the Spirit of Christ, and not another Spirit, and it is the former christological emphasis that seems most often jeopardized today, rather than the latter pneumatological one.

Moreover, if Christ truly is the agent rather than the product of creation, even while standing in his humanity within the created order itself, then only when Christology is misconstrued can such an approach be derided as anthropocentric, for while it may be a denigration of nature to view it as ultimately serving humanity, it is not a denigration but an exaltation of

nature to see it as the stage on which the history of Christ is displayed, for
the value of the stage is not lost but found in the preeminence of the play
and its Author and preeminent Actor. While an anthropocentric view of
nature may lessen creation's dignity, a christocentric view of nature grounds
such dignity.[64] In fact, one could argue that the only way to guard against an
anthropocentric understanding of creation is to maintain a christocentric
and richly trinitarian understanding of creation.[65] Only such an understanding preserves the superabundant richness of the world and superfluous
beauty that delight and serve God and Christ and Spirit in ways that exceed
human appreciation and utilization. Rationalistic and pantheistic versions
of the world can only fail on this score. Deism inevitably makes humanity
lord of this world in God's absence, and pantheism burdens the world with
an impossible task of providing for its own salvation, for the loss of God's
freedom from the world is ultimately the loss of God's power to save it. Such
in the end leads humanity to act as such a savior. What can be left for us,
then, but self-worship?[66]

The first suggestion that I am making is therefore nothing less than that
the doctrine of creation be taken up again in a new way by dogmatics, rather
than conceded as the sole possession of the popular but amorphous religion
and science dialogue within religious studies. It is a call to work from the
center outward, rather than the reverse. This suggestion is *not* meant to deny
that scientific discoveries will impinge on theological questions, nor is it
meant to imply that the relation between dogmatics and natural science will
be (or should be) an easy one of mutual harmony (or of mutual neglect).
Barth himself noted in the preface to his discussion of creation that this
relation between dogmatics and the natural sciences would exercise many a
theological mind.[67] This needs to be remembered by those who fault Barth

---

[64]As Gunton has noted: "What is to be avoided is not all anthropocentrism, but the tearing apart
of creation and redemption, so that redemption comes to appear to consist in salvation out of
and apart from the rest of the world" (*Christ and Creation*, p. 33).

[65]Ibid., pp. 74-75.

[66]It might be added that only in acknowledging a relative and circumscribed special status of
humanity can we truly take up our special responsibility and accountability for the environment
and the well-being of the created order. To deny a special status to humanity among God's
creatures is also to deny a special duty. It is an unwitting justification for ecological irresponsibil-
ity. For a related discussion, see ibid., pp. 32-33.

[67]"There is free scope for natural science beyond what theology describes as the work of the
Creator. And theology can and must move freely where science which really is science, and not

for neglecting such questions himself (regardless of how we judge the validity of such criticisms). Nevertheless, the periphery of the doctrine of creation must not be addressed to the neglect of the center, which is confessional and christological, and which itself must shape the peripheral questions. To labor only at the edges is to ensure that our reflection on creation is not only determined by current scientific theory but also bound to its fate. Part of Barth's ongoing relevance is no doubt tied to his refusal to stake his doctrine of creation on a particular scientific view of the world, a view that now would be quite dated. As we saw, Schleiermacher did not escape this fate with his allegiance to a deterministic closed universe, an allegiance that caused him to make concessions and moves in Christology that now appear not only unnecessary but also unconvincing and contrived.

Second, the judgment that the doctrine of creation ought to begin with its center entails that it begin with the acknowledgment that the God of creation is none other than the God and Father of Jesus Christ, who, with the Holy Spirit, creates the world. What is needed is a thoroughly trinitarian doctrine of creation that includes within it a christological center and pneumatological focus. Whereas a significant amount of literature addressing the interface of theology and science begins by moving from an amorphously described general religious experience to an undefined God, the Christian doctrine of creation is truly trinitarian in shape. As Barth rightfully asserts: "And it is again as this Eternal Father, and not in any other way, that He reveals Himself as the Creator, i.e., in Jesus Christ His Son by the Holy Ghost, in exact correspondence to the way in which He has inwardly resolved and decided to be the Creator. As He cannot be the Creator except as the Father, He is not known at all unless He is known in this revelation of Himself" (*CD* III/1, p. 12). Any revitalization of the doctrine of creation must take place on a solid trinitarian commitment, and creation is thus to be seen in light of every article of the creed.[68]

---

secretly a pagan Gnosis or religion, has its appointed limit. I am of the opinion, however, that future workers in the field of the Christian doctrine of creation will find many problems worth pondering in defining the point and manner of this twofold boundary" (*CD* III/1, p. x).

[68]To read the doctrine of creation under the second article is therefore not to remove it from its rightful home in the first or to deny that it must also be read under the third. It is, rather, to assert that any Christian doctrine of creation must recognize that the God who creates the world does so through the Son by means of the Spirit, that the world is created not only *by* Christ but also *for* him, and that the paradigm and pattern for understanding all communion

In addition, the grammar of the God-world relation must be predicated in light of the unique relation between God and creation in the incarnation of Jesus Christ. In short, it is the incarnation alone that assures us that God takes on a reality other than himself, that he visits a world from which he is distinct. The incarnation grounds both the Christian claim of God's transcendence (which is an ontological claim of freedom rather than a spatial category), as well as the claim that God is not threatened by the world but enters and acts within the world without loss of freedom, identity or the distinction of the Creator and the creation. It is the incarnation that provides the ultimate basis for the Christian conviction that God is both transcendent and distinct from the world and present and active within it, and that provides the way that the Spirit's own transcendence can be understood, thus staving off all types of pantheism (whether Stoic or evolutionary or any other).[69] With this in mind, any Christian doctrine of the creation must move from the identity of the triune God to the identity of the world, for whereas God's identity is necessary and assured, determined not in contrast to the world but in a freely chosen decision for it, it is the world's identity that is contingent and in need of justification. To remember this is to avoid two further errors.

First, while it must be admitted that all revelation is experienced, not all experience is revelatory, and this is oft forgotten. To attempt to ascertain

---

between God and creation is the incarnate Christ chosen for us and we for him before the world began. Furthermore, this principle does not deny a proper, though circumscribed, use for appropriation, such as the affirmation that it is the incarnate Son, rather than the Father or Spirit, who is identified as Jesus Christ and who dies on the cross. The large actions of creation, redemption and regeneration cannot, however, be thus appropriated (for *opera trinitatis ad extra sunt indivisa*). In regard to salvation, we are reminded that the New Testament speaks not of Christ as saving the world so much as that "God was in Christ reconciling the world to himself," and that "no one can confess 'Jesus is Lord' except by the Holy Spirit" (2 Cor 5:18-19; 1 Cor 12:3; cf. 1 Cor 6:11). In light of the New Testament, just as creation cannot be exhaustively subsumed under the first article, so redemption cannot simply be subsumed under the second (or third) article. As Barth relates: "We believe in Jesus Christ when we believe in God the Father Almighty, Maker of heaven and earth. These words of the first article do not make sense if for all the particularity of their meaning they do not anticipate the confession of the second and also the third articles" (*CD* III/1, p. 19). For the history of the development of both informal and formal creeds, see J. N. D. Kelly, *Early Christian Creeds*, 3rd ed. (New York: David McKay Company, 1972).

[69]Such a statement does not deny the role of the Spirit in creation as well, though, as Gunton notes, the "work of the Spirit in creation is less prominent in the New Testament" than that of the Son, or Word (Gunton, "Doctrine of Creation," p. 146).

God's character from a general investigation of religious awareness or the world's order and process is deeply problematic and akin to speculation without constriction. Such can never serve as the basis for a truly Christian doctrine of creation, which can only be rooted in the heart of revelation itself. As Sokowlowski insightfully comments:

> Human reason left to itself will always tend to see the divine as the ultimate principle in the world, whether it expresses that divinity in myths, in scientific theories about the laws of nature and evolution, or in more philosophical formulations of the transcendent. The biblical word of God, the biblical and Christian understanding of God, always has to resist the natural impulse to see the divine as the best part of the world. . . . Christian faith must continually differentiate itself from the natural religious impulse, and it must do so in whatever circumstances it may inhabit at the moment.[70]

Second, and in a related vein, to fail to begin with Christ and the logic of Chalcedon as the paradigm for the relation of God and creation, which recognizes both the unity yet differentiation between God and the world, oftentimes leads to a faulty use of transcendental arguments, in which we move back from general conceptions of the world to specific conceptions of God. Such problematic deductions are readily called to mind: the world is in process, and therefore God is developing as well; or, the world evolves, and therefore God does, too. Such mental maneuvers are remarkably old. For example, consider Canaanite and Hellenic logic, by no means unique: the world is a cycle of life and death, and therefore God is involved in this cycle as well; the world is rife with fecundity and sexuality, and therefore God is tied to and participates in such cycles. At its nadir and its worst, some modern religious literature reminds one of sophisticated Baal worship, evidenced in a return to pagan spirituality that exalts creation at the expense of redemption, failing to realize that to sacrifice God's transcendence is nothing less than to sacrifice God's freedom to save the world.[71] In some accounts, the particularity and uniqueness of Christ is sacrificed for a "cosmic Christ," of whom Jesus is simply one manifestation.[72] The cosmic

---

[70]Sokowlowski, *God of Faith and Reason*, p. xi.

[71]For an example of such a nadir, see Matthew Fox, *Original Blessing: A Primer in Creation Spirituality* (Santa Fe: Bear and Co., 1983).

[72]Matthew Fox, *The Coming of the Cosmic Christ* (San Francisco: Harper & Row, 1988). Fox's ap-

Christ is identified as the immanent divinity in all things, a life principle that fills the world in a return to a revived paganism. As C. S. Lewis once remarked, such advancements are not progress but retrogression.[73] Such problematic alternatives to historic Christian faith should remind us that a perhaps very necessary rethinking of the means by which God created the world does not necessarily mean that God's relation to the world must be rethought in such a way that divine transcendence and discrete activity are thrown overboard as obsolete cargo. Means and relation are two different, but frequently confused, things. Such confusion fosters problematic transcendental deductions, as well as a failure to distinguish natural processes from intentional agency and to recognize that divine and created causality are incommensurable.[74]

Finally, to sum up all that has been said, we should not treat the God of creation in abstraction from the God of redemption. Indeed, only as we

---

proach to these matters is noted approvingly and largely adopted by Rosemary Radford Ruether in *Gaia and God: An Ecofeminist Theology of Earth Healing* (San Francisco: HarperSanFrancisco, 1992), p. 242. See also Sallie McFague, *The Body of God: An Ecological Theology* (Minneapolis: Fortress, 1993). She suggests that the Christian doctrine of the incarnation "be radicalized beyond Jesus of Nazareth to include all matter. God is incarnated in the world" (p. xi; see also pp. 159, 162, 179). For a distinct though similar discussion from the side of science, see Arthur Peacocke, *Theology for a Scientific Age: Being and Becoming—Natural, Divine and Human* (Minneapolis: Fortress, 1993).

[73]C. S. Lewis, *Mere Christianity* (San Francisco: HarperSanFrancisco, 2001), p. 155.

[74]See Tanner's excellent discussion of such issues in relation to Aquinas. She writes: "A being that acts by rational volition . . . is not determined to bring about effects of a single kind like itself. A rational agent acts according to what it knows and not according to what it is; its effects may be various, therefore, and none of them need bear any necessary relation of identity or contrast with its own nature. A being acting deliberately is not a univocal cause, in other words; it need not act so as to produce a simple univocal relation between its effects and itself" (*God and Creation in Christian Theology*, p. 72; also pp. 71-72; for the weaknesses of transcendental arguments in general, see pp. 21-26). That divine and created causality are incommensurable is implicit in the Chalcedonian affirmation that the divine and human natures are without confusion. There is thus an implicit asymmetry and incommensurability between divine and created causality because they are not the action of members of a single class and thus they cannot be brought under a single heading or conception of activity. Is there then a place for apologetic arguments that defend the possibility of discrete divine activity in the world of nature? Yes, there is, insofar as some views of the universe rule out of hand, in an *a priori* fashion, the very possibility of divine agency by means of outdated science. Here knowledge of an open (quantum) universe may correct a closed (Newtonian) one. Yet one should not take such arguments as anything more than the disarming of false objections to Christian belief. They only specify that ruling miracles impossible based on a closed universe is bad science. They should never be taken to mean that God requires or in fact utilizes the quantum level to act. Such a view designates a causal joint that could once more become a gap and therein fails to recognize the ultimate incommensurability of divine and created causality.

know the latter do we truly know the former. As Barth states: "God the Creator is not the supreme being of our own choice and fancy. He is the Lord of the history of Israel" (*CD* III/1, p. 13). Yet today God is at times redefined, the boundaries between God and the world broken down in forms of process and pantheism. Conceptions of the Creator are limited only, it seems, by the metaphorical imaginations of theological writers. Yet if we are to retain the convictions that constrict such imaginative reconstructions, if we are to continue to maintain the transcendent freedom and sovereign activity of God as such inalienable convictions of the doctrine of creation, we must understand the christological grounding for such convictions. The relation between God and the world is not a free imaginative construal; the relation itself is freely defined and determined in God's eternal election to be God for us in Jesus Christ. Such an approach to creation may sound scandalous and hopelessly narrow. But it is no more scandalous and narrow than the New Testament's pronouncement that salvation comes from Israel's son Jesus and only in him. The scandal raised by the confession that the creation exists solely by and for Jesus Christ is but an extension of the scandal of the gospel of redemption and is itself but the logical outworking of the patristic conviction that only the God who created the world can save it and the Christ who saved it is he who created it. To reject one scandal is to reject the other, and examples of this dual rejection are not hard to find.

CONCLUSION

Years ago, Pascal was asked why he believed in God. His simple answer was, "The Jews." At a time when so many looked to the created order for arguments for God's existence, Pascal looked to a particular history as the lens through which to discover the Creator and the meaning of creation itself.[75] He had a good pedigree in this. Michael Buckley, in his magisterial study *At the Origins of Modern Atheism*, states that atheism took its flight in the early modern period precisely when the reasons given for belief in God turned from history to metaphysics. What was remarkable of that time, Buckley

---

[75]For an insightful discussion of Pascal's answer, see James Wm. McClendon Jr., "The God of the Theologians and the God of Jesus Christ," in *Is God God?* ed. Axel D. Steuer and James Wm. McClendon Jr. (Nashville: Abingdon, 1981), pp. 185-205.

notes, is not that atheists found theologians to battle but that the theologians themselves had become philosophers. As he writes:

> The extraordinary note about this emergence of the denial of the Christian god which Nietzsche celebrated is that Christianity as such, more specifically the person and teaching of Jesus or the experience and history of the Christian Church, did not enter the discussion. The absence of any consideration of Christology is so pervasive throughout serious discussion that it becomes taken for granted, yet it is so stunningly curious that it raises a fundamental issue of the modes of thought: How did the issue of Christianity vs. atheism become purely philosophical? To paraphrase Tertullian: How was it that the only arms to defend the temple were to be found in the Stoa?[76]

If theology is not again to succumb to such questioning, the world of nature must once again be seen as the living stage onto which steps its Architect, the Author and Actor of the great drama. The theater itself takes a part in this production, waiting for the revelation of the final curtain; the theater is not only the context for, but also an object of, the salvation enacted within this covenantal performance of redemption which the Spirit is working to bring to completion.[77] This salvation is its hope, as well as the hope of all humankind. In the end, "the play is the thing" whereby we know creation and its King.[78]

---

[76]Michael J. Buckley, *At the Origins of Modern Atheism* (New Haven, CT: Yale University Press, 1987), p. 33.

[77]Rom 8:18-24. The world as the "theater of God's glory" was one of Calvin's favorite metaphors for creation.

[78]With apologies to Shakespeare (*Hamlet*, 2.2.623).

11

Standing Out in the Gifford Lectures

Karl Barth's Non-natural Lectures on Natural Theology

✠

Over the course of the years of 1937 and 1938, Karl Barth gave the prestigious Gifford Lectures in Scotland. That Barth was chosen for such a task was ironic indeed—the world's foremost opponent of natural theology now asked to give the world's most famous lectures on natural theology. This certainly was not the result of an oversight, for there could be no ignorance of Barth's antipathy for natural theology by the time of his invitation. His disdain for natural theology was quintessentially displayed in his famous debate with Emil Brunner in 1934, in which Barth's response to Brunner's proposal of a new natural theology was (in)famously titled, simply, "Nein!"[1] Yet Barth accepted the invitation and the task.

This episode may appear rather odd, but it is not a singular oddity. The history of the Gifford Lectures is itself a strange affair, and not simply because of the selection of Barth to give them. Endowed by a Scottish judge, Adam Gifford, a free thinker who himself possessed quite idiosyncratic religious beliefs, the lectures were, according to Gifford's will, established to address science and "all questions about man's conception of God or the

---

[1]Brunner's proposal and Barth's response can be found in Emil Brunner and Karl Barth, *Natural Theology: Comprising "Nature and Grace" by Professor Dr. Emil Brunner and the Reply "No!" by Dr. Karl Barth*, trans. Peter Fraenkel (Eugene, OR: Wipf & Stock, 2002; first published by the Centenary Press, 1946).

Infinite."[2] An ambiguity therefore resided in the very articulation of their purpose, for as the history of the Gifford Lectures revealed, "man's conception of God" depended on the person being asked, and it is left unclear whether God and the Infinite mentioned are one and the same simply under different designations, or incommensurable and perhaps even rival explanations for the same phenomena behind which they are meant to stand. Indeed, the theme of the lectures could simply be designated as discerning the "ultimate nature of the universe," perhaps a mish-mash of metaphysics and theology.[3]

This ambiguity of topic, along with a concomitant charitable and open-ended directive that established minimal limitations on what could be addressed (the only firm prescription being that the topic be taken up as a natural science), resulted in a trail of lectures in which the lectures themselves seemed to have very little in common with one another, though the general theme of at least most of the early ones was that of natural theology in the broadest sense, an attempt via reason and science to find God.[4] Natural theology was in fact the stated theme of the lectures, and they were to cast light on God without recourse to any special or miraculous revelation.[5] Natural theology had been, however, back on its heels ever since the time of David Hume a century before the Giffords began, and while some of the Gifford lecturers attempted to right the ship from Hume's list, others accepted Hume's arguments and a movement toward an intellectual agnosticism in general. Almost all of the lecturers, however, accepted the general starting point in universal human experience whether or not such experience was thought to point to a god or not.

Barth's radical particularity thus differed greatly from the universal tendencies of such Gifford lecturers. If Barth's own emphasis lay in portraying the particularity of the triune God revealed in Jesus Christ as set over against

---

[2]Stanley L. Jaki, *Lord Gifford and His Lectures: A Centenary Retrospect* (Edinburgh: Scottish Academic Press, 1986), pp. 66-76, quoted in Larry Witham, *The Measure of God: Our Century-Long Struggle to Reconcile Science and Religion—The Story of the Gifford Lectures* (San Francisco: HarperSanFrancisco, 2005), p. 1. Gifford is purported to have said, "Spinoza holds that everything is God . . . I hold that God is everything; if I were to assume a name descriptive of my belief, I should be called a Theopanist" (quoted by Witham, p. 22).

[3]Witham, *Measure of God*, p. 25.

[4]Ibid., p. 2.

[5]Ibid., p. 25.

the sinfulness of humanity, others took a much more general and optimistic approach, highlighting the goodness of humanity and for some its very divinity. For many, man truly was the measure of all things—whether in the personal idealism of Josiah Royce, the developmental anthropology witnessed in James Frazer's lectures that became the famous *Golden Bough* or the empirical psychologism of William James, though an underlying tension always was present between a purely materialist view of the universe and one that retained a belief in God or, and these are of course not the same, in an irreducible spiritual element to reality, a battle that could take different forms, from a row between German idealism and Darwinian materialism, to that of a more general tension if not outright conflict between religion and natural science. Indeed, the Giffords shifted in time from a general focus on philosophy to science as the soil on which a new foundation for natural theology was to be laid.

The purpose here is not to recount the fascinating history of these lectures.[6] Nor is it to defend Barth against the detractors of his lectures and those who reject his rejection of natural theology.[7] It is, rather, to examine and reveal the underlying logic and convictions that governed what Barth attempted in his lectures, which, on the surface, appear to be nothing but a

---

[6]This history is winsomely recounted by Jaki, *Lord Gifford and His Lectures*, and Witham, *Measure of God*.

[7]Such detractors are numerous. For one of the most prominent and influential critics of Barth's view, see James Barr, *Biblical Faith and Natural Theology: The Gifford Lectures for 1991 Delivered in the University of Edinburgh* (Oxford: Clarendon Press, 1993); also more recently Rodney Holder, *The Heavens Declare: Natural Theology and the Legacy of Karl Barth* (West Conshohocken: Templeton Press, 2012); for a response to the latter and to other similar criticisms of Barth's position, see John C. McDowell, "The Unnaturalness of Natural Theology: The Witness of Rodney Holder's Karl Barth," *Colloquium* 44 (2012): 243-55. For an argument more sympathetic to Barth's own, see Andrew Moore, "Should Christians Do Natural Theology?" *Scottish Journal of Theology* 63 (2010): 127-45. An important and developed yet critical defense of Barth's approach is provided by Stanley Hauerwas, *With the Grain of the Universe: The Church's Witness and Natural Theology—Being the Gifford Lectures Delivered at the University of St. Andrews in 2001* (Grand Rapids: Brazos, 2001). A chastened reconstitution of natural theology that is "securely grounded in a trinitarian vision of God" is offered by Alister McGrath and might be more rightly considered a theology of nature; see *The Open Secret: A New Vision for Natural Theology* (Malden, MA: Blackwell, 2008), quote on p. 314. McDowell notes: "Part of the problem with critical readings of Barth's critique of natural theology is that they rarely define what they mean by 'natural theology'" ("Unnaturalness of Natural Theology," p. 245). Very helpful in in this regard and teasing out the various meanings of the term "natural theology" is the excellent discussion of David Fergusson, "Types of Natural Theology," in *The Evolution of Rationality: Interdisciplinary Essays in Honor of J. Wentzel van Huyssteen* (Grand Rapids: Eerdmans, 2006), pp. 380-93.

somewhat dry commentary on a very old Scottish confession. Barth's lectures are most often referenced in regard to their open rejection of natural theology, but there is more going on within them than such a rejection. Barth's Gifford Lectures come into a context of contested convictions, and his rejection of natural theology comes as a challenge to an entire tradition of inquiry.

Theology as a Peculiar Science

Certainly Barth's rejection of natural theology is what is initially most striking about his lectures. Barth related that he could not fulfill Lord Gifford's intent by setting aside all recourse to special revelation, but he went further to question the entire enterprise of the science of natural theology: "I certainly see—with astonishment—that such a science as Lord Gifford had in mind does exist, but I do not see how it is possible for it to exist. I am convinced that so far as it has existed and still exists, it owes its existence to a radical error."[8] Barth proffered his rejection of natural theology by stating that he was a Reformed theologian, not a philosopher or a psychologist, and faithfulness to this calling in itself prevented him from taking up natural theology. Such a refusal, however, was in fact not simply a matter of confessional loyalty but was also predicated on a number of other central convictions that shaped all of Barth's theology.

Barth had already defined natural theology in his debate with Brunner: "By 'natural theology' I mean every (positive *or* negative) *formulation of a system* which claims to be theological, *i.e.* to interpret divine revelation, whose *subject*, however, differs fundamentally from the revelation in Jesus Christ and whose *method* therefore differs equally from the exposition of Holy Scripture."[9] For Barth, theology had to begin with attendance to its proper subject and its proper correlative method, and to stray from either was for theology to betray its heart.

Both subject and method defined, for Barth, what it meant to refer to theology as a science, and theology's status as a science was most famously

---

[8]Karl Barth, *The Knowledge of God and the Service of God According to the Teaching of the Reformation: Recalling the Scottish Confession of 1560*, trans. J. L. M. Haire and Ian Henderson (Eugene: Wipf & Stock, 2005; originally published by Hodder and Stoughton, 1938), p. 5; hereafter cited as *KGSG*.

[9]Brunner and Barth, *Natural Theology*, pp. 74-75.

expressed by Barth in his engagement with Heinrich Scholz.[10] It was not only Barth's rejection of natural theology that set him apart from others who gave the Gifford Lectures, but his entire approach to science. Against a prevailing way of thinking in the philosophy of science of his day, a view echoed in Scholz's reflections on the possibility of a theological science, Barth went resolutely in another direction. Scholz had stated that what determined a field of inquiry as a science (and thus as a valid field of knowledge) was the adoption of and adherence to a set of methodological axioms that were required for the validity of any general scientific method and indeed defined such a method.[11] In other words, what made a field of study a science was its conformity to a universal scientific method as articulated by means of certain fundamental axioms that guided its investigation. Theology was then itself to be tested against this bar. Barth nevertheless stated "point-blank" that this approach to science was unacceptable to theology and could not be embraced by it without the betrayal of its very theme.[12]

This rejection of Scholz's list of scientific criteria and entire approach was necessary for Barth because of a central conviction that he held against the general tenor of his day, and against Scholz specifically, namely, that it is not a universal method that makes a field of inquiry a science, but the proper and respectful attendance to its specific object of study that does so, in turn establishing and marking off a field of study with its own integrity and particular theme. For Barth, this was quintessentially true for understanding the nature of theology as a science, and this theological principle could by analogical extension be applied as a general principle to any particular science. For Barth it was not a universal scientific method that determined the validity of a field of inquiry, but the subject matter of that field that determined the proper method, so that the method of a discipline must conform to the particularity of its object of study rather

---

[10]Barth's response to Scholz and his reflections on theology as a science are found in *CD* I/1, pp. 3-11. Barth had, however, long before wrestled with what it might mean to say that theology is a science and to discern its relation to the other sciences. For the history of this development in Barth's thought, see Clifford Blake Anderson, "The Crisis of Theological Science: A Contextual Study of the Development of Karl Barth's Concept of Theology as Science from 1901 to 1923" (PhD diss., Princeton Theological Seminary, 2005).

[11]Scholz's axioms are recounted by Barth in *CD* I/1, pp. 8-9. See also Scholtz, "Wie ist eine evangelische Theologie als Wissenschaft möglich?" *Zwischen den Zeiten* 9 (1931): 8-53.

[12]*CD* I/1, p. 9.

than a general method be imposed on the object with attendant *a priori* rules of justification.[13] In other words, the distinct subject of a science determines the means by which it is to be approached and examined and thus the particularity of its method. When this is understood, it should be apparent that Barth's particularity runs all the way down, as will become more apparent below.

This conviction that it is the particularity of an object of systematic investigation rather than a universal method of inquiry that determines the status of a field as a science in turn entails a number of ensuing commitments and corollaries. First, if the validity of a field of inquiry is determined by its proper attendance to its distinctive object of study, then it need not adopt or conform to the methodological criteria laid down by a philosophy of science or any other science. Barth came to this conviction not as a general

---

[13]In this move, Barth is not alone insofar as his position has now been echoed by others. Consider the following from John Polkinghorne: "There is not one single, simple way in which we can know everything; there is no universal epistemology. We know the everyday world in one way, in its Newtonian clarity; we know the quantum world in another way, in its Heisenbergian uncertainty. Our knowledge of entities must be allowed to conform to the way in which they actually can be known. If we are to meet reality at all, we must meet it on its own terms. If that is a lesson applying to our knowledge of the quantum world, it would not be altogether surprising if it were a principle that also applied to theology's quest for knowledge of the mystery of God." See Polkinghorne, *Faith, Science and Understanding* (New Haven, CT: Yale University Press, 2000), p. 7. This argument was made in at least one form as early as Aristotle, who argued that the precision required of the results of an investigation could not be stated in advance or in abstraction of the actual subject under investigation, for it is the subject at hand that determines not only the method but also what may be expected in terms of precision. As Aristotle put this, "it is obviously just as foolish to accept arguments of probability from a mathematician as to demand strict demonstrations from an orator" (*Nichomachean Ethics*, 1094b25). For Barth, this matter of precision was not as important as the matter of correspondence, and the nature of theology, as the study of the revelation of a living divine Subject, required that one begin not with indifference but deference, not proud confidence in the powers of reason but with prayer, for the knowledge of God was not pried from the universe's indifferent hand but given by God himself. And because this knowledge was a divine gift freely given yet never a "given" itself, theology always had to "begin again at the beginning," in Barth's oft-used phrase. The knowledge of God was a gift that required a grateful heart for its reception, and a reception that must occur again and again, not only by each new generation but also within the life of each individual, for while this knowledge is not arbitrary but rests on the great faithfulness of God, it always comes, as do God's mercies, "new every morning." The great difference between Barth and Polkinghorne (and by extension Aristotle), however, is that whereas Polkinghorne applies this principle as a general one of science to theology, Barth forms this particular understanding in relation to his discovery of the uniqueness of theology and its incomparable subject matter and only then applies it by analogical extension to the other sciences (cf. Anderson, "Crisis of Theological Science," pp. 326-27). In this, Barth preserves not only the uniqueness of theology's object of study but also the uniqueness of its corresponding method to which one can compare the other sciences only in terms of a formal analogous correspondence and not a specific shared universal method.

principle holding for any science that could then be applied to theology but as a distinct understanding of theology as a science which he then applied to all other sciences.[14] For this reason, theology has its own integrity and need not conform to the guiding investigative principles of the other (natural or social) sciences. It can learn from their devotion to their own particular subject matter, but it cannot conform to their own methods without betraying its own center. As Barth stated:

> The existence of other sciences, and the praiseworthy fidelity with which many of them at least pursue their own axioms and methods, can and must remind it that it must pursue its own task in due order and with the same fidelity. But it cannot allow itself to be told by them what this means concretely in its own case. As regards method, it has nothing to learn from them.
>
> It does not have to justify itself before them, least of all by submitting to the demands of a concept of science [*Wissenschaftsbegriffs*] which accidentally or not claims general validity.[15]

Barth thus continued: "If theology allows itself to be called, or calls itself, a science, it cannot in so doing accept the obligation of submission to standards valid for other sciences." And so, Barth provides the concluding lesson: "The only way which theology has of proving its scientific character [*Wissenschaftlichkeit*] is to devote itself to the task of knowledge as determined by its actual theme [*Gegenstand*] and thus show what it means by true science."[16]

Bruce McCormack insightfully notes that in his refusal to concede to a definition of a universal science, Barth was protecting the integrity not only of theology but also of all sciences against "the totalizing effects of a unified theory elaborated on the basis of a single science (usually physics)."[17] What was at stake, McCormack avers, was "not merely the uniqueness of the 'object' of *theology* and therefore of the methods appropriate to its object;

---

[14]See note 13 above.

[15]*CD* I/1, p. 8.

[16]*CD* I/1, p. 10. The relation between the scientific status of theology and its theme was already articulated by Barth in the second edition of the commentary on Romans: "To be scientific means to be objective [*Wissenschaftlichkeit bedeutet Sachlichkeit*]," for "Objectivity [*Sachlichkeit*] in theology means absolute respect for the particularity of its own chosen theme" (quoted in Anderson, "Crisis of Theological Science," p. 468). This is not to say, however, that Barth had developed this idea as he would by the time of the first volume of the *Church Dogmatics*.

[17]Bruce McCormack, *Orthodox and Modern: Studies in the Theology of Karl Barth* (Grand Rapids: Baker Academic, 2008), p. 285.

what was at stake was the concept of 'science' itself."[18] First some comments on the object of theology, and then on the nature of science—in light of the above, these are intricately related.

For theology, the object of its investigation was not an object among objects but the self-revelation of a distinctive divine Subject in the person of Jesus Christ through the Holy Spirit, who could never be treated as or approached as an object among objects subject to human manipulation and control. God remained Lord even in his self-giving. Thus the "object" of theology was a self-giving Subject, and the method of theological inquiry was unique in that it began not with the examination of an object but the entreaty of a Subject for illumination and revelation. Prayer is thus integral for the theological task, as are humble obedience and faith.[19] Moreover, its method must be seen in its concrete practice as "the exposition of Holy Scripture," in the words of Barth's reply to Brunner, though it included an examination of past expositions as found in the church (confessions and the writings of other theologians), as well as an examination of the church's speech found in its proclamation.[20]

This prayerful, obedient and faithful attendance to its particular subject matter was the basis for Barth's understanding of theology as a science and for his twofold estimation of theology as simultaneously both formally similar and yet entirely materially unique in relation to the other sciences. From one perspective, theology is one science among many and can thus be designated under the general category of "science." In its very human attempt to reflect on what it is given in divine revelation, it can even be designated as, like all sciences, "secular" (*Profanität*).[21] The only formal principle Barth has as a criterion for a science is that it systematically attend to a specific area of inquiry; in this regard, theology shares this minimalist formal criterion with the other sciences and thus stands among them as one field of human inquiry among others, for all sciences are such based on the careful attendance to their subject matter.[22] So Barth could write: "As a

---

[18]Ibid., p. 286.

[19]*CD* I/1, pp. 14, 17-24.

[20]"Dogmatics is the self-examination of the Christian Church in respect of the content of its distinctive talk about God" (*CD* I/1, p. 11).

[21]*CD* I/1, p. 11.

[22]Barth refused to concede the term "science" to the natural or social sciences and retained it for

human concern for truth, it recognizes its solidarity with other such concerns now grouped under the name of science."[23]

From another perspective, however, and one more determinative and significant, theology is set apart from all other sciences as unique due to the distinctiveness of its subject matter and its purpose. Its object of inquiry is no object among objects but a divine and uncreated Subject who remains Lord even in his revelation. In this regard, theology stands in a singular position among the other sciences and cannot be subsumed into a system of sciences as one among others, even as one above the others that provides them with their cohesion and meaning.[24] While all areas of inquiry must "follow after" their object of inquiry, theology requires this in a particularly special way, so that, as McCormack writes, the unique nature of this objectivity "must prevent us from ever construing the 'object' of theology as belonging to a continuum on which the objects of the other sciences are also to be found."[25]

---

theology as well. Barth provides three reasons why theology should not concede the term to another particular science or group of sciences: (1) it is a human area of inquiry after truth as they are, neither inferior nor superior to them; (2) it thus protests against a "quasi-religious certainty" of the term as a general concept of science and thus demonstrates that its meaning is not a settled matter or undisputed; (3) in retaining the name it demonstrates to the other sciences that it does not take the "heathenism of their understanding seriously enough to separate itself under another name," and thus protests against their own protest and rejection, and exclusion, of theology as a valid discipline within their midst. In other words, Barth insists that theology must recognize their status as disciplines that are "part of the Church" in spite of their steadfast refusal to accept such a place and resolute resistance to and perhaps even disdain for such an understanding (*CD* I/1, p. 11). In short, Barth refuses to allow the other sciences to determine the meaning of the term or to serve as the guardians of its meaning. That they do so was, for Barth, a sign of their totalizing sinful ambition and resolute rebellion against their true identity as inquiries after truth under and within the larger canopy of God's good creation, of which more will be said below.

[23]*CD* I/1, p. 11.

[24]Barth writes: "Since the days of Schleiermacher, many encyclopaedic attempts have been made to include theology in the sciences. But the common objection may be made against all of them that they overlook the abnormality of the special existence of theology and therefore essay that which is radically impossible. The actual result of all such attempts has always been the disturbing or destructive surrender of theology to a general concept of science and the mild unconcern with which non-theological science, perhaps with a better sense of realities than theologians with their desire for synthesis, can usually reply to this mode of justifying theology" (CD I/1, p. 10). Anderson perceptively argues that this conviction was intrinsic to Barth's eschatological understanding of theology; see "Crisis of Theological Science," p. 411.

[25]McCormack, *Orthodox and Modern*, p. 287. McDowell adds to this point its corollary for matters of theological method: "Since God is not an 'object' in the sense that things are objects, theological rationality remains relatively independent from these other forms of rationality" ("Unnaturalness of Natural Theology," p. 251).

This understanding of theology as a science, of its similarity to the other sciences in light of a shared formal principle of investigation as a human quest of knowledge and truth, and of its nevertheless unique status among the sciences due to its specific material theme, its particular objectivity (*Sachlichkeit*) and its distinctive and inimitable corresponding means of investigation—this understanding Barth had developed in the first volume of the *Kirchliche Dogmatik* of 1932 and brought with him to Scotland in 1937/1938.[26] Barth entered the fray in his Gifford Lectures not only against natural theology but also against a kind of scientism that made the natural sciences the gold standard and arbiter for what could be deemed a legitimate field of inquiry and valid knowledge. Barth's distinctive convictions thus entailed that he could only reject the natural theology proposed by the Gifford Lectures. He opposed it precisely because it failed to take the true subject of theology as its starting point and did not attend to its proper method, and thus could only turn out as an exercise in speculative metaphysics, cultural anthropology or existential psychology.[27] Whatever theology was, it was not these, in Barth's estimation.

For Barth, theology had to have its own proper objectivity, its own true subject matter, and this could not be self-selected. This was so because of an intrinsic realism in his theological approach. Contrary to Frazer and Feuerbach, who saw the divine simply as the projection, idealization and development of human thought, and who thus reduced theology and religion to anthropology, Barth acknowledged and em-

---

[26]Indeed, as Anderson has shown, Barth had many of these pieces in place long before his debate with Scholz. This viewpoint included a rejection of metaphysics and apologetics as a means to procure knowledge of God, as well as a focus on the particularity of God's revelation against such general avenues of knowledge. But it also included a wariness of scientific positivism and the threat it posed, as well as a conviction that epistemology was distorted when all but the empirical is excluded from its purview not only methodologically in the natural sciences (a move which he accepted) but also as a matter of metaphysical principle ("Crisis of Theological Science," pp. 248, 274-75, 457, passim).

[27]For Barth, a general metaphysics could never achieve knowledge of the living God, but only reveal the limit concept of rational investigation. The Infinite was thus *not* God, not the God who had revealed himself in Jesus Christ, but the designation for that which lies outside the rational and intuitive understanding of humanity, the postulated paired correspondent to the finite side of an antinomy that provides, in Kantian terms, the absolute freedom, unity and final cause that lies beyond our perceived deterministic and pluralistic universe of one cause followed by another in an endless chain, a world that, in both nature and history, is, to all appearances, in Arnold Toynbee's immortal words, "just one damned thing after another."

braced the general criticism of religion as anthropology but stated that Christian theology attended not to a human projection but a divine revelation that broke into history with the person of Jesus Christ. The radical particularity of this revelation excluded Christian theology (and therefore, for Barth, Reformed theology) from attending to any subject matter other than that given to it. Hence, natural theology, which began with a universal aspect of human experience, could only be rejected by Barth as theology, for by its very definition it renounced the particular starting point of God's revelation in the person of Jesus Christ. In short, the science of natural theology was, for Barth, profoundly unscientific. It was so because it was an inquiry in search of an object of study.[28] And no inquiry could be a science that was not only in doubt but also ignorant of its theme of study.

Which is not to say that an object could not be ambitiously proposed. Themes proposed within the Gifford Lectures through the years could include

---

[28]Barth's steadfast devotion to the objectivity of theology is sadly lost on Witham, who mistakenly reads Barth only as given to subjectivism (see *Measure of God*, p. 224). Clifford Anderson has shown that Barth's conviction of particularism and focus on the object of study predates even his break with liberalism; see "Crisis of Theological Science," pp. 226-27. He quotes Barth in 1910: "An object that is not present cannot be analyzed" ("Crisis of Theological Science," p. 227; cf. p. 468), quoted from Barth, "Ideen und Einfälle zur Religionsphilosophie," in *Vorträge und kleinere Abeiten 1909–1914*, ed. Hans-Anton Drewes and Hinrich Stoevesandt (Zürich: Theologischer Verlag Zürich, 1993), p. 131. The distinctive discovery of Barth's break with liberalism was therefore not simply a new adherence to particularism but to its being wedded to a distinct form of realism—that God's reality transcends and is distinct from human knowledge of that reality, whether that knowledge is philosophical, anthropological/historical or psychological. For Barth's realism in this regard, see Bruce L. McCormack, *Karl Barth's Critically Realistic Dialectical Theology: Its Genesis and Development 1909–1936* (Oxford: Clarendon Press, 1995), p. 129; also Anderson, "Crisis of Theological Science," p. 289; for a brief summary of Barth's doctrine of revelation, see McCormack, *Orthodox and Modern*, pp. 109-13. Anderson rightly emphasizes that such realism must be qualified by Barth's ongoing commitment to idealist thought forms that prevent such realism from becoming a form of positivism ("Crisis of Theological Science," p. 522). In other words, such a critical element prevents the lordship of God in his revelation from being sacrificed once again to a form of identification with the creaturely medium assumed by God for divine self-communication such that it become an object liable to domestication, manipulation and human control. While the theme of realism thus requires careful qualification by a critical element, it could nevertheless be argued that it is the inseparable unity of these two themes (particularism and realism) that provide the specific shape of Barth's mature theological program. Perhaps a simpler way and indeed more accurate way to capture all that is intended to be said when we speak of Barth's particularism, realism and critical epistemology is to say that Barth's mature theology was singularly devoted to the conviction and confession of the free and holy Lord revealed in the particular person of Jesus Christ through the Holy Spirit alone, thus remaining Lord even in the act of divine revelatory accommodation.

the history of human mythology, the order of nature or the immediate religious experience of the human subject, represented in the lectures of James Frazer, Arthur Eddington and William James, respectively.[29]

While the diversity of themes is significant, what must also be noted is that some lecturers at times presented claims that overreached what the evidence warranted, that extended beyond the circumscribed limits of their investigation and that thereby betrayed a movement from self-described scientific objectivity into the open advocacy of a particular agenda. Frazer's attempt, and not the last one of anthropology (or sociology, or psychology, or more recently biology) to reduce religion to primitive superstition, a move itself intended in turn to subsume Christian faith into human religiosity in general, and thus into such superstition, was but one example.[30] It was not simply a descriptive program but proposed a normative one, where magic gave way to religion, and both gave way, and *should* give way, in the end, to modern science. All such metaphysical and cultural/sociological/psychological approaches belonged to the anthropological projects that Barth came consistently to resist. For Barth, such metaphysical, historicist and psychological investigations into the sources of human religiosity could not be considered theology per se because they were speculative rather than scientific and could at most provide valuable insight into anthropological phenomena. And it was theology as a distinctive science that Barth was devoted to present in his Gifford Lectures.[31]

Barth's understanding of science ran against the grain not only of the Continental (German) tradition as articulated by Scholz but also of the (Scottish) post–Enlightenment project from which the Gifford Lectures arose.[32] Barth's understanding was radical in its day but is perhaps less so

---

[29]James George Frazer, *The Golden Bough: A Study in Magic and Religion*, new abridgement, ed. Robert Fraser (Oxford: Oxford University Press, 2009); Arthur Eddington, *The Nature of the Physical World* (Cambridge: Cambridge University Press, 2012); William James, *William James: Writings 1902–1910* (New York: Library of America, 1987).

[30]See Witham, *Measure of God*, pp. 70-71. Witham concludes: "While the spirit of anthropology inescapably challenged Christian belief—suggesting it was evolved superstition—the science of anthropology also claimed scientific neutrality. Yet its association with debunking religion is indelible, and for many that is the true legacy of the 'science of man'" (p. 75).

[31]And so Barth can state in his lecture on the first article of the Scottish Confession: "The Confession does not *conceive* its object at all, it *acknowledges* it" (*KGSG*, p. 13).

[32]Alasdair MacIntyre brilliantly examined this project in his own Gifford Lectures—*Three Rival Versions of Moral Enquiry: Encyclopaedia, Genealogy and Tradition* (Notre Dame, IN: University

in our own. The dream of a universal scientific method, a general approach to inquiry articulated in formal logical methodological principles that would hold across all fields of investigation thus providing an absolute line of demarcation between science and pseudo-science, as well as between the rational and the superstitious, is at an end. Even those who defend science (meaning, as it is now generally referenced, the natural sciences) against the literary and deconstructionist barbarians at the gate realize that such a dream is dead.[33]

THEOLOGY AS A PARTICULAR CONFESSION

Besides Barth's rejection of natural theology and commitment to particularity, there is a further element of Barth's project in the Gifford Lectures that is often overlooked. Barth's proposal is marked by particularism in the very means by which he conceives, constructs and organizes the lectures. That Barth chose to structure his lectures as a running commentary on the Scottish Confession of 1560 implicitly tells us how far Barth has removed himself from the Enlightenment project of natural theology to which Lord Gifford subscribed. Barth's commitment to explicating his theme in conversation with the Scottish Confession illustrates his commitment to confessional particularity and a contextual understanding of faith and reason.[34] Barth's views regarding confessions have been described earlier in chapter

---

of Notre Dame Press, 1990). Describing the philosophical project of Gifford's day, which he investigates through the particular lens of the ninth edition of the *Encyclopaedia Britannica*, a work in which its guiding convictions and principles come to mature expression, MacIntyre writes: "What then was a science taken to be within this particular framework? Sciences were generally taken to be individuated by their subject matter, *not by their methods*" (pp. 19-20, emphasis added). Reminiscent of the earlier discussion of Scholz, MacIntyre relates that all sciences were therefore ruled and defined by adherence to a formal method articulated by means of a number of necessary logical elements (see pp. 19-20). MacIntyre's lectures are an attempt to explain why this project could not and did not succeed.

[33]For such a staunch and able defender against said barbarians, see Susan Haack, *Defending Science—Within Reason: Between Scientism and Cynicism* (Amherst, NY: Prometheus Books, 2003); and Haack, *Manifesto of a Passionate Moderate* (Chicago: University of Chicago Press, 1998). Haack attempts to provide a definition of science and thus a line of demarcation that separates it from non-science.

[34]Barth explains his project in this way: "In responsibility towards what was 325 years later offered 'to the whole population of Scotland,' I am letting John Knox and his friend speak in their *Confessio Scotica* of 1560. This is not to take the form of an historical analysis of the Scottish Confession, but that of a theological paraphrase and elucidation of the document as it speaks to-day and as we to-day by a careful objective examination of its content can hear it speak" (*KGSG*, p. 10).

eight above, so I will not belabor expounding them here. But they do need
to be related to the topic here being addressed.

Barth rejected the Enlightenment (and thereby modern) project dedicated to knowing God apart from the contingencies of history. There were,
of course, important reasons why this project was undertaken in the first
place, and they should not be lightly dismissed, though they will not be rehearsed here.[35] Yet the project itself was in Barth's estimation ultimately a
betrayal of a central truth of the gospel, that is, that God has chosen the
particular to shame the universal, a truth which could only be a stumbling
block to the intelligentsia not only of Paul's time but also of every time, including Barth's own. The reverse side of this obverse and primary truth was
that we ourselves only stand within a particular time and not above it; there
is no time-less perspective, no God's-eye view for us that transcends history.
Barth's commitment to particularism in revelation, seen in his firm commitment to the singular revelation of God in Jesus Christ and to the specific
witness to this historical revelation in the Holy Scriptures, was wedded to a
particularism in regard to confession—that is, theological reflection and
exposition took place, like revelation itself, within a particular place and
time as undertaken by a particular people. Barth was committed to a form
of theological practice that recognized that specific confessions produced
by a particular community of faith (itself the embodiment of a specific ecclesial tradition) were inescapable for theological reflection.

Not surprisingly, then, Barth approached his exposition of God's revelation in Christ witnessed in Holy Scripture in his Gifford Lectures through
the prism of a particular confession (the Scots Confession) produced in a
particular place (Scotland) within a particular tradition of theological inquiry and confession (that of the Reformed churches, and implicitly and
more broadly, the tradition of the Reformation). The irony of this may be
lost on many. Barth was, in essence, repudiating the universal project of
natural theology in the Gifford Lectures by reminding his hearers that that
project was itself in reality a specific historical *Scottish* theological project

---

[35]See James M. Byrne, *Religion and the Enlightenment: From Descartes to Kant* (Louisville, KY:
Westminster John Knox, 1997); Jeffrey Stout, *The Flight from Authority: Religion, Morality and
the Quest for Autonomy* (Notre Dame, IN: Notre Dame Press, 1981); Stephen Toulmin, *Cos-
mopolis: The Hidden Agenda of Modernity* (Chicago: University of Chicago Press, 1990).

(regardless of its extension beyond Scottish borders). But it was not the only one Scotland had produced, and as Barth implicitly argued, not its most compelling one.[36] Barth was arguing that such a project was in fact quite problematic, not least of all because it forgot its preceding alternative. And reminding it of this alternative and explicating it was precisely Barth's goal and what he felt could be his particular contribution to the history of the Gifford Lectures, rather than arguing against natural theology per se. As Barth stated, his lectures would not present an argument against something but one for something else:

> They [the lectures] will not therefore be devoted to the refutation of "Natural Theology." This is not only because this aim would be incompatible with good faith towards Lord Gifford's will. The decisive reason is that the Reformation teaching does not live by its antithesis to "Natural Theology" in the way in which the latter lives by its antithesis to Reformed teaching. Even if there were no "Natural Theology," Reformed teaching would be just as it is. It lives independently by its positive content. For this reason we must turn our attention to this positive content—and we must do so for the sake of our proposed service to "Natural Theology" as well. If it is to know whom it is contradicting and if it is really to have the opportunity once more of measuring itself by its most dangerous opponent, it must not hear exclusively or even primarily this opponent's denial of it, but must first and foremost hear the positive affirmation of that opponent, in order that then and from that position it may perhaps also understand the denial which is directed against it.[37]

What Barth therefore argued, not surprisingly in light of his means of engagement with the atheism of modernity (and Barth always saw natural theology and atheism as cousins within the household of modernity), is that *natural theology is a parasite of confessional Reformed theology while confessional theology has no dependence on natural theology*. When seen in this

---

[36]Further, as James Barr has noted, Barth deliberately chose the Scottish Confession rather than the Westminster Confession (Barr, *Biblical Faith and Natural Theology*, p. 7). Barth's choice thus displays not only a debate with the Enlightenment project of natural theology but also an internecine conflict within the history of Reformed theology itself. In brief, Barth rejected any systematic attempt to incorporate natural theology with Christian theology, whether Catholic *or* Protestant (see *KGSG*, pp. 8-9). Barth would later trace the incorporation of natural theology in the Reformed tradition to the Gallican and Belgic confessions (see *CD* II/2, pp. 127-28).

[37]*KGSG*, pp. 9-10.

light, Barth's claim that he would not argue against natural theology is, it must be admitted, somewhat disingenuous. For while Barth left these opening chapters behind and committed himself only to present a particular confessional theology, his argument against natural theology had already been stealthily made. It is not a drawn-out, developed, detailed or direct assault, but rather a quiet kicking out of the stool. In short, Barth's argument, as covert as it may be, and however brief it may appear, is a powerful one: natural theology has no true integrity as a science because it is but a parasitic reaction against Reformed theology and is at best an abstraction and perversion of it, whereas Reformed theology alone has a "positive content" which allows it to carry on independently regardless of the program natural theology may follow. And the only "proof" Barth offers for the Reformation position itself is nothing more, or less, than a presentation and description of its content. This is, nonetheless, itself a form of argumentation, yet one that attempts not so much to directly engage its opponent on its own soil as to display its inferiority by overshadowing it with a richer alternative. It may be overreaching to claim that Barth's lectures are an attempt to reclaim Scotland for the Reformation from its captivity to the modern Enlightenment project of natural theology—but not by much.

Barth's argument against natural theology is in fact analogous to and foreshadows the kind of argument that Alasdair MacIntyre made against the modern project in his own Gifford Lectures.[38] Barth simply seeks to outnarrate rather than outdebate natural theology and believes the narration itself will reveal the feebleness of natural theology in light of the richness of the dogmatic convictions of the Reformed tradition.[39] It must be admitted, however, that this constructive proposal is Barth's own particular reading of the tradition, for he does acknowledge that the original Reformers were not

---

[38]MacIntyre, *Three Rival Versions of Moral Enquiry*. That Barth made such an argument seems entirely lost on Barr—see *Biblical Faith and Natural Theology*, pp. 7-8. It is perceptively intimated by Hauerwas when he writes that "as Barth uses it, the language of the church is itself already an argument just to the extent that his descriptions and redescriptions cannot help but challenge our normal way of seeing the world" (*With the Grain of the Universe*, p. 182).

[39]Barth is not so naive, however, to think that the problem of a turn away from God to focus on humanity is endemic only to the modern period; see *KGSG*, p. 17. Yet he can state: "The modern world has failed to hear the warning of the Reformed confession precisely at this point and has thought fit to exchange the mediaeval conception of the world as geocentric for the much more naïve conception of the world as anthropocentric" (p. 17).

altogether consistent in their rejection of natural theology. Moreover, Barth deliberately chose the Scottish Confession rather than the Westminster Confession as the object of his explication. So one must recognize, once again, that Barth was not only conducting an engagement with the Enlightenment project but also attempting to bring the Reformed tradition into consistency with its own best insights—and hence Barth sides with the Scottish Confession over against the Westminster one, an argument for the promise and coherence of the faith as explicated by the Scottish Confession.

Barth was not, however, simply returning to a staid premodern orthodoxy espousing timeless theological (Reformed) truths or rejecting modernity in its entirety. He was a child of the modern historicist turn, fully aware as much as anyone of the contextual nature of any theological claim (and it was this historicist element of late modernity that itself caused him to reject early modernity's claims of a timeless rationality). Moreover, he was committed to the relative, rather than absolute, authority of confessions, relativized not only by their contextual nature but more precisely by the Holy Scripture that is not only illumined by them but which also must stand over them in judgment. Barth was not returning to a precritical, premodern position on the truth value of confessions. More accurately, one could say that in light of his commitment to an ecclesially embodied and confessed faith firmly rooted in place and time, and to a particular rationality embodied in a tradition of inquiry rather than to a universal and decontextualized view of reason, Barth moved to a position that might rightly be seen as postmodern, regardless of remaining commitments to certain strands of (Kantian) critical idealism. This statement is further warranted when we look at a third element of Barth's Gifford Lectures.

THEOLOGY AS A POLEMICAL EXERCISE

If the first element of Barth's approach to the Giffords is Barth's particular understanding of theology as a science that precludes a systematic integration of natural theology, and if the second is an implicit argument against natural theology by means of an embrace of a view of faith and reason that are contextualized, the third element is a rejection of attempts by the other sciences to put forth systems of thought that attempt not only to illuminate the world as studied within their sphere of competence but also to provide metaphysical explanations of all of reality. Barth opposes all such scientism and attendant grand metanarratives on theological grounds. His judgment was pointed and stark—in the end, such totalizing scientistic or philosophical metanarratives are but new forms of idolatry and enslavement in new modern dress. To quote Barth at length:

> The gods so-called, which the proposition about the "ane onelie God" [in the Scottish Confession] was designed to combat, are, however, also the gods and godheads of all the human ideologies and mythologies, philosophies and religions. With the well-known ambition of a devoted father, man decks the children of his self-assertion with the same authority with which he has previously decked himself. These are the systems by means of which he proposes— at least in phantasy and fancy—to exercise his divine freedom and lordship. They might also be described as costumes, each one more beautiful than the other, which man dons in turn in his rôle as the one and only reality. And just as fathers must sometimes accommodate themselves to their children, and just as each costume constrains the actor to adopt a definite attitude, so the systems woven in man's phantasy and fancy come to possess and keep a definite power over him. His conception of the world and thus his world become full of ideas and principles, points of view scientific, ethical and aesthetic, axioms, self-evident truths social and political, certainties conservative and revolutionary. They exercise so real a dominion and they bear so definitely the character of gods and godheads, that not infrequently devotion to them actually crystallises into mythologies and religions. (Universities are the temples of these religions). But each one of these claims at the moment to be the one and only reality with monopoly over all systems. It is now considered impossible to abandon them either. Service and honour are offered them also and it is believed that the hope of salvation should be put in them. To recognize the one and only God means to make all these systems relative. "We acknowledge ane onelie God" means that the principles and objects of these systems, whatever they may be, are in reality no gods or at best gods so-called. Are they to be annihilated? Perhaps not at all, perhaps not yet. But the end of their authority is within sight. When the knowledge of God becomes manifest, they can no longer possess ultimate credibility, and real, serious and solemn reverence cannot be shown them any longer. "What askest thou Me concerning the good? One is good" (Matt. 19, 17). "The destruction of the gods" comes down upon them then. In any case they can henceforward prolong their existence only as symbols and hypotheses, perhaps as angels or demons,

perhaps only as ghosts and comical figures. This makes clear to us how it was possible for the early Christians to have been accused of atheism, and the Christian church would be in a better position if she had remained suspect of atheism in this sense of the word in modern times as well. All that we can say is that this is not the case. The church has much rather played a most lively part in the game of dressing up in different costumes a mere counterfeit of the one and only reality.[40]

This passage is replete with provocative and pregnant judgments and assertions that lie at the heart of Barth's understanding of humanity's project to know itself and its world. First, Barth notes that apart from the knowledge of God, humanity proposes "ideologies and mythologies, philosophies and religions," theoretical systems of explanatory power constructed in order to provide overarching descriptions of intelligibility, meaning and purpose for the world or elements therein. These "systems" do not simply arise from humanity's creative activity but in turn come to enslave and restrict humanity itself, and here Barth's argument prefigures those made in more recent times by persons for whom the "principalities and powers" are a primary way by which to understand the fallenness of the world.[41] That Barth was not simply speaking of primitive religion is unquestionably evident when one notes that he explicitly mentions that the temples of such mythologies and religions are modern universities. These systems of thought that are created, maintained and guarded by the modern university in turn become objects of hope and salvation but which in reality are part of humanity's captivity.

To confess the one true God, Barth states, is nothing less than to relativize these systems' importance and certainly to call into question the absolute claims they make (and, in this, also to relativize the authority of their

---

[40]*KGSG*, pp. 18-19. This form of argument was not unique to Barth's Gifford Lectures; it is further developed in his discussion of the "lordless powers" in *The Christian Life: Church Dogmatics IV, Four Lecture Fragments*, trans. Geoffrey W. Bromiley (Grand Rapids: Eerdmans, 1981), pp. 213-33; see esp. pp. 213-16.

[41]For biblical references to such powers, see Col 1:16; 2:15; Eph 6:12; cf. Eph 3:10-11; Rom 8:38-39; Tit 3:1. Formative works for contemporary discussion of the powers are those of Walter Wink, *Naming the Powers: The Language of Power in the New Testament* (Philadelphia: Fortress, 1984); *Unmasking the Powers: The Invisible Forces That Determine Human Existence* (Philadelphia: Fortress, 1986); and *Engaging the Powers: Discernment and Resistance in a World of Domination* (Minneapolis: Fortress, 1992). Also, see Barth's discussion of the "lordless powers" in *The Christian Life* (note 40 above).

guardian temples). It is not that all such descriptions are to be entirely abandoned or condemned—Barth is not proposing, for example, that all theories
and laws of the other sciences are inherently false and need be "annihilated"
(though it must be admitted that Barth's discussion regrettably leaves such
nuanced and relative judgments largely off the table and thus in question).
But such theoretical frameworks, whether modest theories or large ideo-
logical constructs, are not divine, and insofar as they not only methodologically but also metaphysically preclude God, they are abstractions at
best and demonic at worst. They are the latter specifically when they are
given an authority that extends beyond their limited sphere of explanation
and are put forward as ambitious descriptions of the meaning of the world
as a whole, metaphysical constructs that in reality are but new mythologies.
They are blatantly so when they set themselves up as direct rivals to Christian
faith and reject God outright. Christians rightly oppose such new divinities
with a healthy dose of skepticism and atheism. For Barth, that Christians
have failed in this regard displays their own proclivities to wear the "costumes" of human fabrication that bind them and blind them to their true
confession of the living God.

There is an intrinsic and at times explicit polemic notable here. Barth is
opposing what he calls the "costumes" with which we array ourselves. This
is perhaps a strange metaphor for what Barth truly seems to be referring
to—which are quite broadly the theoretical models, conceptual systems,
ideologies and overarching narratives of meaning that we as humans creatively produce and tell ourselves in order to understand and make sense of
our world and our place within it.[42] As noted, in the end these theories,

---

[42]Barth's polemic is seemingly directed not only against natural theology but also against all
forms of explanation (and here Barth seems to have in his sights not so much the theories of
the natural sciences but of the social ones) that attempt to provide a comprehensive picture of
the world and that exclude the particular revelation of God. When Barth thus pronounces that
"if there were a special Reformed doctrine of *man*, a special Reformed anthropology, it could in
point of fact only consist in the doctrine of *sin*" (*KGSG*, p. 46), this should not be taken to mean
that he denies the integrity of human life and history or of the ethical and moral import of the
human subject, though many have read Barth this way. More accurately, what Barth rejects is
any attempt to understand these areas of human life apart from and abstracted from God's
revelation where such an approach is in reality a principled rejection of such revelation and
assertion of autonomy. In other words (and this takes shape in the later volumes of the *Church
Dogmatics*), for Barth anthropology is rightly understood only when it is a subcategory within
and dependent on a larger frame of reference, which is in truth Christology.

systems and conceptual schemes may be somewhat benign or even very valuable and beneficial (for instance, one might think of Kepler's laws of planetary motion, germ theory or the principles of economic theory). But they may also be much more ambitious and even insidious (the political ideology of National Socialism, for instance). Yet even those most beneficial and modest are revealed as requiring openness to future revision, and as but partial truths of the whole. Even the grandest are relative at best, and insofar as they put themselves forward as totalizing and final metaphysical descriptions of all reality, they become idolatrous, for they extend beyond their limited sphere of description to become overarching narratives that set themselves up as rivals to the knowledge of the one true God. In so doing, they reveal themselves to be objects of service, honor and salvific hope, and thus indeed of absolute allegiance, which is but another term for worship.

This description certainly illuminates Barth's opposition to National Socialism as an extreme case of such a malevolent "costume." But there are metanarratives of our own day that fit this description and that Barth would no doubt oppose if he were here today. For instance, when natural selection is no longer seen as an illuminating description of aspects of biological life and becomes rather a metaphysical description of all of reality, we witness such an ambitious and mythological "costume." So when in reference to natural selection Daniel Dennett writes, "Darwin's dangerous idea is reductionism incarnate, promising to unite and explain almost everything in one magnificent vision"—and which, for Dennett, includes not only explaining but also explaining away religion of every type, including the Christian faith—we are presented with a particularly garish costume, woven of the coarse fabric of materialistic scientism.[43]

---

[43]Daniel Dennett, *Darwin's Dangerous Idea: Evolution and the Meanings of Life* (London: Penguin, 1995), p. 81. For Dennett's extension of such ideas to the realm of religion, see his *Breaking the Spell: Religion as a Natural Phenomenon* (London: Penguin, 2006). For a particularly pointed and incisive response to Dennett, see David Bentley Hart, "Daniel Dennett Hunts the Snark," *First Things*, January 2007; and Hart, *Atheist Delusions: The Christian Revolution and Its Fashionable Enemies* (New Haven, CT: Yale University Press), chap. 1. A similar metaphysical picture proposing the all-encompassing power of a scientific materialism wedded to natural selection is provided by E. O. Wilson in *Consilience* (New York: Alfred A. Knopf, 1998), esp. pp. 238-65. Even if Wilson's picture is rejected, however, one must sympathize with him, for the Christian faith presented to him in his youth had no serious intellectual component positively to engage his newfound love for the sciences (see pp. 3-7). Thus by his own admission he traded the Christian faith for a scientistic one.

Such strange pictures of the world, Barth states, take on a life of their own, and as they do, humanity moves from the role of the creators of such powerful explanatory theories to being their captives. These theories-*cum*-ideologies become humanity's masters as they form us to become persons who unquestionably adopt a picture of the world abstracted from seeing it as the creation of a good and wise Lord. Such a picture of the world becomes all-encompassing, but insofar as it succeeds, it does so only by defining whole areas of the world out of existence if they do not fit the prescribed picture (or, at the very least, by extending explanatory descriptions from one sphere where they are useful to areas where they are at best very limited, or even trivial, useless or ludicrous—for example, extending natural selection, useful in biology, to areas of mathematics and astrophysics). Such forms of explanatory expansionism, which is but the observe of a kind of ontological or methodological reductionism, in the und distort rather than illumine the world in which we live. They are themselves a kind of impoverishment. They do, however, have a kind of seductive power nonetheless that appeals to human ambition and hubris. How else could one explain how a view that denies the very reality of consciousness is even taken seriously and argued by self-aware and self-reflective persons?[44]

For Barth, the gospel prophesies against and protects us from falling prey to theoretical idols of our own making, whether these exist in the realm of the natural or social sciences, or beyond. Insofar as such grand illusions can be recognized as such not only in the light of the gospel but also by a number of perceptive persons who note their inner inconsistencies, strange alliances can be formed. Thus, despite their tremendous differences (as so incisively set forth by Stanley Hauerwas in his Gifford Lectures), both Barth and William James shared a common rejection of a scientific reductionism comprised of

---

[44]For such a denial of consciousness, see Daniel Dennett, *Consciousness Explained* (Boston: Little, Brown and Co., 1991). John Searle captured the bizarreness of Dennett's argument in the closing lines of his own review of Dennett's work: "I am a conscious reviewer consciously answering the objections of an author who gives every indication of being consciously and puzzlingly angry. I do this for a readership that I assume is conscious. How then can I take seriously his claim that consciousness does not really exist?" Daniel C. Dennett, reply by John R. Searle, "'The Mystery of Consciousness': An Exchange," *The New York Review of Books*, December 21, 1995. The same holds true for those explanations that maintain that human agency and personal intentions and explanations can be eliminated or subsumed into physical laws and impersonal causes. For an insightful discussion of such questions, see Diogenes Allen, *Christian Belief in a Postmodern World* (Louisville, KY: Westminster John Knox, 1989), pp. 165-81, esp. pp. 167-71.

both metaphysical commitments to materialism and methodological ones displayed in a search for a single ontological description of reality.[45]

Indeed, while Barth's rejection of this form of triumphalism is perhaps more implicit in his Gifford Lectures, though evident in the long quotation above, James's rejection of such reductionism is open and powerfully expressed in his own lectures—perhaps the most famous lectures ever given—published as *The Varieties of Religious Experience*.[46] James's rejection was bound with his staunch commitment to a knowledge of the particular over general abstraction in religious matters, though a particularism that was still much too general and anthropological for Barth.[47] It was evidently displayed in his open disdain of a "medical materialism" that attempted to reduce religious and spiritual experience simply to lower-level chemical or biological phenomena. As James wrote:

> Medical materialism finishes up Saint Paul by calling his vision on the road to Damascus a discharging lesion of the occipital cortex, he being an epileptic. It snuffs out Saint Teresa as an hysteric, Saint Francis of Assisi as an hereditary degenerate. George Fox's discontent with the shams of his age, and his pining for spiritual veracity, it treats as a symptom of a disordered colon. . . . All such mental over-tensions, it says, are, when you come to the bottom of the matter,

---

[45]Whatever their differences (and these were serious ones), James and Barth did share at least two significant convictions. First, they were skeptical of large totalizing philosophical discourses and focused on particularity, though of two very different kinds. For Barth, this particularity was christological and focused on the unique and incomparable divine revelation in Jesus Christ that relativized all human perspectives; for James, it focused on the single individual and the uniqueness as well as limitations of the finite person. Second, both Barth and James saw the world in a pluralistic fashion. This was not a thoroughgoing relativism but a recognition that we are bound to systems we create to understand the world, and these systems are many rather than one, and they are fallible. As evident in the discussion of "costumes" above, however, Barth went beyond James in stating that we are captive to these systems that in the end exert a power and thus mastery over us and that we are therefore in need of deliverance from them. In so doing, Barth introduced sin and eschatology as epistemological categories that found no place in James's thought despite the latter's emphasis on human finitude, fallibility and the resultant need for epistemological humility, all elements of epistemology that Barth shared. Both Barth and James thus rejected the dominant systems of an abstract idealism (Absolute Idealism) and a scientific materialism but did so for different reasons. James rejected these for humanistic ones—to preserve individuality, creativity and diversity (Witham, *Measure of God*, p. 84). Barth rejected them as affronts to the revelation and lordship of God and that in their fallen form enslaved human persons. For an insightful comparison of the epistemologies of James and Barth along similar though not identical lines, see Clifford Anderson, "A Pragmatic Reading of Karl Barth's Theological Epistemology," *American Journal of Theology and Philosophy* 22 (2001): 241-69.

[46]Found in James, *William James*.

[47]Ibid., p. 3. See note 45 above.

mere affairs of diathesis (auto-intoxications most probably), due to the perverted action of various glands which physiology will yet discover.[48]

James rightly saw that such thinking was a two-edged sword that cut both directions and in doing so did not illumine but undermined all forms of understanding and reason—a "convenient hypothesis" of mind-body reductionism that in the end explained nothing by explaining everything.[49] Conceding that the experience of Paul may well have included a seizure of some kind, and readily acknowledging that all spiritual experiences of the persons named above took place within them as physical organic beings, James nevertheless continued:

> But now, I ask you, how can such an existential account of facts of mental history decide in one way or another upon their spiritual significance? According to the general postulate of psychology just referred to, there is not a single one of our states of mind, high or low, healthy or morbid, that has not some organic process as its cognition. Scientific theories are organically conditioned just as much as religious emotions are; and if we only knew the facts intimately enough, we should doubtless see "the liver" determining the dicta of the sturdy atheist as decisively as it does those of the Methodist under conviction anxious about his soul. When it alters in one way the blood that percolates it, we get the Methodist, when in another way, we get the atheist form of mind. So of all our raptures and our drynesses, our longings and pantings, our questions and beliefs. They are equally organically founded, be they of religious or of non-religious content.[50]

James then concluded and put to rest such silliness, but alas, not for all time:

> To plead the organic causation of a religious state of mind, then, in refutation of its claim to possess superior spiritual value, is quite illogical and arbitrary, unless one have [sic] already worked out in advance some psycho-physical theory connecting spiritual values in general with determinate sorts of physiological change. Otherwise none of our thoughts and feelings, not even our scientific doctrines, not even our *dis*-beliefs, could retain any value as revela-

---

[48]Ibid., p. 21.

[49]Such large theories, Karl Popper famously said, bear the problem that they explain so much that in the end they explain nothing. This seems true not only of the "medical materialism" James was opposing but also of Dennett's extension of natural selection as the magic key to understand all of human phenomena.

[50]James, *William James*, pp. 21-22.

tions of the truth, for every one of them without exception flows from the state of their possessor's body at the time.[51]

To translate James's point into the language of today's popular form of this argument: if religion is a product of a cultural evolution that seems to propagate itself in light of selective processes (*a la* memes), then under this grand metaphysical picture of natural selection, atheism (and all thought) is the product of the same process, and rationality and argument dissolve as the reasons we give for our beliefs are biologically determined and meaningless. As James realized, this kind of super-theory is an acid that burns all the way down until all we are left with is that whatever is, is. James's rejection of such simplistic materialism should be required reading for all of those so enthralled by the reductionistic and triumphalistic bombast of today's atheistic scientism, one in great need of redemption from a seemingly complete captivity to a particularly idiosyncratic if seductive form of the genetic fallacy.[52]

The purpose of this excursus on James is but to show that Barth's theological position can appropriate into itself the arguments of others, and that the approach he takes in the Gifford Lectures need not entail a wholesale rejection of non-theological positions or portray the work of the human mind simply as producing "costumes" in the worst sense of the word. In this, James's thought may be seen not simply as a rival, but an ally, to Barth's own theological program. It illustrates that Barth's project is misunderstood if taken to assert that theology is insulated from engaging other philosophical positions. There can be, according to Barth, a kind of "good apologetics,"

---

[51]Ibid., p. 22.

[52]See Dennett, *Breaking the Spell*, p. 25. Dennett claims James as one of his philosophical heroes, but one wonders if he has taken James's rejection of material reductionism seriously enough. James's arguments on this point can only frustrate and problematize the reductive and triumphalistic scientism of Dennett's overarching attempt to explain all religious phenomena via Darwinian natural selection in *Darwin's Dangerous Idea*. Anderson writes of Barth's own attitude toward materialism in the period of the second edition of the commentary on Romans: "Barth's alliance with the materialists was critical, not constructive. While he regarded the materialists as the guardians of the secularity of the natural and the historical world, he rejected metaphysical constructions built on materialism. That is, he rejected materialism as a worldview. Of course, Barth also rejected the concept of a 'Christian worldview.' He considered the struggle over worldviews to be misguided. Both sides take up positions within the sphere of the temporal, ignoring the eternal. Both sides thereby wind up divinizing the temporal—the materialists by intention, the philosophical theologians as a necessary consequence of their unintended denial of the true Creator" (Anderson, "Crisis of Theological Science," p. 455).

and one not only comprised of polemical attacks against other positions (which, as we have seen, Barth certainly had no hesitation to offer), but also where one can dialogue with and constructively draw on the positions of others—but only if it is done with a clear understanding of theology's own goal and identity, and with a recognition that such apologetics and polemics are "an event and not a programme."[53] Such common ground, while not granted a more fundamental or foundational status than theology's own proper claims, could be acknowledged and appreciated, however limited it may be.[54]

And with regard to James and Barth, it is of course limited. This is in no small way due to the fact that Barth differed greatly from James's own naturalization and psychologizing of religion, as well as from his individualism, traits that marked James as, for all of his American differences from his European interlocutors, still a part of a liberal project that Barth rejected.[55]

---

[53]CD I/1, p. 31, CD II/1, pp. 7-9.

[54]At the very least, a consideration of Barth's actual practice should put to rest the idea that Barth spurned rational argument. When confronted by a questioner as to what place he had for reason in his theology, Barth curtly replied, "I use it." See Karl Barth, *Karl Barth Letters 1961-1968*, ed. Jürgen Fangmeier and Hinrich Stoevesandt, trans. Geoffrey W. Bromiley (Grand Rapids: Eerdmans, 1981), p. 294.

[55]One way that James greatly differed from European commentators on religion was his rejection of the search to distill religion down to a particular essence, whether this be Schleiermacher's "taste for the infinite" (in the *Speeches*) or the "feeling of absolute dependence" (in the *Christian Faith*), or Otto's sense of the holy or, in James's term, any other single "religious sentiment." See *Varieties of Religious Experience*, pp. 32-33. Here again we see James's pluralism and attention to the particular that cannot be brought under one heading or phenomenon to capture the rich variety of religious experience. As James notes, "there is no ground for assuming a simple abstract 'religious emotion' to exist as a distinct elementary mental affection by itself, present in every religious experience without exception" (*Varieties of Religious Experience*, p. 33). Yet where James continued in the modern vein was his unquestioned assumption that all religious experiences could seemingly be traced back to a common source (see Hauerwas, *With the Grain of the Universe*, p. 62). Moreover, James also saw the deepest source of religion in feeling (see *Varieties of Religious Experience*, p. 68). Where Barth differed greatly from James was that whereas James saw his focus of study to imply not only a plurality of subjective responses but also of religious objects, for Barth theology proper had but one object, the revelation of God in Christ. Here is the greatest dividing line between Barth and James—for Barth, the subject of theology is the revelation of the triune God; for James, the subject of religion is the religious subjectivity of the individual person. Barth thus focuses on the divine objectivity given in revelation; James remains agnostic as to the objective reality behind religious experience (allowing "divinity" to be defined in the broadest sense possible) and focuses on the religious experience in the human subject itself. James therefore has little place for institutional religion and restricts himself to what he calls "personal religion" (*Varieties of Religious Experience*, pp. 34, 36-38). He provides a working definition of the religion he was examining: "Religion, therefore, as I now ask you arbitrarily to take it, shall mean for us the feelings, acts, and experiences of individual men in their solitude, so far as they apprehend themselves to stand in relation to whatever they may consider the divine" (*Varieties of Religious Experience*, p. 36). His Gifford Lectures are in this light rightly

But it is also the case because, as Hauerwas has recounted, James himself fell prey to but another form of reductionism.[56] This reductionism is not a methodological one that reduces religion to scientific description. Rather, James reduced religious practice to its subjective activity and experience and cut it off from an examination of its true objective ground, that is, the reality of God. As Hauerwas articulates this,

> Whether the God to whom prayer is directed exists does not seem to bother James. What makes prayer authentic is not the status or character of the one to whom one prays, but the subjectivity of the one who is praying. The difficulty, of course, is whether James's understanding of such subjectivity is the same as the understanding of the one who is in fact doing the praying, given that the latter at the very least assumes that there is a God to whom he or she prays.[57]

When James is thus combined with the American Transcendentalist tradition, we see the origins of the current American fascination with spirituality and disdain for organized religion, and a significant reason why the phrase "spiritual but not religious" has become a self-description for a significant part of the American population. But the manner in which this phenomenon is approached and analyzed, that is, as the contrast between organized institutional religion and individual spirituality, scarcely gets at the real issue, and is, rather, the confusion of a symptom for the disease. At the heart of the postmodern, and contemporary American, fascination with a spirituality unfettered from social embodiment is the strong bifurcation of the objective and subjective poles of faith with a swallowing up of the first into the second, a kind of faith in faith itself, or perhaps better, a celebration of a religiosity pointing to no referent outside of its own spiritual experience—an awareness of awareness itself. Such religiosity can only rightly end in the singing of Walt Whitman's celebratory hymn "Song of Myself," and while

---

understood by Hauerwas as taking the form of a "phenomenology of religious experience" (Hauerwas, *With the Grain of the Universe*, p. 60). And it was this approach that makes intelligible and revealing Hauerwas's claim that for James, as for the modern period generally, "Christianity makes sense only as disguised humanism," and theology is really at root anthropology (*With the Grain of the Universe*, p. 64; also p. 116). It was against such modern views of domestication and the reduction of theology to the examination of human subjectivity that Barth so strongly objected.

[56]Hauerwas, *With the Grain of the Universe*, p. 65.

[57]Ibid., p. 66.

James himself seemed ambivalent about Whitman's solipsistic spiritualism emptied not only of God but also of moral consciousness, he could provide no means to allay or delay it.[58] Such is no accident. As Hauerwas rightly notes, "It does not seem to occur to James that attending to the how of what it might mean to be forgiven is not separable from what Christians think God has done for the world in Christ."[59] Or that the need for forgiveness arises only when we are confronted by a God who is not ourselves in the first place. Despite its remarkably amenable features, James's empirical psychology of religion itself becomes another human costume, though, as I would argue, not all costumes are created equal, and some are much more amenable to the gospel, and some much more insidious, than others. Such relative judgments were not Barth's strength, though he could make them (especially in relation to political systems, of which he favored democracy). At the very least, they are not made in Barth's discussion of "costumes" in his lectures.

Despite such shortcomings, the easily missed element of Barth's objection to such "costumes" was his contention that in their exclusion of God and exaltation of human reason and freedom, they ironically ended in denigrating the human person and leaving humanity at the mercy of and in slavery to fatalism and existential despair. However counterintuitive it may seem, the harsh judgment on anthropocentricism is in the end for Barth the only means by which human dignity can be preserved. Reductionism, as well as other mythologies of humanity's own making, has always led to a loss of human dignity, and such is the particularly tragic end of their fallen nature, in Barth's view. Large meta-theories either subsume the self into a frighteningly impersonal transcendence (as in the absolute idealism of Hegel), celebrate individualism to the point of libertinism and the condemnation and despair such unchecked freedom brings (as in the existentialism of Sartre) or dissolve the self altogether in the "astonishing hypothesis" of the scientific materialism James so ably dispatched, yet which rises again

---

[58]See James, *Varieties of Religious Experience*, pp. 82-85.

[59]Hauerwas, *With the Grain of the Universe*, p. 72. Hauerwas insightfully notes that this was so because James's convictions about Christianity preceded and did not follow from his pragmatism. This truth reveals once again that theological convictions do not so much follow from scientific investigation but shape the manner in which such investigation is carried out, circumscribing the possibilities of its conclusions and the form of their articulation.

reborn in new forms, such as that articulated by Francis Crick: "The Astonishing Hypothesis is that 'You,' your joys and your sorrows, your memories and your ambitions, your sense of personal identity and free will, are in fact no more than the behavior of a vast assembly of nerve cells and their associated molecules. As Lewis Carroll's Alice might have phrased it: 'You're nothing but a pack of neurons.'"[60] The judgment on these "costumes" is for Barth not a misanthropic denigration of scientific or any other human achievement, but the necessary first step of humanity's liberation. God kills to make alive; God's judgment serves his mercy. To hear God's Word of liberation may take the form, in our day, of telling us that there is more to us than can be captured by the fact that we share 75 percent of our DNA with a pumpkin.[61]

BETWEEN THE (MODERN AND POSTMODERN) TIMES

The lesson to be drawn from this admittedly wandering narrative is that for Barth particularism cannot be divorced from realism, just as realism cannot be divorced from particularism. Barth's attempt not to tear apart what, in his mind, God has irrevocably joined together, constitutes his particular contribution to the Gifford Lectures. In light of such a view, one can say that all exploits in natural theology as witnessed in the Giffords were predicated on a divorce of one kind or the other, namely, to sacrifice particularity while retaining a theological realism, or, more common recently, to sacrifice realism while focusing on (cultural) particularities—in other words, to trade Christian theology for either metaphysics or anthropology.

---

[60]Francis Crick, *The Astonishing Hypothesis: The Scientific Search for the Soul* (New York: Touchstone, 1994), p. 3.

[61]For an irreverent and witty deflation of the reductionistic myth, it would be difficult to top the obituary of Crick written by Mark Steyn, "The Twentieth-Century Darwin: Francis Crick (1916–2004)," *The Atlantic* (October 2004), pp. 206-7. Turning Crick's reductionism on itself, Steyn, with tongue firmly in cheek, concludes: "But even if Francis Crick is 75 percent the same as a pumpkin, the degree of difference between him and even the savviest Hubbard squash suggests that as a unit of measurement it doesn't quite capture the scale of the difference" (p. 207). Another incisive and brief deflation of such reductionary thinking is given by C. S. Lewis, "Meditation in a Toolshed," in *God in the Dock* (Grand Rapids, Eerdmans, 1970/1999), pp. 212-15. Lewis provides the following example of reductionism's self-refutation: "The cerebral physiologist may say, if he chooses, that the mathematician's thought is 'only' tiny physical movements of the grey matter. But then what about the cerebral physiologist's own thought at that very moment? A second physiologist, looking at it, could pronounce it also to be only tiny physical movements in the first physiologist's skull. Where is the rot to end?" (p. 215).

These alternatives correspond, in essence, to what MacIntyre has termed the projects of "Encyclopedia" (namely, a commitment to reject all forms of particularity in favor of universal reason) and "Genealogy" (an embrace of particularity but at the price of realism and truth). In this sense Barth, like MacIntyre, rejects both, and his thought is thus not easily captured by typical modern or postmodern categories (realism/antirealism; foundationalism/non-foundationalism, etc).[62] Barth is no naive realist or advocate of rationalism or foundationalism, and he gives full voice to humanity's ways of world-making in the theories and systems it proposes and devises— theories and systems not simply read off of nature and history but creatively proposed and imposed on them. But neither does Barth dissolve the world into these systems such that epistemology is reduced into matters of politics or that the objects of which the sciences speak are themselves relegated to the mythological [63] Barth may reject the Enlightenment claims

---

[62]At the very least, a recognition of Barth's understanding of contextual reason, his embrace of pluralism and fallibilism and his understanding that the most important categories of the mind were socially constructed, should greatly qualify what is too often taken as a given, that is, the importance of Kantian critical idealism for Barth's thought. It certainly did play a role in the development of his early theological epistemology. But as time went on, Barth became less "modern" in this way, too. At the very least, he became more centered on the expansive question of how God overcomes the socially constructed systems of not only our intellectual but also our cultural and political life than on the epistemological question of how he overcomes the limitations Kantian categories placed on the understanding.

[63]Barth therefore would not go so far as Paul Feyerabend when the latter writes that it is only the context that determines meaning to the exclusion of reference itself, and then goes on to say that for this reason, the Greek gods must be judged as real as scientific quarks: "we either call quarks and gods equally real, but tied to different circumstances, or we cease to talk about real things altogether." See Paul Feyerabend, *Farewell to Reason* (London: Verso, 1987), p. 125. Nor would Barth go so far as to accept Feyerabend's principle of relativism: "For every statement, theory, point of view believed (to be true) with good reasons *there exist* arguments showing a conflicting alternative to be at least as good, or even better" (p. 76; cf. p. 297). Of course, such a principle makes scientific progress an unintelligible concept, such progress itself being but an illusion masking what is in reality but alternative epistemological and, really, social models. Nothing that Barth says about the "costumes" or "lordless powers" need imply such a thoroughgoing antirealism or relativism, though it does imply the relativization of their descriptive capacity and explanatory power. Yet even in Feyerabend (like Overbeck?) Barth might find an unlikely ally in at least certain respects, such as Feyerabend's own recognition of the problems of totalizing metanarratives. He writes: "When I was a student I revered the sciences and mocked religion and I felt rather grand doing that. Now that I take a closer look at the matter I am surprised to find how many dignitaries of the Church take seriously the superficial arguments I and my friends once used, and how ready they are to reduce their faith accordingly. In this they treat the sciences as if they, too, formed a Church, only a Church of earlier times and with a more primitive philosophy when one still believed in absolutely certain results. A look at the history of the sciences, however, shows a very different picture" (p. 264). Barth might indeed be sym-

to universal reason, but neither does he deconstruct the sciences to be nothing other than the constructions of the powerful. Each is forced to submit to a real objectivity that imposes itself on us even as we impose an order of knowing on it. And no science is so forced to submit to its object as is theology.

It must also submit to all the ramifications of what such an objectivity reveals. One of the most important is that Barth does not think that the knowledge of God is simply a matter, as one person has noted, of "epistemic access."[64] Rather, Barth maintained that the knowledge of God revealed the grounds not only of its possibility but also of its natural impossibility, and, as noted above, Barth makes two distinct claims in his discussion of the knowledge of God in the Gifford Lectures that do not find a place in most natural theologies. One is that the problem of the knowledge of God is not simply a matter of determining a proper epistemological method but of overcoming sin.[65] The second claim is that such knowledge cannot be separated from eschatology and the need for reason itself, including the sciences themselves, to be redeemed. Barth provides a thoroughly theological (rather than philosophical) epistemology in his lectures, and he applies it by analogical extension to general scientific and philosophical concerns. In other words, the "costumes" that he mentions are often idolatrous and false because they are fallen, and even if benign (as far as we can tell), they are at the very least incomplete and insufficient because they lack integration, though this integration can come only at the end of time. Theology thus

---

pathetic to such an "atheism" and demythologization. See also Anderson, "Crisis of Theological Science," pp. 497-98. Anderson writes: "If Barth's concept of the boundaries between university disciplines was modernistic, then his understanding of the relationship between theology and the other faculties of the university was postmodern" ("Crisis of Theological Science," p. 498). McCormack, who is perhaps more inclined to read Barth as a "modern" theologian than some others, himself writes: "The justification for a faculty of theology in the university lies in its willingness to bear witness to an eschatological disclosure of the ultimate foundation of all the disciplines and, in so doing, to the meaningfulness of all the disciplines in spite of their inability to demonstrate their foundations" (*Orthodox and Modern*, p. 288).

[64]As used by Andrew Moore, who writes: "Use of natural theology in apologetics can reinforce the view that what humans most need is epistemic access to God. But in fact the gospel tells us that God has found access to us and that he has done so by slipping beneath the radar of our defences against him and even in defiance of our apologetic strategies" ("Should Christians Do Natural Theology?" p. 135).

[65]See the discussion of these points by W. Travis McMaken, "The Impossibility of Natural Knowledge of God in T. F. Torrance's Reformulated Natural Theology," *International Journal of Systematic Theology* 12 (2010): 329-30.

serves not only to stand against the idolatrous claims of metaphysical
systems that exclude and indeed pronounce against the knowledge of God
but also to remind the other sciences that even the most benign and benef-
icent of theories await further confirmation and integration. This eschatological conviction was the basis of Barth's opposition not only to scientism
but also historicism.[66] And it is these themes of the fallenness of our attempts at knowledge (not only of God but also of the world) and their incompleteness that remain missing from natural theology but which are
central to the Reformation heritage that Barth espouses.

POINTING BEYOND ST. BENEDICT

In the particular shape of their criticisms of the modern project, and in their
rehabilitation of a contextual reason within a tradition of inquiry, the Gifford
Lectures of MacIntyre and Barth have much in common. Barth certainly has
more in common, I would argue, with MacIntyre's project than that of
James.[67] Both Barth and MacIntyre saw the modern university as in need
of a good bit of demythologization. In the estimation of both, the university
was not a united front for universal reason and shared epistemological commitments but the arena of conflicting and irreconcilable disagreement,
though their assessment of this disagreement differed, for Barth cast this
situation in a theological light, whereas MacIntyre's analysis was a philosophical one. For Barth, the modern university was the temple of the secular
religions arising from modernity's proposed "ideas and principles, points of
view scientific, ethical and aesthetic, axioms, self-evident truths social and
political, certainties conservative and revolutionary," an august but not
atypical outcome of the Pauline narrative of fallen powers gone astray
wreaking havoc on human unity and community.[68] For MacIntyre, such
diversity displayed the hopeless reality of a state of affairs in late modernity
in which (particularly for the humanities but also for the social sciences)

---

[66]See Anderson, "Crisis of Theological Science," p. 475. He writes: "Theology bears witness to the
   inability of the sciences to provide an account of human knowledge as a whole. In more contemporary terms, theology testifies to the inability of the sciences to come up with a comprehensive 'theory of everything'" (p. 496). This fact grounds Barth's insistence on the "secularity"
   of the sciences (p. 484).
[67]Though it is significant and notable that all three share important commitments to fallibilism,
   as well as oppose and reject a separation of fact and value and of theory and practice.
[68]KGSG, p. 18.

"warring positions" find no resolution, an outcome due to the fact that while each contested position "characteristically appears irrefutable to its own adherents," it nevertheless "seems to its opponents to be insufficiently warranted by rational argument," for the very standards of rationality themselves are part of what is in dispute. The ironic result is that "the wholly secular humanistic disciplines of the late twentieth century . . . reproduce that very same condition which led their nineteenth-century secularizing predecessors to dismiss the claim of theology to be worthy of the status of an academic discipline."[69]

Against those who see Barth's approach to theological investigation as hopelessly parochial, one can only say that it at least openly espouses its standpoint and acknowledges the conflict between its position and that of the more "universal" forms of natural theology. MacIntyre may well have sympathy for this. For both Barth and MacIntyre, the modern university places a veneer of universal consensus that exists only in name (*uni*-versity) over what is, in reality, a lack of consensus amid competing factions and positions no less parochial in what is in reality a *multi*-versity (Marxist; feminist; deconstructionist; et al.; need one even begin to list them? Could one list them all?). Without apology, Barth begins with a distinct object of study as understood within a particular tradition of inquiry, a tradition which is, in MacIntyre's famous phrase, a "historically extended, socially embodied argument,"[70] and he engaged in such an argument that was not only his own Reformed tradition but also within the larger Christian one, with Protestant liberalism on his left and Roman Catholicism on his right, and with natural theology as a third thin alternative which Barth found strange, mistaken and ultimately parasitic on the more substantial Protestant and Catholic visions.

Yet here too the shared ground, though significant, is also limited. Barth and MacIntyre have serious differences in material commitments and what they propose to set over against the modern project, not least the difference between MacIntyre's Aristotelian and Thomist retrieval and synthesis and Barth's own staunch Reformed and Protestant vision. Barth would have little

---

[69]MacIntyre, *Three Rival Versions*, p. 7.
[70]Alasdair MacIntyre, *After Virtue*, 2nd ed. (Notre Dame, IN: University of Notre Dame Press, 1984), p. 222.

sympathy for placing Aristotle once more at the center of the theological project, and perhaps even less for thinking of the task of theology *solely* in terms of the retrieval and extension of a tradition, which, to Barth, could once again be seen as the domestication and confusion of divine revelation with the historical medium of its appearance and transmission, the naturalization of revelation into the means of its historical mediation. Barth would also be suspect of a tradition that placed at its heart the inculcation of virtues, which in his estimation would but reintroduce all of the problems of self-justification the Reformation reacted against. In short, and whether entirely fair or not, Barth's concerns with MacIntyre's project would perhaps not differ very much from those he expressed regarding Roman Catholicism.

Without going into a further detailed comparison of Barth and MacIntyre's projects, this much at least might be said. Barth differs from MacIntyre in that he ultimately does not locate the compelling power of a tradition within the tradition itself, or even on the winsomeness and compelling nature of the form of its social embodiment. Here he differs not only from MacIntyre, who focuses especially on the first, but also from Hauerwas, whose emphasis is on the second. In other words, Barth refuses to locate the ultimate power of the Christian tradition within the tradition itself, or to locate the compelling power of the gospel solely or primarily in the truthfulness of its communal life as church. For Barth, the ultimate power of the Reformation argument he is making in his lectures rests in the end not in the intrinsic winsomeness of its presentation and in its ability to outnarrate its rivals, nor even in its social embodiment in a community of witness.

For some, this fact reinforces their fears that Barth leaves us with a deficient ecclesiology, or worse, a deficient pneumatology—usually these are two sides of one coin. Such deficiency entails that Barth fails to provide an ecclesial life rich enough (particularly a rich enough sacramental life) to sustain this tradition of inquiry, and indeed Christian witness, through time. This is certainly at the heart of Hauerwas's concerns and criticisms of Barth's theological project, in the end.[71] For while Hauerwas is sympathetic to Barth's singular focus on the subject of theology and to the method Barth follows, he believes that Barth has not provided a rich enough context for

---

[71]Hauerwas, *With the Grain of the Universe*, pp. 178, 199-200. Hauerwas's criticisms borrow from and follow those offered by Reinhard Hütter.

such theological reasoning to flourish and to take shape in witness.[72] Such matters were addressed in the first chapter, and they need not be rehearsed again.[73] Rather, I want to end with one small observation regarding the lectures of MacIntyre and Barth and the consideration of one final difference.

To read MacIntyre's estimation of late modernity and its new "Dark Ages" of moral barbarity and darkness is to read a sobering assessment that, while not altogether devoid of hope, is marked by an implicit fear. Already in *After Virtue*, MacIntyre famously concluded:

> What matters at this stage is the construction of local forms of community within which civility and the intellectual and moral life can be sustained through the new dark ages which are already upon us. And if the tradition of the virtues was able to survive the horrors of the last dark ages, we are not entirely without grounds for hope. This time however the barbarians are not waiting beyond the frontiers; they have already been governing us for quite some time. And it is our lack of consciousness of this that constitutes part of our predicament. We are waiting not for a Godot, but for another—doubtless very different—St. Benedict.[74]

By the time of the publication of his later Gifford Lectures, even such hope seems to have darkened a bit. As MacIntyre wrote in the introduction to *Three Rival Versions*:

> The experience . . . of participating twice over in the discussion of these lectures [at Yale and Edinburgh] strongly reinforced the conclusion that such lectures can no longer be presented whether on the basis of presupposed agreements or with the purpose of securing general agreement. The most that one can hope for is to render our disagreements more constructive. It was with that aim that I delivered these Gifford Lectures; it is with the same aim that I publish them.[75]

---

[72]Hauerwas ties this to Barth's rejection of Catholic sacramentalism (*With the Grain of the Universe*, p. 199).

[73]Before leaving this topic, however, it could be said that in light of the examination of Barth's discussion of "costumes" and the "lordless powers" here given, Hauerwas's statement that Barth thought "that Christian faithfulness should not involve challenging false notions of science, morality, or art on theological grounds" seems wide of the mark (*With the Grain of the Universe*, p. 203).

[74]MacIntyre, *After Virtue*, p. 263.

[75]MacIntyre, *Three Rival Versions*, p. 8.

One senses a different demeanor at the end of Barth's own lectures. Barth ends with the following:

> The teaching of the Reformation is only rightly understood when it is realized that its Confession of faith must end with prayer and therefore naturally must begin with prayer too, and that the only prayer possible at this place must be the one found here, "Arise, O Lord," and "give Thy servants strength"—the prayer for God's Word and Revelation, and the prayer for faith and thus in the first instance and in the second a prayer for God's own action, which alone makes amends for what we ourselves shall do badly on all occasions, however hard we strive after right knowledge of God and right service of God. The church, by praying and praying thus, declares that she puts her trust not in herself but in the comfort and hope, whose name is Jesus Christ—and in the power of the name of God the Father, Son and Holy Spirit, the one true God, to whom alone all Honour and Glory is due. By praying and praying thus the church declares that she is crossing the gulf by the one real bridge. *Without prayer of this kind Reformation teaching would have no real foundation.* All its statements, strictly speaking, can only be understood, if one allows oneself to be called by them to prayer of this kind. Natural Theology has this advantage over the teaching of the Reformation that it has no need of prayer of this kind, and requires neither to begin nor end with it. What it claims to know about God, the world and man can most certainly be known without such prayer. Is this an advantage? I wish to leave this question open, after having indicated once more the dimension to which men must turn their gaze if the statements of Reformed Theology are not merely to be heard and discussed, but recognized as the Words of Truth.[76]

Reading this passage in light of those before, one senses that perhaps there is a difference between philosophical optimism in the power of a tradition and its communal embodiment, and theological hope that looks to something beyond the tradition and community itself. One has to decide in the end whether this is simply a deficient pneumatology and ecclesiology or, in contrast, a quite high one. Certainly Barth hems the knowledge of God and the service of God behind and before with prayer. It is, in fact, this introduction of prayer as the foundation of knowledge of God, with all that it implies, that perhaps should be seen as the most striking thing about Barth's

---

[76]*KGSG*, pp. 244-45, emphasis added.

Gifford Lectures (rather than his rejection of natural theology). And of course these, too, are related, but it is the first that grounds and gives the rationale for the second, rather than the second giving rise to the first. This is, it must be admitted, a very odd kind of foundationalism.

Years ago I gathered with a number of graduate students and others in a home where philosophy and theology were discussed. The occasion was the presence of a young visiting scholar from Europe whom I (regrettably) have forgotten. He was pressed on all sides by the fervent questions of graduate students who wanted to know how theology was to address the pressing concern of God's existence and its demonstration to a postmodern, pluralistic, increasingly secular world. I will never forget his answer. "I just think that God's existence is God's problem." I suppose this is a poor argument, though it may be a kind of witness.

12

A Concluding Postscript to
Schleiermacher's Christology

✟

Friedrich Schleiermacher's *Glaubenslehre* is the product not only of theological genius but also of a deep desire to explicate and maintain the unique status of the Redeemer, Jesus Christ, and his ongoing significance.[1] The recognition of the primacy that Schleiermacher gives to Christ has caused Martin Redeker to posit that the very center of Schleiermacher's theology is Christology,[2] and it is not difficult to see that the success of Schleiermacher's theological program is intimately connected with the fulfillment of Schleiermacher's christological intent. From the beginning, however, many have questioned whether Schleiermacher was successful in his aim. F. C. Baur charged Schleiermacher with sacrificing the historical Jesus to an archetypal ideal,[3] while D. F. Strauss contended that both Schleiermacher's dogmatic and exegetical work rendered not a portrait of Jesus of Nazareth but the

---

This chapter appeared in an earlier form (*sans* the epilogue) as "Between Heaven and Earth: Schleiermacher's Christology in View of Intrasystematic Tensions and Relations within the '*Glaubenslehre*,'" in *Schleiermacher's "To Cecilie" and Other Writings by and About Schleiermacher—New Athenaeum*, vol. 6, ed. Ruth D. Richardson (Lewiston, NY: Edwin Mellen Press, 2001), pp. 179-95. Reprinted with permission.
[1]All following references and quotations, unless otherwise noted, are taken from *CF.*
[2]Martin Redeker, *Schleiermacher: Life and Thought*, trans. John Wallhausser (Philadelphia: Fortress, 1973), p. 149.
[3]F. C. Baur, *Die christliche Lehre von der Versöhnung in ihrer geschichtlichen Entwicklung von der ältesten Zeit bis auf die neueste* (Tübingen: Osiander, 1838), pp. 614-48. For a summary of Baur's various criticisms of Schleiermacher, see Peter C. Hodgson, *The Formation of Historical Theology: A Study of Ferdinand Christian Baur* (New York: Harper & Row, 1966), esp. pp. 43-54.

Christ of Schleiermacher's Moravian childhood.[4] While the force of such criticisms must be appreciated, the criticisms themselves do not detract from the fact that Schleiermacher's theology centers on Christology.

Yet to label Schleiermacher's theology as christocentric is perhaps a misnomer; at the very least, the use of such a term must be explained. There are at least two ways in which a theology might be christocentric. One of these is to understand and explicate all doctrines in light of the doctrine of Christ. In such a theology, Christology functions in a formative and hermeneutical manner, shaping and determining the understanding of all other theological *topoi*. Another way is to understand Christology as the central focus and fulfillment of all other doctrines, the pinnacle, so to speak, of the theological edifice. While Schleiermacher's theology, like many others, contains a dynamic interplay between these two approaches, his Christology functions primarily in the second sense. That is to say, Schleiermacher's Christology does not regulate the unfolding of all other doctrines, but elements of other doctrines, and especially those of God and creation/preservation, exert a counterinfluence on Christology. So Richard Niebuhr's designation of Schleiermacher's theology as christo-morphic is still a viable alternative to that of christocentric:

> The reader will not find Schleiermacher justifying all that he says about God and man by his doctrine of Christ. Christology is not the archimedean point by means of which *The Christian Faith* moves all the other doctrines of theology before the reader's view. It is not the absolute center about which everything else revolves. . . . In *The Christian Faith* the redeemer is only one among a plurality of objects of theological knowledge, but at the same time he is paramount and central as the agent who reforms and shapes anew the Christian's relations to God, the world and himself.[5]

An understanding of Schleiermacher's Christology thus requires an attendance to its intricate relationship with the other elements of the dogmatics. Specifically, Christology in the Second Part of the *Glaubenslehre* must be seen in light of the First Part. The purpose here is to examine the

---

[4]D. F. Strauss, *The Christ of Faith and the Jesus of History*, trans. and ed. Leander E. Keck (Philadelphia: Fortress, 1977), p. 4.
[5]Richard R. Niebuhr, *Schleiermacher on Christ and Religion: A New Introduction* (New York: Charles Scribner's Sons, 1964), pp. 211-12.

manner in which Schleiermacher's exposition of Christ as Redeemer and as Second Adam, the completion of creation, is influenced by his understanding of earlier doctrines. In so doing, it will become evident that the problems of Schleiermacher's Christology arise in large part because of his understanding of other dogmatic topics, especially the relationship between God and the natural order. Such an investigation will then lead to the discovery that the second identity of Christ as Second Adam overshadows the first of Christ as Redeemer. After such an examination is made, one will be in a better position to evaluate Schleiermacher's Christology in light of his dogmatic intention.[6]

SIN, THE FALL AND HUMAN NATURE

While references to Christ are interspersed throughout *The Christian Faith*,

---

[6]At this point it is appropriate to respond to the charge that might be raised contending that the construal of Schleiermacher's Christology given above is inaccurate, and that in fact, Schleiermacher's Christology serves a much more determinative role in shaping the doctrines of the First Part, such as that of creation. Robert Sherman has defended this position, arguing that Schleiermacher's doctrine of creation should not be seen as derived from a general God-consciousness that is independent of the specifically Christian consciousness, but that such a general consciousness is itself an abstraction of the specifically Christian one; see Sherman, *The Shift to Modernity: Christ and the Doctrine of Creation in the Theologies of Schleiermacher and Barth* (New York: T & T Clark, 2005), pp. 13-40. In effect, Sherman is calling attention to the fact that the *Glaubenslehre* is a distinctively Christian and systematic work: all parts are structured in a seamless manner to present a specifically Christian faith. Schleiermacher's doctrine of creation is therefore not a generic (although monotheistic) one to which is attached a specifically Christian doctrine of redemption, but creation is presented itself in view of a whole which is determined by the distinctively Christian consciousness. Sherman recalls that Schleiermacher himself asserted that he could reverse the order of the First and Second Parts. Yet in fact Schleiermacher did *not* reverse the order, and one reason which he gives for not doing so, which Sherman himself notes, is his belief that only the present organization could adequately address the issue of reconciling Christian faith and free scientific investigation. And it is this external (non-dogmatic) preoccupation that provides warrant to assert that Schleiermacher's theology is not simply concerned with internal dogmatic questions, and that such external concerns shaped the character of Christology by means of their direct effect on the doctrines of creation and preservation. Such a point does not imply that Schleiermacher formulated his doctrine of creation directly from concepts borrowed from natural science (see Niebuhr, *Schleiermacher on Christ and Religion*, p. 241); neither does it deny the validity of Sherman's general argument. What it does justify, however, is the current investigation which posits that the tensions within Schleiermacher's Christology are primarily created by earlier positions outlined in the *Glaubenslehre* and that a reversal of the First and Second Parts may well have led to significant differences in the resulting work. Finally, we might note that even those who defend Schleiermacher's Christology recognize that the *Glaubenslehre* is as much concerned with the relationship between divine and natural causality as with christological formulations; see Jacqueline Mariña, "Schleiermacher's Christology Revisited: A Reply to His Critics," *Scottish Journal of Theology* 49, no. 2 (1996): 177-200, esp. pp. 185-86 and n. 16.

the heart of Schleiermacher's Christology resides in the Second Part, and specifically §§86-99, although, because Schleiermacher considers Christ's person and work (or, in his terms, his "Dignity" and "Activity," §92) to be mutually definitive, this might be extended through §105. These sections fall within the category of propositions that are descriptions of human states of mind, or reflections on the self-consciousness, which Schleiermacher holds to be the fundamental type of dogmatic propositions (§30). It is here that Schleiermacher attempts to establish the unique status of Christ in relation to the work of redemption and the completion of human nature.

In §88 Schleiermacher claims that the redemption that gave rise to and is transmitted via the Christian community is effected through the communication of Jesus' sinless perfection (*unsündlichen Vollkommenheit*). This sinless perfection of Jesus consists in his perfect and absolutely potent God-consciousness (*ungehemmte Kräftigkeit des Gottesbewußtseins*, §88.4). It is Jesus' sinless perfection, his pure and unhindered God-consciousness, which allows him to perform the work of redemption. Redemption is the removal of sin, in effect opening up humanity to a new possibility of communion with God. Schleiermacher's understanding of sin in relation to Jesus' God-consciousness poses a difficulty for his Christology, however.

Schleiermacher has defined the uniqueness of Christ as well as his sinlessness in terms of his completely potent God-consciousness. Sin is therefore anything that hinders the God-consciousness (§66.1).[7] Yet by defining Jesus' unique status, in effect his difference from all other persons, in terms of his God-consciousness, Schleiermacher seems to have made sin an intrinsic element of human nature. This problem could perhaps be ad-

---

[7]Schleiermacher rejects any position which would see sin as the breaking of divine commands, which requires divine retribution for such deeds and which then posits the punishment for such infractions as demonstrated in a vicarious death undertaken by Christ on the cross; see, for example, the discussion of God's justice (§84) and Christ's death in relation to sin (§104.4). Hans Graß summarizes Schleiermacher's attitude toward such views, stating that Schleiermacher has no place for such sacrificial and vicarious notions of atonement, for divine wrath or for a feeling of divine abandonment by Christ: "Dem Opfertod selbst, dem Blut Christi eine Bedeutung zuzuschreiben, lehnt Schleiermacher ab. Von einem Erleiden des göttlichen Zorns will er nichts wissen. Daß Christus sich am Kreuz von Gott verlassen gefühlt habe, ist für ihn ein unmöglicher Gedanke, wie er ja überhaupt von einem ernsthaft angefochtenen Christus nichts wissen will." Graß, "Die Durch Jesum von Nazareth vollbrachte Erlösung. Ein Beitrag zur Erlösungslehre Schleiermachers," in *Denkender Glaube: Festschrift Carl Heinz Ratschow* (Berlin: Walter de Gruyter, 1976), p. 157.

dressed by referring to the traditional understanding of original sin, in which Christ is differentiated from sinful humanity by his unique sinlessness, yet the sinfulness of humanity is not intrinsic to the very definition of human nature but arises out of the fall. Schleiermacher, however, has rejected this option. Human nature has not undergone a change through the fall but has remained ever and always the same: "If then, on the one hand, we discard the view that a change took place in human nature itself, but, on the other, still maintain that an incapacity for good is the universal state of men, it follows that this incapacity was present in human nature before the first sin, and that accordingly what is now innate sinfulness was something native also to the first pair" (§72.4, *CF*, p. 301). This is not to deny the original goodness of humanity. But for Schleiermacher this is a logical, and not a chronological, distinction. Sin is recognized in light of the imperfect though good capacity of God-consciousness in a person, but both equally cohere in human nature itself. Instead of an original and perfect nature which was lost and replaced by a sinful nature, Schleiermacher posits a "human nature universally and without exception— apart from redemption—the same . . . a timeless original sinfulness always and everywhere inhering in human nature and co-existing with the original perfection given along with it . . . the simple idea of an absolutely common guilt identical for all" (§72.6, *CF*, p. 303).

It is important to understand why Schleiermacher believes the traditional understanding of the fall should be rejected. A human nature truly changed through sin would in effect betray a limitation of the omnipotent sovereignty of God, setting up a will independent of God which could thwart the divine purpose, thus rendering the feeling of absolute dependence an illusion (§80.4; cf. §81). I will return to this topic when taking up the theme of Schleiermacher's understanding of the God-world relationship, but for now a full explication of this point must be set aside and it must simply be noted that for Schleiermacher the fall as traditionally understood entails a frustration of the divine purpose. If this is the case, however, Schleiermacher must recognize sin itself as part of the divine plan, and he must face the implication that God is the author of sin.

Schleiermacher addresses this question in §§79-82. His discussion can be summarized along the following lines. First, Schleiermacher acknowledges that God, as the cause and ground of all that exists, is for this reason the author of sin. God is, however, not the author of sin in the same sense that he is the author of redemption, for sin has only a transitory existence on the way to redemption's fulfillment. We might say that God has penultimately ordained sin as necessary only because of redemption's ultimate aim. Schleiermacher cannot admit a "divided sphere of causation," or the recognition that God is not ultimately sovereign over all. Instead, he writes:

> As against this, our own theory is that sin was ordained only in view of redemption, and that accordingly redemption shows forth as the gain bound up with sin; in comparison with which there can be no question whatever of mischief due to sin, for the merely gradual and imperfect unfolding of the power of the God-consciousness is one of the necessary conditions of the human stage of existence. (§81.4, CF, p. 338)

Because sin only exists in light of redemption, we can even say that sin has no real existence for God, since sin is only the imperfection of the God-consciousness in light of its completion in Christ and redemption.[8] So then, in what sense does sin exist? Schleiermacher asserts that sin is our recognition that our own God-consciousness is imperfect, unable to subjugate all sensible moments to itself and thus standing in need of the redemption effected by Christ's own perfect God-consciousness. God has ordained sin then only as that recognition in us of our own defective God-consciousness and the need for the redemption which Christ, as the embodiment of an absolutely potent God-consciousness, can bring. Schleiermacher writes (with echoes of Spinoza):

> [T]here is no reality in, nor any divine idea of, the bad . . . the bad as an actual antithesis to the good has no existence at all, and that therefore that displeasure with the bad which is wrought in us by the divine causality is, strictly speaking, only our own displeasure in the fact that the effective power of the God-consciousness falls short of the clearness of our apprehension. (§83.3, CF, p. 345)

Both sin and redemption thus spring from one divine will, although only redemption adequately describes the divine purpose.

---

[8]Evil also may be said to have no real existence for God but only arises from our limited perspective of the divine purpose (see §82).

Having traced this necessary if tortuous route, we can now see what difficulties such views of sin and human nature pose for Christology. Two distinct problems come into view. First, by defining Christ as one free from the conflict between the God-consciousness and the sensible self-consciousness that is fundamental to human nature, Schleiermacher has problematically separated Christ from what appears essential to humanity. Second, and correspondingly, Schleiermacher's account of sin has subsumed it into the divine purposes and thus has not only weakened its offensive force but also has made the very conception of redemption questionable, for it appears as if Christ's work is better described as the completion of the creative act than the restoration of a lost state.

In light of the prior difficulty, Schleiermacher does indeed apply himself to answering the question of Christ's continuity with humanity. First, Schleiermacher denies that sinfulness is intrinsic to human nature, describing it rather as a "derangement" or "disturbance" (*Störung*) of human nature (§68.3, *CF*, p. 278; §94.1, *CF*, p. 385). This answer, however, is difficult to reconcile with his claim above that "the gradual and imperfect unfolding of the power of the God-consciousness is one of the necessary conditions of the human stage of existence" (§81.4, *CF*, p. 338). Of more importance is Schleiermacher's attempt to establish a continuity between Christ and humanity by means of a distinction between a divine activity and a human receptive capacity, thereby making this human capacity that both Christ and all other persons share definitive for understanding human nature. This capacity consists in the ability of human nature to receive into itself an absolutely potent God-consciousness (§89.3; cf. §88.4). While this line of reasoning initially may seem promising, it provides but a questionable answer. To posit a receptive capacity as the definitive aspect of human nature is to say nothing really about humanity and everything about divinity; it is an empty concept. This is especially evident when we realize that Schleiermacher denied that this capacity could be self-actualized because sin exists not only in the individual but also is corporately transmitted: sin is a "corporate act of the human race" (*Gesamttat des menschlichen Geschlechts*, §93.3; cf. §87.3). That is to say, no person could ever attain a completely potent God-consciousness not only because of the internal subjugation of the God-consciousness to the sensible self-consciousness which is an ele-

mental part of human life and nature, but also because of the external corporate nature of humanity which both propagates sin and thereby involves
all persons and actions in corporate sin and guilt. The capacity could only
be fulfilled through a divine activity, and this is in fact the case with Christ.
So instead of bridging the gap between Christ and humanity, the concept of
capacity seems rather to widen the gulf between them. Certainly this cannot
be said simply on the basis of Schleiermacher's claim that Christ is sinless.
Traditional Christologies also portrayed Christ as the fulfillment of perfect
humanity, and thus definitive of it. Sinfulness was not seen as an intrinsic
element of human nature, and thus Christ's sinlessness does not call into
question his full humanity. Yet Schleiermacher's claim, again, that "the
gradual and imperfect unfolding of the power of the God-consciousness is
one of the necessary conditions of the human stage of existence" (§81.4, *CF*,
p. 338) seems itself to imply that "sin" is elemental to human nature.

It should therefore come as no surprise that Schleiermacher's defense
against the second charge made above, namely, that redemption has become
such an attenuated concept that it is in danger of being subsumed into creation, is equally problematic. For if we consider the fact that Schleiermacher
has combined sin and redemption under one divine decree, primacy must
go to the one creative act, not to redemption. And this is in fact what we find
in the *Glaubenslehre*. Because sin and evil have no real existence for God,
Christ's appearance as the work of redemption is only the effect of his appearance; it is not the purpose for which he came. So the redemption Christ
brings is in fact the possibility of a new relationship to God, not in a restor-
ative sense but as the completion of the creation itself. It is thereby for this
reason that the person of Christ is defined ultimately not by his work of
redemption but by his completion of human nature. Christ as Redeemer is
overshadowed by Christ as Second Adam. The implications of this will be
considered below.

It was earlier noted that redemption could not arise merely from the
natural corporate life of sin. Jesus' perfect God-consciousness was, according to Schleiermacher, not the product of this corporate life but had
a supernatural origin (*übernatürlich gewordenen*, §88.4). This assertion
does not in and of itself, of course, make Schleiermacher's Christology
deficient with regard to Christ's human nature. Traditional Christologies

also held that Jesus was not simply the product of historical forces and human generation but that his existence was the result of a unique divine act. In light of Schleiermacher's earlier expressed understanding of the God-world relationship, however, Christ's supernatural status raises other distinct quandaries, best appreciated in light of his understanding of creation and preservation.

CREATION, PRESERVATION AND THE GOD-WORLD RELATIONSHIP

In §37 and §38 Schleiermacher explains the relationship between the doctrines of creation and preservation. Because these doctrines are not differentiated in the religious self-consciousness, they may be combined, yet Schleiermacher retains each for historical and explanatory reasons. In effect, however, he does subsume creation into preservation, for he relates that finite reality should not be understood as arising from a special divine act which is differentiated from the ongoing relation of God to the world, since all finite existence arises out of one eternal and divine decree.

Schleiermacher also asserts that earlier dogmaticians such as Quenstedt have recognized divine preservation and natural causation as the same thing viewed from different perspectives (§46.2, *CF*, p. 174). This is *not* pantheistic. Schleiermacher strongly contends that God is not the totality of finite existence but is totally antithetical to the world and God's causality is totally unlike the reciprocal causality of the natural realm (§46, §49; cf. *CF*, p. 192). Because, however, the ground of our feeling of absolute dependence, which is in fact the divine causality, extends to include all of finite existence, we can conclude that the divine causality is "equal in compass to finite causality" (§51, *CF*, p. 201). The feeling of absolute dependence itself arises out of the consciousness that all finite reality is determined by and contingent on the interdependence of nature (*Naturzusammenhang*, §46). This placement of the finite causality under the scope of the divine causality may be expressed as the divine omnipotence (§54, *CF*, p. 211).

Such a relationship between the divine causality and the natural order makes miracles especially problematic. No longer do miracles display divine omnipotence; rather, a true miracle would refute God's sovereignty by destroying the constancy of the causal nexus. Only the stability and constancy of the natural order provide the basis from which the feeling of absolute dependence can arise. For this reason, the religious significance of any fact will never entail that it be explained in such a manner that frees it from any dependence on the system of nature. An act of God can never be an act independent of the *Naturzusammenhang*, for the divine causality and the natural order of relations are coextensive (§47). Schleiermacher concludes that for this reason, which agrees with the findings of natural science, the very conception of the "absolutely supernatural" (*schlechthin Über-natürlichen*) should be abandoned. His rejection of miracles thereby parallels his rejection of the traditional fall; both would sacrifice the divine omnipotence demonstrated in the constancy of nature and would thereby imply the imperfect realization of the divine purpose.

It is important to consider the full weight of Schleiermacher's argument. A true miracle is not only a scientific embarrassment. A true miracle would destroy the system of nature, the reality of the divine omnipotence and the feeling of absolute dependence, which arises and is made possible only because of the interdependence of nature and its corresponding constancy. In effect, a miracle would render the religious possibility an impossibility; a miracle could lead only to absurdity and atheism. This then allows us to see Schleiermacher's assertion that Jesus is not the product of corporate nature in a new light, for Jesus' appearance as a *"wunderbare Erscheinung"* (§93.3), if truly an absolute miracle, would spell the end of the natural order and all that it entails.

Schleiermacher must then confront two equally problematic realities. First, the God-consciousness of Jesus cannot be the product of the natural (and sinful) order of existence. On the other hand, Jesus' appearance cannot be a miracle in the traditional sense. Such an understanding could only betray a divine capriciousness (cf. §13.1). This difficulty lies at the heart of Schleiermacher's Christology and combines a number of dogmatic concerns. On one level, this difficulty is that of explaining how Christ could be both the singular, unsurpassable ideal (*Urbildlichkeit*) and historical. On another level, it is the attempt to explain Christ as a uniquely self-determined individual versus the product and sum total of natural, social and historical forces.[9] On yet another level, it is Schleiermacher's attempt to explain Jesus

---

[9]It must be remembered that Schleiermacher has articulated the thesis that no event's religious significance can be explained by divorcing it from the natural order, for the divine causality and

as both divine and human, or, from another angle, to avoid both docetic and ebionitic heresies. Schleiermacher's greatest christological challenge lies in reconciling these two paradoxical positions.

We can begin to approach Schleiermacher's attempt to solve this dilemma by noting that his assertion that Christ's appearance was miraculous is always qualified by reminding his readers that this is so only in the sense which he outlined in §13 (§§88.4, 93.3). In this section Schleiermacher explains that the appearance of any new religious community (and its founder) cannot simply be explained in terms of its historical environment; the community must introduce something new.[10] The appearance of such individuals and the communities they create should not, however, be understood in a purely supernatural sense, for while their appearing exceeds historical explanation, it is still due to a divinely ordained "law" (*Gesetz*) which though indiscernible is necessary for human progress (§13.1). Christ's appearance can be explained in a similar way, although with a significant qualification, namely, that while other religious leaders shall pass into oblivion, Christ's person and influence are universally and eternally unsurpassable. Nevertheless, Schleiermacher can speak of Christ's appearance as a "natural" fact for at least two reasons: (1) the capacity in Christ to receive the perfect God-consciousness is not unlike that which all persons share; and (2) even if this realization is only a human possibility and cannot be

---

the natural order are coextensive (§47). In the introduction to the *Glaubenslehre* Schleiermacher stated that religious figures, though seemingly original and unprecedented, can be explained in terms of their historical environment (§10). This is not a simple determinism, for the divine causality ordains freedom within the world as well as natural causation (§49.1). In fact, the feeling of absolute dependence can only arise if a limited spontaneity exists. But this does not undermine the fact that all finite phenomena, including human individuals possessing freedom, are ordained by God to arise from within the natural realm. So Schleiermacher can write that "no particular thing, since it always belongs to the world, can in itself be regarded as divine revelation. For just as the dawning of an archetypal idea in an individual soul, even if it cannot be explained by the previous states of that very soul, can certainly be explained by the total state of the society to which the individual belongs: so even the men who are credited with divine descent always appear as determined by the character of their people, and thus it is from the total energy of the people that their existence is to be explained or comprehended" (§10, *CF*, p. 51). If Christ, then, could be explained in such a way, he could in no way be the archetypal ideal and a unique revelation, for as conditioned by the world system his influence could only be reciprocal and thus his significance could only be temporary. He would fade into history and could be left behind (cf. §93.2, *CF*, p. 380).

[10]Here Schleiermacher is applying himself to the question of historical determinism earlier discussed in §10; see note 9 above.

historically realized apart from a divine act, the actuality of this capacity experienced by Jesus must also be understood as a human action and the highest development of a (theoretically possible) human ideal.

In evaluating Schleiermacher's argument thus far we can pass over these last two points, for they fall under the criticisms of such a human capacity outlined earlier. What is of more interest is Schleiermacher's conception of "law" as used here.

GESETZ AND THE ETERNAL DECREE

Schleiermacher invokes the concept of "law" as explaining the appearance of the Redeemer in §89.2. This law is, in effect, a concept that represents Schleiermacher's understanding of how the supernatural and natural are combined. Schleiermacher believes he can overcome the paradox between the two, and the dilemma posed earlier of Christ as both unique and historical, by eliminating the difference between the natural and supernatural. He does this by explaining that Christ's appearance is a supernatural act that becomes natural, that is, historical. This unique conception may seem as if it has solved Schleiermacher's quandary on its own, but we must note that Schleiermacher believed this idea applied not only to Christ but also to creation itself.[11] This causes one to wonder what is left of the uniqueness of Christ if everything is supernatural.

Ultimately, this fusion of the natural and the supernatural leads us to the heart of Schleiermacher's solution to the problem posed above. This solution rests in subsuming both creation and Christ's appearance into one eternal divine decree; the mystery of the two is located in the "unity of the divine thought" (§88.4, CF, p. 365).

This is Schleiermacher's most brilliant move. By locating creation and Christ's appearance within one eternal decree he can maintain Christ's unique and "miraculous" appearance as divinely instituted and not subsumed into historical causes, yet retain its historicity in that Christ's ap-

---

[11]"Whenever I speak of the supernatural, I do so with reference to whatever comes first, but afterwards it becomes secondly something natural. Thus creation is supernatural, but it afterwards becomes the natural order. Likewise, in his origin Christ is supernatural, but he also becomes natural, as a genuine human being. The Holy Spirit and the Christian church can be treated in the same way." Schleiermacher, *On the* Glaubenslehre: *Two Letters to Dr. Lücke,* trans. James Duke and Francis Fiorenza (Atlanta: Scholars Press, 1981), p. 89.

pearance is the completion of a truly historical and human ideal, that is, one that is realized in history in a human person. Christ is thus the completion of human nature:

> If the impartation of the Spirit to human nature which was made in the first Adam was insufficient, in that the spirit remained sunk in sensuousness and barely glanced forth clearly at moments as a presentiment of something better, and if the work of creation has only been completed through the second and equally original impartation to the Second Adam, yet both events go back to one undivided eternal divine decree and form, even in a higher sense, only one and the same natural system, though one unattainable by us. (§94.3, *CF*, p. 389)[12]

Christ is thus the Second Adam, the completion of human nature, and thereby the one who defines what human nature is to be.

Schleiermacher's understanding of Christ as the Second Adam allows him to resolve the above paradox to a great degree. Still, this resolution has not come without cost, and problems still remain. First, at this point it should be clear that Christ's role as Redeemer is completely overshadowed by Christ as the completion of human nature. Not only is the idea of redemption greatly subdued, but also the ongoing significance of Christ is questioned. If he is the fulfillment of human nature (and this alone defines his uniqueness), what relationship can he have with those before and after who do not themselves realize the ideal? And if those after do realize it through the mediation of Christ, what is Christ's ongoing significance? It appears that there are no fully acceptable answers to these questions.[13]

---

[12]Graß comments on this point, noting that creation and redemption thus are folded together in one undifferentiated divine election: "Dabei sieht Schleiermacher Schöpfung und Erlösung in einem Zusammenhang, indem er beide auf *einen* ungeteilten göttlichen Ratschluß zurückführt, ja in einem Naturzusammenhang stehend sieht, der freilich von uns aus unerreichbar war. Denn die Erscheinung Jesu ist für Schleiermacher ein Wunder, allerdings das einzige Wunder, das er gelten läßt." See "Die Durch Jesum von Nazareth vollbrachte Erlösung," p. 154.

[13]Such a conclusion is not merely an assumption. Maureen Junker-Kenny has shown that the shift in emphasis from understanding Christ in the role of Redeemer to that of the Second Adam, the fulfillment of creation, was a deliberate move on Schleiermacher's part in writing the second edition of the *Christian Faith*. This shift in emphasis between the first and second editions was intended to give Christ a role of universal, and not only particular, significance. But in so doing, Junker-Kenny contends, Schleiermacher was not able to maintain the uniqueness and ongoing significance of Christ: "Even if it is through the mediation of Christ, all that happens in the history of salvation is that human nature finally attains its own essence. To have mediated something already possessed and known cannot assure Christ's principal position that Schlei-

This leads to a second difficulty. Even if Christ's appearance is established by the same eternal decree that gave rise to all of humanity, Christ's independence from the sinful corporate life of historical existence, along with his status as a new, or second, creation (§89.2), seems to place a fundamental distinction between Christ and humanity in such a way that the question of his identification with other persons once again arises.[14] To speak of two stages of creation is itself problematic in view of the fact that the divine causality is both grounded in a single divine decree and is directed toward the nature system as a whole. As such, it cannot be directed toward any individual in a separate and discrete action, and this then makes the unique status of Christ, as a single historical person, difficult to maintain.[15]

Before we simply conclude that Schleiermacher's Christology falls short of asserting the full humanity of Christ, however, we must note that any such

---

ermacher wants to defend. Although Schleiermacher's Christology looks back toward Christ as the factual starting-point of the new humanity, there is no substantial distinction in Jesus to justify his ongoing importance for the process he inaugurated: the significance of Jesus consists in realizing the divinely affirmed essence of humanity, not in communicating something radically new in the history of the human race. The singular fact that in one particular life God's self-revelation towards humankind was realized here disappears within the evolution of humanity. Christianity is absorbed in religion in general." See Junker-Kenny, "Schleiermacher's Transcendental Turn: Shifts in Argumentation between the First and Second Editions of the *Glaubenslehre*," *Neues Athenaeum* 3 (1992): 37-38; cf. pp. 33-41. Junker-Kenny's point is perhaps overstated, and her reference to the evolution of humanity may betray a failure to see the creation completed in Christ as located in the eternal divine decree (cf. Niebuhr, *Schleiermacher on Christ and Religion*, p. 257). Her overall argument is, nevertheless, both forceful and compelling. It is interesting that even Mariña's able defense of Schleiermacher's Christology falters at precisely the issues here discussed. While spending considerable time justifying Schleiermacher's method and explaining the importance of Christ as the fulfillment of human nature and creation, Mariña's defense neither defines nor significantly addresses redemption or Christ's role as the Redeemer and does not provide any special argumentation for the ongoing significance of Christ.

[14]This point is easily illustrated with the following quotation: "The origin of every human life may be regarded in a twofold manner, as issuing from the narrow circle of descent and society to which it immediately belongs, and as a fact of human nature in general. The more definitely the weaknesses of that narrow circle repeat themselves in an individual, the more valid becomes the first point of view. The more the individual by the kind and degree of his gifts transcends that circle, and the more he exhibits what is new within it, the more we are thrown back upon the other explanation. This means that the beginning of Jesus' life cannot in any way be explained by the first factor, but only and exclusively by the second; so that from the beginning He must have been free from every influence from earlier generations which disseminated sin and disturbed the inner God-consciousness, and He can only be understood as an original act of human nature, i.e. as an act of human nature as not affected by sin" (§94.3, *CF*, pp. 388-89).

[15]Schleiermacher will later argue that justification itself is a single decree; it is not to be understood as directly applied to individuals (§109, *CF*, p. 501).

charge must be qualified. We should remember that Christ was the fulfillment of a human ideal; that is to say, Christ was the fulfillment of human nature and thereby was a part of the created order. He was thus the fulfillment of a human possibility, albeit a theoretical one. Christ was not the incarnation of an eternal divine Subject (for, and this is not unimportant, Schleiermacher famously rejected traditional Nicene and Chalcedonian conceptions of the incarnation) but came into existence through a divine eternal decree. We should also remember that the antithetical relationship that Schleiermacher has articulated as existing between God and the finite world makes the idea of any true divine incarnation suspect, if not impossible.[16] So in *this* sense, Schleiermacher's Christology may be deemed to slight the divinity of Christ and perhaps be designated ebionitic.[17]

---

[16]For illustrations of this antithesis, see *CF*, pp. 155, 174, 192-93, 196, 228-32, 673: "there can be no relation of interaction between creature and Creator."

[17]It might be rejoined that my argument here ignores Schleiermacher's explicit assertion that "to ascribe to Christ an absolutely powerful God-consciousness, and to attribute to Him an existence of God in Him [*ein Sein Gottes in ihm beilegen*], are exactly the same thing" (§94.2, *CF*, p. 387, and *Christliche Glaube*, vol. 2, p. 45; see also §100.2, *CF*, pp. 426-27; §101.2, *CF*, 432-33). A full examination of this point would take us too far afield, but we can outline some observations that should demonstrate that such a statement cannot be understood to imply any type of true divine incarnation. First, the antithetical relationship between God and the world outlined above prohibits the very possibility of God in any way entering either into the causal nexus or time. Second, we should notice that while the religious self-consciousness requires that the feeling of redemption stem not merely from an exemplary figure but requires an ideal (*Urbildlichkeit*, see §93, *CF*, pp. 378-79), it requires a human ideal, that is, the productivity of the Redeemer is necessitated by the fulfillment and perfection of a distinctly human possibility. For this reason, Schleiermacher's extrapolation from the perfect God-consciousness to a real presence of God in Jesus betrays two of his own dogmatic principles: 1) it attributes a dignity to Christ higher than his activity requires (§93.2), and 2) it introduces a proposition into the dogmatics which, because not ultimately given and derivable from reflection on the distinctively Christian self-consciousness, can only then be seen as a speculative principle (see §16 Postscript).

These conclusions are further substantiated if we remember that in the feeling of absolute dependence God is never given as an object but is only the *Whence* which makes the relation between the God-consciousness and the sensible self-consciousness possible. This statement is not intended to deny Schleiermacher's realism but to clarify that God is never himself given, that is, present, in such experience. Even in Schleiermacher's philosophical thought, seen in the *Dialektik*, this understanding is upheld. Thandeka illustrates this matter when she states: "In this 'element' or 'feeling,' the transcendent ground or the highest essence itself is represented in human consciousness. Schleiermacher, however, was clear that this is a *representation* and not the ground itself." Thandeka, "Schleiermacher's *Dialektik*: The Discovery of the Self That Kant Lost," *Harvard Theological Review* 85, no. 4 (1992): 449; cf. p. 451. Thandeka here refers to the following passage from the *Dialektik*: "Diese transcendente Bestimmtheit des Selbstbewußtseins nun ist die religiose Seite desselben, oder die religiose Gefühl, und in diesem also ist der transcendente Grund oder das höchste Wesen selbst repräsentirt." Schleiermacher, *Dialektik*, ed. Ludwig Jonas, in *Schleiermacher's sämmtliche Werke*, vol. 3.4.2 (Berlin: Reimer, 1839), p. 430.

SCHLEIERMACHER'S CHRIST—SUSPENDED BETWEEN
HEAVEN AND EARTH

Ultimately, the problems of Schleiermacher's Christology are derived from his understanding of God and the divine-world relationship. Because God is antithetically related to the world, and because the relation between the divine and natural causality precludes discrete divine acts, a true incarnation, God entering the temporal causal nexus, is impossible in Schleiermacher's system. Instead, Schleiermacher defines Christ's unique status as the realization of a perfect human ideal, that is, a perfectly potent God-consciousness. Jesus' significance and uniqueness is thereby dependent on the fact that no other person could ever attain this ideal, and this in turn makes sinfulness (God-forgetfulness) an intrinsic element of human nature. Christ thus appears to be placed in a mutually antithetical relationship to both God and humanity. Because his ideal identity is based not on the incarnation of a divine Subject but a divine-human relationship that cannot be disturbed without sacrificing his perfect God-consciousness, Christ is precluded from experiencing seemingly fundamental elements of human life, such as conflict

---

Why then does Schleiermacher make such an equation between Jesus' God-consciousness and a divine existence within him? Mariña proposes the following: "The existence of God in Christ is just this pure consciousness of God, mediated through absolute dependence, in which the spontaneous self experiences God. The question naturally arises as to why *consciousness* of God should be equated with an *existence* of God in Jesus Christ. The answer lies in Schleiermacher's idealism, in which it is presupposed that to the extent to which something is known or interiorized, to this extent knower and known must be identical" ("Schleiermacher's Christology Revisited," p. 198). This account is provocative but entirely problematic, and not least because it collapses the God-world distinction. But more pointedly, God is *never* given in the self-consciousness as an object that can be *known*, that is, an object of consciousness. To put things this way is to confuse knowing and feeling and to bring God into the realm of reciprocal relationships implying that God is an object of the finite realm on which we can exert a reciprocal influence. Such an idealist epistemology can never apply to God. A more promising avenue is to see Schleiermacher's move as one that identifies Christ's consciousness more closely to a form of *activity* than *knowledge*, and in turn equates Christ's activity with divine action. This appeal to *actualism* rather than *idealism* is closer to Schleiermacher's real intent (see CF §94.2, p. 387, where he states that "God's existence can only be apprehended as pure activity"). Nevertheless, as the epilogue below will explore, this route is also deeply problematic (and may itself confuse acting and feeling, as the aforementioned idealism confuses knowing and feeling).

My own conviction is that Schleiermacher's equation of God-consciousness with divine being in Jesus is a holdover from more traditional Christologies which Schleiermacher rejects, but that he retains this element both to shore up his arguments for the ideal and unique status of Christ and to provide a basis from which he can salvage the doctrine of the Trinity which otherwise would to have been abandoned, something Schleiermacher was not willing to do. Regardless, his equation of these elements has not been done successfully when judged by his own dogmatic criteria.

and temptation (cf. §§93.4, 98). Moreover, because a true incarnation is impossible, God can only be said to be functionally, and not really, present.[18] In the end, Schleiermacher's Christology raises more questions than it answers. It is questionable that it is able to affirm the full humanity of Christ, in that Christ can never truly participate in ordinary human experiences of conflict and doubt. Moreover, it fails in maintaining the divinity of Christ insofar as Christ remains the realization of a human ideal (for no real incarnation is possible) and its attempts to address this matter are ultimately unsuccessful by Schleiermacher's own dogmatic criteria.[19]

We can speak, however, only in relative terms when we describe Schleiermacher's Christology as slighting Christ's humanity or divinity. For such ways of speaking historically originated to describe relationships between the divine and human natures in Christ's person in light of a hypostatic union, whereas Schleiermacher rejected such traditional Chalcedonian categories and such talk of a discrete act of a divine Subject entering into history to take on creaturely reality, just as he also eliminated a corresponding supernatural-natural distinction. What is certain is that Schleiermacher's Christ can only questionably be described as true man (human) or as true God. He exists between heaven and earth but belongs to neither.

In conclusion, it must be acknowledged that while much ground has been covered, many questions remain and many crucial areas of Schleiermacher's Christology have been neglected. Little has been said about the distinctive nineteenth-century problem of relating the archetypal ideal and the historical that Schleiermacher was forced to address especially in relation to the criticisms of Baur.[20] The person-forming activity of the divine God-

---

[18]Schleiermacher's Christology is thus adoptionist, although only in an eternal sense. God's unique selection of Christ for a special divine purpose takes place in the one and eternal divine decree, not in a temporal decision or historical act.

[19]See note 17 above. Junker-Kenny reaches even stronger conclusions: "The reason for the shortcomings of the Christology of the *Glaubenslehre* can be found in its doctrine of God. For Schleiermacher, it would mean to attribute arbitrariness to God if one went beyond God's total causality and conceived of specific divine acts. Thus, as his explanation of the concept of revelation already made evident, the idea of a specific act of God's self-revelation is excluded. God's initiative to communicate God's self and to risk a history of freedom with humanity becomes unthinkable. The effect on Christology is that any specific identification of God with the person and story of Christ is impossible" ("Schleiermacher's Transcendental Turn," p. 40).

[20]For a discussion of this problem in relation to Kant, Schleiermacher and Herrmann, see Brent W. Sockness, "The Ideal and the Historical in the Christology of Wilhelm Herrmann: The Promise and the Perils of Revisionary Christology," *Journal of Religion* 72 (1992): 366-88.

consciousness of Christ in relation to his human passivity has also received little attention. Nor is here offered an exhaustive account as to why Schleiermacher made his distinctive moves. To address this would require an explanation of Schleiermacher's detailed critiques of traditional Christologies and other doctrines such as that of creation and the fall.

Nevertheless, the primary purpose of this examination is more restricted and need not address these questions. It has focused on demonstrating the influence of Schleiermacher's other dogmatic doctrines (specifically, his conceptions of God, the relationship between God and the world, sin and election) on his Christology. In the light of such an investigation it becomes apparent that Schleiermacher's christological problems stem primarily from constrictions placed on his Christology by earlier dogmatic convictions. It is now possible to conclude that Schleiermacher's Christology, though brilliant in its attempt to overcome traditional christological quandaries, has not resolved or eluded them but has translated them into a new dogmatic framework, and something essential seems to have been lost in translation.

Epilogue to the Postscript

While the arguments above are significant enough to call into question Schleiermacher's christological project, there have of course been attempts to revive and defend Schleiermacher's Christology. To my mind one of the most innovative, insightful and plausible of these positive interpretations is that of Kevin Hector.[21] Hector provides a re-reading of Schleiermacher's Christology in view of what he takes to be Schleiermacher's actualism, that is, an attempt to see the relation of divine and human in Christ not in terms of substances or self-defined entities but in terms of events, activities and relationships.[22] Whereas Schleiermacher is often read as providing a "low" Christology that sacrifices Christ's uniqueness, Hector reads Schleiermacher as providing a "high" Christology that speaks of a real presence of God in Christ, regardless of his renunciation of Chalcedonian categories. The key to understanding Schleiermacher's conception of such a presence, Hector

---

[21] Kevin Hector, "Actualism and Incarnation: The High Christology of Friedrich Schleiermacher," *International Journal of Systematic Theology* 8 (2006): 307-22.

[22] Ibid., 307-9, drawing on the work of George Hunsinger, *How to Read Karl Barth* (New York: Oxford University Press, 1991), p. 30.

argues, is to understand it in terms of a divine actualism wherein, in Hector's words, "every moment of Christ's life repeats the pure act of God's being, such that Christ *is* God incarnate."[23] So while Schleiermacher is often seen as offering a low Christology, particularly by traditionalists, and yet one too high for thoroughgoing liberals committed to historical relativism, Hector offers a different way to understand Schleiermacher's intention, claiming that Schleiermacher was actually "trying to find a way of talking about Christ as God incarnate, in which (a) Christ is fully human; (b) God is really incarnate in that humanity; but such that (c) God remains free from our counterinfluence."[24] In short, Hector argues that for Schleiermacher God is pure activity, and Christ is God incarnate precisely because Christ, too, is pure activity, the divine activity reproduced specifically in Christ as God's pure act of love whereby God establishes fellowship with us.[25] This presentation of Schleiermacher's Christology as best understood in light of an actualist (rather than essentialist) metaphysics is an intriguing argument, and Hector presents it with a winsome cogency and clarity. He writes:

> Christ is the One who reproduces God's pure, loving act in human history, and is therefore God incarnate. The key to this reproduction is Christ's God-consciousness, which functions as the organ by which God's pure act is apprehended and turned into Christ's own activity. God-consciousness, on this account, is that which makes it possible for God to become incarnate in a human, because only a God-conscious, rational creature can receive and reproduce God's activity.[26]

Hector is quite persuasive in arguing that this view summarizes what Schleiermacher intends, achieved and indeed took to be a proper Christology, though one might have lingering reservations about whether Schleiermacher's seemingly direct equation of the perfect God-consciousness of

---

[23]Hector, "Actualism and Incarnation," p. 308.

[24]Ibid., p. 309.

[25]Ibid., pp. 310, 313. Hector writes: "Every moment of Christ's life perfectly instantiates God's pure activity, because at every moment Christ apprehends and reproduces that activity" (p. 313).

[26]Ibid., p. 311. Hector maintains that rather than "de-supernaturalizing the term 'divinity' by saying something like, 'the only thing that can count as "divine" in a human is the awareness of how dependent we are upon God,'" Schleiermacher is up to something else: "If my interpretation is right, Schleiermacher is saying something quite different: that 'perfect God-consciousness' can be equated with 'divinity' precisely because Christ's God-consciousness is the human organ through which God's activity becomes incarnate" (p. 312).

Jesus and the presence of divinity in him should be interpreted as Hector does, namely, not as an equation of the two but as the first being an organ that mediates the second, the God-consciousness the capacity that makes the presence of the divine possible. The difficulty of settling this question may itself boil down to the underdetermination of meaning of a particularly brief and seemingly straightforward yet nonetheless cryptic sentence by Schleiermacher.[27] Yet, even if this is the case, and Hector is correct in his interpretation of Schleiermacher's intention and achievement, the question remains: Should we follow this path in our own christological thought? For when we begin to look at these sentences we are confronted with a host of serious difficulties, none of which undercut Hector's penetrating reading, but all of which greatly call into question whether Schleiermacher's road is the way we should travel.

First, we are confronted with whether Schleiermacher's God-world relationship outlined earlier really allows him to say such things coherently, and on at least two counts. First, how can such a conception of a real divine presence *in* Christ stand in light of Schleiermacher's primary and basic presupposition earlier noted that "there can be no relation of interaction between creature and Creator" (*CF*, p. 673)? This is a serious question worth pondering. Yet even if we reconcile ourselves to this conundrum by quoting passages from the *Christian Faith* (§13.1, *CF*, p. 64) or from Schleiermacher's *Life of Jesus* where he asserts that "it has always been assumed in Christian faith that a union with God is possible in terms of man's essence,"[28] we are still left with a second question of how we can speak of this as a unique and thus discrete activity of God when God's activity is, according to Schleiermacher, universally effected and not to be identified with any particular event, for God's activity pertains to the whole, all finite existence arising out of one eternal and divine decree. In view of this, what does it mean to say that Christ *uniquely* "reproduces" God's loving act in history when history

---

[27]Namely, Schleiermacher's statement that "to ascribe to Christ an absolutely powerful God-consciousness, and to attribute to Him an existence of God in Him, are exactly the same thing" (§94.2, *CF*, p. 387; see also §99.1, p. 418).

[28]Quoted in fact by Jacqueline Mariña, "Christology and Anthropology in Friedrich Schleiermacher," in *The Cambridge Companion to Schleiermacher*, ed. Jacqueline Mariña (Cambridge: Cambridge University Press, 2005), p. 156. Mariña provides another sympathetic account of Schleiermacher's Christology worthy of consideration and critical reflection.

itself is the uniform expression of God's act of will, which itself is described by Schleiermacher only in terms of uniform causal relations, and never in terms of divine character or motivation, much less discrete miraculous action?[29] It is therefore difficult to see how identifying Christ's activity specifically and uniquely with God's activity can be accommodated within a theology that sees *all* activity as divine activity insofar as all is dependent on God and his creative action and where divine causality is "equal in compass to finite causality" (§51, *CF*, p. 201).[30] Christ is simply the apex (and can we still speak intelligibly of such a thing?) of a universal and eternal activity, or causal nexus, and one where divine preservation and natural causation are co-extensive (§46, *CF*, p. 174).

This set of questions then leads to further specifically christological ones. Though Hector retains the term and argues for a true "incarnation" in Schleiermacher's Christology, can we speak of a divine incarnation simply by replacing "natures" with "activities" if we exclude the crucial aspect of affirming a divine *Subject* who enters uniquely into history (something, as seen above, Schleiermacher himself rejects as impossible)?[31] Moreover, isn't Schleiermacher's understanding of the divine in Christ better termed an indwelling than an incarnation, anyway? Even if we were to prefer the second to maintain the uniqueness of Christ's relation to God, is it truly the best term to speak of a presence of a divine activity in the human person, or perhaps better, of a convergence of the two? So once again, coming full circle, even if we say farewell to classical metaphysics and its language of "natures" and embrace "activities," can we really abandon the language of a divine *Subject* in Christ and still speak intelligibly of an incarnation?[32] It is not at

---

[29]For Schleiermacher's exclusion of such elements of divine character and motives and strict adherence to questions of causal activity, see Edwin Christian van Driel, "Schleiermacher's Supralapsarian Christology," *Scottish Journal of Theology* 60 (2007): 266.

[30]This is not even to address the question of whether divine causality is in any way distinguished from divine activity for Schleiermacher.

[31]Furthermore, Schleiermacher in the *Speeches on Religion* as well as the *CF* distinguishes "feeling" not only from knowledge but also from activity (§3, *CF*). If so, then it seems problematic to equate Jesus' "God-consciousness" (a *feeling* of absolute dependence) with Jesus' *activity*. One has the suspicion that here Hector may have fallen prey to a category mistake in equating them if seen against the background of Schleiermacher's own understanding of religion as distinct from the realm not only of knowledge but also of activity. See note 17 above.

[32]Such questions become all the more pressing when one considers that one sympathetic interpreter of Schleiermacher's Christology begins to examine Christ's perfect God-consciousness by providing a metaphor for it in human preaching, thus likening the potency of Christ's God-

all clear that the concept this term conveys makes sense within Schleiermacher's system, for he has rejected the very christological underpinnings that make such a term coherent and comprehensible.[33]

Yet let us move on from such intricate christological inquiries. For even if we were to grant that Schleiermacher could answer such objections (and that is conceding a lot), we are still left with other equally serious and troubling, though not unrelated or necessarily original, questions. What are we to make of the fact that Christ's "God-consciousness" (a human capacity, even if perfectly actualized in Christ) is, in Hector's words, the "*organ*" by which God's activity is "*apprehended and turned into*" Christ's activity?[34] Can the perfection of a human capacity really become (or if not become, actualize) a divine presence (for Schleiermacher of course directly equates them, as witnessed earlier)? Is it not the case that here we are really dealing with anthropology, not Christology? And is it also not the case that we must admit to an unsettling suspicion that what is really going on for Schleiermacher may well be not that God's activity is "turned into" Christ's activity, but that Christ's activity, as the perfect human ideal, is now turned into God's activity, for as we saw above, and this fact cannot be brought to and impressed on the mind often enough, nothing in Schleiermacher's own dogmatic convictions surrounding redemption requires a divine, rather than perfectly realized human, ideal for such redemption to occur?[35] Yet in the

---

consciousness to that of a preacher who is inspired. Having experienced God's presence through our act of preaching, Catherine Kelsey concludes: "Somehow God did something better or bigger than our best effort, yet God worked through that effort. Rather than a 'God-and-me' experience, the experience is one of 'God-through-me-toward-others'" (Catherine L. Kelsey, *Thinking About Christ with Schleiermacher* [Louisville, KY: Westminster John Knox, 2003], p. 9). Kelsey goes on to state that such fleeting experiences of inspiration have been shared by writers, visual artists, performers, novelists, potters and musicians, and that when he thought about Christ, "Schleiermacher was thinking about a man whose life was an unbroken series of those moments. Christ's entire life was like those precious moments that we receive as fleeting gifts of grace" (p. 9). Even granting that this matter of degree may be qualitative and not only quantitative, one is hard pressed to think of such inspiration or indwelling as a personal incarnation. One would have to stretch language to the point of breaking to deem it so. This point should also be apparent when we begin by speaking of metaphors in human experience for Christ's perfect God-consciousness. Once we begin to speak of metaphors for the incarnation, we have already left the uniqueness and mystery of the incarnation far behind. Kelsey herself is not unaware of such problems (p. 19).

[33]Schleiermacher seems to have reduced Christ's divinity from that of a Subject to that of a power (§96.3, *CF*, p. 397).

[34]Hector, "Actualism and Incarnation," p. 311, emphasis added.

[35]See note 17 above.

end, how can we even know it is one and not the other with any certainty? For here the movement from heaven to earth seems equally interchangeable with that of earth to heaven.

All the more is this the case because where the Fathers and the Reformers spoke with one voice of the Holy Spirit as miraculously and singularly joining the divine and human in Christ, Schleiermacher, according to Hector, speaks of a human organ that unites the divine and the human in Christ, which, moreover, is alone capable of making this possible from the human side, for "only a God-conscious, rational creature can receive and reproduce God's activity."[36] But again, can a human capacity, even if perfectly actualized, ever have the power to be equated with a divine activity and presence? Isn't this, to put it mildly, a category mistake? Hector is right, maybe even more right than he fully knows, when he states that for Schleiermacher it is the God-consciousness, a human capacity and thus potentiality actualized in Christ, that truly is "that which makes it possible for God to become incarnate in a human." But we should make no mistake—such language of potentialities and possibilities reveals that here we have a modern, but nonetheless faithful, rendition of a *potentia obedientialis*. Yet one cannot oppose the one in medieval Catholic thought and support it here in Reformed guise.[37]

The problems continue. If all persons have the capacity to receive into themselves an absolutely potent God-consciousness by virtue of the human nature they possess (*CF* §89.3; cf. §88.4), then it is unclear why any person or all persons could not be the Redeemer instead of Jesus himself, Christ's role being one that anyone or all could take up intrinsically, save for God's eternal and hidden decree that it in fact be Jesus who achieves this.[38] It

---

[36]Hector, "Actualism and Incarnation," p. 311.

[37]Those who might quickly object should consider Hector's own summarization of Schleiermacher's thought: "In order for God to become incarnate in a creature, that creature must be able to perceive God's activity and reproduce it—and only humans, with their *innate God-consciousness,* have this *ability*" ("Actualism and Incarnation," p. 311, emphasis added). To the language of potentialities and possibilities we can now add that of innate capacities and intrinsic abilities. Is an objection to such language really staved off by simply reminding oneself, perhaps placating oneself, that this can only happen by a divine act?

[38]This is a point made by van Driel. He writes: "According to Schleiermacher, Christ's human nature is completely identical to ours. The only difference between him and us is sin; but sin is not an essential part of human nature. Christ's and all our individual human natures are open to the sinless life; in all of us 'reside the possibility of taking up the divine into itself, just as did

should come as no surprise, then, that when Christ is conceived in this way, a conception in which the direction of divine and human activity is difficult to discern, that the line between Christ and the church, as well as that between Christ and the Christian, is also now a permeable one. Indeed, their relation is a reversible one, the second term an extension of the first, for as reversibility holds in Christology, so it also holds in ecclesiology and the life of the Christian. Indeed, despite Schleiermacher's attempt to maintain the uniqueness of Christ, such a claim seems in danger of dissolution. Hector reminds us that for Schleiermacher the basis of Christ's divinity rests on the fact that his activity is a reproduction and thus identification with divine activity, and that correspondingly our activity is a reproduction and thus identification of Christ's own. Hector writes:

> It is not enough, however, for Christ to have lived a sinless life; if we are to be redeemed, the power of this life must somehow be communicated to us. Christ does so by drawing us into the activity of his life—he not only acts upon every circumstance of his own life, he also acts upon us, in such a way that *his* activity becomes *our* activity.[39]

Yet if true, then it must be admitted that all the walls of distinction have fallen to the ground. For if "God's pure activity is perfectly reproduced in Christ's life," such that Christ's activity *is* God's activity, and this is in fact the basis of Christ's divinity, then it seems to follow straight away that if "*his* [Christ's] activity becomes *our* activity," then God's activity is in the end our own.[40] It should not be surprising then that for Schleiermacher the church is an extension of Christ's life, the Christian's redeemed consciousness a replication of Christ's own, the Spirit of Christ the possession of, and indeed indistinguishable from, the spirit of the church and the Christian. In the end,

---

happen in Christ." But if that is the case, God did not have to choose Jesus to be the Redeemer. He could have chosen any of us" ("Schleiermacher's Supralapsarian Christology," p. 269). Driel continues on to state that rather than imparting redemption to us through the mediation of Christ, God could have communicated this immediately to all, for "since all humans have a potency to receive such impartation, God could have imparted Godself to all of us directly" (p. 269). It is not at all certain that Schleiermacher's feeble response to such a charge is adequate to meet it; see §13.1, *CF*, p. 64.

[39]Hector, "Actualism and Incarnation," p. 318.

[40]Ibid., pp. 312, 318, respectively. Hence this conclusion seems to follow the trail of basic logic:

    A.   God's activity = Christ's activity (p. 312)

    B.   Christ's activity = Our activity (p. 318)

  Therefore, C.   God's activity = Our activity

Christ is subsumed into the church, and thus into Christian experience. This is theosis with a vengeance, for it is a theosis in reverse, Christ taken up into the church's life and subsumed within it.[41] Hector sums up:

> Christ is perfectly receptive to God's pure act and perfectly reproduces it as his own action; in redeeming us, Christ makes us receptive to his pure act so that we can reproduce it as *our* action. Christ's work, therefore, is a repetition of his person.[42]

Now once again, if this is true, two things seem to follow almost deductively: our activity is God's activity, and the church (as well as the Christian) is a repetition of Christ's person. The distinction between Christ and the church, and that between Christ and the Christian, seems blurred beyond relief.[43]

In working out the full implications of Schleiermacher's Christology, Hector has done a great service. His rendition of Schleiermacher's Christology is not mistaken. Far from it. It is because it is so correct in its incisive revelation of Schleiermacher's inner convictions, so keen in laying bare its true dogmatic intent and achievement, so perceptive in its explication of a

---

[41]Schleiermacher's Christology thereby stands at the beginning of a tradition and makes later statements by those who follow in this tradition intelligible, such as that of Paul Tillich: "And, without the reception of Jesus as the Christ by the church, he could not have become the Christ, because he would not have brought the New Being to anyone" (Tillich, *Systematic Theology*, vol. 2: *Existence and the Christ* [Chicago: University of Chicago Press, 1957], p. 135). One wonders if here the reversal of the relation of Christ and the church has found full voice and reached its conclusion. As Tillich also writes: "Although appearing in a personal life, the New Being has a spatial breadth in the community of the New Being and a temporal dimension in the history of the New Being. The appearance of the Christ in an individual person presupposes the community out of which he came and the community which he creates. Of course, the criterion of both is the picture of Jesus as the Christ; but, *without them, this criterion never could have appeared*" (ibid., p. 136; emphasis added).

[42]Hector, "Actualism and Incarnation," p. 319.

[43]For sake of comparison, Barth himself could also speak of a unity of Christ and the church, and of Christ and the Christian, in his understanding of the *totus Christus* and the *unio cum Christo*, respectively. But the difference—and the one that makes all the difference—is that such a relation for Barth was always a unity-in-distinction, one in which the walls of differentiation though not of participation between Christ and the church, as well as between Christ and the Christian, were absolute, where such unities could not rival, replace or be confused with, but only witness to and reflect, the one unsubstitutable and unique and irreplaceable union of God and man in Jesus Christ. It was this unity of God and humanity in Christ that was in the end the basis for all other relations of God to the world, and one that both established and revealed that all such relations were irreversible and asymmetrical. For Barth's own distinctive christological logic as it pertains to ecclesiology, see Kimlyn J. Bender, *Karl Barth's Christological Ecclesiology* (Aldershot, UK: Ashgate, 2005; reprint, Eugene, OR: Cascade Press, 2013).

christological logic in which God's activity and Christ's activity and our own activity flow seamlessly one into another, that the logic itself must in the end be set aside, the achievement itself be sincerely admired but nevertheless abandoned, the convictions respectfully if quietly left behind to history. Hector's account is perhaps as good as any of the recent attempts to grasp and defend Schleiermacher's project, and ironically, it is also because and not in spite of this the most incisive argument for why that project must in the end be rejected.

Yet, once more into the breach. Let us, again just for sake of argument (and only for its sake), grant that, even if Schleiermacher could not resolve all such quandaries and contradictions here presented to our satisfaction, he has at the very least succeeded in presenting a theologically consistent Christology within the strict parameters provided by his view of the world, one that rejects traditional christological answers, one that respects an eternal covenant of religion and science, one predicated on a closed and deterministic universe, in short, one consistent with the modern view of the world as he holds it, a view that is the coat which Schleiermacher is convinced one as a modern person must wear and in which one must live and move and have one's being.[44] Yet even if all of this is conceded, we are *still* here at the end left with the question of why we should accept such a constriction in the first place. Maybe what really must be done is simply to take off the jacket. Schleiermacher's conviction of religious feeling, one dependent and indeed defined by a view of the world in which knowledge, activity and feeling are kept distinct in strict ledger columns; one in which any discrete divine action would undermine the feeling of absolute dependence, thus undercutting religion's ground; one in which religion is precisely the examination and realization of a human ideal; and one in which Christ must be understood within (and *only* within) these strict parameters— perhaps these presuppositions themselves should be jettisoned as now antiquated cargo. Or, to stay with our first metaphor, maybe it is time that we took the jacket off and embraced a less constraining garment with more elbow room. For even if some retain such a taut and heavy coat, continuing to assert that something like Schleiermacher's picture of God and

---

[44]Even Paul himself in Acts could entertain such Stoic ways of thought in a positive fashion (Acts 17:28).

the world is the one we must inhabit if we are to be intellectually responsible and culturally relevant, we are still left with the embarrassing admission that this is not the picture that Scripture paints. For it paints a picture of a God who enters into the world, into time and its vicissitudes, a God who acts in discrete events however perceptible or imperceptible to us, a God who exists not apart from the world as an inferred "Whence" but bears the name "Emmanuel," God with us. This is a world where the spheres of human knowledge and morality and feeling flow into one another with no respect for hard and fast disciplinary boundaries, just as they flow together in human life, where to love God with one's mind and soul and heart and strength are messily bound into one, where God is not simply the source of a uniform and timeless causality but of a great and timely drama. This is a world not only of the Redeemer's uninterrupted blessedness but also crucified agony, where the cry of dereliction is not an embarrassment to be explained away but a holy mystery to be revered, and one where, though almost entirely peripheral to Schleiermacher's picture, the resurrection features most prominently, objections to miracles be damned.

We are confronted with the possibility that we may need to take the questions posed to our world by the "strange new world within the Bible," in Barth's memorable phrase, at least as seriously as we take our own. If so, then much of the modern project, where Kant's relegation of God to a moral postulate, and Hegel's relegation of God to a rational postulate, and Schleiermacher's relegation of God to a religious postulate, will not do.[45] Even Schleiermacher's superior Christology (certainly to that of Kant and also to that of Hegel, not even mentioning Strauss) cannot redeem the larger project, for it can be argued that for Schleiermacher, in the end, Christ himself is a postulate to make sense of the church's experience of redemption, as God is a postulate for Kant to make sense of our moral experience. Perhaps we should move on (with a full appreciation of the past, both its real achievements and failures) to a different project altogether.

The foremost heir of Schleiermacher's project in Barth's day was Barth's own teacher, Wilhelm Herrmann. After his famous break with his teachers,

---

[45]In speaking of the religious consciousness explicated by Schleiermacher, Keith Clements can therefore explain that "God is the correlate of this religious consciousness" (Clements, ed., *Friedrich Schleiermacher: Pioneer of Modern Theology* [Minneapolis: Fortress, 1991], p. 38).

Barth always looked on Herrmann (as he did Schleiermacher) with an ir-reducible mix of sincere and reverential respect and undaunted and critical wariness. Whether Barth was always fair to Schleiermacher in every respect is a live question, and perhaps the same might be asked with regard to Herr-mann. But *what* Barth's position was on the Christology and theological program of both is little open to doubt. Looking back on the theology of Herrmann, Barth saw the conclusion of a century's attempt to provide a way ahead that traded a central truth for relevance to an age.

In an essay examining Herrmann's theology written in 1925 after his break with liberalism was a settled issue for him, Barth turned a new eye on the thought of his former teacher. Barth zeroed in on a single sentence from Herrmann's *Dogmatik*: "*In the power of the man Jesus* we apprehend God himself working upon us."[46] The reader who has traveled through this chapter cannot help but be struck by how similar this sentence from Herr-mann about our human subjectivity is to Hector's language regarding Christ in Schleiermacher:

> Christ is the One who reproduces God's pure, loving act in human history, and is therefore God incarnate. The key to this reproduction is Christ's God-consciousness, which functions as the organ by which God's pure act is *ap-prehended and turned into* Christ's own activity.[47]

But if there is any question of how Barth might estimate the latter, we need only consider his actual response to the former sentence by Herrmann. Barth is far from convinced by Herrmann's claim, and breaks from a de-tached evaluation to a strident judgment:

> That is monophysite and it is impossible. In the power of *the man Jesus as such* we never "apprehend" God himself. That power, if so isolated it existed at all as a conceivable entity (which it is not), would be an historical influence which would necessarily diminish as the square of the time-space-distance, like any other historical potency.[48]

For Barth, this was as true of "the man Jesus" as it is for us—there is no

---

[46]Karl Barth, "The Principles of Dogmatics According to Wilhelm Herrmann," in *Theology and Church: Shorter Writings 1920–1928*, trans. Louise Pettibone Smith (New York: Harper & Row, 1962), p. 264.

[47]Hector, "Actualism and Incarnation," p. 318, emphasis added.

[48]Barth, "Principles of Dogmatics According to Wilhelm Herrmann," p. 264.

way from earth to heaven, for the road traveled is of the Son into the far country, not of a man to the stars. There really cannot be any doubt as to how Barth would assess these sentences describing Schleiermacher's Christology in light of how he spoke of Herrmann's own sentences concerning us. We need only substitute Schleiermacher's "God-consciousness" for Herrmann's "power of the man Jesus" to have our answer, since for Herrmann, as for Schleiermacher, the distinction between Christ and us is a matter of degree, remembering also that Schleiermacher could equate such consciousness with a power (§96.3, *CF*, p. 397). Barth not only would doubt the reality of such an isolated consciousness of the man Jesus as he did such an isolated power, but also would argue that even were it to exist, it would, as a historical entity, only lessen in potency as time continued onward.

In the same essay addressing Herrmann, Barth summed up what he saw as the only way ahead, and it was one very different from the road Herrmann had taken:

> Here no other "way" whatever exists except the road from above downwards. Orthodox Christology is a glacial torrent rushing straight down from a height of three thousand metres; it makes accomplishment possible. Herrmann's Christology, as it stands, is the hopeless attempt to raise a stagnant pool to that same height by means of a hand pump; nothing can be accomplished with it.[49]

Later he would sum up these differing approaches succinctly: "There is a way from Christology to anthropology, but there is no way from anthropology to Christology" (*CD* I/1, p. 131).

Those who might think that Barth's maturation in Christology in his later years dispelled or changed *this* judgment in light of his newfound and consistent attention to the humanity of God can only be mistaken. No matter what paths were taken (or that others might take beyond him) in the latter volumes of the *Church Dogmatics*, there were paths abandoned in his early years that Barth would never travel again. However much Barth's theology changed from the time he wrote those words in the first volume of the *Church Dogmatics*, he never abandoned *that* conviction. Moreover, however much Barth corrected himself in moving to a position that embraced and

---

[49]Ibid., p. 265.

took seriously the humanity of God (and if there was a strength to the neo-Protestant project, that was certainly one), he never reversed course on a fundamental commitment to begin with God. And so, even though Barth came to take seriously the "The Homecoming of the Son of Man" (*CD* VI/2, §64.2), the road traveled always began as "The Way of the Son of God into the Far Country" (*CD* IV/1, §59.1). Whatever their similarities, here Barth and Schleiermacher traverse two very different roads.

Accepting Barth's criticisms of Schleiermacher need not mean that we overlook Schleiermacher's noble attempt to maintain the uniqueness of Jesus in an age increasingly defined by historical relativism, this attempt itself being his own idiosyncratic commitment to embrace the scandal of particularity. Certainly Barth learned much from Schleiermacher, sharing with him not only an anti-speculative and anti-historicist impulse but also a firm commitment to christological particularity. Barth always looked with respect on Schleiermacher, but if we are honest, it was always more of a respect of Schleiermacher's intention and project than his accomplishment.[50] And as all persons learn in time, we are finally judged by our actions rather than our intentions. Hector is correct that Schleiermacher attempted to produce a "high" Christology, but it is a road that moves from below to above, and all such attempts hit a celestial ceiling.

In the end, Hector's study is not only perceptive and astute in its portrayal of Schleiermacher's christological content but also judicious in the conclu-

---

[50]So even with all of his appreciation for Schleiermacher expressed late in life in his "Concluding Unscientific Postscript on Schleiermacher," Barth nonetheless concluded: "However, it must not be overlooked that after praising everything worthy of praise in my writings on Schleiermacher, I still had ringing in my ears the venerable 'Apostles' and Nicene Creeds. Theologically speaking, I could not revert to Schleiermacher" (Karl Barth, *The Theology of Schleiermacher*, ed. Dietrich Ritschl, trans. Geoffrey W. Bromiley [Grand Rapids: Eerdmans, 1982], p. 267). He later continues: "Until better instructed, I can see no way from Schleiermacher, or from his contemporary epigones, to the chroniclers, prophets, and wise ones of Israel, to those who narrate the story of the life, death, and resurrection of Jesus Christ, to the word of the apostles—no way to the God of Abraham, Isaac, and Jacob and the Father of Jesus Christ, no way to the great tradition of the Christian church. For the present I can see nothing here but a choice. And for me there can be no question as to how that choice is to be made" (pp. 271-72). Barth would not, however, make this into a final judgment (pp. 274-75). Nevertheless, with the judgment he did make, he showed that he never really moved from his initial one made in 1922, that is, that Schleiermacher stood outside of the tradition running from Jeremiah, to Paul, to Luther and Calvin, and to Kierkegaard, and thus a tradition Barth claimed as his own (see Karl Barth, *The Word of God and Theology*, trans. Amy Marga [London: T & T Clark, 2011], pp. 182-84).

sions it draws about Schleiermacher, of which it offers three.[51] First, "Schleiermacher is a church theologian, and not primarily an apologist or philosopher." True enough, though as we saw above, external (non-dogmatic, that is, non-theological) convictions did constrain his thought and profoundly shape his project.[52] While all theological thought must come wearing its cultural and philosophical dress, some theology is more concerned about adapting to reigning cultural assumptions than others.[53] Nevertheless, with such qualifications, the first conclusion is a sound one. Second, Hector judges that Schleiermacher "was not dim-witted, as some facile criticisms of his theology take him to be." Indisputably, irrefutably true—he was and remains the greatest and most brilliant proponent among those who propounded a Christology that turned from Nicea and Chalcedon to find another way, a way from below to above. He not only stands at the head of that tradition but also remains its greatest representative. And third, Hector concludes, "we can learn from his theology." Absolutely. But there's the rub: What do we learn? Hector states that Schleiermacher was not an apologist but a dogmatic theologian. That may well be the case, though there comes a point where one can legitimately wonder how many dogmatic theologians must serve as his apologists.[54] No less, one wonders if this task is worth the

---

[51]See Hector, "Actualism and Incarnation," p. 321.

[52]See also Georg Behrens, "The Order of Nature in Pious Self-Consciousness: Schleiermacher's Apologetic Argument," *Religious Studies* (1996): 93-108. He writes: "While *The Christian Faith* is principally a work of dogmatic theology, it is also our most important source for the apologetic agenda of the later Schleiermacher, namely to offer some guarantee of a harmony between authentic Christian doctrine on the one hand, and the presuppositions and results of natural and historical science on the other" (p. 94).

[53]This point seems irrefutable. P. D. L. Avis writes that "it seems to me completely illusory to suppose that Christian theology can be carried on, or even exist at all, in total independence of historical thought-forms and conceptual systems" (Avis, "Friedrich Schleiermacher and the Science of Theology," *Scottish Journal of Theology* [1979]: 30). But some theologies wear these garments provisionally and lightly, and with a certain degree of critical freedom, whereas others are constrained by what they accept to be their unyielding tightness and rigidity, and Schleiermacher did his dogmatic work in a pretty tight jacket. In the end it seems safe to say that Schleiermacher was more occupied to shape his theological content to fit the garments of modernity, whereas Barth was more intent to shape and tailor the garments to fit the theological form.

[54]If Hector's article has a weakness, it is the strained attempt at the end to reconcile Schleiermacher's Christology with a notion of Christ's pre-existence and harmonize and incorporate it into a conception of "God's eternal triunity" and a more robust trinitarianism. If any of the above criticisms hold, then this becomes hard to take except as a case of special pleading (see Hector, "Actualism and Incarnation," pp. 320-21). Hector concludes his essay: "If we are interested in constructing a post-essentialist theology, this [Schleiermacher's Christology] seems like a good

effort. It depends, I suppose, on what one thinks we learn from Schleier-macher. For some, what one learns about is deemed to be the most sophis-ticated and exquisite, the most meticulously and brilliantly engineered, of all hand pumps.

---

start" (p. 322). Yet one may without any duplicity be open to and even embrace the proposed project without agreeing with the conclusion drawn.

Author Index

Subject Index

Finding the Textbook You Need

The IVP Academic Textbook Selector
is an online tool for instantly finding the IVP books
suitable for over 250 courses across 24 disciplines.

---

ivpacademic.com